CLARA SCHUMANN
AN ARTIST'S LIFE

Da Capo Press Music Reprint Series

MUSIC EDITOR
BEA FRIEDLAND
Ph.D., City University of New York

CLARA SCHUMANN
AN ARTIST'S LIFE

BASED ON MATERIAL FOUND IN
DIARIES AND LETTERS

BY

BERTHOLD LITZMANN

TRANSLATED AND ABRIDGED
FROM THE FOURTH EDITION

BY

GRACE E. HADOW

With a New Introduction by
ELAINE BRODY

VOL. I

ILLUSTRATED

DA CAPO PRESS · NEW YORK · 1979

Library of Congress Cataloging in Publication Data

Litzmann, Berthold, 1857-1926.
  Clara Schumann: an artist's life, based on
material found in diaries and letters.

  (Da Capo Press music reprint series)
  Reprint of the 1913 ed. published by Macmillan,
London.
    1. Schumann, Clara Josephine Wieck, 1819-1896.
  2. Pianists—Germany—Biography.
  ML417.S4L72 1979   786.1'092'4 [B]   79-20823
  ISBN 0-306-79582-5

This Da Capo Press edition of *Clara Schumann:
An Artist's Life* is an unabridged republication
of the English translation published in London
by Macmillan & Co., Limited and in Leipzig by
Breitkopf & Härtél in 1913, supplemented with
a new introduction by Elaine Brody.

Published by Da Capo Press, Inc.
A Subsidiary of Plenum Publishing Corporation
227 West 17th Street, New York, N.Y. 10011

INTRODUCTION

Child prodigy, pianist, composer, teacher, wife, mother, counselor and friend to many distinguished personages of her day, Clara Schumann (1819-1896) in the course of her life played many roles. For decades her accomplishments were overshadowed by the vast achievements of her husband, but the time is now ripe for a reappraisal of her worth. The diverse activities in which she excelled place her unquestionably in the forefront of those women who, throughout history, have not only fulfilled their customary domestic obligations but have moved into the professional arena to compete successfully with men. Of these, a few rare individuals manage to do both concurrently. She is one of them.

Clara Wieck was born in Leipzig into an unhappy household. Her mother, née Marianne Tromlitz, was the granddaughter of Johann Georg Tromlitz, flute maker, player, and composer. An accomplished pianist, Fräulein Tromlitz had been the pupil of Friedrich Wieck (1785-1873) before they married. Wieck, a stern perfectionist, completed studies in theology but left the ministry after preaching one sermon, deciding instead to devote his life to music. Early in his career, Wieck managed a piano factory, supervised a music-lending library (from which young Richard Wagner borrowed books), and finally settled into teaching, becoming an outstanding pedagogue whose students included his daughters Clara and Marie as well as Robert Schumann and Hans von Bülow. His rigid authoritarian personality first drove away his wife and later his daughter and son-in-law.

Marianne Wieck left her husband when Clara was four-and-a-half years old, and the court awarded Friedrich custody of the child from the time she was five. Within a year Marianne married the musician Adolf Bargiel (d.1841) earlier a good friend of Wieck himself. Much like the children of divorced couples today, young Clara was shepherded back and forth between her parents, as each regularly warned the other not to spoil her. Food, clothing, discipline, and morals all became subjects of contention as the parents continued to battle even after their separation. Clara loved both and accepted her fate with dignity and with an understanding that belied her years. While still a child, she was thus forced to become completely self-reliant. Yet, despite this inner strength, in later years Clara bemoaned the loss of her mother's love when she needed it most; on several occasions, moreover, this dutiful daughter would also find herself torn between her father and her husband.

In 1839, after protracted delays and in defiance of her father's wishes, Clara announced her intention to marry Robert Schumann. During their stormy courtship, her mother, now settled in Berlin, offered temporary solace and comfort. Frau Bargiel opened her home and extended her hospitality to Robert, who was in Berlin for a time without his beloved Clara.

Wieck regarded his daughter as an extension of himself. Her success would prove the value of his method; her fame redounded to his reputation as a teacher. When their relations became strained, he found a substitute in her step-sister Marie (Wieck's daughter by his second marriage to Clementine Fechner), whom Clara loved, but whose talents she suspected were not as extraordinary as her father liked to imagine. When she voiced her concern and told him he would ultimately be disappointed, he peremptorily dismissed her comments. Wieck was an old-fashioned, conservative father who demanded respect and obedience from his children. He scrupulously taught them the value of work, indolence being as foreign to his nature as it would always be to Clara's.

Posterity continues to regard Wieck as a mean and hateful person who stood between two young lovers, delaying their cherished marriage. The reality of the situation demands that we understand his reluctance to allow his daughter Clara, already a famous pianist with an international reputation, to spend her life in a union with a minor composer, a pianist *manqué*. (He had already injured his finger.) To forestall this eventuality, Wieck made several stipulations with regard to Schumann's annual income and his savings. Furthermore, he attempted to safeguard Clara's own earnings so that in the event of a financial crisis for the couple, her fortune would remain intact. After several years of impatient waiting, these obstacles became insurmountable and the young people resolved to marry when Clara attained her majority. Except for the attitude of her father, their marriage in 1840 was cause for much celebration, and the event inspired Schumann to compose a number of magnificent Lieder.

Schumann's fame spread, prompting Wieck in 1843 to make several conciliatory overtures which both young people quickly heeded. Recognizing Clara's strong ties to her father, Robert took the necessary steps to bring them together again. From Dresden, where he now lived, Wieck reminded Robert in a letter that, musically, they had always been on the same side. When Schumann first arrived to study in Leipzig, Wieck had written to his mother, vouching for his talents and his ability to succeed in the profession of music. "Good teachers are hard to find," Wieck had explained, adding that most are unfamiliar with the literature and cannot perform the pieces they are teaching. A man with Robert's background, he concluded, would be in a position to earn a nice living and the young man should certainly consider music as his profession. For Robert, it was hard to forget such support!

With the gift of hindsight, we may judge that Wieck was correct about his son-in-law and daughter. Their wedded bliss lasted only thirteen years. During this time Clara gave birth to eight children and continued intermittently to teach, tour, and perform. After several bouts of depression and an attempted suicide, Schumann entered the asylum at Endenich near Bonn early in 1854, while Clara tried to carry on without him.

The best of Robert Schumann's compositions, the finest of the keyboard pieces and the Lieder, date from the period before 1841. In his remaining years, Schumann composed a variety of works in all genres, but none compares with his earlier compositions. We can only speculate on the reasons for the decline in quality of his later pieces; it is not inconceivable that the problems of a two-career family played havoc with Schumann's peace of mind. Clara's father believed that she should sacrifice everything for her career or at least marry a man who could provide financial security while she extended her professional activities; her husband held a completely different point of view. Schumann was pleased that he could discuss his music with Clara and that she performed his pieces before an ever-widening public. Still, he wanted her to stay at home, near him. He believed he could offer sufficient financial and emotional support for Clara and that she should have no need of the additional gratification of a virtuoso career. Early in their marriage Clara deferred to Robert, but problems soon arose.

Usually they had at least two pianos in their home, sometimes three, placed in far distant corners of the house. Yet when Robert was composing, Clara could not practice lest he be distracted. Without practicing, she could not accept engagements, although at times her performances were their only source of income. In the early years of their marriage, Robert accompanied her on tour. When inspiration deserted him in rented rooms and hotels, he decided in despair to return home while Clara continued without him. Robert was dismally unhappy when they were apart, but he needed peace and time to write really fine works. He could not force the creative process.

From previous experiences, Clara was well aware that she did not enjoy traveling alone. Once, before their marriage, when Wieck was determined to keep the young people apart, he insisted that Clara go unaccompanied to Paris, while he remained in Leipzig. Wieck assumed she would discover her dependence on him to deal with agents, music dealers, publishers, and patrons. She would certainly be helpless without papa. But this maneuver had the opposite effect. It brought Clara closer to Robert, who regularly advised her about finding a traveling companion, guarding against lechers, and generally avoiding the pitfalls common to artists on tour. His admonitions remind us of Mozart's letters to his wife Constanze, when she visited the spa while he remained in town.

And so Clara remained at home after their marriage, but professional isolation did not agree with her. She needed to perform; she wanted to go out among people, enjoying the thrill of public performances. She could not understand, even later, the reluctance of her daughter Elise, a good pianist who made her debut with Clara in a performance of her father's *Andante and Variations for Two Pianos,* to continue as a performing musician. Elise complained that the pre-performance tension was more than she could bear and turned to teaching instead. Clara, too, suffered from nervousness, but in the aftermath of a performance, she always felt it was worthwhile.

Much of Clara's time and energy was spent in mothering Robert. Fortunately, her disposition lent itself to the task. When Robert was institutionalized, she immediately assumed the role of

pater familias. It was she who decided where the older children
would attend school. She urged Ferdinand to apply himself to his
studies so that he could maintain a tradition, a level of work of
which the family could be proud. She cared for her ailing daughter
Julie, who died before reaching adulthood, and she tended to
Johannes Brahms who had but recently (1853) arrived to study
with her husband. For Brahms, she remained an alter ego, some-
body with whom he could discuss his works, his performances, his
ideas, and his activities. She performed the same services for
Joseph Joachim, until he met and married the singer Amalie Weiss.
From the Mendelssohn family, she received support: emotional,
psychological and, when necessary, financial. Both she and Robert
adored Felix and named their youngest son—whom Robert never
saw—after him. The young couple were deeply grieved at the news
of Felix Mendelssohn's death, as well as the death of his sister
Fanny the following year.

Although they lived with and through one another, Clara successfully maintained her independent opinions on music and musicians. Robert, for example, accepted Richard Wagner and his
music but complained that "Wagner is such a bore. He talks of
nothing but himself!" Clara insisted that Wagner was taking
music in the wrong direction. She could not tolerate him or his
music. Her relationship with Liszt, who tried valiantly to help her
at all times, particularly after Schumann's death, was rather more
complex. She did not care for him or for his works, which she regarded as too flamboyant. She admired his abilities, particularly
his remarkable skill in sight reading. "What he does *prima vista*
takes all of us hours of practicing to achieve," she complained. She
abhorred the chaos that invariably surrounded them in Liszt's
presence. Robert usually took his side, but when Liszt, once in

Vienna, spoke disparagingly about Mendelssohn's music, Robert asked him to leave.

In concerts, Clara emerged as the foremost interpreter of middle and late Beethoven. In 1836, barely eighteen years old, she played the *Appassionata* for an untutored audience and revealed its extraordinary beauty. She introduced Chopin's music in cities where his pieces had not yet been heard. She loved the works of Bach, but she played them most often for herself. Her working repertory, which is listed in the second Litzmann volume, is staggering in size and scope.

When Brahms despaired at the lack of critical and public acceptance of many of his new pieces, she reminded him of Robert's frequent comment: "In ten years, things will change." She also performed his compositions regularly in private soirées for select, influential, persons. She spoke favorably of them to journalists and did not hesitate to admonish even her good friend Jenny Lind for not showing the proper appreciation of Brahms's Variations.

The material found in the two volumes here reprinted derives from forty-seven books of diaries and journals, the earliest begun on 7 May 1828 by Wieck for his daughter and the later ones kept alternately, one week by Clara and the next by Robert. They chronicle the daily life of two musicians at mid-century and of Clara's activities and associates during the forty years she outlived her husband. Valuable information on nineteenth-century performance practice and on music in a socio-historical context appears side by side with specific details about the harried, exciting life—musical and personal—of Clara Schumann.

We learn, for example, of Clara Schumann's guidelines for practicing (playing everything from memory and then later checking the rough spots), her preparation for performances, and the nightmare of memory lapses while on stage. She expresses her irritation with poor orchestras, weak conductors, unprepared players, and rude audiences. She was annoyed by the bravura style that seemed to please the public; as an afterthought, though, she wondered whether or not Robert should write a crowd-pleaser for her programs. She describes her friendship with young Pauline Viardot, whose unconventional *ménage à trois*—Turgenev, her lover, was installed in the house with Viardot's husband and children— made Clara uncomfortable. She demonstrates an overwhelming reverence for Schröder-Devrient, particularly in her role as Fidelio (a performance that motivated Richard Wagner to become a musician). She felt compelled to implore Schröder-Devrient not to continue on the concert platform when her voice was clearly past its prime.

Clara was bitter at the Viennese publisher Haslinger who, in enlarging the scope of his *Anzeiger,* made it more difficult for Robert to sign subscribers for his *Neue Zeitschrift für Musik,* and she showed surprise that Parisian audiences enjoyed Schumann's music sooner than his countrymen. She preferred Pleyel's pianos although the Erards as a family had been so kind to her that she was reluctant to express herself on the subject in public. She disliked Berlioz—"an intense man who asked me so many questions"—and his music, although Robert felt otherwise on both counts. She ultimately decided to forgo composition when she realized that her works could not compare with her husband's. She gives a vivid account of the sometimes exciting but mostly frustrating musical scene in Leipzig, Vienna, Hamburg, Dresden, Berlin, Weimar, Erfurt, Amsterdam, Rotterdam, The Hague, Copenhagen, St. Petersburg, and other cities.

The events of Clara's life become first-hand experiences as we read her observations of the musical world. In her chosen profession and in her role as wife and mother, she succeeded as well as any liberated female of the twentieth century. Readers of her recollections will find themselves inescapably drawn to this artist who carved her own role model because there was none she could emulate. All of us can rejoice in her achievement.

Elaine Brody
New York University
June, 1979

Editor's Note: The present reprint has been offset from the first (1913) English-language edition. The numerous typographical errors in the original volume, minimally reflected in their errata lists, have not been corrected because it would have required resetting the entire work.

CLARA SCHUMANN
AN ARTIST'S LIFE

BASED ON MATERIAL FOUND IN
DIARIES AND LETTERS

BY

BERTHOLD LITZMANN

TRANSLATED AND ABRIDGED
FROM THE FOURTH EDITION

BY

GRACE E. HADOW

WITH A PREFACE BY

W. H. HADOW

VOL. I

ILLUSTRATED

MACMILLAN & CO., LIMITED
ST. MARTIN'S STREET, LONDON
AND BREITKOPF & HÄRTEL,
LEIPZIG 1913

E. Fischer 1832

Eleonor Wiert.

TRANSLATOR'S PREFACE.

The task of translation can never be a light one, since every language has not only its own peculiar shades of meaning, but also its own peculiar charm — a fragrance which evaporates as soon as the national frontier is crossed. This is especially true of the German of Robert Schumann. His delicate, poetic imagination found perfect expression in the language of his hero, Jean Paul, and the endeavour to render his love letters, and still more his poems, in another tongue is foredoomed to failure; the original words alone fitly express the poet's thought. In the following pages an attempt has been made to give as far as possible the spirit of the German, but only a poet could hope for success in such an enterprise, and I am conscious of many shortcomings. It is with great pleasure and the warmest gratitude that I acknowledge my indebtedness to Miss H. C. Deneke and to Miss Eugenie Schumann, both of whom read through the manuscript and gave me much valuable advice and criticism. Miss Schumann went through the translation word by word, and to her never wearying patience and consideration is due whatever in it there may be of good.

It was unfortunately found necessary to turn the original three volumes into two in the English edition, and by so doing the balance of the whole had necessarily to be re-adjusted. Prof. Litzmann in his prefaces explains the principle which underlies the whole work. I have endeavoured to interfere as little as possible with his method, though some slight changes were necessary in order to avoid any abrupt break between the volumes, vol. ii of the German edition being divided between the two volumes of the English edition. It is with sincere apologies and deep regret that I have ventured to make what omissions were called for by reason of space, and I have to tender my thanks to Prof. Litzmann for his courtesy in permitting such changes.

Cirencester 1912.

Grace E. Hadow.

PREFACE.

The reproach is commonly brought against musical biographies that they are monotonous: and indeed the life of the musician has not often afforded much scope for incident or variety. If he be a composer he treads the accustomed course of early struggles, hard-earned victories and posthumous fame: if he be a virtuoso his career is one triumphal progress which leaves little to record except the successive trophies that he has planted and the successive laurels that he has won. The concentration required by his art removes him in some degree from the stir and stress of public events: for the most part he dwells in an ideal city of his own and breathes the more freely when he has shut its gates upon the world.

To this it may be added that the biographers of our great musicians have too often tended to merge the historian in the advocate. They are full of a generous enthusiasm for their subject; they are anxious above all things to present it in an attractive light; but they sometimes neglect Cromwell's advice to Sir Peter Lely and spoil their portrait by giving it a classic regularity of feature. No doubt every biographer is something of a partisan: — it is no use writing a man's life unless you think well of him: — but the worst of all ways to arouse interest in your hero is to represent him on a faultless paladin and to treat as a paynim and a miscreant everyone who ever offered him the least opposition. No man can build the monument of departed greatness if he is using up all the stones to pelt his adversaries.

It may be said that the interpretation of character is less important in music than in any other arts or pursuits because music is more detached than they from the concerns of everyday life. But this is a false inference. The character of the musician is probably moulded by fewer external influences than that of the poet, but it is not less faithfully reflected in his work. And one reason why the work of the musician is the more difficult to comprehend is that it has received less assistance at the hands of the biographers and historians. The great biographies of Bach and Haydn, of Mozart and Beethoven, though free from the fault of extravagant partisanship are perhaps a little inclined to be cold and scientific: they give us admirable studies of the conditions under which these composers wrought: they give us some of the best technical criticism ever written: what they rather withold is that spark of human insight and sympathy through which the whole of a man's life and work becomes illuminated. All genius is beyond explanation: it is too divine for our imperfect standards and our clumsy formulae: yet there is a meaning in the statement that we are nearer understanding how Gœthe came to the second part of Faust than how Beethoven came to the Choral Symphony.

It is for this reason that a special interest attaches to Dr. Litzmann's Life of Clara Schumann. As an example of musical erudition it is in no way comparable to the great biographies mentioned above: it would, indeed be far from making any such claim: its chief value lies in the vividness of the story which it has to relate and in the remarkable studies of character by which that story is illustrated. For these Dr. Litzmann has been specially fortunate in his materials. There are full diaries, there are frequent letters, there are reminiscences of relations and personal friends, and throughout

them all there breathes an air of truth and simplicity and
candour which is seldom to be found in diaries and not always
in correspondence. No doubt much of the ground is already
familiar: some has been recently traversed by the admirable
volume of Miss Florence May[1]): but there still remains a good
deal of new and valuable information and the whole story
has been wrought into a coherent picture by judicious selec-
tion and arrangement.

The central group consists of four persons — Wieck, Clara
and Robert Schumann, and Brahms. Of these Wieck is in
many ways the most interesting study. We are long past the
period of regarding him as a mere pedant with an unreasoning
antipathy to his son-in-law: but until the appearance of Dr.
Litzmann's work, and of Miss May's introductory chapter, it
was impossible to form a just estimate of his curiously varied
and complex character. Brought up in extreme poverty and
educated for the Lutheran Church he learned early the lessons
of that solid and rather dour self-reliance which remained with
him throughout his life. With no genius for composition, and
with not enough musical training to give him great executive
skill, he had nevertheless the soul of an artist; he imperilled
his career both at school and at college by "devoting too
much time to music"; after taking a theological degree as a
preparation for the ministry he preached a single trial sermon
and immediately abandoned, on conscientious grounds, the
vocation upon which he depended for a livelihood. Opportunity
soon showed that he possessed a remarkable talent as a teacher:
he obtained a series of private tutorships, left them to give
pianoforte lessons, married, and added to his other avocations
the charge of a piano-factory and of a lending-library of music.

---

1) "The Girlhood of Clara Schumann." It carries the story on to 1840.

As a pianist he was virtually self-taught — for the half dozen lessons from Milchmayer can hardly count as serious education: — among the pupils whose genius he helped to form were his daughter Clara, Robert Schumann and Hans von Bülow [1]).

Such is the man as he stands at the opening of this biography: — upright, masterful, energetic, capable alike of tenderness and of fierce anger, eager for affection yet too proud to ask it, a genuine artist, a wise and sympathetic teacher, wounded and perhaps embittered by the quarrel which after eight years of marriage drove his wife from the home, pouring forth all his hopes, all his devotion, all his pride and love upon the little daughter whose name he had deliberately chosen as a presage of her future renown. From her fifth birthday, when she first came into his charge, he surrounded her with a more than paternal care. He gave her daily lessons and as much close companionship as a busy life could afford: he even kept for her a diary, couched in correct autobiographical form and containing not only the record of her progress but the most pungent comments on her occasional misdeeds: —

"My father who had long hoped in vain for a change of disposition on my part noticed again today that I am still lazy, careless, disorderly, obstinate and disobedient, and that I play as badly as I study."

So says the diary on October 29th 1828, when the criminal was nine years old and, what is the more remarkable, had just played for the first time at the Gewandhaus and had

---

1) It may be added that when the Leipsic Conservatorium was established Mendelssohn made every effort to secure Wieck as Professor of the pianoforte and it was only on his refusal that the post was offered to Moscheles.

"won much applause". It was on this occasion that the débutante, on setting out for the concert-room, was put by mistake into an omnibus conveying some dancers to a country ball. When she arrived at the Gewandhaus, very late and very nervous, she was met by her father with a paper of sugar-plums and the grave reassurance "I quite forgot to tell you, Clärchen, that people are always taken to the wrong house the first time they play in public". It is the sort of explanation which would have delighted Lewis Carrol.

We can trace a further development of Wieck's character when, in 1831, the concert-tours began: his joy in his daughter's triumphs, his rage at official stupidity, the sardonic humour that notes down, with their appropriate replies, the "seventeen questions which were asked him seven hundred times at Hamburg": —

Q. When did your daughter begin?
A. Never.
Q. How old is your daugther *really*?
A. That is written under her portrait.
Q. Do not your daughter's fingers hurt her?
A. You forget that you are speaking of Clara Wieck.

and so on, up to the climax: —

Q. Does your daughter like playing?
A. There is an end of everything — even of answers.

It is noticeable that although he firmly upheld the "classical" school of Clementi, and had the greatest dislike of mere dexterity he allowed Clara during these early years to study many bravura pieces, particularly those of Herz and Hünten which Schumann afterwards killed in the Neue Zeitschrift. A possible explanation may be found in another "question and answer" which is recorded in the diary. Someone asked him whether his daughter did not play "anything of Hummel,

Kalkbrenner or Beethoven" — a significant collocation. The
reply was "yes, but only at home". And indeed when we
study the concert programmes of 1830 we are forced to the
conclusion that Wieck knew his public[1].
At the same time it must be admitted that he was doing
as much as anyone to reform and educate the popular taste.
He brought up his daughter on the practise of Bach and
Beethoven; he made her study Chopin when the rest of Germany, led by Rellstab, was laughing at the "crazy stuff", he
was one of the first men, outside Vienna, to appreciate
Schubert. Yet all this sensitive artistic discrimination was
controlled by a sturdy prudence and directed by a keen eye
to the main chance. Music was to be an ideal, but it was
to be none the less a profession and a career: there must
be no extravagance, no fanaticism, no leading of forlorn hopes;
but a wise and well-regulated life devoted to noble pursuits
and surrounded by adequate comfort. When in 1830 Schumann
threw up his law-classes and announced to his mother that
he wished to become a musician, Wieck wrote her a letter
full of sympathy and insight and solid reasoning, in which
there occurs the following paragraph: —

"Without committing myself further at present I declare
that the piano-virtuoso (if he does not happen to be the most
famous composer whose name has been honoured for years)
can earn his living only if he gives lessons — but then very

---

1) Miss May: (op. cit p. 186) says that the first performance of the
Appassionata at a Concert was that given by Madame Schumann in
1837: thirty years after its publication. There was in Paris, at this time,
an outburst of enthusiasm for Beethoven, but it was mainly directed
towards the Symphonies and especially No. 7. And even here the Conservatoire, according to Berlioz, remained hostile. See his Autobio-
graphy ch. XX.
2) See the whole letter, pp. 18—31.

easily and well. Good intelligent teachers who have received an all-round education are wanted everywhere, and it is known that people pay 2—4 thalers an hour in Paris, Vienna, St. Petersburg, Berlin, etc. and 6—8 thalers in London. I am educating my daughter to be a teacher first of all, though — child as she is — she is already far superior to all other women-pianists in the world for she can improvise freely: but I do not allow this to mislead me in any way. Robert would be able to live very comfortably in such places as a piano teacher since he has a small income of his own. For I should be sorry to think that he will eat up his capital."

Two years later Schumann permanently crippled his hand, and his chances of a career, as teacher or virtuoso, were gone for ever. His compositions, though they were welcomed by such critics as Liszt and Grillparzer, had not yet attained any success with the public; the Neue Zeitschrift, which he started in 1834, brought him much applause but a scanty income; and we can well imagine Wieck's feelings when in the summer of 1837 this unwelcome suitor asked him formally for his daughter's hand. It is fair to hold that his refusal was not mainly selfish. No doubt he could ill accept the prospect of parting from the daughter whose genius he had trained and whose companionship had been, from her childhood, his constant solace and delight; but the weight that lay heaviest in the scale was his firm conviction that the marriage would prove disastrous. He had known what poverty meant; he had fought his way out of it by sheer determination and energy; in his eyes Schumann was an "imagination-man", a dreamer of dreams, endowed, may be, with the talent that should deserve success, but not with the mastery that should command it. The event showed that his forecast was erroneous, but given the time and the circumstances it was not unreasonable. He had keen memories of an unhappy marriage: his natural temper was cold and passionless: it would have been little short of a miracle if he had understood.

He began with direct refusal. When that weapon broke in his hand he offered conditions which, perhaps, were meant to be prohibitive: during three miserable years he grew daily more peevish and more embittered. In 1839 he proposed, as an open challenge, that his daughter should wait until she was of age and in the meanwhile travel on another concert-tour with him; and when this proposal was declined he froze into a black hatred the story of which is almost too pitiable to record. For a time he forgot his honour, his manliness, his probity; everything except the sense of defeat and the desire of revenge.

The marriage was allowed by the law-courts against his plea, which indeed brought him nothing but the unsuccessful defence of a libel-action. He accepted it in grim silence and even when news came to tell him of the birth of a grand-daughter he showed no sign of relenting. But, in 1843, when the outlook seemed hopeless, Madame Schumann received an unexpected letter which said: —

"I continue to have a genuine and undisturbed love of art, and it follows that the work of your talented husband cannot remain unconsidered and unrecognised by me. I will prove this to you by asking you to let me know in advance when there is any chance of my hearing in public some of your husband's latest compositions, which are so much praised by connoisseurs. I would come to Leipsic on purpose."

and ended: —

"Come to Dresden soon and bring your husband's quintet with you."

Later in the same year, when Schumann had established his reputation with Paradise and the Peri, there came a second letter addressed to him: —

"We were always united where art was concerned. I was even your teacher: my verdict decided your present course for you. There is no need for me to assure you of my sympathy with your talent and with your fine and genuine aspirations.

In Dresden there joyfully awaits you

Your father

Fr. Wieck."

It is very characteristic of Wieck that, after barring his front-gate against the rebels he should invite them in through the door of the music-room. He had opposed Schumann from a genuine disbelief in his powers, and with a sort of Stoic justice withdrew when he found that he was in the wrong. The reconciliation was cordially accepted, and despite occasional clouds, was never again seriously impaired. Sometimes his irritable pride was wounded by an offer which he took for patronage: sometimes his anger was roused by a momentary failure or disappointment, but his daughter's affection for him remained unbroken till the end, and the words in which she records his death[1] are at once the noblest and the most fitting monument to his memory.

When Schumann made acquaintance with Clara Wieck she was nine years old, he was nineteen, and the affection which sprang up between them seems, at first, to have been like that of the younger sister for the big brother at the University. He was an admirable playfellow, good at devising games and inventing riddles, and telling the most romantic ghost-stories: it is easy to realise how much sunshine he must

---

[1] October 6th 1873. See Vol. II p. 301.

have brought into that rather frigid and formal household.
He had already given ample indication of that vein of sentiment which ran so deeply through his character, but it was
traversed by a boyish gaiety and good-humour, and by a
whimsical sense of fun which may well have been its natural
counterpart. When in 1829 he migrated to Heidelberg —
ostensibly to attend Thibaud's lectures, really to "practise the
piano for seven hours a day" and to write the "Papillons"
and the "Abegg" variations — he entered on his new work
with the same cheery and buoyant temper, and the diary of
his first vacation is one long record of adventure and high
spirits.

Then, in close succession, came two calamities the effect
of which on his early life can hardly be overestimated. In
1832 came the accident which ruined his career as a virtuoso
and which befell at a time when he had begun to doubt his
prospects as a composer. A few months later followed the
death of his sister-in-law Rosalie Schumann, who ever since
her marriage had been his most intimate friend and coun-
sellor. The news entirely prostrated him; for some days
he feared the loss of his reason; and when medical aid
restored him to health he returned with an enfeebled will
and a darkened outlook on life. Five years later he can
hardly bear to speak of his sorrow [1].

It is certain that his feeling for Clara Wieck had already
ripened into something far warmer than admiration. But at
a period of such deep depression and mistrust he may well
have thought that this "bright particular star" was unattainable.
While she was winning triumphs from Paris to Berlin he was
sitting at home with a crippled hand and a desk-full of un-

---

[1] See the letter of February 11th, 1838. Vol. I pp. 70—73.

successful compositions: he did not know enough of human
nature to realise that if she loved him his weakness would
have been an irresistible appeal. So from sheer unhappiness
and need of companionship he drifted into betrothal with
Ernestine von Fricken: a betrothal which brought him for a
time some measure of consolation, and then died away as
quietly as it had begun.

By 1834 he had recovered confidence in himself and his
art. His compositions, which now included the Carnaval, the
Toccata, the two great piano-sonatas and the two sets of
'Paganini' caprices, were beginning, through the instrumentality
of Clara Wieck, to attract the attention of connoisseurs: the
Neue Zeitschrift, though it brought him little income, yet gave
him the opportunity of making his mark as the first musical
critic in Germany. To this was added the cordial friendship
of Mendelssohn, who settled at Leipsic in 1835 and was received
with a hero-worship which ennobled everyone that it touched.
So came into existence the honourable society of the Davidsbund: — Florestan and Eusebius, Raro and Felix Meritis and
Chiarina who was best and dearest of them all: once more
Schumann could feel that life was good, that it meant art and
comradeship and affection and the promise of an even richer
guerdon to come. The winter of 1835 brought him nearer
the fulfilment of his hopes: in the summer of 1836 he proposed
marriage and was accepted.

We are told that, with all a lover's optimism, he had taken
Wieck's consent for granted, and there can be no doubt that
he was deeply wounded by his disappointment. During the
last three years he had become if not famous at any rate
honourably known, he had won an established position, he
had learned to trust his own genius, — in any case to a
newly accepted suitor there is no such word as fail. Wieck,

however, maintained a stubborn opposition, and in face of that barrier his courage was not always at its height. He was, indeed, the last man in the world who should have been subjected to such a trial. From his gentle sensitive nature every blow drew blood. To his transparent honesty of purpose even the most innocent finesse was abhorrent. Throughout his life he never pushed his own interest, or fought in his own quarrel, or attacked anyone save, now and again, an artistic malefactor. It was a hard stroke of fortune that placed him in circumstances from which only a "strong trampling man" could emerge unscathed.

And as we read the history of the next four years we see how deeply he was indebted to the power and foresight of the woman who afterwards became his wife. She moulded all that was best in his plans, she soothed him in despondency, encouraged him in hope, and quieted by her own sweetness and dignity his rare moments of jealousy or ill-humour. It is easy to judge him too severely: it is not so easy to maintain that any other man, with so much at stake, would have borne himself better. At any rate by this time the story has been fully (perhaps too fully) revealed, and the reader is well provided with the materials for drawing his own conclusion.

In the autumn of 1840 the cloud passed away, and the Schumanns entered on a married life as noble and beautiful as that of the Brownings at Casa Guidi. During its first few years Schumann's health improved, and his genius came to its climax in that series of masterpieces which extends from the "year of songs" to the mystic chorus of the second part of Faust. Even the terrible disease which clouded the last decade of his life could neither sour his temper or degrade his ideals. No doubt it made him more hesitating in judgement more shy and silent in his dealings with his fellow-men; it caused the irresolution which hindered his career at Dresden and entirely ruined it at Düsseldorf[1]); but it never seems to have extorted from him one bitter word or one unkindly action. His "enmities" were all in the cause of art, — as for instance when he quarrelled with Gradener for refusing to drink to the memory of Jean Paul, or turned Liszt out of his house for disparaging Mendelssohn[2]), — and even these were forgotten as soon as the outburst was over. He seems to have been incapable of hate or envy: he bore opposition with patience and repaid friendship a thousand-fold. When he felt that the final tragedy was approaching he himself made preparations for going to the asylum, lest in the darkness of insanity he might do some hurt to those whom he loved: his last act, before it fell, was to compose music to a theme which had been "dictated to him in a vision by the spirits of Schubert and Mendelssohn". His intervals of health at Endenich were entirely occupied by memories of his art and solicitude for his family and his friends: when the moment of release came it set free one of the gentlest and purest souls that have ever appeared on earth.

During all these dark days of anxiety and sorrow Madame Schumann found comfort and support in the friendship of Johannes Brahms. He had come to Schumann in 1853 with a letter of introduction from Joachim, had at once been received into the intimate circle, and was by this time treated almost as a son of the house. His warm and affectionate nature, his uprightness and honesty rendered him doubly sympathetic to the great artists in whom these qualities were so conspicuously present: his genius, mature even in boyhood, was welcomed by them with an admiration marred neither by patronage nor by rivalry. From the first he was "der der

---

1) See Vol. II ch. 1.
2) See Vol. I pp. 466 and 395.

kommen musste", the pioneer of the new paths which Schumann could no longer hope to tread; each new work of his as it appeared was hailed by them not only as an achievement but as a presage of future advance; and his own buoyancy and vitality repaid in no small measure the love which they showed him. "His nobleness of mind", writes Madame Schumann in 1855 [1]) "his clearness of vision lend one wings".

There can be no better illustration of the comradeship that subsisted between them than can be found in the first cloud by which it was temporarily darkened. On July 1st 1858 she writes to protest against a letter of "cold philosophising" and "unjust reproaches" "which have hurt me more than anything has done for a long time". The letter of Brahms to which these words were an answer is a warning to her that she is setting too high a price upon his talent — that her praise of it is accentuated by personal affection: —

"You demand too rapid and enthusiastic a recognition of talent which you happen to like. Art is a republic, you should take that as your motto. You are far too aristocratic . . . . do not place one artist in a higher rank and expect the others to regard him as their superior, as dictator. His gifts will make him a beloved and respected citizen of the abovementioned republic, but will not make him consul or emperor."

Cold philosophising, no doubt; for very few men are so dispassionate about their own merits. But it is a curious and significant subject for mutual reproach. Nor is the end of the letter less noticeable: —

"Do not look upon my folk-songs as more than the most casual studies, or you will be much dissatisfied. But perhaps in one or two of them you may see gleams of better things. You should improve the accompaniment: try to make it freer."

_____

1) See Vol. II p. 100.

When we realise that Brahms was, at this time, the greatest living writer of song-accompaniments we cannot but wonder at the modesty with which he submits his work for censure and correction. Schubert, one of the most genial of men, is only known to have accepted criticism twice in his life and both times with a bad grace: Chopin, who would torment himself for weeks over a single phrase, shrank (perhaps in consequence) from the least breath of adverse opinion: Brahms endures good-temperedly to be told that one of his melodies is "like Hiller" and that his pianoforte passages are occasionally dry. It is true that the praise is cordial and the blame tactfully administered, but it is a tribute to the sincerity of both artists that they could discuss so intimate a matter with a frankness so plain-spoken and so unreserved[1].

This is the more noteworthy because, on other grounds, the friendship was not always uninterrupted. Brahms, with all his greatness, had a freakish humour which sometimes pushed the jest beyond the verge of offence, and which once at least was the occasion of a serious quarrel. At the same time, though singularly open-minded in all that concerned his art, he was, like so many musicians, hyper-sensitive to the fear of a personal rebuff. When he was helping Madame Schumann to prepare the first great edition of her husband's works she happened, for some reason, to omit a few pianoforte pieces on which he had bestowed especial care, and the fancied neglect rankled in his mind long after she had forgotten the circumstance from which it arose. "I feared," he writes "that you did not wish to see my name coupled with his": — a sentence which shows how deeply the misunderstanding must

1) Madame Schumann was not the only critic whose verdict Brahms accepted with equanimity. See for many other instances his correspondence with the Herzogenbergs.

have penetrated. Well she might write in her diary (December 16th 1886) "I was full of sad thoughts about Brahms this afternoon . . . . . How lonely one must feel when one is no longer in touch with one's best and oldest friends". Yet these were after all but episodes: touches of human weakness which could mar but not destroy the affection of so many years. The good sense and good feeling of both prevailed in the end[1]), the memory of a common sorrow brought them once more together, and the last years of their friendship were as serene and unruffled as the first.

Indeed it is no exaggeration to say that Madame Schumann's attitude towards Brahms, as revealed in this biography, is like that of a wise and loving mother towards a brilliant, affectionate and rather wayward son. Her character, always strong, had been finely tempered by the vicissitudes of her girlhood and by the joy and the tragedy of her married life: the trials which would have broken a more dependent spirit only confirmed in her the gifts of kindness and fortitude, of humility and self-reliance. Perhaps the two most conspicuous of her qualities were her warmth of affection and her unswerving justice. We can trace them already in the motherless girl whose keenest delight was in her father's approbation, and whose first tears were shed on hearing herself undeservedly applauded. Through the chequered and involved drama which preceded her marriage it was she who carried the issue in her hands: who decided between competing projects, who adjusted irreconcileable claims, and who bore with admirable sweetness and patience a persecution that must have wounded her like a poisoned weapon. After marriage she subordinated her own life, as far as was possible, to that

---

1) See the three letters of September, October 1892 (Vol. II pp. 417 —419).

of her husband; though she was the more famous artist of the two she always gave him precedence, and she was far more shocked than amused when at one of her recitals an ill-informed patron asked her "And is your husband also musical?" Indeed there is a typical story that once she gave up practising for many days, with an important concert in view, because "Robert was composing in the study and must not be disturbed". The greatest work of her career was to establish his reputation, and in so doing she built her own imperishable monument.

Her relations with his intimate friends was always frank and cordial. First came Mendelssohn, whose arrival at Leipsic in 1835 opened a new musical horizon: later came Joachim to whose executive genius her own was perhaps most closely akin, and of whose character hers was in many ways the counterpart. With Liszt the Schumanns were never entirely at their ease: Madame Schumann in particular seems to have noticed from the outset a touch of insincerity in his music which even his amazing power as a virtuoso was not wholly able to conceal. But to every artist the house-door stood open, for every genuine gift there was welcome and admiration, every triumph was shared with whole-hearted and ungrudging pleasure. It is ill speaking about the jealousy of musicians when we read what she says of Schröder-Devrient and Jenny Lind and Stockhausen, of the great pianists who were her contemporaries, and of the composers from Chopin to Brahms whose works she interpreted.

No doubt, like everyone else, she had her antipathies, among which we may regretfully notice some of our countrymen whom her husband held in esteem. In 1839 she writes from Paris.

"Do you want me to play Moscheles, Bennett, and (what is the third called?) Potter? I should be sorry to play the

first for he is dry, at least in his new compositions: very
sorry to play the second (I simply cannot conceal from
you that I cannot like his compositions) and the third? I
know nothing whatever of him, but he does not sound very
hopeful."

Vieuxtemps, too, she disliked, thinking his work flashy and
superficial, as indeed it is: while poor Ella who conducted
the Musical Union concerts is dismissed as "knowing no more
of music than a baby". But her severest censure was always
visited on compositions of which she thought the moral tendency unwholesome. A scene from Berlioz' Romeo and Juliet
seemed to her "really devilish music"; the repute of Wagner
was in her eyes merely "a passing intoxication" and she
warmly supported Joachim when in 1876 he aroused some
enmities by refusing to attend the Bayreuth Festival. But in
no adverse judgement was there ever a touch of personal
feeling. It was always easier for her to praise than to blame,
and her verdict, on whichever side it lay, was carefully and
maturely considered.

Her compositions were episodes, side-issues in her life, and
there is no need that they should here be described in any
detail. They are indeed too derivative in character to add
very greatly to her reputation. The early scherzos are closely
reminiscent of Chopin: the smaller pianoforte lyrics often
recall Mendelssohn's Lieder: the Preludes and Fugues, admi-
rably written for the keyboard, are studies in the manner of
Bach — except for one prelude where Chopin unexpectedly
reappears: — the later compositions all show more or less
the dominating influence of Schumann. But though there is
in them no striking originality they are far too good to be
neglected. Three of the songs are included in Schumann's
Liebesfrühling, and are well worthy of their place: the cadenzas

to Beethoven's C minor and G major concertos and to the
D minor Concerto of Mozart are in their kind masterpieces:
the variations "on a theme of Schumann" and on Haydn's
"Emperor's Hymn" are brilliant in the best sense of that
misused term: the pianoforte romances show a good deal of
poetic feeling. Her most elaborate composition is the Piano-
forte Trio in G minor op. 17: a pleasant, clear, melodious
piece of work, written with freshness and charm, and presenting no great difficulties either to the performers or to the
audience. It is entirely free from triviality or sentimentalism,
it says what it has to say in simple and unaffected language,
and it might well be used to replenish the not overwealthy
stores of our concerted chamber-music.

As an executive artist she took high rank — perhaps the
highest — among the great pianoforte players of her time.
There were, in the days when some of us were young, many
pianists whom London specially delighted to honour: — Hallé
reserved and self-contained, always faithful to his text, and
always exquisitely pure in tone: Bülow, epigrammatic, incisive,
a little hard, a virtuoso of wonderful skill, a musician of keen
intellectual powers, too disdainful of his audience to be wholly
sympathetic: Rubinstein, turbulent, miraculous, defiant of all
laws, a storm of passion which swept you from your feet like
a whirlwind. (But no-one combined all her gifts: none could
reconcile such warmth of emotion with such inherent reverence for the chastity of art.) She was as incapable as Joachim
of trick and artifice; in her playing, as in his, there was an
essential nobility which would never stoop to conquer. Her
technique might serve as a model to many famous virtuosi
of to-day. She never seemed to raise her hands from the
keyboard, the notes even in staccato passages, were pressed
rather than struck, her strength of arm was concentrated

more in the wrist than in the elbow. As a natural consequence her loudest volume of tone was neither harsh nor
strident, there was no "edge" to it, no feeling of shock or
impact, but a rounded beauty which filled the ear without
ever setting it astrain. Still more wonderful was her cantabile.
Of many great pianists it is high praise to say that their
melodies are crystalline: hers were liquid, a continuous flow
of sound which swelled and eddied and rippled with all the
loveliness of a living voice. Yet finest of all was her power
of interpretation: the sympathy which mediated between composers and audience, which revealed the creative genius as a
great actor reveals Shakespeare or Gœthe, not by obtrusion
of personality but by due subordination and control. To
hear her play Schumann's C major Phantasie, and follow it,
on recall, with Warum or Träumerei or the Schlummerlied
was to realise once for all what was meant by romance
in Music.

In many directions, too, she was a pioneer to whom later
musicians are deeply indebted. She studied Bach at a time
when, to the public, his work was almost entirely unknown.
She was the first to play Beethoven's Appassionata in a
concert-hall, and to convince many unwilling sceptics that his
later sonatas were neither laboured nor obscure. While the
critics were warning Germany against Chopin she was teaching
it to understand him: she played Mendelssohn's Lieder as no-
one has ever played them since, and gave their first impetus
to the pianoforte works of Brahms. It may be true that in
Schumann's music she found her closest and most intimate
inspiration: it is natural that this should be so, for on this
point all the circumstances of her life converged. But to say
that is not to disparage her breadth of knowledge, her cathol-
icity of taste, and the magnetic insight with which she at-

tracted and held all the strength and purity of the art which she served.

A gift so personal is not readily transmitted, yet in the greatest of her pupils we may find something of the spirit by which she was animated, and something at any rate of the ideals which she kept in view. Since her death there has followed a remarkable change in the whole structure and idiom of music, a change which has set us enlarging our vocabulary and revising our critical standards. On all historical analogy we may expect to find that some of it is bravado, some a passing fashion, and some a real advance on intelligible lines of evolution. But with us, as with our forefathers, the real touch-stone is sincerity, "not newness", as Ruskin said, "but genuineness"; and in applying this test we may well follow the example of one who maintained untarnished the faith that was in her, and who by sheer force of character and genius has handed it on as an heritage to the generations that are yet to come.

W. H. H.

AUTHOR'S PREFACE.

That the portrait of Clara Schumann should be painted
not by a musician but by an historian of literature calls for
a word of explanation and perhaps of apology. May I therefore be permitted to give a brief account of the circumstances
which have finally led me, after long hesitation, to obey the
call of necessity and of impulse and to undertake a work so
far removed from my usual sphere?

About a year after the death of Clara Schumann, her eldest
daughter asked me, in the name of her brothers and sisters,
if I felt disposed, with the help of the letters and diaries left
in their hands, to write the biography of her mother.

Although from childhood I had been fortunate enough to
experience in the daily intercourse of my parents' house the
wonderful fascination which Clara Schumann's personality
exercised upon all who knew her, and the suggestion was
therefore extremely tempting from both an artistic and a
psychological point of view, yet, upon mature consideration,
I then felt myself bound to give an unqualified refusal, as I
felt I had not the peculiar technical knowledge of music necessary for the biographer of an executive artist. I suggested,
therefore, that the guardian of this rich treasure should herself undertake the work and from her parents' letters and
diaries put together a book of the kind which S. Hensel produced for the Mendelssohns in his *Familie Mendelssohn*. And
I gladly offered to give help and advice.

Unfortunately insurmountable obstacles prevented this suggestion from being carried out. In the autumn of 1898, how-

ever, Fräulein Marie Schumann succeeded in finding in Julius
Allgeyer, the biographer of Anselm Feuerbach, a man whose
long intimacy with the Schumanns — dating, as it did, from
Düsseldorf days — as well as his many-sided artistic and
musical culture marked him out as peculiarly fitted for such
a task. The septuagenarian flung himself into the work with
youthful fervour and whole-hearted devotion.

At the end of a year the first part of the biography, down
to the last two years of Clara's girlhood, was in manuscript.
Then, in September 1900, Allgeyer died.

And now for a second time the Schumann family begged
me to give the help which I had promised, to edit Allgeyer's
work and to write the concluding chapter of a volume which
was to bear his name and stamp. This request I felt it impossible to refuse without trangressing the limits within
which I had offered my assistance. But when, in the
spring of 1901, I began the work, I found unlooked-for difficulties. Soon I realised that not only had the final chapter
to be written, but that Allgeyer's manuscript needed alterations on so many important points that in the end it
would be practically a new work. Thus unexpectedly and
contrary to his first intention the editor was forced to become author.

The manner in which the book originated has not been
without its influence upon the style of the first volume. Carefully as I have attempted to modify the work of my prede-
cessor — going over it page by page, striking out here and
inserting there — yet numerous passages great and small were
taken over as they stood. And it cannot be denied that this
has resulted in a certain duality of style which the reader
cannot fail to notice, though it is to be hoped that this is not
sufficiently obtrusive to be disturbing.

My alterations are due partly to difference of temperament, partly to the fact that I have drawn more largely than All- geyer upon the diaries and have kept more strictly to their actual words. These diaries, indeed, afford the biographer the most valuable and characteristic material imaginable. There are 47 volumes which throw almost unbroken light upon the inner and outer life of Clara Schumann from the day of her birth to the day of her last illness, March 26th 1896.

On the first page of the first volume stand, written in Friedrich Wieck's hand, the words: "My diary, begun by my Father, May 7th 1827, and to be continued by Clara Josephine Wieck." In truth, the first volume, though Clara almost al- ways speaks in her own person, is written by Friedrich Wieck, and during all the years of girlhood, though sometimes Clara alone holds the pen and sometimes she alternates with her father, the diary reflects, not her thoughts and opinions, but her father's. Not till the summer of 1838, and more especially after the journey to Paris which marked the actual breaking free from her father, does Clara's personality make itself more and more evident and exact its due attention. Then came her marriage with Schumann and the practice of husband and wife keeping the diary for alternate weeks. This, how- ever, lapsed into desuetude and Schumann, under the ever increasing pressure of creative work, let himself be replaced by Clara, in whose hands — after the Russian tour of 1844 — the work was left altogether.

Next in importance to the diaries come the countless letters to and from Robert and Clara Schumann, most of which — and above all Clara's letters to Robert — are now published for the first time.

But a portrait of Clara Schumann must be drawn not only from such material as this, but also from all those contrib-

utory details which go to make up the impression of a personality, and in particular from a presentation of her inner
life, since only by laying bare the individual qualities of heart
and character can we understand how Clara Schumann came
to be accepted as a queen by more than two generations of
German artists.

Never, perhaps, has the very essence of her nature been
better understood and expressed than by Allgeyer in the
beautiful words with which he touches on this subject in the
preface which he sketched. They may well form the close of
this introduction, and at the same time stand as a memorial
to the excellent man who, alas! is no longer here to enjoy
the reward of his faithful work:

"In whatever character, in whatever relationship to the
world at large Clara Schumann shows herself in her correspondence, whether as daughter, sister, friend, betrothed, wife,
mother, artist, colleague, or teacher, everywhere and always
it is the absolute humanity combined with the fathomless
depths of a pure woman's soul which attracts and touches
us. This poetry of heart, as we may call it, which breathes
from her whole being spoke through her art, in the spiritual-
ised language of sound, to the soul, the feeling, the heart of
those who had ears to hear ... After what has been said,
the prominent position held by Clara Schumann in the musical
life of our day needs no explanation, we think first of the
woman. ... But in truth the biographer has fulfilled his task
only if he has succeeded in making the figure of this great
artist stand out clearly, and through her inmost being has
revealed her personality as a whole, showing her as an
example of noble, pure, and true womanhood."

Interlaken September 1st 1902.

Berthold Litzmann.

TABLE OF CONTENTS.

Vol. I.

ERRATA Vol. I.

p. 2 l. 18 for *sum* read *sense*.

p. 5 l. 25 for *premilinary* read *preliminary*.

p. 14 l. 5 for *in* read *is* (before the word *unapproachable*).

p. 15 l. 6 for *Hunten* read *Hünten*.

p. 19 l. 17 for *understake* read *undertake*.

p. 25 l. 33 for *bronce* read *bronze*.

p. 27 last line but one delete comma after *concert*.

p. 29 l. 10 for *misunderstool* read *misunderstood*.

p. 29 l. 24 for *keys-board* read *key-board*.

p. 30 l. 27 for *pianistes* read *pianists*.

p. 33 l. 10 after *among* insert *the*.

p. 33 l. 14 delete comma after *here*.

p. 33 l. 17 for *Moxert* read *Mozart*.

p. 33 l. 21 for *letter* read *better*.

p. 35 last line, for *distracteds* read *distracted*.

p. 50 *played* should come immediately after *Bahrdt*, instead of after *Variations*.

p. 51 l. 1 for *Darus* read *Carus*.

p. 54 l. 1 for *includig* read *including*.

p. 54 l. 8 for *by* read *be*.

p. 57 l. 16 for *peacably* read *peaceably*.

p. 58 l. 6 for *hand* read *hard*.

p. 58 l. 11 for *too* read *to*.

p. 58 last line for *enferred* read *inferred*.

p. 59 l. 32 for *think* read *thick*.

p. 64 l. 3 for *ove* read *love*.

p. 65 l. 16 for *Bank* read *Banck*.

p. 67 l. 6 for *daughthers* read *daughters*.

p. 74 l. 20 for *ordor* read *order*.

p. 79 l. 18 for *terrible* read *terribly*.

p. 80 l. 11 for *ABCH* read *ASCH*.

p. 81 l. 4 insert *were* after hours.

p. 84 l. 29 for *heard* read *head*.

p. 91 l. 15 for *notwithstandig* read *notwithstanding*.

p. 105 l. 21 for *stet* read *this*.

p. 110 l. 9 for *chould* read *should*.

p. 110 l. 25 for *ahe art* read *a heart.*
p. 110 l. 29 for *promissed* read *promised.*
p. 116 l. 21 for *faitfully* read *faithfully.*
p. 116 l. 23 for *your* read *you* (before the word *of*).
p. 124 l. 8 for *moonshire* read *moonshine.*
p. 124 l. 12 delete *your.*
p. 125 l. 25 for *thoroughy* read *thoroughly.*
p. 126 last line for *Henseltist* read *Henseltists.*
p. 128 l. 4 for *Belive* read *Believe.*
p. 128 l. 18 for *unknow* read *unknown.*
p. 136 l. 14 of poem, for *wonders* read *wonder.*
p. 138 l. 8 for *there* read *these.*
p. 138 l. 9 insert *I* before *suggest.*
p. 138 l. 10 for *you* read *your.*
p. 138 l. 12 for *fisrt* read *first.*
p. 145 l. 24 insert *of* after *recollections.*
p. 147 l. 5 for *were* read *where.*
p. 147 l. 17 insert *of* before *Buda-Pest.*
p. 148 l. 5 insert *have* before *the heart.*
p. 150 l. 18 for *heared* read *heard.*
p. 156 l. 2 from bottom, for *on* read *an.*
p. 156 l. 3 from bottom, for *artistes* read *artists.*
p. 157 l. 23 (also p. 277 l. 32) for *Rakemann* read *Rackemann.*
p. 160 l. 20 insert *the* before *future.*
p. 161 l. 3 of poem, for *no es* read *notes.*
p. 162 l. 33 (and 163 l. 33) for *Hasslinger* read *Haslinger.*
p. 166 l. 24 for *an* read *and.*
p. 170 l. 15 for *ether* read *other.*
p. 171 l. 25 for *here with* read *herewith.*
p. 171 l. 29 delete *a feeling.*
p. 178 l. 23 for *shouded* read *shrouded.*
p. 184 l. 15 for *lefter* read *letter.*
p. 189 l. 12 insert *with* before *your.*
p. 190 l. 15 insert *of* before *your.*
p. 191 l. 1 for *braggast* read *braggart.*
p. 192 l. 32 for *dit* read *did.*
p. 194 l. 26 for *managable* read *manageable.*
p. 202 last line, for *greateness* read *greatness.*
p. 203 l. 4 for *Frenchwoma* read *Frenchwoman.*
p. 203 l. 6 for *Frenchwomann* read *Frenchwoman.*
p. 203 l. 23 for *lear nto* read *learn to.*
p. 207 l. 12 for *hat* read *that.*
p. 211 (note) for *had been* read *afterwards.*
p. 215 l. 30 for *sorrows* read *sorrow.*

p. 222 l. 4 from bottom, insert *to* before *write*.
p. 223 l. 18 for *forget* read *forgot*.
p. 226 l. 4 for *your* read *you*.
p. 226 l. 18 for *at* read *as*.
p. 236 l. 8 insert *and* before *Henriette*.
p. 239 (note) *they* .... *conception* should come between *that* and *it*.
p. 240 l. 3 from bottom, insert *the* before *Fantasie*.
p. 241 l. 1 for *to* read *of*.
p. 242 l. 6 for *day but to* read *but to-day*.
p. 274 l. 6 for *livliest* read *liveliest*.
p. 274 l. 19 for *Nocturno* read *Notturno*.
p. 274 l. 26 for *hypocondriacism* read *hypochondriacism*.
p. 279 l. 2 for *witicism* read *witticism*.
p. 280 l. 16 for *ies* read *lies*.
p. 287 l. 12 for *humain* read *human*.
p. 289 l. 15 insert *at* before *all*.
p. 291 l. 9 for *behave* read *behaves*.
p. 297 l. 14 for *mariage* read *marriage*.
p. 298 l. 3 for *genus* read *genius*.
p. 301 l. 4 from bottom, for *versitality* read *versatility*.
p. 302 l. 14 for *writen* read *written*.
p. 303 l. 2 from bottom, for *interpretive* read *interpretative*.
p. 306 l. 10 insert *the* after *was*.
p. 310 l. 28 insert *of* before *so*.
p. 311 l. 3 for *naïvly* read *naïvely*.
p. 311 l. 22 transpose *et* and *nos*.
p. 318 l. 5 should be l. 1.
p. 329 l. 7 for *eve* read *Eve* and insert *formed* directly after it.
p. 335 last line, for *und* read *and*.
p. 342 l. 23 insert *a* before *symphony*.
p. 353 l. 6 *to her* should come at the end of the line above.
p. 353 l. 21 for *negociation* read *negotiations*.
p. 358 l. 25 delete *of*.
p. 359 l. 8 delete *are*.
p. 360 l. 20 delete the second *of*.
p. 383 l. 3 from bottom, insert *of* after *house*.
p. 383 l. 13 after 1849 substitute comma for full stop and read *the* for *The*.
p. 384 l. 6 for *discrepencies* read *discrepancies*.
p. 390 last l. for *insistantly* read *insistently*.
p. 398 l. 5 from bottom, for *medecine* read *medicine*.
p. 399 l. 5 from bottom, for *recurrance* read *recurrence*.
p. 417 l. 18 for *exclamation* read *exclamations*.
p. 420 l. 1 of foot-note for $E\sharp$ read $E\flat$.

Errata.

p. 428 l. 17 for *hignesses* read *Highnesses.*
p. 429 l. 6 insert *to* before *associate.*
p. 434 l. 12 for *house* read *houses.*
p. 437 l. 12 for *part* read *put.*
p. 438 l. 26 for *conducter* read *conductor.*
p. 442 l. 4 for *over-stain* read *over-strain.*
p. 448 last line of foot-note for *diano* read *piano.*
p. 453 l. 2 delete the 2nd *the.*
p. 462 l. 22 for *tableau* read *tableaux.*
p. 462 l. 28 for *Prophete* read *Prophète.*
p. 463 l. 14 for *ritardantos* read *ritardandos.*
p. 465 l. 3 etc. for *Egger* read *Eggers.*
p. 466 l. 4 for *one* read *once.*
p. 467 l. 14 for *beast* read *least.*
p. 470 l. 6 from bottom for *entsusiasm* read *enthusiasm.*
p. 470 l. 8 from bottom, insert *is* after *It.*
p. 474 l. 30 for *an* read *a.*
p. 475 l. 5 for *and* read *at.*
p. 476 l. 5 for *Kuntsch* read *Kuntzsch.*
p. 478 l. 5 from bottom, delete inverted comma.

CHAPTER I.

CHILDHOOD.

1819—1834.

"I was born at Leipsic, Sept. 13th 1819, in the house *Zur hohen Lilie* in the new *Neumarkt*, (to which my parents had moved at Easter 1818) and received the name of Clara Josephine. My godparents were a notary named Streubel, a friend of my father; Madame Reichel, a friend of my mother; and Frau Cantorin Tromlitz of Plauen, the mother of my mother Mariane Tromlitz. My father[1] kept a musical lending-library and carried on a small business in pianofortes. Since both he and my mother were much occupied in teaching, and beside this my mother practised from one to two hours a day, I was chiefly left to the care of the maid, Johanna Strobel. She was not very fluent of speech, and it may well have been owing to this that I did not begin to pronounce even single words until I was between four and five years old, and up to that time understood as little as I spoke. But I had always been accustomed to hear a great deal of piano playing and my ear became more sensitive to musical sounds than to those of speech. I soon learned to walk, and in my third and fourth years could go out with my parents and cover miles of road.

My inaptitude for speech, and my want of concern in all that was passing round me, often caused my parents to complain that I was dull of hearing. Even up to my eighth year this

---

1) Friedrich Wieck, born 1785, died 1873.

defect was not entirely cured, although it improved as I came
to speak better and to take more notice of what was going on.

At Easter 1821 my parents moved to a house in the *Salz-
gässchen*, and it was here that I was fated to lose my mother.
She left my father on May 12 1824 and went to Plauen to
arrange for a legal separation."

With this harsh dissonance begins the record of a life which
in later years was to pour its full music before innumerable
multitudes and to round on a close of perfect and unalloyed
harmony. It was her father's hand which traced these lines
on the opening pages of her diary: that loving stern hand
which with unbroken singleness of purpose, moulded the girl's
life and thoughts, and yet with utter callousness bruised the
most intimate and tender of her feelings. The few cold words
in which he narrates, for his daughter's reading, the disaster
of his marriage, show little care for the pain with which she
was one day to see them, if indeed they were not intended to
widen her sum of the estrangement.

Wieck's right to the custody of his daughter began at her
fifth birthday. Accordingly for a few months she accompanied
her mother, together with her little brother Viktor [1]), (born in
the spring of 1824) on the strict understanding that she should
return to Leipsic by September 13th. There is a pathetic
letter in which Frau Wieck asks leave to bring her back in
person: a permission which Wieck refused. At the same time
he certainly allowed some freedom of intercourse between
them. In 1825 Frau Wieck married a music-teacher named
Bargiel and came with him for a year's residence in Leipsic.
During that year Clara frequently visited her mother, carrying
with her on one occasion a stiff, characteristic note which
begins 'Madame, I send you the dearest thing left me in the

---

1) *Translator's note*: Her brothers Alwin (born Aug. 27 1821) and
Gustav (born Jan. 31 1823) remained at Leipsic.

world', and continues with injunctions that 'she be told nothing which can arouse her suspicions', that 'she be given little pastry', that 'her conduct be better supervised than it was at Plauen', and that 'she should not be allowed to hurry when practising'.

"On September 18th," so runs the diary, "my father began to give me regular piano-lessons. Already, some months before my mother took me with her to Plauen, I had learned to play several exercises without moving the hand and had picked up a few simple dance-tunes by ear, but this was all that I could accomplish since I could neither speak myself nor understand others.". Wieck cannot refrain from adding bitterly "During the few months at Plauen my mother, in this respect at all events, was not of the slightest use to me."

For her musical gift Clara was as much indebted to her mother as to her father. Mariane Tromlitz, who had been Wieck's pupil before she became his wife, was a good musician[1] and a capable pianist. But it was Wieck to whom his daughter owed her musical training. He was one of the greatest teachers in Germany, cordially acknowledged as master by Schumann, von Bülow and many others: he had made up his mind before Clara's birth that if she proved to be a girl she should be a famous artist, he deliberately chose her name as a presage of future renown, and the fulfilment of the presage was the chief work to which he dedicated his life.

"On October 27th of this year my father began to teach me together with Therese Geyer and Henriette Wieck." This was an experiment by which he hoped to diminish the difficulty which she found in speaking and in understanding what was said. As a matter of fact her power of speaking improved now with extraordinary rapidity, and she also

---

1) She was the granddaughter of Johann Georg Tromlitz the famous flute-maker, flute-player and composer.

displayed a remarkable memory, especially for music, and could play by heart and remember for a long time every little piece which she had tried over once or twice. These lessons lasted till Easter 1825. During this time she played according to Logier's system [1]), but her father also taught her by his own method [2]). By this method she played without notes at first, but at the same time learnt to write them down, though she went to no school and "did not know a single letter". By degrees she learnt to play all the scales, major and minor, in quick succession, with both hands together, and also to play triads in every position and every key. At the same time her father made her play by ear a number of little pieces which he wrote for her, since the training of the ear and the study of expression in contra-distinction to mere mechanical dexterity, formed the essence of his applied theory of musical education: as he himself says:

> The artist's first rule
> Is that skill is a tool;
> But your art's put to shame
> If skill is the aim.

Wieck believed that in this way the dull work of learning to read from note was made as little irksome as possible.

As a result of thoroughly practising her father's method Clara became so familiar with the key-board that when later

---

1) According to Logier's system the {difficulties of technique were made easier, and organic defects, such as stiffness and lack of flexibility of the fingers, were overcome by means of the "*Chiroplast*", a contrivance attached to the key-board to accustom the pupil to the best method of holding body, arms, and fingers.

2) Friedrich Wieck expressed — in pithy language which recalls the wisdom of popular proverbs — the substance and aim of his teaching, and above all the grounds and principles of his theory of music-teaching, in a pamphlet whose contents should be laid to heart by every student of music today: "*Piano and Song, a didactic and polemic work* by Friedrich Wieck" (Leipsic, Leuckart) and his thoughts on music as an art in his, "*Musical Proverbs and Aphorisms*". (Ibid. 1871.)

on she played from note she seldom found it necessary to watch her hands and could steadily follow the notes with her eyes. By this means in a short time she achieved a readiness in playing from note which was marvellous for her age. Also she had no difficulty in keeping time, although it was not until her eighth year, when she learned mental arithmetic at school, that she understood the correct way to count time. From the time she was six she went to school regularly, but for not more than from three to five hours a day, for her father now not only gave her an hour's lesson himself every day, but made her practise the piano daily for two hours more.

In the winter of 1825—1826 she went for the first time to the large subscription-concerts in the *Gewandhaus*. "I heard," says the diary, "a grand symphony of Beethoven's, amongst other things, which excited me greatly. Also I heard some big choral works, which interested me very much."

Her education was, so her father thought, greatly helped, during the following year (down to September 1827) by his pupil, Emilie Reichold from Chemnitz, in whom Wieck was specially interested, and who gave a concert at the *Gewandhaus* in the autumn of 1826. She made Clara read through a number of pieces, and also study some more carefully, in the course of which, as the diary reprovingly remarks, she had, "much to suffer" through the "contradictoriness" of the pupil "which I seem to have inherited". In the year 1826 Clara learned a great many duets playing mostly the bass part.

At the end of the year — after a course of premilinary exercises to make the hand capable of stretching — she first began to play octaves with both left and right hand. At six years and ten months (July 23rd 1826) she played with an accompaniment for the first time; taking the bass part of Haslinger's little *Concerto for four hands with Quartet accompaniment*.

A few weeks later she went to the theatre for the first time, and saw Ludwig Devrient as "the poor poet" in Kotzebue's piece of that name, and as "Elias Krumm", "which", says the diary, "I did not understand"; and in addition to these she saw Spohr's *Berggeist*, "which filled my thoughts for a long time, although I did not understand it either".

The year 1827 brought a substantial advance. "In 1827", remarks the diary, "my perception of music began to develop more and more quickly, and I could distinguish the keys with fair certainty simply by ear, nor was I unacquainted with the first elements of theory, I could quickly find the sub-dominant and dominant chords in every key, and could modulate at will or at command (as the chords led me) from major and minor keys through the diminished seventh, by using the leading-note of the dominant. My playing also improved, my attack was good, firm and sure, and my fingers strengthened so rapidly that I could now play difficult pieces for two hours on end with fair persistency, and my father often praised my aptitude for natural and good execution, which I always liked. "But", the inexorable diary continues, "I very easily became obstinate over it and my desires were limitless — (so my father says)!"

The daily practising was now extended to three hours, and the hand was specially trained and strengthened by new exercises in trills.

In May she began her first study of a concerto with orchestral accompaniment, Hummel's *Concerto in G-major* Op. 73, which she had mastered by July. At the same time the diary tells us of little attempts at composition. "My father says that most of them were correct rhythmically, and the bass was tolerable; at least I did not double the major third in the chord of the dominant and I avoided fifths and octaves which always sound so ugly to me." She now began to notice the difference between good and bad pianos, specially liked

Andreas Stein's, and complained bitterly "if my father did not happen to have one now and then". But she condescended to play on any piano of from six to six and a half octaves, "which does not worry me". Square pianos however were emphatically declined, "because as a rule they have not sufficient tone". "My father assures me that I have already a powerful and good touch, with which the plumpness of my hand and the flexibility of my fingers (apart from any movement of the elbows) have not a little to do."

In direct connection with this, Friedrich Wieck incorporated with his daughter's diary — *sub specie aeterni* — his own programme of musical education, and added to this an expression of opinion, addressed to his friend Andreas Stein of Vienna, which fulfilled the threefold purpose of justifying his method, warding off the suspicion of enthusiasm, and spurring on the heroine of the book to fresh artistic efforts by a word of qualified praise which she was intended to overhear. "In my opinion" the word run "my daughter Clara will become a capable pianist: her attack and touch are already good, she has the right feeling for execution a good ear, some real musical talents, and a retentive memory. Her tone will be further developed as much as possible by the use of the best instruments, and perhaps I may add by the teaching of her father. Already she can play difficult studies artistically and with a round pure tone. But I do not wish her to kill herself (musically) by over-practise. Nearly all our virtuosi have done this — pianists in particular — they have practically no feeling or understanding left, but only a base pleasure in their own mechanical dexterity, nor, can they take any delight in hearing others play, but only in playing themselves!!" [1]

---

[1] The fable has often been spread abroad in the musical world that Clara was kept at the piano by her father as long as her physical strength would endure. The origin of this legend goes back to Franz

This impersonal appreciation and recognition of what had been reached so far, is followed a few days later by some characteristic remarks which must have been less pleasing to the subject of the diary: "My father specially blames me now for a certain jealousy of disposition — love of pleasure — childish sensitiveness — and a curious inclination never to enjoy the present time or present possessions. This last troubled my father the most, because it made me appear seldom contented, since a perpetual 'But' or 'If' got in the way."

If such demands as these made upon a child of eight, show an austere discipline only to be looked for in a much older person, the father's complaint, which follows a few months later, "over my entrance into the awkward age," at the same time shows a ray of humour which softens the rugged pedagogy; and the remark "that it is beginning to pass", affords proof how little rooted in this child's nature were the faults which were being blamed.

This was the point of mental and musical development which Clara had reached when on Sept. 9th 1827, four days before her eighth birthday, she played the E♭ major concerto

Liszt who was one of Clara's sincerest admirers. La Mara, without mentioning his authority, states that they left her so little leisure for play and recreation, such as child-nature delights in, that she was obliged to steal the few moments in which she caressed her beloved little kittens, behind her father's back. The present quotation, drawn from the most authentic source ought at last authoritatively to put an end to such statements. Anyone who knows Wieck's writings and the brilliant results which, up to his 88th year, accompanied his activity as a teacher, knows that to over-strain a pupil so cruelly, would be to pour contempt on one of the fundamental principles of his method of teaching. He really valued study only when it was begun with perfectly fresh, or well-rested powers. Clara was never compelled to practise more than three hours a day. She had to thank this circumstance for the fact that throughout her life she was spared from the chief suffering of the modern musical world, — nerves.

of Mozart before a select audience at a concert rehearsal. The accompaniment consisted of two violins, two violas, a violoncello, a flute, and two horns. Let us hear her own words, sent to her mother, Frau Bargiel, at Berlin, over this, her most recent appearance in public:

The letter — the first, by the way, that Clara ever wrote in her life — is remarkable for its precocious hand-writing, a peculiarity which may well be connected with the technical development of the little hand, and for the happy childishness which runs through it in spite of all.

"Dear Mother

You have as yet read nothing from me, but now I can write a little I will send you a little letter, which will please you. I had presents on my eighth birthday from dear Bertha and from my dear Father, from dear Father I got a beautiful dress, and from Bertha I had an ashcake and a plum-cake and a lovely knitting-bag. And I played Mozart's $E\flat$ major concerto which you used to play, with orchestral accompaniment, and Herr Mathäi, Lange, Belka and a lot of others played with me. It went very well and I never stuck at all, only my cadenza would not go easily, where I had to play a chromatic scale three times, I was not a bit frightened, but the clapping troubled me. Emilie Reichhold and M. Kupfer played too, The day before my birthday I went to Malger with Father. Please give my love to Grandmamma, and my brothers send their love to you. Now you will write to me, won't you?

Leipsic   Your obedient daughter
Sept. 14th Clara Wieck.
1827

Dear Mother

I will come to see you soon and then I will play a great many pieces for four hands with you. And I have sung and played through ever so many operas already, such as *Oberon, Die Schweizerfamilie, Der Schlosser, Die Zauberflöte*, which I have seen in the theatre too. My dear Father has ordered me a beautiful piano

from H. Stein in Vienna, because I have been industrious and
can play and sing at the same time all Spohr's songs, and the
concerto went without a mistake.

Good-bye   C."

In February 1828 the diary goes on to speak of a large
musical evening "At Home" which Friedrich Wieck gave and at
which Clara played, among other things, four polonaises of
Schubert, with her father. Soon after the expected piano
"of six octaves" arrived from Vienna, and at the same time
she received a Physharmonica[1]) of three octaves: "on which",
says the diary, "I can improvise".

She appeared more and more in public, though not chiefly
in the concert-hall. Thus the diary speaks on March 31st of
a gathering at Dr Carus's where she played a trio of Hummel's,
Op. 96, and adds, "I made fewer mistakes than the gentlemen
who accompanied me." Easter-time in particular, gave the
young performer many opportunities of appearing before artists,
and colleagues from other places. And while she herself,
like a true child, enjoyed the Easter festivities and conscientiously reports that she has seen "the wax-works, the elk,
Weisse, the juggler from Paris, the horse-breakers, and the
Panorama of Gibraltar", she continues, "I have played and
sung before a great many people this Easter, among other
things J. Schmidt's variations Op. 56, Moscheles' rondo No. 30,
and *Die Forelle* by Schubert".

It was possibly at this gathering at Carus's house that the
first meeting took place with Robert Schumann, who had
come to Leipsic a few days before (March 25th)[2]), and as he
was closely connected with the Caruses, may well have been
one of the guests.

Ostensibly Robert Schumann came to Leipsic with the
intention of studying jurisprudence. At the same time his

---

1) An instrument which had just then been revived by Anton Häckel.
2) Cf. *Jugendbriefe* p. 18.

remarkable talent for music, which had long ago manifested itself, was not to remain uncared for. He visited the Caruses, and thanks to them, appears immediately to have come into close touch with Friedrich Wieck, whose lively, stimulating disposition, as well as the extraordinary proficiency of his nine-year-old daughter, made Robert determine to become his pupil for piano. Before long he was the daily companion and recognised favorite in Wieck's house, and Clara's friend in particular; for no-one could invent new riddles, tell beautiful fairy-tales, or make one shudder at dreadful ghost-stories, so well as he.

On July 3rd of the same year Friedrich Wieck married for the second time. He married Clementine Fechner, a daughter of Pastor Samuel Traugott Fechner of Grossfärichen in the Niederlausitz. Clara and her two brothers, Alwin and Gustav, were present at the wedding.

Three days after this event Clara, accompanied by her father and her new mother, set out for Dresden, where they had many friends. "I was amazed at Dresden", the diary tells us, „and also at the beautiful country round; but I liked even better to be in the Simons' garden with little Ida and Thekla, and the lamb, or under the cherry-, and gooseberry- and currant-trees. I enjoyed myself thoroughly until the 15th, when we left again." Besides this, she was well-received among the musical circles of Dresden, and was allowed by her father to play in the Institute for the Blind, among other places. It was indeed, a preparation for her first public appearance, which took place in the *Gewandhaus* on Oct. 20th, at a concert given by a Fräulein Ernestine Perthaler of Graz in Styria. Clara played the treble in Kalkbrenner's variations Op. 94, with Emilie Reichold. "It went very well, and I did not play any wrong notes, but got much applause", says the diary.

She had a little adventure too, which the diary mentions briefly, and which she used afterwards to describe with much humour. One of the chief delights of these early appearances in public was the beautiful "*Gewandhaus* coach" in which the performers were accustomed to be fetched in state. Therefore when on the evening of the great day, they announced "the carriage for Fräulein Clara is ready", she went down with the servant in a very exalted frame of mind. It was a dreadful disappointment when instead of the beautiful, wellknown glass-coach she found waiting for her a vehicle something like an omnibus, which she had to share with several strange girls, all dressed in their best. The servant put her in, and off they went. But who can describe her amazment and uneasiness when, after passing down a few streets, the carriage stopped, and after a minute or two of waiting, a new, beautifully-arrayed guest joined them, and this was repeated over and over again in the following streets. This was surprising enough, but uneasiness grew to anxiety when she noticed that the carriage was obviously going in an entirely different direction from the one that she wanted. At last she took heart and shyly asked the lady sitting near her: "This is not the way to the *Gewandhaus*, is it?" "To the *Gewandhaus*? No; we are going to Eutritzsch." At this, overcome by her fate, she began to cry softly to herself. But all at once loud shouts were heard behind them — the carriage stopped, Clara was taken out, and the proper glass-coach soon appeared, and did really take her "to the *Gewandhaus*". The fact was that there was a country ball to which the porter's daughter, who was also called Clara, had been invited, and to which the guests were fetched from their houses by this vehicle. It had come to fetch the wrong Fräulein Clara. But naturally these experiences, first the disappointment and then the anxiety, had frightened the young débutante out of her childish confidence, and she arrived at the place of performance, where her father was already anxiously waiting for her, very much upset, and in tears. But if ever Friedrich

Wieck showed himself an inspired educationalist, it was at this moment. He saw what was at stake if Clara could not be quieted before she had to appear. And as if nothing had happened, he came towards her with a paper of sugar-plums in his hand and said: "I quite forgot to tell you Clärchen, that people are always taken to the wrong house, the first time they play in public."

But a harsh discord followed the "great applause". Nine days after this concert the master expresses his discontent with his pupil, in drastic term: "My father, who had long hoped in vain for a change of disposition on my part, noticed again to day that I am still lazy, careless, disorderly, obstinate, and disobedient, and that I play as badly as I study. I played Hünten's new variations Op. 26 to him so badly, without even repeating the first part of the variation, that he tore up the copy before my eyes, and from to day onwards he will not give me another hour, and I am to play nothing but scales, Cramer's *Études* Bk. I, and Czerny's trilling-exercises."

Violent as was the family thunderstorm, it soon passed over. By Nov. 5th the lessons had already begun again, "after I had faithfully promised to improve".

The year ended with the composition of a waltz for the taciturn old servant, the guardian of her earliest years, who must have been much edified by this musical greeting.

One February evening in 1829 Clara's father heard at the *Gewandhaus* that Paganini had arrived, and was going on to Berlin the next morning. He and several others quickly decided to try and persuade this rare guest, "the greatest virtuoso of our time", to give a concert in Leipsic. At first there was promise of success, but it came to nothing through "the obstinacy and narrow-mindedness of the concert-directors". "And so Paganini went away again", the diary relates, "and we looked after him with melancholy faces and longing eyes, and shall have to go to Berlin now if we want to hear him."

Friedrich Wieck did go, and the impression which Paganini's art made upon him was simply over-powering. "Never", he wrote in Clara's diary, "had he heard a singer who moved him so much as an adagio of Paganini's. Never has an artist been born whose greatness in unapprochable in so many different ways." Loud therefore was the joy when at last, in October of that year, they really succeeded in getting Paganini to give a concert in Leipzic.

"On the evening of Sept. 30th," runs the entry in the diary, "Paganini came, and now I shall hear the greatest of all artists."

The first concert took place on Oct. 5th. On the morning of the preceding day, Wieck, accompanied by his daughter, called on the master, who not only recognised him at once, but also received his little colleague very kindly. "I had to play to him, on a wretched old piano with black keys which had been left behind by a student; I played my polonaise in $E\flat$, which he liked very much, and he told my father that I had a vocation for art, because I had feeling. He at once gave us permission to attend all his rehearsals — which we did."

The days which now followed, were the most stirring and crowded which her life had known hitherto. The concerts took place on the 5th, 9th, 12th, and 16th of October, and on each evening Clara, full of reverence and exaltation, sat with her father in the closely-packed audience. Twice she sat on the stage, as guest of the artist, who also treated her very kindly at the rehearsals, having a chair brought up for her, for instance, and, when opportunity occurred, presenting her to critics from other places, such as Rellstab and Elsholz from Berlin; while Clara on her side, was able, by means of this privilege, to introduce older musicians whom she knew to the master. One afternoon she found an opportunity of playing to Paganini again; this time not on an old instrument, but

on a new one which Wieck had caused to be put in the place
of the other, during the first concert, so that he might show
Paganini an attention and be of some service to him. She
and her father played an unfinished rondo for four hands on
four themes from Paganini's concertos, written by her father's
friend, Krägen[1]), and Hunten's rondo for four hands on *Elisa-
betta.* "He praised me," says the diary, "but told me that I
must not play too restlessly and with too much movement of
the body."

The diary says very little of the impression made upon
her personally by his playing, it only makes a quite general
remark among other things on the first evening that Paganini's
cantabile with passages in double notes, and the rondo scherzoso
of the Kreutzer "were beyond all description". Later, only the
programmes were given. Nevertheless every line shows how
deep and powerful was the impression made by this first meeting with a great artist. At parting he gave her for her album a
sheet of paper containing four bars from his scherzo, and the
harmonization of the chromatic scale in contrary movement
"al merito singulare di Madamigella Clara Wieck". On the
departure of "the greatest artist who has ever been in Leipsic"
the nine-year-old little "Madamigella" gave the four-year-old
little son of Paganini two bunches of white and purple grapes,
and received as a reward a squeeze of the hand from the
master, while the two fathers kissed each other.

In the latter months of this year the noise of the great
world sounded ever nearer and louder in her child-life. She
began to think of artistic fame as the object of life, childishly
but yet in a shape that could be grasped. Nor were tactless
warnings wanting. A clerical relation to whom she played,
remarked unctuously: "You can do much, my daughter. Never
forget that the greatest art is virtue." "I will often say this

---

1) Court pianist to the king of Saxony. Died 1879 in Dresden.

to myself," the diary remarks. But in the mean time she looked out into the world which was to be hers without any serious doubt or anxiety. The first intimation of this appears in the diary for 1829. "Father has promised to take me to Dresden, towards Easter 1830, where I am to play in private houses [1])."

The journey was undertaken on March 6th. The visit proved so satisfactory from the outset that it extended to four weeks. The warmest interest was shown by the family of Hofrat Carus, whose influence and friendship Clara had chiefly to thank for her reception by the court and the aristocracy of Dresden. Thus she twice played to the Princess Louise, once in the presence of the future King John and his wife. Another time she improvised before this same Princess on a theme which was given her from *La Muette de Portici*. In a letter to his wife[2]) at this time, Wieck writes: "We are having an unexpectedly favourable reception here. Every one thinks not only Clara's musical development but her technique very remarkable. People do not know which to admire most, the child or the teacher. I am afraid lest the admiration and notice should have a bad influence on Clara. If I see any harm, I shall leave at once, so that she may return to her middle-class surroundings, for I am too proud of her simplicity to exchange it for any honour in the world. People find her very lovable: she is still the same simple, natural child, but she often shows deep understanding and rich imagination; she is unruly, but noble and sensible. When playing she is incredibly self-possessed, and the larger the company, the better she plays."

"Yesterday," says another letter, "Count Kospoth asked her to go there next Monday in order to play duets with his wife, who is among the finest woman-pianists in Germany. She

1) For the repertoire, see below,
2) Printed by Kohut, *Fr. Wieck* p. 55.

answered 'I will come; but are you sure your wife can play?' 'Yes, certainly,' he replied. 'Well take me to her then, and I will make her acquaintance.' .... Yesterday we played together before a large audience, and although the grand piano was remarkably hard to play upon, she played Herz's variations through, as well as possible. At the end, the whole company applauded. She stood there, quiet and grave, and said: 'There now! you are clapping, and yet I know I played very badly'; and she burst into tears. That is the only time, up to now, that she has cried."

Clara returned to her parent's house from her first tour as an artist, the richer by many pleasant memories and also by a number of little ornaments which had been given her.

At this point a course of theory, given by Cantor Weinlich[1]), was added to her musical studies, and for the first time we find J. S. Bach and his fugues, in her daily programme. When, by the beginning of September, she had finished her musical grammar, Weinlich started her on counterpoint. She at once composed her first four-part song, *Schwäne kommen gezogen*, and some two- and four-part chorales.

Matters had reached this stage when Robert Schumann came to lodge in the two rooms in Wieck's house looking on the *Reichsstrasse*[1]). He had spent three terms at Heidelberg, in the interval, studying jurisprudence. Hating law in his heart, he had decided on it only in accordance with the wishes of his mother, who could see a guarantee of future happiness only in the study of a profession which would enable him to win his bread. But eventually there broke in upon her son the certainty that his real vocation was that of a musician. Schumann's letters to his mother throw a clear light upon this crisis[2]). By his own suggestion the

---

1) *Cantor* of the Thomasschule in Leipsic. Wagner was also among his pupils.

2) P. 113—124 in the *Jugendbriefe Robert Schumann's* (Breitkopf & Härtel).

decision was made dependant upon Wieck's counsel and judgment.

Wieck's answer to the questions of Schumann's mother[1]), which was as characteristic of him, as it is of high interest on account of the opinion which it pronounced upon the young Schumann, ran as follows:

"Honoured Madam

I hasten to answer your esteemed favour of the 7th inst., without futher assuring you in advance of my warmest sympathy. But my answer can only be quite short, since I am pressed by business of various kinds, and since I must talk over the greater part of it with your son, if a satisfactory result is to be attained. My suggestion would be that in the first place (for many and far-reaching reasons of which I hope to persuade your son) he should leave Heidelberg — the hot-bed of his imagination — and should return to our cold, flat Leipzic.

At present I merely that say I pledge myself to turn your son Robert, by means of his talent and imagination, within three years into one of the greatest pianists now living. He shall play with more warmth and genius than Moscheles, and on a grander scale than Hummel. The proof of this I offer you in my 11-year-old daughter, whom I am now beginning to present to the world. As to composition, our Cantor Weinlich will no doubt be sufficient for present needs. But —

1) Robert very mistakenly thinks "that the whole of piano-playing consists in pure technique"; what a one-sided conception! I must almost infer from this either that he has never heard an pianist of genius in Heidelberg, or else that he himself has advanced no further in playing. When he left Leipsic he knew better what belongs to a good pianist, and my 11-year-old Clara will show him something different. But it is true that for Robert the greatest difficulty lies in the quiet, cold, well-considered, restrained conquest of technique, as the foundation of piano-playing. I confess frankly that when — in the lessons which I gave him — I succeeded, after hard struggles and great contradictoriness on his

---

1) This letter of his mother's is printed in J. von Wasielewsky's *Biographie Robert Schumann's* p. 60—61.

part, after unheard-of pranks played by his unbridled fancy upon two creature of pure reason like ourselves, in convincing him of the importance of a pure, exact, smooth, clear, well-marked and elegant touch, very often my advice bore little fruit for the next lesson, and I had to begin again, with my usual affection for him, to expound the old theme, to show him once more the distinctive qualities of the music which he had studied with me, and earnestly to insist on my doctrines (Remember that I cared only for Robert and for the highest in art). And then he would excuse himself for the next week or fortnight or even longer; he could not come for this or that reason, and the excuses lasted — with a few exceptions — until he went to a town and to surroundings which in truth are not designed to restrain his unbridled fancy or quiet his unsettled ideas. Has our dear Robert changed — become more thoughtful, firmer, stronger, and may I say calmer and more manly? This does not appear from his letters.

2) I will not understake Robert (that is if he means to live wholly for art in the future) unless for a year he has an hour with me almost every day.

Why? For once I ask you to have unquestioning confidence in me. But how can I do this now that I have a business in Dresden as well, and at Christmas am going to found a similar one in Berlin, and within a year shall make a tour with my daughter to Berlin, Vienna, and probably also to Paris? What will Robert's so-called Imagination-man say to it, if the lessons (lessons in touch, with an unemotional theme) have to be stolen from me, and he is left to himself for from 3 to 6 weeks, to go on the right direction? Honoured lady neither of us can tell that; Robert himself knows best; he alone can say if· he really has any determination.

3) Without committing myself further at present, I declare that the piano virtuoso (if he does not happen to be the most famous composer whose name has been honoured for years) can earn his living only if he gives lessons — but then, very easily and well. Good, intelligent teachers who have received an all-round education are wanted everywhere, and it is known that people pay 2—4 thaler an hour in Paris, Vienna, St Petersburg, Berlin etc. etc., and 6—8 thaler in London. I am educating my daughter to be a teacher first of all, though — child as she is — she is already far superior to all other woman-pianists in the world, for she can improvise freely — yet I do not allow this to mislead me

anything. Robert would be able to live very comfortably in such places, as a piano-teacher, since he has as small income of his own. For I should be sorry to think that he will eat up his capital.

But I wish to know if Robert will decide at once to give lessons here, since teaching needs years of training?

Robert surely remembers what I demand from a good piano-teacher? That is one question which I cannot answer: nor can I say whether Robert also himself can answer it.

4) Can Robert determine to study dry, cold theory, and all that belongs to it, with Weinlich for two years? With instruction in the piano I always combine lessons in the practical study of simple chords[1]) by means of which I impart a beautiful and correct touch etc. etc. — in a word everything that is not, and never will be found in any piano-school.

Has Robert condescended to learn even this small amount of theory, although in any case my lessons are sufficiently interesting? I must say, No. Will Robert now decide like my Clara to give some hours every day, to writing exercises in 3 and 4-part composition? It is work, which almost wholly silences the imagination — at least such a one as our Robert enjoys — ?

5) If Robert will not do all that I have said, then I ask: "What part will he play, and what outlet will his imagination find?"

From the frankness with which I have spoken of this, even if it has not been possible to treat it fully, you can easily see that I know how to appreciate the confidence of both of you, and shall know how to deserve it later, if your son comes back to Leipsic, when he and Dr Carus can discuss everything with me more fully and we can advise together.

Your son will excuse me for not having answered his letter to me. My business and the education of my daughter must excuse all such neglect on my part, as well as the haste in which I have written this letter.

Most honoured friend, do not be anxious — compulsion is of little use in such matters: we must do our part as parents; God does the rest. If Robert has the courage and the strength to clear away my doubts when he is with me, — and they might

---

1) Wieck wrote many exercises on simple tonic and dominant chords as studies for improving the touch of his pupils.

practically be removed in six months (so that in the contrary case everything would still not be lost) — then let him go in peace and give him your blessing. In the mean time you will be awaiting his answer to these few lines the writter of which respectfully signs himself   Your most devoted servant

Fr. Wieck."

Schumann, whose mother at once placed him in possession of this letter, did not hesitate for a second as to what he should decide. His declaration reached Wieck and his mother [1]) by return of post. In writing to the latter his exultation at being at last permitted to become an artist, shows itself with special fervour. Carried away by this conviction he returned to Leipsic, not only to become Wieck's pupil once more, but also to live in the house of his honoured master.

With Wieck's plans for Clara's immediate future we have already been made acquainted through his letter to Schumann's mother, and he was man enough to translate his words into action. The preliminary was the concert in the *Gewandhaus* in which Clara first appeared as a concert-giver, which had been planned for the beginning of September, but on account of the public disquietude had been postponed at the eleventh hour, and now took place on Nov. 8th. "On Nov. 8th", says the diary, "I gave the first concert of my own in the *Gewandhaus* here. I played to the satisfaction of my father and of the public [2]). My bows were not very successful, except for the first; they were too quick."

Two days later the following notice appeared in the *Leipziger Zeitung*: "On Nov. 8th the 11-year-old pianist, Clara Wieck,

---

1) The letter to his mother, dated Heidelberg Aug. 22nd 1830, is among the *Jugendbriefe* p. 120.

2) She played Kalkbrenner's *Rondo brillant*, Op. 101, with the orchestra, *Variations brilliantes*; Op. 23, by Herz, and then took part in a *Quatuor concertant* for 4 pianos by Czerny, concluding with variations of her own upon an original theme.

gave a concert in Leipsic. The excellent and remarkable performance of the young pianist, both in playing and in her compositions, aroused universal admiration and won her the greatest applause."

The clear profit of the concert was about thirty thaler. "I gave my father 20 thaler for his trouble," runs the diary, "and I am sorry that he will not take more, but from now on I shall frequently treat my family at the *Kuchengarten*" [1].

Encouraged by this, Wieck travelled to Dresden with Clara at Christmas, in order to give another concert there. He had at first to contend with many obstacles. In spite of this, the first concert took place on the 10th of January, with the royal band, in the Hotel de Pologne; on the 25th Clara played a solo in the theatre before and after the presentation "*Doktor und Apotheker*" in the presence of the court; and there was a second concert in the Hotel de Pologne with crowded audience and constantly increasing applause. On her last appearance in the "*Conversation* [2]" she was greeted with applause the moment she appeared. New and influential friends were also made in Dresden society, and new ties were formed. In contrast to these successes Wieck notes with ironic delight some envious slanders which were being circulated about Clara as well as about himself: that she could neither read nor write, that she had to practise 12 hours a day, that she was not 11 but 16 years old but she might come to something if she had any other teacher than her father.

Back in Leipsic Clara at once took up her studies in theory again, including a course of lessons in instrumentation and in reading scores. Besides this she practised the violin in order to get some knowledge of this instrument as necessary in composing for orchestra. Further, she studied Czerny's "*Guide*

---

1) *Translator's note*: A place of entertainment in Leipsic.
2) *Translator's note*: The name given to a series of private concerts.

to the Art of Improvisation", which she grasped quickly, so that it gave her no trouble to improvise on a given theme every day. Naturally she found scanty leisure among these various branches of study to compose for herself; but nevertheless her first official composition — a volume of four polonaises for piano — appeared during this year, published by Hofmeister of Leipsic [1].

Among the favoured few to whom she gave a copy, was "Herr Schumann, who has lived with us since Michaelmas 1830, and studies music".

The time left her after her studies in music, was devoted to exercise in the open air, on which her father always set the highest value, and to which he had kept her which strict regularity.

This summer was noteworthy for her as she first began to work at Chopin.

"Chopin's Variations Op. 2," she writes in the diary, "which I learnt in eight days, is the most difficult piece of music which I have ever seen or played. This original, inspired composition is still so little known that is has been considered incomprehensible and unplayable by nearly all pianists and teachers. At the next concert that I give, here, or in Berlin, or anywhere else, I shall play it in public for the first time."

These words point towards further plans on a large scale, a concert tour for which Wieck had been making preparations for some time, for which he had already succeeded in bespeaking the recommendation of honourable and right honourable personages in Dresden, and the ultimate goal of which he intended to be Paris. On this account Clara had to pay special attention to her French. Clara's attack of measles in August, and the outbreak of cholera at Berlin in September were suf-

---

1) In the 24th number of the *Iris* of 1830 a notice by Rellstab appeared which was not unfavourable to Clara but which strongly blamed the father for permitting the publication.

ficient to change the plans and the route, but not to stop the journey, which was undertaken on Sept. 25th, and on the 26th brought them to Weimar.

At noon on the following day the two travellers were standing expectantly before the house in the *Jungfrauenplan* with the hope of seeing Gœthe, and they had the pleasure of receiving a friendly acknowledgement of their respectful greeting. But for this, their first impressions of Weimar were anything but favourable. von Spiegel, the *Oberhofmarschall*, who evidently knew nothing of the artistic fame of father and daughter, contemptuously and unkindly declined to render them any assistance, and above all refused them permission to play in the theatre. Genart, the Oberregisseur, whom they had asked to receive them at a certain hour, refused them admittance; and Wieck therefore gave up as perfectly hopeless idea of calling the upon Hummel, his nearest colleague. "Culture reigns here", he remarks bitterly, "but also great egotism and obstinacy, as well as a certain stiff, courtier-like pride and etiquette there is self-opinionatedness in art, and especially in piano-playing; the newest piano-music is not known even by name." In reality things were not quite so bad as they appeared to the enraged piano-teacher.

Immediately after these disillusionments Wieck made acquaintance with Geheimrat Schmidt, a "musical nobleman", who proclaimed himself an enthusiastic admirer and student of Beethoven, who received Chopin's variations with the finest understanding, and for his part did everything he could to smooth the way for the new art which in the person of little Clara was knocking at the gate of the city of the Muses. In this way in the course of the next few days, the travellers came to know a number of distinguished, artistic people, above all Heeser, the choir-master, Petersilie, the magistrate, Professor Töpfer, Coudray, the director of public works, and Dr. Froriep; while Clara at the large private parties at

Schmidt's, at Frau Germar's (wife of Major Germar), and at Froriep's, found opportunity to awaken in her personality and her playing a lively interest which grew into enthusiastic admiration. The first and best result of this was that Gœthe, whose attention was called to them by Coudray, sent to ask the travellers to call on him. "On Oct. 1st at 12 o'clock," the diary tells us, "we had an audience with the 83-year-old Minister, his Excellency von Gœthe. We found him reading, and the servant took us in without further announcement, as he had made an appointment with us the day before for this hour. He received us very kindly: Clara had to sit by him on the sofa. Soon afterwards his daughter-in-law came in with her two very clever-looking children of 10 and 12. Clara was now asked to play and as the piano-stool was too low Gœthe himself, fetched a cushion from the ante-room and arranged it for her. She played Herz's *La Violetta*. While she was playing more visitors arrived and she then played Herz's *Bravura-Variations*, Op. 20. Gœthe estimated these compositions and Clara's playing very justly, spoke of the pieces as bright, French, and piquant, and admired Clara's intelligent rendering.

With this entry another saying of Gœthe's, added in the diary, stands in apparent contradiction, but in any case it is flattering to Clara: "Clara's interpretation makes one forget the composer".

The best proof of the interest which Gœthe took in Clara was the invitation to repeat the visit on the 9th of October. "Clara played her duet with Herr Götze, Hünten's rondo for four hands with me, and her variations . . . Gœthe spoke to us several times most kindly. Once he said to Clara: 'The girl has more power than six boys put together'."

On October 11th Gœthe sent Clara through Coudray a bronce medal of himself and a sheet of paper with the words: "In kindly remembrance of Oct. 9th 1831. Weimar. J. W. Gœthe."

A second sheet for her father ran, "In recognition of a masterly musical entertainment. Weimar Oct. 9th. J. W. Gœthe." The medal was placed in a box, on which was fastened a paper with the inscription in Gœthe's hand: "To the gifted Clara Wieck."

At the same time Gœthe wrote to Zelter[1]): "Yesterday a remarkable phenomenon appeared before me: a father brought his daughter (a pianist) to see me. She was on her way to Paris and played some recent Parisian compositions; the style was new to me, it demands great ease in execution, but at the same time is always light; one listens readily, and enjoys it. As you are certain to understand the sort of thing, please explain it to me."

Now that Clara had played in Gœthe's own house there soon arose in all circles in the town, a desire that she should give a public performance. Herr Schwabe, the mayor, gave them permission to use the town hall without payment. Accordingly a concert was arranged there for Oct. 7th.

The day before, Wieck and Clara experienced a peculiar satisfaction. That dread potentate, von Spiegel, who had sent them about their business so ungraciously, came with a command that they were to appear at court that evening. The Grand Duke sat by Clara at the piano, and let her play to him and the company till nearly 10 o'clock. She was rewarded by unmixed applause from all of them, her improvisation being specially admired. The concert in the town-hall took place before a brillant assembly of 500 hearers. A number of ladies grouped themselves round Clara on the platform. No-one could re-member such a success. The applause which bordered on acclamation constituted a veritable triumph over her opponents, the great men of the place, Hummel, Eberwein, Lobe, etc. etc., whose absence was remarked by everybody.

---

1) *Briefwechsel zwischen Gœthe and Zelter* No. 821.

Indeed, as occasion offered, their good friends gave them plenty to do. In excellent spirits Wieck describes in the diary two scenes with the wife of Geheimrat Schmidt, who reproached him most bitterly for not allowing Clara enough liberty for childish games and intercourse with companions of her own age. The lady became more and more impassioned, Wieck irritated in his most sensitive feelings as a father, and by the doubt cast upon his wisdom as a teacher, most decidedly declined any interference with the method of education which he had practised with a clear conscience for years. The lady snapped out that as a punishment he should not have a single one of the letters of introduction which her husband had provided for him. "So we parted from each other in a rage," the diary concludes, "and she kept the letters of introduction, and I kept — Clara Wieck, with leaves from the albums of Paganini and Gœthe. And so God guide us on. God's will be done."

After Clara, "loved by all and bidding farewell in tears," had written her name in some twenty albums, they left Weimar for Erfurt on Oct. 12th.

But in the course of their wanderings they could not again repeat the happy days at Weimar; indeed even the iron-willed, obstinate man who stood by Clara's side, sometimes lost heart under the difficulties of his hard undertaking and in the struggle against indifference and intrigue.

It was very suggestive of the state of music in the city of Erfurt that the only dealer in musical instruments, Suppus by name, had no piano for sale or hire in his shop.

After an evening party at which Clara had performed and at which there had been a good deal of disturbance while she was playing, Wieck writes in the diary: "Both the audience and the instrument are unworthy of Clara's playing". An attempt to give a concert, would neither have paid them nor have added to their reputation. Nevertheless Wieck decided to remain there for some days in order to deal with his vast correspondence and at the same time to give both himself and Clara a little rest. It was at this time that he made acquaintance with an appreciative music-lover, Professor Mensing who wrote to him, enclosing a number of letters of introduction: "I take the liveliest interest in your charming little girl. Her education does you honour in every respect, and I am convinced that she is already the greatest woman pianist and that she will soon leave all other performers behind her: I even believe that she is ordained to make the art of music still more sublime."

These are noteworthy prophecies at a time when the domination of virtuosity made musical life suffer almost everywhere from a mere external facility which aimed at nothing but superficial effort. It needed fine musical insight to hear in Clara's bravura-playing, as it then was, the future inspired interpretess of the sublime. Encouraged by Mensing to undertake the further journey to Cassel, Wieck determined to follow his advice. "I have decided therefore," he writes in the diary, "to take Clara to my old friend Spohr, and he shall say if I have done well." With this object he wrote to Spohr from Erfurt, and after allowing himself to dilate upon Clara's past history continued: "I flatter myself that I am known to you from Leipsic, and will only add that with all my experiences of youthful talent I would not presume to ask for your countenance still, if I could show in Clara nothing more than the usual infant prodigy who with pain and labour has learnt a few concert pieces."

I can say that I have trained Clara, as far as music is concerned in the magnificent school of Field, to which the so-called Viennese school always seems to me entirely subordinate, without neglecting the fashionable piquant and frivolous French method. I will leave connoisseurs to speak of the extraordinary applause with which Clara has been greeted in the above mentioned towns and most recently in Weimar, and I will only assure you that according to the judgment of all the many kind people who learnt to know Clara more intimately, I appear also to have succeeded in keeping her and her childlike innocence free from all over-education and over-strain."

The next town in which the travellers stayed was Gotha. Wieck warned by his experiences in Erfurt, was soon convinced that if one means to have genuine success and not "to be most pitifully misunderstool, wounded, and neglected" one must seek the large cities and fair-sized towns alone, unless a small but cultured court like Weimar offers a refuge.

In the mean time they were asked to perform at a private musical club. Great were the delight and the applause of the company at Clara's playing, but almost equally great the continuous disturbance while she played. When in the middle of a cadenza a lady allowed herself to be given tea in the noisiest fashion, Clara lost the thread and recollected herself again only after an interval. According to her father's opinion she played and improvised more magnificently than ever on this evening, because after long deprivation she once more sat a good piano, which her father had ordered from Leipsic [1]. Before now she had been obliged to play on a small piano with a black keys-board and the "raised notes" unusually narrow.

Wieck abandoned an intended expedition to Eisenach on receipt of a warning menage, that a local artist played the Pixis concerto which his daughter was to have played.

He replied in his usual blunt fashion: "If they do not care to hear my daughter play this concerto and to submit her rendering to a comparison, she is quite capable of playing in its place another concerto by Field or Moscheles, which may

---

1) On these journies Wieck also looked after his business interests as dealer in musical instruments.

not have been heard in Eisenach. She can also play Chopin's great bravura fantasia in which he represents the whole life and doings of Don Juan, in the most original manner, a work which it has hitherto been considered impossible to interpret in the spirit of the composer. My Clara might well count on receiving the same recognition in Eisenach that was granted to her in Dresden, Leipsic, Altenburg, Weimar, and other places."

Instead of going to Eisenach, Wieck accepted an invitation for himself and Clara to Arnstadt. Here they soon found that they were no strangers. Hardly had they arrived when they received a command from the Prince who lived there, to give a concert. The whole royal family, and the Grand-Duke of Weimar and the Prince of Reuss, who were there on a visit, were present. They found also among the inhabitants themselves a great feeling for art and most friendly and kindly sympathy.

On the day of their departure from Gotha — to which they had returned from Arnstadt — there appeared in the *Gothaischen politischen Zeitung* (No. 208) a most flattering article on Clara's performances, in which greatly to Wieck's annoyance (as it came too late) an eager desire was expressed, that "the marvellous child who hitherto has allowed herself to be heard only in a restricted circle, would also permit the art-loving public of this place to be delighted by her skill." "Clara Wieck", it concluded, "not only equals and perhaps surpasses in skill the well-known pianistes Belleville and Blahetka — for she plays with most amazing ease and elegance, and at the same time with a certain greatness of style, the most difficult pieces, whose full interpretation has till now been considered to some degree impossible — but she also surprises us most delightfully with her own delicate, charming, and often original compositions . . . . With all this, Clara Wieck is no hot-house flower, nothing about her is forced;

her extraordinary skill is but the early development of the impulse of that great musical genius which is in her."

On Nov. 3rd they arrived at Cassel. Of their visit to Spohr Wieck reports:

"Clara played her *Variations* No. 2 to him in his music-room where he has his winter quartets, and where a fairly good Streicher piano of 6$^1/_2$ octaves stands. He praised them very much, especially for their originality, but thought that the finale was two bars too short, and Clara has now added these. Then he fetched his wife and his daughter and Clara played her *Scherzo in C.* In this also, Spohr wished for a coda. Then she gave Chopin's *Variations* Op. 2, to which they all listened with the greatest amazement. Spohr praised the composition as remarkably imaginative and original, but he found Clara's playing so broad and sustained, and at the same time so brilliant and solid, that he could hardly listen to the end of each variation without discussing it with his wife. It it however, difficult to make Clara's talent appreciated on all sides, and I am continually doubtful whether to let her play something of her own, or of Herz or Field or Pixis, or simply improvise. Much depends upon the first impression, and how difficult it is to gauge the point of view of a music-lover, his disposition, his humour at the moment, and to make the most favourable impression with a piece."

In the evening they were taken to the *Cäcilia,* a choral society under the direction of Spohr. Hauptmann played from the full score, Clara played among other things her *Scherzo in C* with the coda added by Spohr's wish, and won universal applause. Spohr in particular, who turned over for her, admired anew her broad, sustained playing, and thought that under her hands the piano became a different instrument. Moritz Hauptmann wrote[1]) at this time to his friend Hauser at Munich:

---

1) *Briefe von Moritz Hauptmann* p. 83.   Leipsic, Breitkopf & Hærtel.

"There is a little pianist here now, Clara Wieck from Leipsic. The girl plays beautifully; she is 12 years old and except for her playing quite a child."

Thanks to Spohr's unwearied efforts Clara was finally able to play on the occasion of the first court concert. Spohr himself led her to the piano. How greatly the Elector was pleased with her playing was shown by the fact that after the concert he himself promised her father to let Clara have the opera-house, and expressed his pleasure at the thought of hearing her again. At 10 o'clock it was time for dinner, and they dined at the royal table. A ball followed in the magnificent new ball-room, which had been finished only a short time before. Clara stayed till 2 o'clock. Wieck sums up the whole in the reflection: "This court concert was full of honour for us, and who knows if we shall find that again. Thank God all such things leave no impression on Clara."

On Nov. 29th the first concert in the opera-house[1]) took place before a full house and in the presence of the whole court. A second was stopped by the revolts which broke out in Cassel on Dec. 7th. A private concert, however, took place on Dec. 13th in the Stadthaussaal and, in spite of the continued unrest, met with a success which was scarcely to be expected under the circumstances. When at last they had to leave Cassel, Spohr gave Clara the following weighty letter of recommendation:

"At the request of the father of the young artist, Clara Wieck, I gladly express in the following lines, my recognition of her extraordinary talent. Although now-a-days it may not be an entirely rare thing for a child of her age already to have acquired remarkable mechanical skill in piano-forte playing, yet hitherto, this has never been combined, as in her, with such

---

1) The Elector sent Clara 15 ducats for the court concert, and 8 for the performance in the theatre.

broad execution, the right accentuation, and perfect clearness united with the finest lights and shades of touch. Such is her skill that she plays the most difficult works that have been written for the instrument, with a combination of certainty and ease which is to be seen only in the greatest living artists. Her playing is further distinguished from that of the ordinary prodigy in that it is not only the result of rigorous, classical training, but also springs from her own heart, as is testified by her compositions which, like the young artist herself, are among most remarkable newcomers in the world of art."

The next halting-place on their journey was Frankfort on Maine. The reception afforded to Wieck and Clara by the musical leaders here, was cold and distant. Aloys Schmidt told them when they came, with respect to Clara's repertoire, that she would not succeed in Frankfort unless she played works by Mozart and Beethoven. Schnyder von Wartensee, who was no less chilling at first, became more sympathetic after he had heard Clara play. Schelble, the director of the *Cäcilienverein*, where she was to have an opportunity of making her playing letter known, did not take the slightest notice of her. Only Kapellmeister Guhr, and Ferdinand Ries met them in a friendly and helpful spirit. The prospect of a concert disappeared: nobody troubled about them, or wanted to hear Clara play, so that Wieck breaks out into bitter complaints: "What difficulties there are in the way of giving concerts! If I find such petty and disagreable people in the next town it shall be the last concert of mine. A miserable spirit governs this place, and many are envious of us. At this rate threshing is better than concert-giving."

Meanwhile the New Year, 1832, had dawned, and brought with it a cheery greeting from home, a letter from Robert Schumann. The masterless pupil had naturally followed his honoured teacher and his gifted little friend, in spirit thus far

on their wanderings, with full sympathy, and he writes to
Wieck on Jan. 11[th 1]):

"In the first place accept my best wishes for Clara's success.
In truth, easily as the world forgets, it seldom overlooks
the extraordinary; it is, if I may say so, like a herd of cows
which looks up when it lightens, and then placidly goes on
grazing: such lightning flashes were Schubert, Paganini, and
— now Clara.

You would hardly believe how much I miss you and her."

To Clara herself he writes:

"Dear, honoured Clara

I could not repress a gentle smile yesterday, when I read in
the *Didaskalia*: '*Variations* by Herz, etc. etc. played by Fräulein
Clara W.'; forgive me honoured Fräulein, and yet there is a prefix
which is better than any — and that is none at all: Who would
say, Herr Paganini, or Herr Gœthe? I know you are a wise person
and understand your old moon-struck charade-maker — Well then
dear Clara! I often think of you, not as a brother thinks of his
sister, or as friend of a friend, but rather as a pilgrim thinks of the
picture above the distant altar. I have been in Arabia during
your absence, in order to be able to relate all the fairy-tales which
might please you — six new stories of doubles, 101 charades,
8 amusing riddles, as well as the lovely, horrible robber-stories,
and that of the white ghost — ugh, ugh! how I am shaking! —
Alwin has grown into a very comely boy, his new blue coat and
the leather cap like mine, suit him very well. There is nothing
remarkable to say about Gustav, except that he has grown so remarkably that you will be surprised, for he is nearly as tall as I
am. Clemens is the drollest, dearest, most self-willed little boy,
who speaks like a book and has a most sonorous voice: he has
grown very much too. Alwin will some day devote himself to the
violin. As to Cousin Pfund[2]), there is certainly (except for me)
no man in L. who longs for Frankfort as much as he does. —
Have you been composing? and what? I often hear music in my

---

1) Printed among the *Jugendbriefe* p. 161.
2) Later, the well-known performer on the kettle-drum.

dreams — then you are composing. I have got to three-part fugues
with Dorn[1]; besides this a sonata in B minor and a book of *Pa-*
pillons are finished; the latter appear in print within a fortnight.
. . . The weather is glorious today. — How do you like the Frankfort apples? And how is that *F* in alt in Chopin's *Spring Varia-*
tions getting on? My paper is coming to an end. — Everything
comes to an end, except the friendship with which I am Fräulein
C. W.'s warmest admirer
                                           R. Schumann."

At last, on Jan. 25th, the long-planned concert at Frankfort
got under way. None of the Frankfort singers had been willing
to undertake the customary vocal numbers at it. Only on
the day of the concert itself, the singing mistress, Gleichauf,
and her pupil, Fräulein Rauch, were good enough to fling
themselves into the breach. The latter sang Clara's setting of
Tiedge's poem, *"Der Traum"*. Wieck makes the following
entry in the diary: "God be thanked, it is all over! What an
unsympathetic public, so cold, so soul-less! — not to be warmed;
and Clara — I must say — played more magnificently than ever.
She was in the right frame of mind, her powers at their best,
and played *con amore*. She did win applause indeed, that is
true, but it was not enthusiastic as it has been hitherto. The
orchestra gave her the most applause both at rehearsal and
at the performance by knocking with their violin-bows, which
was very cheering and answered very well."
Darmstadt, to which the two travellers now turned their
steps, was in every respect the opposite of Frankfort. A single
letter from Wieck had sufficed to smooth all paths; every
arrangement had been made for their reception and for Clara's
appearance. They arrived on the 3rd of February, there was
a rehearsal on the 4th, and a performance on the 5th. Here,
however, her father complains of Clara that though good at
times yet on the whole she played coldly, was distracteds

---

1) Schumann's teacher of counterpoint.

without interest, without the finer lights and shades, and incomprehensibly in the tuttis, when the orchestra faltered and failed to come in right, she did not once help them. Nevertheless the applause was very great, and almost each separate variation was clapped.

After a short rest in Mainz, the journey to Paris now followed, on Feb. 11th. They arrived on Feb. 15th, after four days and nights of discomfort.

"Great God! what a journey! what hardships during these four nights on the way to Paris! And now we are here, we are much hampered by our inability to speak French!"

The whole misery of overtired travellers, who are almost beside themselves among half-unpacked boxes in a strange land, is expressed in these words. And in spite of the fact that Wieck's brother-in-law, Eduard Fechner, had done his best for them and had got them rooms in the Hôtel de Bergère, rue de Bergère, Faubourg Montmartre, they found everything "quite different from what we expected".

It was certainly very daring to venture — armed with only a few introduction, good as these were — with a half-grown child on ground which he did not know from his own experience, and in a region in which honour and riches might possibly be found, but dangers of many sorts certainly lurked. And yet it is easy to understand why Friedrich Wieck was eager to take Clara to Paris on this first journey. Not only was Paris the home, or at least the dwelling-place, of Chopin, Herz, Pixis, and Kalkbrenner, that is of the composers of the day on whose works Clara had hitherto chiefly relied in order to give illustration of her art, and from whom she could already count on a friendly welcome, but the Paris of that time was the chief focus of the musical life of the world. Here ambitious, self-confident, musical youths were to be found side by side with the great lights. Here was prevalent an exchange of musical stimulus such as was hardly to be found anywhere else at that time; and staying in Paris therefore, meant for the future of a great musician, not only a kind of higher diploma in musical education, but at least as much the bond of personal intercourse with all the famous heroes of the international musical world. And however much the young men and youths from all the great countries, who found themselves here together, giving and taking, the Meyerbeers, Chopins, Mendelsohns, Liszts, and Hillers, might be in advance of the specific French school of music, both in desire and in power, however artificial and obsolete many of them considered the fashionable method of voice-production and piano technique in France, yet on the whole musical Paris had an inspiring and stimulating effect on all of them.

Our travellers found this also, after they had got over the first discomforts, and when the first personal ties were formed with Parisians and with foreigners. In the comparatively short time that they were there — from Feb. 15th to April 16th — a flood of new impressions poured upon them, too rapidly perhaps for a child who in spite of her fine artistic skill had yet remained a child, and by her father's wish, should so remain; though at the same time she gained by this means a freer point of view in judging various artistic personalities and tendencies, which was certainly not without value in her own development.

It was in the nature of things that in this great world-market the quiet little girl from Leipsic — and many people did not know in what country that was — should find herself rather among the spectators and hearers who stood at the edge of the circle than, as hitherto, on German ground, the centre of interest. Where Mendelssohn and Chopin, Liszt and Hiller, were in the foreground and were working in the fullest strength of their youth, Clara Wieck could only expect to be heard once in a way when they happened to be silent. And this hearing she won for herself chiefly through the quiet, gentle attractiveness of her childish nature, which awoke in the musical salons a purely human interest in the little artist, and which, when she came to express herself, developed above all things an increasing wonder at the artistic seriousness and ripeness of 12-year-old child.

Clara, perhaps even more than her father who speaks of it with saturnine humour in the diary, suffered under the stiffness, monotony, and length of the evening assemblies which for the most part did not begin until 10 o'clock and lasted on beyond midnight, and at which a mass of good and bad music was usually poured out by good and moderately good artists in rapid succession, without as a rule any particular appreciation of either one or the other being shown by the public. Both father and daughter were naturally most interested in Chopin; they were several times in the same room with him apparently without ever having opportunity for closer personal intercourse. "Chopin", said Wieck to Schumann, after their return, "is a handsome fellow, but Paris has made him slovenly and careless in himself and in his art." At Abbé Bertin's they heard him play his concerto in E minor, "Quite in Field's manner", Wieck wrote of it in the diary, "if I had not known whose it was, I should have taken it for a work of Schumann's; it is not suited to a mixed audience for many passages are new, tremendously difficult, and not brilliant according to the prevailing fashion. On the same evening (March 14th) Mendelssohn's octet was played. This, or another similar evening, when they were in company with Mendelssohn, Chopin, and Hiller, became associated in Clara's mind with a merry, riotous scene in the artists' room, where these three amused themselves by bear-fighting. More serious, naturally, was the meeting with the acknowledged matadors of the Parisian musical world, among whom Meyerbeer in particular seems to have expressed himself kindly and sympathetically in respect of Clara's art, while Kalkbrenner, Pixis, and Herz, his closest "colleagues", were inclined to maintain an "affable retirence". Meeting Paganini again gave them special pleasure, and he on his side greeted his friends from Leipsic with his old kindness. Unfortunately however, the plan of letting Clara appear at his concert had to be abandoned on account of his illness. Father and daughter were much pleased by the friendly way in which Erard met them, he placed a piano at Clara's disposal, an offer which was the more thankfully accepted by her since the kind of piano in use, even in the best houses, was far below her most modest expectations. So much was this the case that Wieck at first seriously debated whether he would not be compelled to teach Clara some other method of playing, because with his method no light and shade and no expression could be brought out of these "tough bones", as he called them. In this manner, at a concert that Chopin gave at Kalkbrenner's, in three "fairly small rooms in which were crowded from 300 to 400 people", they first heard his *Variations* Op. 2 played, "so that they were hardly recognisable on this tough and stubborn piano of Kalkbrenner's, playing on which is nothing but a struggle". Above all, Wieck could not approve of the Parisian technique either in singing or in piano-playing, though he thoroughly recognised the merits of the orchestra both in ensemble and in solo-playing, admired both the beauty of the tone and the exact execution, and only occasionally blamed a tendency towards niggling.

With the exception of Kalkbrenner, Felix alone found complete favour in his eyes, as a player of Beethoven. One thing which especially surprised the travellers was the predeliction of the Parisians for Beethoven. "The French at present affect to love Beethoven above everything", writes Wieck in the diary, "everyone here lives for, and demands nothing but — Beethoven." In the concerts at the Conservatoire as well as in private circles Beethoven was always represented, and frequently by several works. That in spite of this Wieck

judged the artistic insight and taste of the Parisians somewhat contemptuously, is comprehensible when one reads the
descriptions of what usually took place at these musical evenings, of which an example taken from a letter of Wieck's to
his wife may be given [1]):

"You should see me at the soirées (most pedantically
attired by Fechner beforehand) with yellow gloves and a white
stock, my hat always in my hand careering about from 10 at
night till 2 in the morning, half French, half German, and
half despairing, perpetually straining my ears in order not to
miss anything. Child, you would not recognise your Friedrich,
for you never saw a more interesting-looking lackey. Just so
well do my sturdy boots and shoes (they are made something
after the fashion of the ferry-boats in which one used to cross
the Mulde near Wurzen) fit with my blue frock-coat with the
velvet collar and little brass buttons, and black trousers. In
this get up I look something like a young oak in the *Rosenthal*[2]). We have heard Kalkbrenner; he is the greatest; he
comes the nearest to my ideal. I will tell you something of
our conversation after Clara had played several of her own
compositions, upon his heavy piano which is hardly bearable.

Kalkbrenner: 'C'est le plus grand talent!' He kisses her.
Picture to yourself a handsome, very vain man, and his wife,
a true Frenchwoman, young and very rich, who sits by the
fire and fans herself with a new-fangled French fan, and then
says: ,But it is a pity that she will be ruined as a pianist in
Germany.'

I: 'She will not be ruined, for I shall not let her out of
my own hands.'

Kalkbrenner: 'I beg your pardon sir, in Germany you all
play in one style, that is to say in the groping method of the

---

1) *Translator's note*: Printed by Kohut, *Fr. Wieck*, p. 59.
2) A public garden in Leipsic.

Viennese school of Hopp and Hummel, as did Czerny, Ciblini, Pixis, Hiller, and in a word all those who have come here from Germany.'

I: 'I really must beg that you will consider me the first exception, for I am the greatest enemy to this system; I am well acquainted with Field's method, and I have taught my daughter and my pupils by this principle alone.'

Our conversation continued for some time in this manner, and time will show him who was right.

To complete this is added, also from the diary, the vivid description of a great soirée which took place on March 2nd at the Princess Vandamore's.

"A great soirée at Princess Vandamore's. It was remarkable. What a place for it! There was an audience chamber decorated with heavy, old-fashioned tapestries, which with its adjacent rooms was a veritable emporium of porcelain, huge old vases, cups, figures, stuffed birds etc. etc. Here we found nothing but princes, ambassadors, and ministers as audience. Clara made a beginning upon an old, English, ramshackle piano whose every note jerked and quivered. Clara made it do, however, and played so well that Kalkbrenner, who was there too, often cried 'bravo', and the whole large assembly applauded. An Italian sang next (not a professional) with so much expression, declamation, vivacity, and in a word such perfect technique, that she could not but be reckoned among singers of the first rank, though her method was that of the latest frivolous, coquettish school, with all its merits and defects, its eternal ritardandos and cadenzas. Later, she sang various little Italian and English chansonettes and accompanied herself with an unusual ease and a taste such as I never before heard. Then two famous and learned doctors sang a duet with almost equal ease. Kalkbrenner accompanied them with never-failing beauty of tone and great charm.

As we entered the room, a Spaniard in national costume lay almost at full length on two chairs among the ladies. He was a guitar-player, but what a one! I never conceived such playing as his. He did inconceivable things, and played with true Southern fire. Naturally this handsome young man in his costume, with what I might call his insolent nonchalance, and this talent, which he tried to turn to the best account, especially among the ladies, by incessant coquettries, was most successful in his performance. I did not consider it advisable that Clara should play again at the end, when many people had already left, but excused myself to Kalkbrenner on the score of the instrument. Under such circumstances one must know how to master one's vanity and keep oneself from doing too much, rules which the Italian and the Spaniard did not entirely understand."

It is intelligible that both travellers, in spite of the wealth of interesting impressions and events which poured upon them, should have been anything but comfortable in the midst of these doings; they felt at home only in one house, that of Madame Bonfil, where things were less stiff, and which was frequented only by really musical people. All the same a share in the great social functions was importants if they were to attain the chief object of their journey and attract the attention of the influential connoisseurs of the day, thus preparing the way for a concert. As a matter of fact, before Clara appeared in public, the *Constitutional* had noticed the young artist in a very appreciative manner, so that now a concert of her own no longer seemed too great a venture. Her performance at a musical soirée, which Franz Stöpel, who was an eager and notorious champion of Logier's method and who lived in Paris, arranged at his school of music on March 19th, might be considered as a preparation for this, but according to Wieck's comment there was "no remarkable attendance" at it. All the more did they set their hopes upon the concert itself, which was planned for April 9th, and for which a room in the Hôtel de Ville was hired and printed circulars of invitation were sent out to all friends and patrons, at the end of March. Then suddenly cholera broke out and in its wake came disturbances in the streets. At one stroke the situation was altered. The travellers determined to leave immediately after the concert, and eventually, since terror of infection was frightening everybody out of Paris, was given it with Schröder-Devrient's help, on the appointed day in a much smaller hall (that of Stöpel's school), and to a much smaller audience than had been expected. For the first time Clara played — according to the Parisian custom — entirely by heart, and improvised in public. As was only to be expected under these conditions, the practical result was very small, but the artistic success was all the greater.

On April 13th they left Paris and passed through Metz, Saarbrück, where they had to spend several days in quarantine, Frankfort, where Clara fell ill and they were compelled to stay, Hanau and Fulda, and finally at 11—30 a. m. on May 1st 1832 they arrived safely back in Leipsic. "A quarter of an hour later, Clara was cleaning knives in the kitchen", says the diary.

It is like a scene from a fairy-tale. The glass coach and the golden clothes have disappeared and the child, Cinderella, stands on the hearth and dreams of the past and the future. And the prince?

In his daily notes in the *Record of my life in Leipsic* Robert Schumann writes under May 2nd:

"Early yesterday Clara and Wieck arrived; Gustav and Alwin told me at once."

On the 3rd: "Now I have him again. But though it may have been absent-mindedness or fatigue, he seemed to me weaker in every respect than he was before, only his pride, his fieriness, and the rolling eye were the same. Clara has grown prettier and taller, stronger and more self-possessed, and speaks German with a French accent which Leipsic will soon drive out of her. She played the new *Caprices*[1]); it sounded to me like an hussar[2]). Her childish originality shows itself in everything, thus she likes the third *Papillon* best[3])."

May 4th: "There was a gathering of friends at the *Brand*[4]). Wieck was very polite, Clara childishly simple. We went home very late. Clara and I arm in arm. She plays now like a trooper. *Caprices* they are not, but *impromptus* or *Wieck's moments musicals*."

May 7th: I went to the menagerie with Clara, Pfund, and the children. What grace, naturalness, and agility there is in a panther; study that! Clara was foolish and frightened.

May 9th: I played and worked at the intermezzis at home. I shall dedicate them to Clara.

May 16th: Clara plays Field's concerto divinely; but the *Papillons* uncertainly and unsympathetically.

May 23rd: Clara and the *Papillons* which she has not quite mastered. She has caught the spirit, only her rendering is not quite delicate enough, full of soul and sound sentiment it is. — At the *Brand*; Clara in very high spirits.

May 25th: Clara played Bach's second fugue to me, clearly and plainly and with (undecipherable) play of colour. The fugue into which living colour is introduced is no mere piece of skill, but a work of art. The old man grumbles at her want of vanity. There is some truth in it. In the evening I went with them and Rosalie[5]) to the *Wasserschenke*[6]). There

---

1) *Caprices* of Clara's, printed by Stöpel in Paris, at later by Hofmeister in Leipsic.

2) The natural result of becoming accustomed to playing on stiff Parisian pianos.

3) R. Schumann's Op. 2.

4) A garden restaurant in Leipsic.

5) Wife of Schumann's brother, Karl.

6) *Translator's note*: another restaurant in Leipsic.

we discussed many things in the most lively manner, and with all our hearts. — Clara did not know if a duck were a goose or a duck. We laughed over it a great deal. — To thee, my friendly guardian angel, I return my childish thanks for this spring.

May 26th: Clara played the last movement of Moscheles' concerto in E ♭, but carelessly — though here and there one caught delicate glimpses of the rain-bow, afterwards she played the great *Bravour-Variations* by Herz, better than formerly — and then the *Papillons*. Clara has got hold of them correctly and with spirit, and so renders them, with few exceptions. Wieck acted as interpreter, and pointed out harlequin and the deeper meaning of the masque.

"Now Madame," he said to Rosalie, "does not Clara represent your Robert well?"

May 27th: As Clara was playing Field's concerto enchantingly, an angel came in, Frau Carus[1]; later Rosalie came. I have never heard Clara play as she did to day — everything was masterly and everything beautiful. And she played the *Papillons* almost better than yesterday.

May 28th: There was a soirée this evening in Monsieur Wieck's salon. In the fugue of Bach's, which Clara had to play, the right people were not present. The audience did not seem to me to understand the *Papillons* properly, they looked at each other foolishly and could not grasp the rapid changes. Besides, Clara did not play so well as on Saturday, and must have been tired mentally and physically. Towards 11 o'clock she played again, more carelessly but with more spirit! Clara was very charming and lively, but there was that tiresome prying Pfund.

1) Agnes Carus, the wife of a Professor of Medecine. She was an excellent singer, who had already, in 1827, inspired Schumann to compose.

May 29th: This evening I tore through six Bach fugues, arranged as duets, at sight, with Clara. I gave the Dutch maiden[1]) a soft and gentle kiss, and when I came home, about 9 o'clock, I sat myself down at the piano and ideas poured from me till veritable flowers and gods seemed to stream from my fingers. The idea was C. F. G. C.[2]).

June 1st: Clara is being very self-willed just now, towards her step-mother, who is certainly the worthiest of women. The old boy scolded Clara. All the same he will soon be under Clara's thumb; already she gives orders like a Leonore — though at the same time she knows how to beg and coax like a child.

June 4th: Clara was self-willed and tearful; a few words of blame, spoken gravely and as from a superior, would have a good effect upon her whims, and would be sure to awaken vanity, which, when it ripens into pride, is so necessary to artists."

He wrote to Wieck at this time[3]): "Every day on which I am not able to speak to you or Clara, makes a gap in the record of my life in Leipsic." Gœthe in one place speaks of his time at Strassburg, as "those wonderful, happy days of infinite possibilities". Even such a dawning promise of approaching happiness seemed to be softy stealing out of the distance and spreading over these spring days and weeks.

For Clara the time which followed, after the short pause for rest which her father allowed her was well-filled and rich in duties and work. Besides her brother Alwin's piano lessons, which her father handed over to her by, the middle of May, there were lessons in counterpoint twice a-week from Musikdirektor Dorn in addition to her daily studies, and public life again made its claim upon her.

---

1) Agnes Carus.
2) The opening bars of the Impromptu Op. 5.
3) *Jugendbriefe* p. 180.

On July 9th and 31st she gave two concerts in the *Gewand-haus*, at which in spite of the oppressive heat there were good attendances and great applause. Particular attention was attracted by the fact that she played everything by heart, and there were not wanting clever people who declared that it was only possible for her to play such difficult pieces in this way, because she could see the keys! But in August a long article, "Reminiscences of Clara Wieck's last concert in Leipsic", appeared in Herlossohn's "*Komet*", in which it said among other things:

"Within the space of three weeks Clara Wieck has played in public a concerto by Pixis, the *Don Juan Variations* of Chopin, the *Bravour-Variations* by Herz, Hummel's *Sentinella* Op. 51, a duet by Beriot and Herz, the polonaise from the concerto in $E\flat$ major by Moscheles and Herz Op. 48. In each of these performances she gained, to a greater or less extent, deserved applause, and if her playing is not grounded only upon mechanical skill but is strewn with blossoms grown by her own genius, this and the characteristic of playing everything entirely from memory, deserve all the more recognition and admiration." "Belleville's tone", it says in another place, "pleases the ear without going further; Clara's touches the heart and peaks to the emotions. One is poetic, the other is the poem." This article, signed R. W. came from the pen of Robert Schumann[1]).

Still more flattering perhaps, was an incidental judgment of Rellstab's in the "*Iris*" (No. 41) according to which it was impossible in theory to decide with respect to a particular question of musical technique but "we must bow to the authority of the great pianists from Clementi to Clara Wieck". And yet it happened that this 13-year-old famous pianist, "stuck

---

1) *Gesammelte Schriften über Musik und Musiker* Vol. I, 4th ed. by J. G. Jansen 1891 p. 6.

several times" in playing a little scherzo for a game at a children's party on her birthday. She thought it was not surprising: "So many little girls there to listen — and having to play on my birthday."

The winter made still greater claims. Clara appeared again at the first subscription concert, on Sept. 30th, and played among other things Moscheles' concerto in *G* minor. Her acquaintance with the composer and the pleasant way in which each impressed the other personally as well as artistically, was the result of Moscheles' visit to Leipsic in October. Of less importance, at first sight, seemed a little concert tour in November, which took them to Altenburg, Zwickau, and Schneeberg. And yet Nov. 18th, when the "grand concert" took place in the hall of the *Gewandhaus* at Zwickau, had peculiar importance not only for the Zwickau lovers of music at that time, but for Clara's future; for not only did she win literal storms of applause from the audience in Herz's *Bravour-variations*, so that during the performance the people forced their way among the orchestra desks, but on this occasion Robert Schumann's name appeared for the first time with hers in public. In the second part of the concert the first movement of a symphony[1]) was played, without however attracting any honour in its own country. It passed over the heads of the inhabitants of Zwickau without making the faintest impression. But this journey on which Schumann accompanied the Wiecks as far as his relations at Schneeberg, had an importance of its own in addition to this.

"Clara will give you plenty of food for thought", Schumann had written to his mother on Nov. 6th[2]). Her son's accounts and letters had already prepared her to a great extent and aroused her interest in the 13-year-old marvel who came into

---

1) Which was never published.
2) *Jugendbriefe* p. 194.

personal contact with her friend's mother and brothers for the first time during this visit to Zwickau. And there one day, something wonderful happened. Schumann's mother was standing by the window with Clara. Robert passed below and nodded up to them both. With a sudden, over-powering rush of emotion, she drew the childish figure to her and said softly: "Someday you must marry my Robert." As yet these words were mere sound to Clara, but they made a deep and indelible impression upon her.

They had hardly got back to Leipsic when Clara fell sick of scarlet-fever, from the effects of which she did not fully recover until the New Year (1833). She helped herself through the period of convalescence by learning the hitherto unknown art of sewing, in the practise of which she took great pleasure.

From these days dates the first letter of Clara to Schumann, who was paying a visit to his relatives in Zwickau, and who had made her promise when he left that she would send him news of the doings in Leipsic during his absence.

Leipsic Dec. 17th 1832.

"My dear Herr Schumann

Aha! I hear you say; now we have it. This is the person who never thinks of her promise again! Oh! she remembers it very well. Read now, and hear why I did not write to you before.

On the very day — a few days after our return — when I was to have played at Molique's[1]) concert, I got scarlet-fever, and until a few days ago I had to stay in that wearisome bed. But it was only a slight attack and already I can be up for several hours every day, and have played the piano again. But I was not able to play in the *Gewandhaus*. Herr Wenzel had to accompany Mozart's aria, after Herr Knorr had refused. He was dreadfully nervous and began too softy and timidly; but for that he got through it very well.

---

1) A famous violinist of the time.

LITZMANN Clara Schumann. I.

I played to Hermstedt[1]) and Molique; since then they have not appeared again, for fear of infection. But you, dear Herr Schumann, must not let yourself be prevented from coming here, for everything will be over by the New Year I am playing in the *Gewandhaus* on Jan. 8th, and immediately after that I am playing Hummel's septet, for which everything is prepared already. I wager that the time would not have seemed long to you here, as it probably does in Zwickau; one concert follows another: Grabau sings divinely — ... Ah! what a lot af news I had to tell you. But I will not do it, or else you will stick at Zwickau; I know you. I will just make you curious, so that you shall long for Leipsic. But out of pity I will tell you one thing, since the time must hang so on your hands.

On Saturday my Father was at the *Euterpe.*

Listen: Herr Wagner[2]) has got alread of you; a symphony of his was performed, which is said to be as like as two peas to Beethoven's symphony in *A* major. Father said that F. Schneider's symphony, which was given in the *Gewandhaus*, was like the freightwaggon which takes two days to get to Wurzen always keeping to the same track, and a stupid old waggoner with a great peaked cap keeps on growling to the horses: "Ho, ho, ho, hotte, hotte." But Wagner drives in a gig over stock and stone and every minute falls into a ditch by the road, but in spite of this gets to Wurzen in a day, though he looks black and blue.

At this *Euterpe* the famous young Bahrdt Herz's *Bravourvariations*, played on an upright piano making them sound like five intensely melancholy adagios. You must let my father describe it and imitate it to you more particularly. Although father shakes his head very doubtfully over my further appearance, yet I mean to try and play again. — Father helped me with this part of my letter[3]).

---

1) Pianist and *Hofkapellmeister* at Sondershausen.

2) Richard Wagner.

3) On Jan. 10th 1833, Schumann wrote to Wieck from Zwickau: "The symphony comparisons in Clara's letter have caused much laughter in Zwickau, and especially the naïve parenthesis: Father helped me with this part of my letter." To me it was exactly as if Clara had whispered something in my ear.

Herr D. Darus greets the beloved Fridolin[1]) a thousand times (You will know who this beloved Fridolin is) and he is to send the songs and the symphony soon.

Well! you are a pretty fellow to leave your linen behind in the carriage! Have you got it back from the driver?

I am looking forward to Christmas very much, and the piece of cake that I am going to save for you, is already waiting for you, so that it may be eaten by you, although it is not baked yet.

Give my love to everybody, and write me an answer very soon, only write nice and clearly[2]).

Hoping to see you here very soon, I end my letter and remain

Your friend Clara Wieck."

By the beginning of the year 1833 Wieck's happiness at home had already received a severe blow. Clemens, Clara's youngest brother, and the darling of her and of them all, passed away in his father's arms on Feb. 5th after an illness of barely four hours, only just over three years old.

In order to give himself and his family a change, Wieck took them all to Dresden, at the same entering his elder sons, Alwin and Gustav at the Free-Masons' Institute there. Clara gave a concert during this visit, and she also played at a large soirée at Count Baudissin's, with whose family, from this time onwards, she always had the friendliest relations.

After their return Clara in addition to her playing, studied singing more seriously than she had done before, as a special means of musical education. Her father gave her a daily singing-lesson himself.

Clara had at this time a special affection for the songs of Carl Maria von Weber, which she called her daily bread. At the same time she continued with her wonted ardour her lessons in theory and her essays in composition. In the course

---

1) This was the name that Schumann bore among his circle of friends in Leipsic.

2) Schumann wrote a very illegible hand.

of the summer she finished — in addition to a number of little pieces for the piano — her rondo in B minor, as well as "*An Alexis*"; besides the chorus of the "*Doppelgänger*" and several caprices. Finally she even had the courage to try her skill on a grand concerto of which she planned the first movement, and in addition to this began an overture. These compositions besides showing the characteristics of the age and borrowings from elsewhere and in parts a childish tone, give proof also of remarkable effort, industry, and knowledge, and from among their numerous technical difficulties sounds here and there a note of awakening musical thought.

If we were obliged to depend solely upon Wieck's comments for information concerning the year 1833, we should have to consider it empty and uneventful in comparison with the year immediately preceding it. As a matter of fact we learn from other sources that the contrary was the case, though less with regard to external successes than in respect to Clara's general development.

The one-sidedness of Wieck's accounts sprang from the nature and character of the man. It was not that he was deaf to the finer and more spiritual impulses of development in the life even of a child — the gift of humour alone, with which he was so richly endowed, proves that he had the true teacher's capacity for training character —, but his restless, busy spirit always laid most stress upon the practical side of life, this chief interest, to which every other gave way, sprang from his anxiety that life should be founded on a sound basis. This anxiety was the immediate result of his own past. He had worked his way up from the deepest distress and poverty to a respected place in life, and had learned to love the possession of it, not so much for its own sake, but as the most powerful means by which he could do his work in the world. Even in his 88th year he wrote to his grandson, Felix Schumann, "In the deepest poverty I vowed to God that if

He freed me from anxiety as to means of livelihood, or even made me well-to-do, I would dedicate my whole life to the education of humanity and above all to training poor and deserving musical talent."

He carried on Clara's musical education therefore, not only for the satisfaction of his ambition as a teacher of music, but also for the practical advantage of preparing a brilliant future for her in life. Certainly he had both reason and justice on his side, if only the endeavour had not at times led this otherwise excellent man into absurdities. About this time the management of the *Gewandhaus* gave him just cause for energetic insistance on his point of view. As there was a deficit, they made an attempt to cut down by half the honorarium which they had agreed to give Clara. Wieck answered briefly: "As the house was always filled to over-flowing on the three occasions when my daughter appeared, she cannot share any responsibility for this deficit. Clara will always by ready to play for nothing, for any deserving object, but I cannot submit to any reduction of the honorarium when it is a question of playing for money. You are at liberty to consider this as my whim."

The management now requested Clara, from this time on, to play twice in the winter for a fixed sum of 25 thaler; Wieck replied: "I am not in a position to make fixed engagements. I can complete Clara's general education only at the expense of her brothers and sisters unless by means of her talent she makes my expenditure possible by the addition of 3—400 thaler in the course of the winter; and for this I need perfect freedom in the choice of times for the necessary concert tours. I am glad that the management attaches some value to Clara's performances, and, should circumstances permit, I will not fail to show myself ready to oblige, and I will suppress my pride as an artist, and waive my rights, if the management finds itself disposed to give me, my wife, and Clara, free entrance to the concerts, includig the days when the latter is not playing."

Soon after this, Clara gave a concert of her own in the *Gewandhaus*. In writing to the management, Wieck speaks of "Clara's general education", but leaves uncertain what he includes under this head. The question arises, how during these constant week-long and even month-long absences Clara's education other than musical could by carried on. It is perhaps remarkable that her father, a man of university education himself, never mentions this subject in his notes. Only lessons in French and English conversation are mentioned there; and there had special importance for him on account of the tours in foreign lands which he planned for the future. It might seem as if he did not specially care for a schooling which aimed exclusively at information, and as if in the education of youth, he attached higher value to intelligence and to a thorough cultivation of understanding, character, and heart. The result of this was indeed, that in later years Clara often lamented that in her one-sided, musical education many other things had been neglected whose want she felt, and could now no longer supply. Yet she might well comfort herself. The life, rich not only in music but in every sort of mental stimulus, which she had lived from her earliest childhood and her continual intercourse with famous men, were of advantage to her general mental development. In many respects her mental progress, in advance of her years as it was, would at least have proved superior to the scrappy education of the German girls of the day; if not in actual knowledge of school-books, yet certainly in a richer philosophy of life, a more varied experience, and an immediate education by life itself.

This maturity showed itself in Clara's choice of girl-friends. First among these, came the two daughters of Friedrich List, the political economist, who a short time before had returned from America and had settled in Leipsic as American consul. Clara felt herself specially drawn towards Emilie List, who was the elder by a year: a bond of affection which she was to keep throughout her whole life. Emilie List also was, at an early age, removed from the narrow restrictions of German life at that time, and thanks to her father's vast sphere of activity, had been transplanted to distant lands and strange corners of the world. Thus she had early been enabled to develop her mind on many sides. Her attractive, somewhat grave disposition, as described by Wieck, seemed to him particularly good for Clara.

But even at this time there is no doubt that Clara's interest centred chiefly in Robert Schumann, both as artist and as man. He had returned to Leipsic in March, and had taken a lodging for the summer in *Riedels Garten.*

The letters which were exchanged during this period give convincing proof of the growth and development of the comradeship between the 23-year-old youth and the 14-year-old girl. Robert writes on the 22nd of May:

"Dear Clara

Good morning! In your prosaic town you have hardly an idea of one in *Rudolph's Garden*, and how everything there sings, hums, whistles and rejoices with the finches, right up to my window. Are you not going to walk to Connewitz one of these days? And when? And how unfortunate the people are who have to drive there? Or are you rehearsing with the woman from Vienna[1])? And when? She simply delighted me. But please answer all this by word of mouth. —

Many pretty thoughts come into my head on a morning like this, for example that this warm life will last through a whole June and July, or that the old fellow is a butterfly and the world is his flower on which he sways (this thought seems to me too fantastic) — or that the same sun which shines in my room shines also in Becker's room in Schneeberg, or that I am always pleased

---

1) Eder, a pianiste who gave concerts in Leipsic at that time.

when a sunbeam hops on the piano as if it wanted to play with the sound, which after all is nothing more than light made audible. To speak the truth, I cannot give a reason for all of them.

But in all this do you not recognise a certain

Robert Schumann.

Please enclose your *Variations*, and also those on the Tyrolean air.

May 22ⁿᵈ. 33."

A letter from Robert to his mother, dated June 28ᵗʰ[1]), forms a remarkably charming completion to this spring greeting.

He combines with his remarks about her the information that he had often met Kalkbrenner; "the most refined and pleasant (though vain) Frenchman", and then goes on: "Now that I know the most famous virtuosos (with the exception of Hummel), I know what I did before, and that is a good deal. One expects to hear something quite new from famous men, and after all one only finds one's dear old mistakes dressed up in fine names. Names, believe me, are half the battle. However, I give the palm over all male virtuoses, to two girls: Belleville[2]) and Clara. The latter, who is as devoted to me as ever, is just the same — wild and emotional — she runs and jumps and plays like a child and then all at once says the most thoughtful things. It is a pleasure to see how the blossoms of her heart and mind unfold ever faster and faster, and yet leaf by leaf. As we were coming home from Connewitz together, the other day, (almost every day we walk for two or three hours) I heard her say to herself: 'Oh! how happy I am! How happy!' Who would not like to hear that! — On the same road, there are a great many useless stones in the middle of the foot-path. Now when I am talking I have

1) *Jugendbriefe* p. 208 etc.
2) Emilie Belleville, who was born and died in Munich (1808—1888), was a pupil of Czerny.

a habit of looking up rather than down, then she comes behind me and gently twitches my coat at every stone so that I shall not fall. And all the time she stumbles over them herself."

Some more extracts from their letters. On July 13th Robert who in the mean time has fallen ill of a cold fever, writes:

"Dear and good Clara

I want to know if, and how you are living — there is nothing else in this letter. I hardly wish that you should still remember me, for I fall away visibly every day and shoot up to the height of a dry, leafless bean-pole. The doctor has strictly forbidden me to long for anything, that is for you, because it is too exhausting. But to-day I removed all bandages from the wounds and laughed in the doctor's very face when he tried to prevent me from writing; yes, l threatened to fall upon him and infect him with the fever if he would not let me peacably go my own way. Then he gave in.

But I did not mean to tell you all this, but something quite different — namely a request that you have to grant. Since no electric chain binds us to each other at present or reminds us of each other, I have devised a plan of sympathy — this: to-morrow on the stroke of 11 I shall play the adagio from Chopin's variations and at the same time I shall think of you very hard, exclusively of you. Now the request is that you should do the same, so that we may see each other and meet in spirit. The place will probably be over the little *Thomaspförtchen*, where our doubles [1]) meet. If there were a full moon I should suggest using it as a mirror for our letters. I hope very much for an answer. If you do not do it a string will break to-morrow at 12 o'clock; it will be me. I am too, from my deepest heart,

July 13th /33.   Robert Schumann."

Clara to Robert (on the same day):

---

1) This, and the following allusions to "doubles" refer to a joke of Schumann's, who loved to tell the Wieck children — excited by E. Th. Hoffmann's story — about his mysterious double; a joke which Clara then took to herself. Cf. p. 64.

"Dear Herr Schumann

With great difficulty I have at last, with my mother's help,
made out your letter, and at once sit down to answer you. I am
very sorry that you have been so shaken by the fever, and all
the more since I have learned that you are not allowed to drink
any Bavarian beer, a prohibition which you must find it very hand
to obey. You want to know if I am alive? well you may tell
that by the number of compliments I have sent you already —
to be sure, I do not know if they have been delivered, but I
hope so. How I live, you can easily think for yourself. How can
I live happily when you no longer come too see us! As to your
request I will grant it, and shall find myself at 11 o'clock to-
morrow over the little *Thomaspförtchen*. I have finished my '*Doppelgänger*' chorus, and have added a third part to it. To my great
sorrow I cannot write you a longer letter, as I have so much to
do. Please write to me again. From her heart there wishes you
a quick recovery

Clara Wieck.

I ask you most
earnestly for the 2ⁿᵈ
volume of the *Papillons.*

When I got your letter I thought, now
you too shall write really badly for once,
and I have done so, as you may see.

If you receive this letter without a seal, please write and
tell me.

Clara's next letter speaks of her Op. **3**, the romance which
she dedicated to Schumann.

Here, August 1ˢᵗ 1833.

"Dear Herr Schumann

Sorry as I am to have dedicated the following trifle to you,
and much as I wished not to see the variations printed, yet the
evil has come to pass now, and cannot be altered. Therefore I
ask pardon for the enclosed. Your able re-casting of this little
musical thought will make good my mistakes[1]), and so I beg for
this, for I can hardly wait to make its better acquaintance. You
will see by the title of my *Romance* that my double is not forgotten, though I have not summoned him. Can it be enferred

---

1) Schumann had used the theme from Clara's *Romance* as the basi
of his impromptu Op. 5.

from this (that his influence makes my) '*Doppelgänger*' compositions will be more promising?

Now be quick and get out of doors, so that you can come and see us, especially as Krägen is coming to-morrow. I hope Krägen's presence will cure you of your fever.

Friendliest-greetings from

Clara Wieck.

Krägen has just come."

Schumann replied[1]):

"Leipsic. August 2nd /33.

Dear Clara

For people who cannot flatter, there is hardly a more difficult task than in the first place to write, and in the second to answer, a dedicatory letter. One is entirely overcome — crushed beneath a weight of modesty, regret, gratitude, etc. etc. I would cheerfully reply to anyone except you: 'How do I deserve this distinction? Have you thought it over?' Or I would use figures of speech and write that the moon would be invisible to man if the sun's rays did not fall upon her; or say: 'See, how the noble vine clings to the humble elm, that she — fruitless and flowerless — may drink in his spirit.' But to you I have nothing but a heart-felt 'Thank-you' to give, and if you were here (even without your father's permission) a hand-grip; and then I would say something of the hope that the union of our names on the tittle page, may be a union of our views and ideas at a later day. I am too poor to offer more. —

My work will remain, like many others, a ruin, since for a long time it has produced nothing but erasures. Something else is coming. Ask Krägen, to whom I send greetings, if he will stand godfather to the work, that is if I may dedicate it to him.

As the sky is looking too gloomy to-day, I am very sorry that I cannot come round and have some music this evening. Besides I have spun myself into so think a cocoon that only the tiny tips of my wings peep out of the chrysalis, which might easily be injured. All the same I hope certainly to see you again before you leave.

Robert Schumann."

1) *Jugendbriefe* p. 216.

The journey to which reference is here made, was undertaken on August 7th, and took father and daughter to Chemnitz, Schneeberg, and Carlsbad. Both in Chemnitz and in Carlsbad Clara gave concerts. On the bill of the Carlsbad theatre she was mentioned by the theatre director as C. W. "who happens to be here on her tour from Paris to St. Petersburg".

Her father's 48th birthday occurred whilst they were at Chemnitz. Robert Schumann him gave a great pleasure on that day, by sending him his impromptus (Op. 5) on a theme from Clara's *Romance* (Op. 3). They had just appeared in print, and were dedicated to Wieck.

In September Clara played in the *Gewandhaus* in honour of the opening of the newly decorated hall. But this time the public found so many things to criticise in her performance, that her father did not consider it advisable to let her play again. It was time, he thought, for someone else to play; for constantly to place new luxuries before men, is to make them exacting and supercilious; it was time that mediocrity should teach the public to be humble again.

On Jan. 10th 1834 Clara, who was now 14$1/2$, and her friend Emilie List were confirmed together. Two days later, when she went to her first communion, Friedrich Wieck wrote in her diary:

"My daughter

You must be independent now; that is most important. I have dedicated nearly 10 years of my life to you and your education; it is for you now to think of your duties. Fix your mind then, on noble and unselfish deeds, on doing good, on a true humanity which shall grow more and more at every opportunity, and consider the practice of virtue to be true religion. When you are bitterly misunderstood, calumniated, envied, do not let this lead you astray in your principles. Ah! that is a hard struggle and yet in this consists true virtue. I remain your helpful adviser and friend   Friedrich Wieck."

CHAPTER II.

HOARFROST.
1834—1835.

"On April 21ˢᵗ", says the diary for 1834, "my friend Ernestine von Fricken came here in order to have piano lessons from my father."

The friendship was of recent date. They had made acquaintance only a few weeks before, at a concert that Clara gave in Plauen. Ernestine came with her father, captain Freiherr von Fricken, from their country seat, Asch, to that concert, and on this occasion it was arranged with Wieck that she should shortly enter his house as pupil and boarder. The two young girls seem to have made friends with each other very quickly, which was no wonder if one considers their common musical interests, and the sweet, refined character for which Ernestine was noted by all who came into contact with her. She was three years older than Clara[1]), and so in advance of her in *savoir faire* though not at all in inner development. But the freshly made friendship was to suffer an unexpected interruption, as soon after Ernestine's removal to Leipsic, Clara was taken by her father on a long visit to Dresden in order that she might study theory of music with Reissiger, Musikdirektor there, and have singing lessons from Chordirektor Mieksch. Possibly on her father's side there was at the bottom of this sudden resolution some thought too of breaking off

---

1) Born Sept. 7ᵗʰ 1816.

for a time the daily intercourse between Clara and Schumann, which in all innocence was visibly becoming more intimate, and of nipping in the bud an incipient inclination which he thought boded no good for the future. If this were so, then this very step, as we shall see, was, from his point of view, the most unfortunate measure which he could have tried, favourable as the immediate consequences seemed to be. For Clara's absence, which separated her from Schumann — with one short interval — till September, was as a matter of fact the first thing, the first touchstone, which made clear to them their feeling towards one-another. And the very person to whom she owed the first and bitterest pang in her love-story — her friend Ernestine von Fricken — was by this means destined to lay the foundation of an indestructible and indivisible livelong comradeship, which bade defiance to all the storms that were to come.

"I must tell you", Clara writes to her lover four years later[1]), in speaking of this time, "what a silly child I was then. When Ernestine came to us, I said to her: 'Ah! when only you get to know Schumann! I like him the best of all our acquaintances.' — But she would have nothing to say to it, for she said she knew a gentleman in Asch whom she liked much better. I was quite angry; but I had not long to wait before she became more and more fond of you, and soon it got to such a pitch that I always had to call her when you came. I was glad enough to do so then, for I was only too pleased that she liked you, I wanted her to, and I was satisfied. You always talked to her alone when she came, and you only talked nonsense to me. I was not a little hurt at this, but I comforted myself and thought that it was only due to the fact that you always had me, and also that Ernestine was more grown-up than I was. Strange feelings stirred my heart

---

1) March 2nd 1838 in Vienna.

(young as it was it beat warmly even then) when we went
for a walk and you talked to Ernestine, and sometimes made
a joke with me. It was on this account that my father sent
me to Dresden, where I gained more hope again; even then
I thought 'how happy I should be if some day you were my
husband'."

Something of this yearning, excited, restless frame of mind
is shown in the letter which she wrote from the midst of her
zealous musical studies — she was scoring Mozart's fantasia
with Reissiger — to her friend on his birthday, a few weeks
after her departure:

Dresden June 8th 1834.

"Dear Herr Schumann

To-day, Sunday the 8th of June, on the day when the good
God let fall so bright a musical spark from heaven, and you were
born, I sit here and write to you, although I have had two invitations for this afternoon.

The first thing I have to write is that I send you my good
wishes, that you may not always be contrary — may drink less
Bavarian beer — may not stay behind when others go — may
not turn day into night and *vice versa* — may show your friends
that you think of them, may compose industriously — may write
more for the news paper, because the readers wish it [1]) — and
firmly resolve to come to Dresden etc. etc.

But is it permitted Herr Schumann, to take so little notice of
a friend that you do not even write to her? Every time the post
arrived I hoped to get a letter from a certain Herr Enthusiast, but
ah! I was disappointed. I comforted myself with the thought that
at least you were coming here, but my father has just written to
me to say that you are not coming as Knorr [2]) is ill. Emilie too,
is not coming with him [3]) as she is going to a watering-place —
that is misfortune upon misfortune. Well, one must take things
as they come! I am much looking forward to your new rondo,

---

1) The *Neue Zeitschrift für Musik* founded and edited by Schumann,
came into existence on April 3rd 1834.

2) Knorr was his collaborater on the paper.

3) Wieck visited Clara in Dresden in the latter half of June.

it will give me something to work at. Here in Dresden everybody, and Sophie Kaskel (a pretty girl) in particular, is quite in
ove with your impromptus and practises them industriously. She
— and Becker[1]) and Krägen — are quite unhappy that you are
not coming here, and it is really quite unpardonable of you.

There is a notice fixed to my door: 'Clarus Wieck, officially
appointed contributor to the latest musical paper.' Before long
you shall have 6 pages from me, and then you will have to pay
me a lot.

I hear that Gustav has written to you — Fine stuff I expect!
And you really mean to answer him? In that case I too may expect
an original letter — the handwriting need not be original (i. e.
illegible) — may I not, Herr Schumann? This ingenious, original,
and witty epistle commends to you with due deliberation (you do
not like haste) your friend

                                        Clara Wieck
                                        Clara Wieck
                                        Double."

They met again on July 25th, at the christening of Clara's
little step-sister, Cäcilia, when Schumann and Ernestine stood
as godparents, but this meeting did nothing to set Clara's mind
at rest. Schumann's *Record of my Life in Leipsic* says briefly:
"A christening at the Wiecks'. Clara back from Dresden. She
is sorry to be going away again." The affection between
Schumann and Ernestine had become so marked that in August
Herr von Fricken came to Leipsic to ask Wieck for an
explanation, and finally decided to remove his daughter from
the household. Robert gave her a ring when they parted,
and although nothing was said of any definite engagement, he
considered himself bound, and though in writing to his mother
he speaks of this "Summer Romance", he was evidently happy
in the thought of marrying her. By the end of October his
impatience had driven him to Asch, but apparently the parents
still refrained from formally recognising the engagement, though

---

1) Ernst Adolph Becker, an intimate friend of Schumann's and the
Wiecks', at that time in Freiberg.

in his letters Robert repeatedly speaks of Ernestine as his "betrothed". Early in 1834, however, he received a severe shock when he discovered that Ernestine had deceived him as to her family circumstances, and that she was an illegitimate child whom Herr von Fricken had adopted; while at the same time he began gradually to realise that in his youthful enthusiasm he had exalted her into something far more ideal than she really was. She was warm-hearted and affectionate, but she possessed none of the finer traits of mind and character necessary to hold so richly-endowed a spirit as Schumann's.

"On the 25th Herr Schumann went to Zwickau, that is to Asch", wrote Clara in her diary for October 1833.

A long time was to pass before they were to see each other again. In November, after much deliberation Wieck decided to undertake a more lengthy concert-tour, and on Nov. 11th they set out with Carl Bank, giving concerts at Magdeburg, Schönebeck, and Halberstadt. On Dec. 18th they made a longer halt at Braunschweig.

The chief musical event consisted in four grand concerts with which were combined a number of smaller ones, as well as public and private musical recitals. The brothers Karl and Theodor Müller — the one Konzertmeister, the other Kammermusiker to the Duke — both members of the old, but once world-famous Müller String Quartett, out of sheer admiration for Clara played for her for nothing.

This gave her abundant opportunity not only of showing her knowledge of classical music, but also her power of performing it.

Clara was naturally dependent on her father's suggestions and accustomed to be guided by his decisions. The point of view which he took up in this connection, was — if the truth must be told — not purely artistic. It finds explanation, if not excuse, in the condition of musical taste at the time, which as far as the art of performing was concerned, cared for nothing but brilliancy of execution. Understanding for the works of creative genius, in whose rendering and interpretation it was necessary for the performer to subordinate his own personality to that of the composer, was very rare. Wieck was, truly, artist enough to grasp the greatness of a Beethoven or a Bach; but in his opinion full enjoyment of them presumed a connoisseurship reliance upon which was always joined, for the performers, to the danger of playing with serious loss to an emply or silent house; and this did not accord with his practical views. But on neutral ground, in private circles, before an audience of connoisseurs, he was always ready to prove his good taste, and it satisfied his pride to be able to show the world that Clara was at home, in the best sense of the word, in playing classical music.

An exciting, wearing, successful tour followed. At Hanover, in particular, where they went on Jan. 14th, Clara had great triumphs at the vice-regal court; then at Bremen; but above all in Hamburg, though here they also found plenty of disagreeables and annoyances. The impresario father, who was obliged, day in day out, to deal with grasping speculators, adverse and jealous colleagues indifferent or unfavourable critics and a well-meaning but stupid and ignorant public, was driven almost wild, as is grimly illustrated by the 17 questions "which were asked us 700 times in this town, by that half of the human race which thirsts for knowledge", which he has entered on two pages of the diary that happend to have been left empty.

1. When did your daughter begin?
   Ans. Never. It would take too long to explain more fully the justice of this answer.
2. How old is your daughter *really*?
   Ans. That is written under her portrait which appeared in Hanover in 1835.
3. Do your daughter's fingers not hurt her?
   Ans. You forget that you are speaking of Clara Wieck.

4. Do you not over-strain her?

   Ans. My Clara's appearance gives you the best answer to that.

5. But would she not be merrier if she played less?

   Ans. It is really impossible for me to know. But my other daughthers shall learn nothing — so that they shall not reproach me, or make others reproach me.

6. Does not your daughter play anything of Hummel's, Kalk-brenner's, Beethoven's etc.?

   Ans. Yes — but only in private and — at sight; not here — where she is to shine as the greatest pianist now living.

7. You ought to let her play something of theirs even if it is only a trifle.

   Ans. You will be nearer the mark if you ask your own performers to do that. Clara has only come here in order to let you hear what you could not hear otherwise.

8. Does your daughter sing too?

   Ans. Yes, but only songs, and to a few people, and at home.

9. But I must advise you not to do that — will it not be too much?

   Ans. It might well be too much; but as I have already mentioned, I am careful.

10. Will you not let her sing something?

    Ans. You have just answered that yourself.

11. You must be very happy that heaven has given you such a daughter?

    Ans. Yes; once it was snowing — a wilful snow-flake fell into my arms, and behold — that was this Clara, exactly as she stands before you.

12. Have you more children, equally musical?

    Ans. They have as much talent, but have not been taught.

13. How is that?

    Ans. Because I have only one life to give.

14. But what a pity!

    Ans. As you like.

15. How will Clara play in some years' time?

    Ans. I will take care that she forgets nothing and will always be able to satisfy those who understand.

16. How many hours a-day does Clara practise?
    Ans. She does not play at all by night, and by day —
    very little.
17. Does your daughter like playing?
    Ans. That is the end of everything — even of answers.

And Clara herself? Her father complains once in Hamburg
(on April 4th): "Clara plays with reluctance, and does not want
to do any more. What is an artist without vanity!" And in
consequence of this weariness, which weighed on the limbs
of father as well as of daughter, the tour was not carried
further as had originally been planned, but on April 10th they
began the return journey by way of Berlin. Berlin indeed
was to have been one of their halting-places; but the experiences there of the over-wrought and over-tired impresario,
so enraged him that he quickly shook the dust of the Mark
from his feet, and the inhabitants of Berlin, who had already
received notice of a coming concert, by means Voss's paper
were left to look after him. "Amen — God with us", says
the diary. "We are not going to Berlin, God help me out of
it. Amen, Amen — God be praised[1])."

Her nearest relations seem to have had no idea of what
was passing in Clara's mind at the time; something which
made her reluctance to give concerts grow till it became
unendurable. The engagement between Schumann and Ernestine
von Fricken had shaken her deeply, young as she was. It was
the destruction of a hope which now that she must tear its
roots from her heart she first discovered was a vital part of
her being. But she was firmly resolved to do this, and this
frame of mind compounded of childish petulance, and feverish
agitation over this first sorrow which had fallen upon her like

---

1) Wieck did not love the Prussians at all. "Good God! what is
more horrible," he writes once in the diary, "than to be a mediocre
artist and, in addition to that, from Prussia!"

a thief in the night, explains the nervous excitability and over-wrought merriment of a letter which she sent to her step-mother from Hanover [1]), in which she declares that she has fallen in love with the young 'cellist, Müller, of Brunswick. She wished to forget.

In April the Wiecks returned to Leipsic. One of their first callers was Schumann.

"How well I remember," Clara wrote later [2]), "how you came into the room, that first afternoon after our return from Hamburg, and hardly gave me even a passing greeting, and how I went in tears to Auguste, who was with us, and said: "Oh! I love no one as I love him, and he did not even look at me!"

But she deceived herself; though the greeting may have been casual the impression which her personality made upon him, was not.

"I do not know what you looked like that first afternoon," he wrote later [3]); "You seemed to me taller, more strange. — You were no longer a child with whom I could laugh and play — you talked so wisely, and in your eyes I saw a ray of love lie deeply hidden. Do you know what happened then?" he continues, "I broke free from Ernestine — I felt I must."

This assertion is to be found in Schumann's letters for the year 1838, which are important and noteworthy in more than once connection, and in which he tries to give an absolutely honest account of those passages in his inner life, with whose outer expression we have been made acquainted by the letter quoted on the last page, but the key to whose inner meaning — at all events as far as Schumann's conduct is concerned —

1) Printed by Kohut p. 337, with the wrong date, 1836 instead of 1835.
2) Letter to Schumann dated Jan. 13th 1839, from Nuremberg.
3) Letter to Clara of Feb. 11th 1838.

is yet missing. He has described these confessions which he sent to his beloved, as, "A key to all my doings, to all my strange self". Therefore this turning-point, when we see him freeing himself from the enchantment of the "Summer Romance", and restored to his own nature, is the most suitable place in which to insert this document which sheds new light on past and future. He himself wrote some words — which he had "recently read at the end of an excellent book" — as a kind of motto at the beginning: "He is a fool who trusts to his heart, but do not condemn him."

"Leipsic, Feb. 11th 1838.

My own sweet, beloved girl, now sit down by me, put your head a little on the right side, in the dear way you have, and let me tell you everything.

For some time I have been happier than I ever was before. It must be pleasant for you to know that you have given back the bright, cheerful day, to a man who has for years been preyed upon by the most horrible thoughts, who had a genius for finding out the dark and terrible side of things, who was capable of throwing his life away like a farthing. I will lay bare to you my inmost feelings, in a way in which I have shown them to no-one. You must know everything, you whom I love next to God.

My individual life begins at the time when I first became certain of myself and my talent, decided on Art, and turned my powers into the right direction. That is from the year 1830 onwards. You were then a funny little girl with a fund of perversity and a pair of beautiful eyes; and cherries formed your ideal of happiness. Beside you I had no-one except my Rosalie[1]). A couple of years went by. Even then, in 1833, I began to feel a depression which I feared to face; it was the disappointment which every artist experiences when things do not go as fast as he had fancied they would. I found little recognition, and to this was added the loss of my right hand for playing[2]). Amidst all these dark thoughts and images there now came one dancing towards me, yours and yours alone;

---

1) Wife of Schumann's brother Karl. Already dead in 1833.
2) In consequence of an injury to the middle finger.

it is you, who — without knowing or wishing it — have kept me for many long years from all connection with women. Even then the thought sometimes glimmered in my mind that you might perhaps become my wife; but it all lay too far in the future; however this might be, I had always loved you heartily, as befitted our ages. Of quite a different kind was my love for my never-to-be-forgotten Rosalie; we were of an age; she was more than a sister to me, but there could be no question of being in love. She took care of me, always spoke the best of me, cheered me up, in short thought highly of me. And so my thoughts rested most gladly upon her picture too. This was in the summer 1833. Yet I seldom felt happy; something was lacking; my depression, deepened by the death of a dear brother, grew more and more. Such was the state of my heart when I heard of Rosalie's death. — I can speak but little of this — — during the night of Oct. 17th—18th there came to me all at once the most terrible thought that a man can ever have — the most terrible punishment that heaven can send — that 'of losing reason' — it overpowered me with such violence that before it all comfort, all prayer were silenced as if they were mere scorn and mockery — my breath stopped at the thought, 'Suppose you could no longer think!' — Clara, he who has once been thus annihilated knows no more suffering, or sickness, or despair — then, in constant, terrible excitement, I rushed to a doctor — told him all, how my mind often wandered I know not where, from sorrow, yes, that I could not even guarantee that under such circumstances I should not lay a despairing hand upon my life. Do not be horrified, my angel from heaven; but listen; the doctor comforted me most kindly, and finally said with a smile: 'Medicine is of no use here; make haste and find a wife, she will soon cure you.' I felt lightened; I thought that would be all right; at that time you troubled yourself little about me, for you stood at the parting of the ways between childhood and girlhood. — Then came Ernestine — as good a girl as there ever was in the world — She, I thought, is the one; she will save you. I wanted to cling to some woman with all my force. I became better — she loved me, I saw that — You know all — our separation, how we wrote to each other, called each other ,Thou', etc. etc. This was in the winter of 1834. But now that she was away, and I began to think how all this was to end, now that I learnt her poverty — and however industrious I might be,

I earned but little myself — it began to weigh upon me like a
fetter — I saw no end, no hope — in addition I heard of unfortunate family complications in which Ernestine was involved,
and of which — and for this I very much blamed her — she
had told me nothing all this time. All this taken together overwhelmed me — I must confess that I grew cooler; my artistic
career seemed to have suffered a reverse; the picture of her to
whom I had clung to save myself, haunted me now in my dreams
like a ghost; I thought now of working for my daily bread as
an artizan; Ernestine deserved nothing; I spoke to my mother
again about it and we agreed that after many cares this way
would only lead to fresh troubles."

We may add here a later account whose true meaning is
revealed only in this connection: "You are my first love.
Ernestine had to come, in order that we might be united."

But there was still a long way to go before this goal was
reached, and his entanglement with Ernestine soon proved to
be the obstacle most easily overcome.

The "daily companionship with Clara" [1] to which he gives
prominence in the *Record of my Life in Leipsic* for this
summer, was interrupted at the end of July by a concert tour
of Clara's to Halle, and in August by a visit of Schumann's
to Zwickau. But it was just these separations above all things,
which confirmed Schumann in his belief in the truth and
permanency of his feeling towards Clara, and persuaded him
of the necessity of a final rupture with Ernestine.

On August 28th he wrote from Zwickau the letter which
begins: "From the midst of all the autumn glories and exquisite
skies there peeps out an angel's head which is exactly like
a certain Clara whom I know well," and concludes with the

---

1) In the letter dated Feb. 11th 1838. This passage has been misunderstood to mean that Schumann had already broken off his relations
with Ernestine, in August; as is stated in the footnote to the *Jugendbriefe* p. 256.

words: "You know how dear you are to me" [1]), betraying clearly enough a passion restrained with difficulty.

Clara's playful reply no less clearly betrays her joyful surprise.

Leipsic, Sept. 1th 1835.

"I was just winding my way like a worm through your sonata [2]) which two gentlemen from Hanover wanted to hear, when a letter came to me, and from whence, thought I? Then I read Zwickau. I was very surprised, for when you went away from here you did not give me much hope of such a letter. For two whole hours I have been poring over it, and yet there are still a few spiteful words left which will not get into my head by any means.

All the same you do not know what has been happening to me [3]), the *Rosenthal* has fallen out of favour for I have been out very little since you went away. This is on account of my great industry. You will smile, but it is true. 1. I have finished my score; 2. I have written out all the parts myself, and that in two days; 3. I made a clean copy of my variations in *F*, as well as my *Danse de Fantomes (Doppelgänger* chorus) and *Une nuit de Sabbat (Hexenchor)* for the printers. I have begun to score the concerto, but I have not yet written it out. I have altered the tutti a little.

---

1) Printed in the *Jugendbriefe* p. 266. The opening is transcribed almost word for word from the beginning of the first love-letter *Ges. Schriften* I p. 159.

2) *Grande Sonate pour le Pianoforte* No. 1, Op. 11 in *F*♯ minor. Dedicated to Clara by Florestan and Eusebius. — Already in 1831 Schumann introduces Florestan and Eusebius and Raro conversing, in an article on Chopin, and in 1833 he introduces them in the *Komet* as the *Davidsbündler*. As a matter of fact they existed only in Schumann's imagination. By dividing himself into these three phantoms he gave himself the advantage as a critic of being able to express different views and ideas concerning art and artists and in one and the same work. (G. Jansen's paper, *Die Davidsbündler*.)

3) Schumann had written: "I do not know what has been happening to you, and yet I do know: — *Rosenthal* in the morning, *Rosenthal* in the afternoon, Kintschy in the evening. How you would envy us — — if we told you our plan of campaign: in early morning bathing in the sun on a mountain, in the afternoon sleeping in a valley, in the evening flying up and down the mountains" etc.

You have laid out a very fine plan of campaign, yet I do not envy you it, for very soon this envy would be transferred to you: I too have something of great worth in reserve: 1. Moscheles is coming here, and will stay for several days, and possibly will give a concert; 2. Mendelssohn came here yesterday, and 3., guess, there is coming, Oh joy! your ideal — Francilla Pixis[1])! Now, does not that attract you?

I send a hearty greeting to both the two Graces, whom you have described so poetically for me, particularly to Therese. You asked me to convey greetings to your chosen subjects[2]), but I could not, for they have accompanied their master, as true subjects should, in order to share joy and sorrow with him. I send their master, whom you know well, many greetings through you, and so does the *Davidsbündler Florestan Sonata*, which is looking forward to being made a little easier towards the end of its magic tones — B minor, instead of $F\sharp$ major.

Your Clara Wieck.

Please give your mother kindest remembrances from us all.

A few days later Schumann returned to Leipsic. We have learned from Clara's letter that Mendelssohn had arrived in the mean time in ordor to take his place as conductor of the *Gewandhaus*-concerts. She had already been made to play him Schumann's $F\sharp$ minor sonata. There now speedily developed between the two musicians, who were of about the same age, a warm friendship which was of especial consequence to Schumann, and which he valued highly.

On September 13th the Wiecks' young friends met at their table in honour of Clara's birthday, when Mendelssohn was of course not absent. Clara had received a gold watch as a present from the *Davidsbündler*[3]), Ortlepp offered her an

---

1) Franzilla Pixis-Göhringer, the adopted daughter of Pixis; later an opera-singer in Munich.

2) The *Davidsbündler*.

3) By degrees, all Schumann's most intimate friends, and particularly his colleagues on the newspaper, came to be comprehended under this name.

enthusiasic poem, the champagne flowed, and Clara even rose
to the height of attempting to make an after-dinner speech of
thanks, but did herself more justice after they rose from table,
in her accustomed method of expression. She and Mendelssohn
played his *capriccio* for two pianos, and then gave by heart
Bach's $C\sharp$ major fugue, and, at Mendelssohn's special request,
the scherzo of Schumann's $F\sharp$ minor sonata. He vigorously
refused to listen to anything of Herz's, but played himself a
Bach fugue and other things, imitating very cleverly Liszt's
and Chopin's manner of playing. When he left, he gave Clara
his *capriccio*[1]).

Soon after this Chopin visited Leipsic on his way home.
He came from Carlsbad, where he had been to see his parents.
As he was there only for one day, and did not find Clara at
home, he waited a full hour till she returned in order to
see her and hear her play. She played him Schumann's
$F\sharp$ minor sonata, the last movement of his own concerto, and
two of his *Études*. He over-powered her with praise, and
gave expression to his thanks by handing her one of his latest
works. At Clara's request he also played to her one of his
Nocturnes, with the finest pianissimos but in her opinion with
too much capriciousness. He was even then so ill and weak
that he could play a *forte* only by a convulsive movement of
his whole body. In himself, he struck Clara as a model of
French politeness. On leaving, he expressed his hope and
intention of coming back in the winter. Naturally Schumann
and Chopin also made acquaintance on the occasion[2]).

In the mean time the day was approaching on which was
to be decided the fate of her own concerto. The first rehearsal

---

1) Op. 5 in $F\sharp$ minor.
2) The first of the four *Letters of an Enthusiast* contained in the
Neue Zeitschrift für Musik for Oct. 20th 1835, No. 2 p. 127. (Cf. *Ges.
Schriften* I, p. 162 Note) has added as postscript: "Chopin has been here.
Florestan rushed upon him. I saw them arm in arm, floating rather
than walking. Eusebius."

before the performance took place in the *Gewandhaus* on Nov. 9th. Besides this, she played a *Capriccio brillant*[1]) of Mendelssohn's, with the orchestra, Herz's variations on the Greek chorus from the *Siege of Corinth*, and in conclusion Bach's concerto for three pianos, with Mendelssohn and Rackeman of Bremen.

Four days before the concert the *Leipziger Tageblatt* published an article[2]) — which probably came from the pen of Schumann — in which the attention of the public was called to the unusual character of the treat which was awaiting it; first to the "young mistress" herself, who "is one of the few in whom the higher language of art is innate", then to her work, "which gives us an insight into her deepest soul". With reference to the concerto of Bach, which was also being given for the first time in the *Gewandhaus*, the article says: "It would be an interesting and remarkable experience for dwellers in Leipsic if the spirit of their former fellow-citizen, old Bach, with all his profound, good-humoured, capricious, crabbed, lovableness, should walk into their midst, greeting them, exhorting them, and asking drily: 'How are things going with you now, in the artistic world? See; that is what I was!'"

The pianist had an enthusiastic reception. On the other hand, the success of her own work, kindly as it was received, and in spite of the fact that the *Komet* described it as "written throughout in a grand style", and lauded the interchange of the softest and most tuneful melodies with the fieriest and most fantastic passages, and the poetic unity

---

1) In *B* minor. "Only think, Fanny", wrote Mendelssohn on Nov. 13th, "at Wieck's concert I heard my *B* minor *Capriccio* for the first time (Clara played it like a little demon) and I liked it very well". Hensel *Die Familie Mendelssohn* I p. 421.

2) *Leipziger Tageblatt* of Nov. 5th 1835, included by Jansen — certainly with justice — in the *Collected Works*. Cf. *Ges. Schriften* Vol. I pp. 157, 335.

which governed the whole", perhaps fell somewhat below expectation.

In the fourth of his *Letters of an Enthusiast to Chiara* [1]), Schumann, as Eusebius, sums up the impressions made by Zilia's (Clara's) concerto, scrappily and estatically and yet critically, in the words:

"... The first strains that we heard flew before us like a young Phœnix fluttering upwards. Passionate white roses and pearly lily chalices bent over it, and above nodded orange-blossoms and myrtle, and amongst them alders and weeping-willows threw their melancholy shadows; but in the midst of this shone a radiant girl-face seeking flowers for a wreath. Often I saw skiffs floating boldly over the sea, and but one touch of the master-hand at the tiller, but one pull at the ropes was needed to send them, swift and victorious, across the waves. I heard thoughts which had often not chosen the right interpreter to make them shine forth in all their beauty, and yet the fiery spirit which urged them on, and the longing that swayed them, carried them unhestitatingly towards their goal. And now came a young Saracen hero, like an Oriflamme, and jousted with lance and sword, so that it was a delight to see him; and finally a French dandy skipped by and drew all hearts to his side ..."

The first of the four *Letters of an Enthusiast from Eusebius to Chiara* apeared on Oct. 20th in the *Neue Zeitschrift für Musik* [2]), and ended with the significant words: "Enough for to-day. Do not forget to sometimes look in the Calendar for the 13th of August where Aurora [3]) unites your name with mine."

---

1) *Neue Zeitschrift für Musik* of Dec. 8th 1835 No. 46 (III p. 182). Cf. *Ges. Schriften* Vol. I p. 168.

2) *N. Z. f. M.* III No. 32 p. 126.

3) The three days which followed each other were Clara, Aurora, Eusebius. It was a curious chance that the 15th of August afterwards really was fraught with importance for Schumann and Clara.

Just at this time came an explanation between Clara and Schumann. In the *Record of my Life in Leipsic* after Chopin's name comes the entry, "Clara's eyes and her love", and then, "The first kiss in November". In the end, his growing passion mastered him, and although he had not get broken off his relations with Ernestine, one evening when Clara lighted him down the stairs of her parents' house [1]), he confessed his love, and won an answering confession from the surprised girl. "When you gave me the first kiss," she wrote later, "I thought I should have fainted; everything became black before my eyes; I could scarcely hold the light which was to show you the way." He won this at the cost of a "lover's perjury", for he told her — naturally anxious as she was to be satisfied about Ernestine — that the latter was already engaged to some-one else.

Most important of all was the time that they were together at Zwickau in December. On Nov. 26th Clara had set out on a little concert tour to Zwickau, Plauen, Glauchau, and Chemnitz: On Dec. 4th Schumann joined the Wiecks in his native town. The concert was given on Dec. 6th. The diary says nothing of how she played that evening. Three years later, Schumann writes: "To-morrow it will be three years since the evening when I kissed you in Zwickau. I never forget that kiss. You were most charming, that evening. And then, at the concert, you could not so much as give me one look, you Clara, in your blue dress. I remember it as if it were to-day."

In Schumann's copy of the paper, stands written in pencil in the margin, in his hand, the remark: "What an amazing presentiment!"

1) In the entries which he makes in the *Bridegroom's Book*, which he made for Clara during their courtship, Schumann speaks of "hard partings", and mentions as the first, that "in November 1835, after the first kiss on the stairs of Wieck's house, when Clara went to Zwickau". From this it seems as if the explanation must have occurred on the eve of the journey to Zwickau, i. e. Nov. 25th.

The *Record of my Life in Leipsic* announced at this time: "Agreement. Taken leave of my mother. Broken with Ernestine." It is evident not only Clara's love, but also his conversation with his dearly-loved mother — whom he now saw for the last time, alive — had roused in him the power to come to a decision, to give back her promise to Ernestine, and frankly and honourably to break off a connection to which his heart no longer agreed. Yet according to the accounts given later by Ernestine herself, the final separation does not seem to have followed until the January of the succeeding year. The manner in which she set Schumann free does honour to her character and her heart. "I feel keenly, and cannot conceal from myself," Schumann wrote to Clara from Vienna three years later (Oct. 23rd 1838) "that a wrong was done to her, but it would have been a great and a worse misfortune if it had ever come to a union between her and me. Sooner or later my old love and attachment to you must have re-awakened, and then what misery there would have been; all three of us would have been most terrible unhappy. Thus she was the victim of circumstances, and I by no means ignore my culpability in the matter. But Clara, so far as we can put it right, we will. Ernestine .. knows very well that she had first driven you from my heart, that I loved you before I knew her .... Ernestine often wrote to me: 'I have always believed that you could love no-one but Clara, and I believe it still' — she saw more clearly than I."

However, she did the lovers a real service three years later[1]), when Clara's father tried to make capital out of

---

1) Cf. Ernestine's letter to Wieck, Oct. 3rd 1838, printed by Kohut *Friedrich Wieck* p. 104 etc. wrongly dated 1836. That the letter dates from the year 1838 is shown not only by its allusion to her approaching marriage with another, but also by the letters of Clara and Schumann at the beginning of October 1838. A denial of this sort was certainly necessary in her own interests in view of her approaching marriage.

Schumann's engagement to her, and she by at once absolutely denying all relations except those of friendship and music, deprived Wieck of a weapon from whose use he had promised himself great things. In the end Schumann and Ernestine remained good friends, especially after there had been an explanation in Leipsic. Both he and Clara took a warm interest in her future fate, and greeted her marriage — which followed in November 1838 — with especial joy. In the spring-time of his love for her, Schumann had dedicated to her an *allegro* Op. 8, and had paid her a particularly graceful compliment by composing the *Carnaval*[1]) upon the notes *A B C H*, which formed the name of her birthplace. He offered her — then a newly-made widow — a public token of his friendly remembrance when in 1841 he dedicated a volume of songs to her (Op. 31).

----

1) *Carnaval, Scènes mignonnes sur 4 Notes* (Op. 9).

CHAPTER III.

LOST AND FOUND.
1836—1837.

The year 1835 had ended under good auspices. Schumann's *Record* remarks, after their return to Leipsic: "Happy hours pass in her arms at Wieck's house in the evenings." But these very hours to prove fatal to them. Schumann regarded the situation with remarkable optimism. The only thing which prevented him from frankly approaching Wieck with a declaration of his love for Clara was indeed the fact that he had not yet received the formal release from his connection with Ernestine. He never doubted Wieck's consent for a moment, and others too, shared his opinion. "I must tell you of one mistake," he wrote to Clara later, in the spring of 1838[1]), "which many others, and indeed you yourself made as well as I, in believing that your father had already chosen me years before to be your husband, and had educated me for it. Possibly he never thought of it. But he distinguished me in such a manner before all others, he let us go our own way for so long a time, for instance in the summer of 1835, when he could so easily have hindered us, and when he must have noticed our growing affection, that I believed it even then."

Certainly this was a mistake. Wieck's plans were shaped in quite another direction, and if up to this time — believing

---

1) In the long letter to Clara dated April 14th to April 25 1838.
LITZMANN, Clara Schumann. I.

Schumann to be bound — he had seen no harm in their affectionate intercourse, yet now the altered manner both of Clara and of Schumann frightened him out of his calm, and he quickly decided to try for a second time the method, which he had already tried earlier, of separating them. On Jan. 14th he sent Clara to Dresden again, for a long visit, intending, however, that it should be only the first halting-place in a longer concert tour. Certainly Clara found varied distractions and amusements here, in the friendly circle of the Kaskels, Reissigers, and Krägens, at Court, in the general sociability at festive seasons at the houses of Intendant von Lüttichau, Count Baudissin, and others, and at the theatre, which was being visited by Sabine Heinefetter. And the two concerts, which she gave amid enthusiastic applause at the end of January and in the middle of February — "It was cram full . . the audience clapped their hands sore," Lyser wrote to Schumann, about the second — might well have been expected to occupy all her interest and attention. But all these events were of faint importance in comparison with what was going on in her and around her.

It is suggestive of the great mental excitement in which she found herself, that before her first concert, on Jan. 30th "Clara by God's grace," as Wieck wrote in the diary, was nervous for the first time, and shed "some musical tears", in which perhaps there was more of the anxiety of the lover than of the artist. If, as it appears, no open rupture between her father and Schumann had followed as yet, still Wieck had already given plain expression to his disapproval of their inclination towards each other, and had forbidden the continuance of their intimate correspondence. A light is thrown on this by the entry which Clara adds as "postscript" to the records of January given in her diary: "On the 21st I received from Schumann his latest *Paganini Études*, with a few lines. I was very glad of this token of his regard."

All the same they must both have found opportunity to send each other news behind Wieck's back. On Feb. 4th Schumann's mother died, a heavy, irreparable loss to him and also to Clara, who not only suffered in spirit with her lover at the moment, but who was by this means robbed of a true-hearted, motherly adviser, whom she was to need more than ever. It is curious that Schumann does not appear to have gone to Zwickau immediately for the funeral — possibly he was detained by editorial business. However, between the 7th and the 11th of February he certainly made use of a temporary absence of Wieck's from Dresden — of which Clara must have sent him word — to go to Dresden with his friend and room-mate, Ulex, in order to see and speak with Clara undisturbed; in which matter Clara's friend Sophie Kaskel seems to have been of assistance. During these sad hours of mourning and grief, the lovers renewed their plighted oath not to give each up, come what might. "Two years ago to-day," wrote Schumann to Clara on Feb. 11th 1838, "I took leave of you in Dresden. 'Keep true to me', I said — you nodded your head slightly and sadly, and you have kept your word." [1] There is an echo of these moments in the letter [2] sent to Clara from Zwickau on Feb. 13th, the only one still extant of those which they exchanged at this time, in which the bliss of loving and being beloved makes itself heard above all sound of mourning.

"From the Coach-Office at Zwickau. Past 10 at night
Feb. 13th /36.

My eyes are full of sleep. I have already waited two hours for the flying coach. The roads are in such a bad state that I may not get away before 2 o'clock. — How close you seem to me, my darling, darling Clara, so close that I feel as if I could

---

1) In the *Bridegroom's Book* (cf. p. 78 note 1) this is the third "hard parting". "In February 1837 (a mistake for 1836) Farewell from the Dresden coach-office. Clara in a little red hat. A long separation."

2) Part of it is printed in the *Jugendbriefe* p. 267.

hold you. Once I could always find charming words in which to express the strength of my feelings readily, now I can do so no more. And if you did not know it, I could not tell you. Only love me well in return — will you? — I exact much, for I give much.

To-day has brought me many different emotions — a letter of instructions from my Mother; the news of her death. But behind all the darkness your image always shines, and I bear everything the more easily.

I must tell you too, that my future is now far more assured. It is true that I shall not be able to sit with my hands in my lap, and I have much to do in order to win something which you see every time you happen to pass by a looking-glass — but you too will be glad to remain an artist and no "Gräfin Rossi", that is to say, you will wish to help carry my burden, to work with me, to share joy and sorrow with me. Write to me about this.

My first care in Leipsic will be to bring my external affairs into order; those of the soul need no further ordering; perhaps your father will not draw back his hand when I ask him for his blessing. In truth there is much to think about and to smooth over but meanwhile I trust in our good genius. Fate has destined us for one-another; I knew that long ago, but my hope was not bold enough to tell you of it earlier, or for you to understand.

I will explain more clearly later, what I have been writing to you shortly and scrappily to-day. And perhaps you cannot even read this — know then, this alone, that I love you unspeakably.

The room is growing dark. Passengers are asleep near me. Outside it blusters and snows. But I will bury myself deep in a corner with my heard in a cushion, and think of nothing but you. Farewell my Clara. Your Robert."

How deceptive these hopes were, they were to find only too soon. The letter had not yet reached its destination when a catastrophe broke over the lovers which for years destroyed their dreams of happiness.

Immediately after his return to Dresden, Wieck learnt — from whom we do not know — that Schumann had been there, and that their friends had allowed him to have inter-

course with Clara: "NB." runs the entry in his hand in the
diary for Feb. 14th, "Reissiger's want of principle — his wife —
during my absence Schumann and Ulex occupied the father's
place — Sophie, knowing Clara to be in good hands takes
the boa and goes to the theatre in Clara's stead. Sophie, the
talkative and wiley, becomes the silent, and on my return
looks at me as if it were no business of mine. With difficulty
I drag 'yes' and 'no' out of her. — —"

This outburst of anger gives only a feeble representation
of the scenes which took place, of the insults, accusations,
and threats to which Clara found herself exposed without
defence. In the end, the furious father threatened to shoot
her lover if he ever dared to hold intercourse with her, and
so succeeded in frightening her thoroughly, and making her
give up all the letters which she had received from Schumann,
and promise to break off all intercourse with him[1]).

On Christmas Eve 1835, Schumann had given Clara some
pearls, and her step-mother had said in jest, "Pearls mean
tears". The saying proved only too true. Resolutely determined to keep her troth with Schumann, but terrified by her
father's threats, without any possibility of sending news to
her lover or of hearing from him, daily obliged to listen to
the most violent slanders and calumnies of Schumann, in
which Wieck continually indulged, in addition to this, much
occupied with her artistic duties, and finally, still little more
than a child in years, without the support and advice of any
whom she could trust, she had to bear a test of constancy
and of character to which many a one would have succumbed!

From Dresden they went by way of Görlitz to Breslau,
where they stayed from Feb. 28th to April 3rd, and, in spite

---

1) These letters were not returned to Schumann — as the entry in
the *Record* tells us — till June 1836, when Clara herself asked for her
own in a letter which was, of course, instigated and supervised by
Wieck.

of Wieck's complaints about the "half Poles" and thunderings over their bad reception, seem to have enjoyed a great succes. Clara's own feelings at the time, are naturally not revealed in the diary, which was kept sometimes by her and sometimes by her father. But much can be read between the lines. Thus Wieck complains on March 8th that Clara has "lost every vestige of vanity and might as well give up (all thought of) being an artist". That her condition made him anxious is shown by a plan — which he let drop again — for going with Clara from Breslau to Baden-Baden and letting Clara rest "from playing" and resting himself from his part as "lackey".

Their return to Leipsic, which on April 8th followed a short rest in Dresden, brought no unravelling of the complicated situation. The very fact of being together in the same town without any possibility of speaking to each other, the unavoidable and painful thought that at any moment they might meet in a third place and yet out in a consideration for each other would be obliged — or thought they would be obliged — to behave like strangers, served to give them in reality a sense of separation, which, as we shall see, was sedulously and skilfully fostered by meas of whispered insinuations and aspersions cast on their fidelity. A meeting in the street, an attempt on Schumann's part to speak to Clara, a pressure of the hand which was not returned, apparent coolness on one side, gave them both a feeling of disillusionment and produced a sence of depression which was ably made use of by those interested in the separation!

But before we follow the history of their love any further, it is necessary to spend a few moments on the development of the artist, and to bring before our minds the picture of that Clara Wieck who during these momentous years when the storms of spring raged in her heart, found in the public exercise of her art a support and comfort which her nearest relations would not and could not give her.

Clara's répertoire had been much increased during the last year. New bravura pieces had been added to the earlier ones and in addition to this classical compositions appeared in her concert programmes[1]), giving them a new character. On Dec. 15th 1835 she had played Beethoven's *Choral Phantasie* at the concert in the Leipsic *Gewandhaus*, and as we have already seen, she gave Bach's *D* minor concerto for three pianos, at her own concert on Nov. 9th, with the assistance of Felix Mendelssohn, and Rackemann.

It must not be thought strange that Schumann's name never appears in Clara's concert programmes at this time. Wieck, who could still perfectly distinguish between Schumann the musician, and Schumann the unwelcome suitor, thought his music too difficult for the concert public with whom he had to deal. On the other hand he willingly allowed Clara to have her own way when, in more private musical circles, she tried to preach Schumann propaganda. He did this partly with the ingenious idea of keeping her in sufficiently good spirits for her public performances. In this manner she had, as occasion offered, played from among Schumann's compositions the *F♯* minor sonata, the *Toccata*, the *Carnaval*, the

---

1) We give here extracts from the programmes of the years 1836 —39: Herz Op. 20, 23, 36, 76. Pixis *Grand Concerto* and *Glöckchenrondo*, both with orchestral accompaniment, the latter with an obligato of three bells in addition. Thalberg *Caprice* Op. 15; *Phantasie on a theme from Don Giovanni*; Hensel *Variations on an Aria from Donizetti's "Elisir d'amore"*; *Andante and Allegro* (Poème d'amour); *Études*; *Song without Words* — Clara Wieck, *Concerto with orchestral accompaniment*; *Capriccio* (Hexentanz); Bravurra. *Variations on a theme from Bellinis "Piraten"*; *Scherzo*; *Soirées musicales*. — Chopin, *Op. 2, Concerto in F minor, with orchestra*; *Nocturnes*: in *F♯* major, *B* major, *E♭* major; *Mazurkas*: *B♭* minor, *B♭* major, *F♯* minor; *Études*. — Liszt, *Divertisement* over Paccini's *Cavatina*; Adaptation of the following songe, *"Ständchen"*, *Erlkönig*, *Lob der Thränen*; — Mendelssohn *Capriccio* with orchestra *B* minor Op. 22; *Capriccio A* minor, Op. 33; *Lieder ohne Worte* — Bach, *Preludes and Fuges C♯* major, *C♯* minor, *F♯* major, *D* major; — Beethoven *F minor Sonata*; *Violin Sonata* Op. 47; *Trio* Op. 97.

impromptus, and some other pieces. Her spirits fluctuated according to the reception afforded to this new and original type of music.

They had hardly returned to Leipsic when Clara received a visit from Mendelssohn. On this occasion she played him his new *scherzo*, to his great delight, and he played her two *caprices* which he had just composed.

Meanwhile his famous and striking personality had given fresh stimulus to musical life in Leipsic. His influence made itself felt as much in public as in private. The establishment, by his means, of his friend Ferdinand David as leader at the *Gewandhaus*, gave an importance to violin as well as piano, and above all gave more opportunity for the encouragement of better chamber-music.

The Voigts' house formed a pleasant centre for all these interests. We know that Schumann too, was no stranger there. His *Record of my Life in Leipsic* tells us that he had a great deal of intimate intercourse with Mendelssohn and David. Meetings between him and Clara clearly did not take place in this circle, perhaps because there was a certain rivalry between the Wiecks' house and the Voigts'.

Two visits which concern Clara, belong to the year 1836 — Spohr's and Chopin's. She played her four latest "*Charakterstücke*" to Spohr. His opinion of them was so encouraging, his praise so unmixed, that her love of composing was stimulated and increased to no small extent.

Chopin's visit at once pleased and troubled her. She thought him more ill than ever. He heard her play her Op. 5 and 6, as well as her concerto Op. 7.

He went off very much pleased, carrying with him her Op. 5 — over which he had declared himself especially enchanted and enthusiastic — and leaving a page for her album behind him. Anyone who looks at this Op. 5 more closely will easily be convinced by the lively opening and the beautiful elegiac middle movement, that Chopin's praise by no means sprang from mere gallantry.

Besides Clara, Chopin saw no one in Leipsic this time except Schumann, who writes to Kapellmeister Dorn in Riga on Sept. 14th 1836, concerning this meeting:

"Just as I received your letter the day before yesterday, and was about to answer it, who do you think came in? — Chopin. It was a great pleasure. We passed a delightful day, which I was still celebrating yesterday[1]). —

.. It is pathetic to see him sitting at the piano. You would love him. But Clara is a greater performer and gives his compositions almost more meaning than he does himself. Think of a perfection, a mastery, entirely without self-consciousness."

This was the first time that Clara's birthday festivities were held without Schumann's presence. Moreover her father chose this day to take her to Naumburg, where he had announced a concert for the 16th.

It might easily have become a day of ill omen for Clara for she was knocked down on her way to the concert-hall. It was unfortunate enough that her concert-dress was badly damaged; but in addition she was also severely bruised on head and limbs. Regardless of this, and of the great fright, she gave her performance with perfect self-possession and even sang two songs. But subsequently her left hand swelled very much, and for several days she suffered a good deal of pain. Wieck marks this event with the emphatic words: "We passed unharmed through big cities and — in Naumburg the sword of Damocles hung over the dear head."

With the exception of a short concert-tour to Freiberg in November, Clara now spent her time in Leipsic (till February

---

1) Clara's 17th birthday.

1837), chiefly working at her *Bravura-Variations*, which were designed for her next concert-tour.

This began on Feb. 7th 1837. Berlin was decided on for their first halting-place. This gave Clara the pleasant prospect of being frequently with her mother, Frau Bargiel. It may well have been no small surprise to the latter, when Wieck came in to her one day leading Clara — who had completely grown up since last she saw her — and saying: "Here Madame, I bring you your daughter."

The first few days were occupied with visits and calls of ceremony on Ludwig Berger, Stadtrat Behrens, Bettina von Arnim, Count von Redern, Spontini, etc. etc. They were received with special friendliness and readiness by the two last-named. Free admission to the royal theatres followed as a matter of course.

The diary says of Bettina: "An extremely intellectual, vivacious woman — — — with an entirely false judgment in all that concerns music. But she is bubbling with humour." "It is a disgrace," she said to Clara, "that a 17-year-old girl should be able to do so much."

The trouble of making preparations for the concerts, and the difficulties with the police drew from Wieck many an affecting pious ejaculation and many a hearty curse: "Five times must an advertisement pass the censor. There is no giving a grand concert here, for it would take a man half his life." The professional jealousy of colleagues, and the iniquities of the press were fresh causes of anger. The former were conspicuous by their absence at Clara's concert, and the latter succeeded by means of Rellstab's pen — which now found the programme "monotonous", and now spoke of "half-empty halls" — in troubling and damping the pleasure of both father and daughter in the actual great and ever-increasing success which Clara experienced on this hitherto unfriendly ground. But in spite of all cabals Clara took the musical circles of

Clara Wieck.

Berlin by storm, and on her appearance in the opera-house on Feb. 16th as well as in the various concerts at which she played, either as giver of the concert or as one of the performers, she won the most bountiful applause and great sympathy. Only Bettina did not, in the end, find her to her taste, and she declared that Clara was "one of the most intolerable artists she had ever seen". "How pretentiously she seats herself at the piano, and without notes too! How modest is Doehler on the other hand, who has the music in front of him!"

In addition to all this Clara employed her time, which was already so much occupied by social engagements and concerts, in continuing her education, taking lessons in counterpoint from the illustrious music theorist, Dehn.

But notwithstandig all artistic and material successes, Wieck once more left the Prussian capital in a rage. "The day after to-morrow," he wrote in the diary on March 22nd, "shall be the day when, with intense yearning for better people, saved from this sink of iniquity, we shall mount the coach. I am frightened when I think of what I have done, and carried through — eight performances amidst such struggles against calumnious malice and cunning combined with the greatest possible vulgarity and a shamelessness which surpasses everything." At the moment he forgot the many proofs of understanding and appreciation which they had received in this "sink of iniquity", and above all their kindly reception at court, and the attentions with which the usually cold and superior Spontini and his wife had overwhelmed Clara, even going so far as to let her play to him for two hours on one occasion, when he heard her variations at his special request for the third time; all these attentions being due to a real appreciation of Clara's artistic powers.

Though Spontini Clara also learned to know Raupach whom she found very entertaining.

One might have thought that Wieck's irritated feeling towards Berlin would have made it proportionately easy for
Hamburg — the next point on their journey, where they
arrived on March 27th — to win his approval. But it found
just as little favour in his eyes, and the expressions of his
displeasure, in the diary, even show a certain increased asperity
and overstep the bounds of parliamentary language. Yet he
might well have been content with the reception afforded to
his daughter both in public[1]) and in private. Here, as everywhere her personality, with its combination of great artistry
and womanly charm, overcame indifference and cabals and
disarmed opponents more quickly and thoroughly than all the
rudenesses of the impressario-father. A stay in Bremen followed,
but, disturbed by the influenza which was increasing there
and by the effects of the collapse of several great business
houses, the travellers, who began to feel the fatigues of social
duties, brought their visit to a premature conclusion at the
end of ten days (April 17th—27th), after Clara had appeared
at a concert on April 26th and at a soirée. After a short
rest in Hanover and Brunswick, they reached Leipsic again
on May 3rd: "Herr Banck and mother came to meet us at
Lützschena" says the diary.

Clara was once more in the same place as Schumann, and
yet, so at least it appeared, parted from him by circumstances,
further than ever. Since the February days of the year 1836
they had not exchanged a single word, either written or spoken,
with each other. And if at accidental or — so far as Schumann
was concerned — premeditated meetings there had been a
glance, or a pressure of the hand between them, there had been
no word of conversation. "Only twice", Schumann complains
later, did he hear Clara play, during all this period, and often

---

1) She played on April 1st at a Philharmonic concert, on April 8th
at a concert of her own, and on April 12th in the Theatre.

in the summer of 1836, he used to stand at her door and listen. In May of this same year he had sent her the $F\sharp$ minor sonata which he had dedicated to her — "Piano-forte sonata, dedicated to Clara by Florestan and Eusebius" —. But if he had hoped that this would in any way bring an answer from Clara that should betray her feelings, he found himself bitterly disappointed. In the *Record* for June he notes: "Letter from Clara, and exchange of letters." It is not impossible that this was Wieck's answer to the sending of the sonata. In Clara's diary three lines are crossed out after the words which announce the fact of the dedication on June 11th. We must picture to ourselves what the $F\sharp$ minor sonata stood for to Schumann — "one single cry of my heart for you," he called it later, "in which your theme appears in every possible form" — in order to understand how deeply it must have wounded him that this work born of his passion for Clara awoke no echo: especially when we know that every effort was made on Wieck's side to awaken in him the belief that Clara no longer thought of him. Soon after their return from Breslau, a "friend", Carl Banck, who had the entrée of the Wiecks' house, had already expressed to him his "surprise" at "Clara's levity", "who does not give the matter another thought". "I stood as if faint and broken-down", he said later; in the first transport he even replied that if this were so, he was glad to be free from her, for she must be a worthless woman, but he added, "But she would never let you know what was going on in her heart."

But neither these tale-bearings nor the disillusionment of the following months had been able seriously to shake his faith in her loyalty, to say nothing of his love for her, though there were times when, in deep depression of spirit, in one of those paroxysms of "deadly anguish of heart" of which he complains and in which he did not know what to do with himself, he thought that in the utter absence of all prospect of success it would be his duty to renounce her. This is the explanation of the passage in a letter[1]) to his sister-in-law Therese, dated Nov. 15th 1836: "Clara loves me as warmly as ever, but I have wholly given her up." At the opening of 1837 the idea of resigning her began to gain more and more lasting power over him, and made him determine, though at the cost of bitter suffering, on a complete separation. "The darkest time," he wrote to Clara in January 1838[2]), "when I knew nothing of you and tried hard to forget you, was about a year ago next February. At that time our spirits must have been estranged. I had given you up. But then the old pain broke out again — and I wrung my hands — then I said to God on many a night — 'In mercy let but this one thing pass away, without my going mad.' I expected at one time to see your engagement announced in the papers — I hurled myself on the ground, and cried aloud — then I wished to cure myself, to compel myself to fall in love with a woman who had already half drawn me into her nets."

He remained under the spell, not of this woman, but of this renunciatory despairing frame of mind until far into the spring, indeed, until the beginning of the summer. "In March last year," he writes to Clara in 1838, "the thought that I had lost you, came over me again with full force." Even in June the idea once more came to the surface — though it was only passing — that he would "revenge himself" on Clara "for her indifference" by paying court elsewhere.

"At that time our spirits must have been estranged," writes Schumann, with some justice. For in Clara's attitude to Schumann at this time, down at all events in the few remarks of hers which have come or to us, a certain estrangement, or rather a tendency to become critical of him, is unmistakable, which if it had lasted might well have been fatal

---

1) *Briefe. Neue Folge*, p. 71.
2) Letter of Dec. 31st 1837, and Jan. 1st 1838.

to the happiness of both. If we ask for an explanation of this wavering of her mind, we find it not only in the continued separation from Schumann but also in a certain person who for a long time had frankly considered himself called upon to assist the domestic policy of Wieck and his wife in every way, and to sow distrust and jealousy between Clara and Schumann. This Carl Banck, who in the spring of 1836 had already tried to set Schumann against Clara, who had been Clara's singing-master since the end of May, and who was openly favoured and welcomed by the parent Wiecks as being able to divert her mind from her lover, employed his position of confidence with Clara to set her against Schumann. Clara, when she heard from Schumann of the scene in the spring of 1836 wrote later in just indignation: "Thus did he abuse my friendship. This was his gratitude for the genuinely friendly letters which I wrote to him from Berlin? I cannot but be amazed at so evil a heart! He tried to deceive you, and slandered me! Certainly it is true that I always spoke of you with indifference, after I had seen how scornfully he laughed when the tears come into my eyes as he spoke of you with so little consideration." "Indeed", she adds, "I have often spoken of you with some vexation in order to relieve my feelings when you so seldom wrote about me in the paper, I even did it in order to pretend that I had forgotten you. But it was not so; I never forgot you."

This irritation against Schumann — which also finds occasional expression in her diary for the winter of 1836/37 — was indeed often a mask to conceal her real feelings and to prevent those around her from learning the truth. Just because she loved Schumann, every occasion which so much as appeared to give others a right to hold him in slight estimation, irritated and oppressed her. Above all this accounted for her discontent that Schumann "wrote for the paper so seldom". This was a cause for surprise which even during their engagement often roused Clara to gentle reproaches clothed in the form of questions designed to spur him on, reproaches which may be traced to the continual contemptuous remarks made by Wieck on this subject to which Clara had to listen every day. She fancied that she had genuine cause for anger on two occasions when she belived herself to have been deliberately slighted by Schumann; a belief in which naturally she was only too strongly confirmed by all the household and by her friends.

At the beginning of 1837 Clara's piano concerto (Op. 7) had been published by Hofmeister; she counted for certain on the fact that Schumann would not allow anyone to deprive him of writing about it in the paper. Instead of this, a critique appeared on Feb. 17th not by Schumann but by C. F. Becker, who managed the affair very clumsily, saying that there could be no question of real criticism "since we have to do with the work of a lady". Certainly it was only tactful of Schumann, in the face of his notoriously strained relations with Wieck, to let the notice be written hy some one else. On the other hand, Clara, irritated as she was by Wieck's continual pinpricks concerning Schumann's indolence and indifference, and deeply wounded in her proper pride as an artist by Becker's foolish manner of speaking, thought herself the more justified in reproaching her friend for his silence because in the next number (Feb. 24th) there appeared an enthusiastic criticism by him, of his friend Sterndale Bennett's latest concerto. Schumann's favourable opinion of the latter had always been a bone of contention between him and the Wiecks, and that Schumann should have opened the first number of the New Year with an article of his own upon this Bennett, had already been taken by Clara, as her diary makes clear, as being in part "a defiance of us".

She considered herself, however, even more deeply injured by an article which appeared in the *Neue Zeitschrift* for the

19th of May: "A statement to Jeanquirit in Augsburg concerning the last artistic-historical ball at the editor's" [1]); not because Carl Banck, the faithful friend of the Wieck's, was depicted in this article in the most ridiculous fashion under the easily recognisable anagram "de Knapp", but because in the figure of the pianist Ambrosia she thought she had found a wholly ill-natured caricature of herself — an opinion to which (false as it undoubtedly was) she held long and obstinately in spite of Schumann's earnest asseverations and striking proofs of the contrary. But Schumann had intended to hit and to wound Banck. And here we can clearly see that in addition to his general opinion of Banck both as an author and as an individual, of which numerous instances are to be found in his letters later, the rumours which were then current concerning Clara's inclination towards him, played an important part. He could not know that these rumours were entirely without foundation notwithstanding the intention of Wieck and Banck, and that it had never entered Clara's head to take any greater interest in Banck. But although no danger threatened in this direction, yet in view of the systematic assiduity with which Banck exerted himself to disturb their peace and to sow mistrust between them, it was a fortunate dispensation that shortly after Clara's return he found himself compelled to leave Leipsic. It was a remarkable irony of fate that Wieck, who regularly made use of false weapons in his struggle against Clara's unfortunate love for Schumann, found himself, in May 1837, compelled to make friendly but clear representations to this young friend of the house that he was endangering his daughter's peace of mind. The Moor had played his part, had done all he could to estrange the lovers completely, and now he could go [2]). Whatever may have been the plans for

---

1) *Ges. Schriften* 4th ed. Vol. II p. 21—26.
2) *Translator's note*: The reference is to Schiller's *Fiesco* Act III Sc. 4.

the future which Banck cherished, in view of the father's
unmistakable expressions of intention he held it wisest to vacate
the field. And so he disappeared from Leipsic one day, to
the astonishment of all the uninitiated, amongst whom in this
instance was Clara, who could not understand this apparently
motiveless and sudden departure.

On June 11th Clara went to Dresden with her parents, and
when, a fortnight later, they returned to Leipsic, she stayed
behind at Major Serre's country house, Maxen, which lay not
far from Dresden, and there in the cheerful, musical society
which was part of the Serres' daily life, she enjoyed a recreation
after the fatigues of the winter, which really did her good.
For the first time for a long period the entries in the diary
for this date breathe a permanent cheerfulness, as if she
had a presentiment that happiness was standing ready to knock
at her door. In high spirits she laughs at her good friend
Krägen, who comes out every day with cart-loads of opera-
overtures arranged as piano duets, or at a silent admirer from
Copenhagen who found himself in difficulties among the high-
spirited, mischievous young people. Here also, Schumann's
name is mentioned again for the first time, and in quite a
different tone from the last occasion. Wieck had written that
the pianist, Miss Laidlaw, without knowing that Schumann,
whom she admired, was the composer, spoke in his presence
of the $F\sharp$ minor sonata as "mad stuff", and declared that she
never heard of such obscure people as those whose works
Clara Wieck played, such as Henselt, Liszt, Eusebius, and
Florestan. "I can vividly picture the quiet expression of the
last-named," the diary comments with satisfaction.

But on August 2nd she was roughly frightened out of this
holiday frame of mind by a message from her father telling
her that he had announced a concert for her on Aug. 13th.
"I must, whether I like it or not," she writes with gloomy
resignation. She did not suspect that Wieck, entirely against

his will, was on the point of opening a way to the fulfilment of the most secret and the warmest wishes of her heart. It arose through a morning concert at the Exchange, in which Clara was to appear before the Leipsic public again after an interval of two years. And Robert Schumann was also a member of this public. In the programme stood the "$F\sharp$ minor sonata by Florestan and Eusebius". And if, a year ago, he had missed an answering echo to this heartfelt cry for his beloved, now he received the most princely recompense for all that torturing privation, for now the answer came back to him in his own language: under her hands his tones became something new, which spoke of new love, new life. It is true that for the first moment he was startled by the choice of *this* piece, for the last few weeks he had been struggling with the determination to win Clara, cost what it might. "l thought," he wrote later, "that you could love me no longer, since you could do what a man would have trembled to do." But indeed she was brave as a man, that day; and if during the time of their separation her want of self-confidence had made the trial harder for her and for her lover than it need have been, she made up for it now. "Did you never realise," she wrote later, "that I played because I knew no other means of showing you what was in my heart? I could not do it secretly, so I did it in public. Do you think that my heart did not tremble at it?" Certainly Schumann was right when he called her "a brave woman".

In the same letter of later days, in which Clara paints her feelings on this 13th of August, she writes: "I was unspeakably miserable on that day, I felt at variance with the world; we went for a walk but I saw no trees, no flowers, and no meadows; I saw nothing but you — and yet I did not see you, I might not see you."

This attitude of mind is only too comprehensible, for immediately before the concert Clara had taken a step of whose consequent difficulties she was well aware. On Aug. 10th she had written in her diary: "Arrival of my dear friend Becker from Freiberg." Ernst Adolf Becker, at that time Berg-schreiber, that is, examining magistrate in the mining office at Freiberg[1]), a close friend of the Wiecks, and no less of Schumann's, a passionate enthusiast for music, whom only a short time before Clara had constantly met at the Serres, had come over from Freiberg for her concert. Clara, who had absolute trust in his loyalty to her lover, had at last plucked up heart to speak to him frankly of Schumann and of their relations. She had asked him, after he had set her mind at rest by his entire conviction of Schumann's unalterable fidelity, to beg Schumann to return the letters which she had sent back to him by her father's orders in June 1836. If Schumann was still able to doubt the reasons for her choice of the $F\sharp$ minor sonata, this request, which Becker conveyed to him, and which healed the wound which he had received when the letters had been returned the year before, was a proof of loyalty and love, which made him abandon the reserve to which he had hitherto clung. She can no longer have the old letters, he told her through Becker, but she can have new ones.

With this verbal message came the first new letter, dated on the day oft he concert, and a bunch of flowers[1]) and thus the bonds which had been torn asunder in February 1836 were now knitted together firmly and inseparably for life.

That doubt still struggled in his breast is betrayed by these words written on the outside: "After many days of silence full of pain, hope, and despair, may these lines by received with the old love. If it exists no longer, please return this letter to me unopened."

---

1) *Briefe. Neue Folge* p. 388.

2) Afterwards she kept a spray from this in the *Remembrance Book* that Schumann gave her.

The letter itself ran:

"Aug. 13th 1837.

Are you still firm and true? Indestructible as my belief in you is, yet the stoutest heart may become confused when nothing is heard of the being whom one loves best in the world. And you are that to me. A thousand times I have thought it all over, and everything said to me: 'It must be, if we will, and act.' Write me a simple 'yes', if on your birthday itself (September 13th) you will give your father a letter from me. Just now he is well disposed towards me, and will not thrust me away if you beg for me.

I am writing this on Aurora's day. Would that nothing but a dawn parted us. Above all things hold fast to this: it must be, if we will, and act.

Do not mention this letter to anyone, or everything may be ruined.

And do not forget that, 'yes'. I must have this assurance before I can think of anything further.

I mean all this as it stands, with my whole soul, and sign it with my name

Robert Schumann."

"Ah! my God! my feelings when Becker brought me the first letter!" Clara wrote in July, the following year[2]: "It was cold, serious, and yet so beautiful, so grave in just the right way, it made me unspeakably happy, and yet at the same time I was hurt by the words outside which told me to return the letter unopened if I was not the same that I had been two years ago. You were a little hard, and even had sore doubts as to my love, which I never had of yours, not even when there seemed to be cause for it."

And then this "brave woman" sat down and wrote an answer in which playful humour and deep seriousness are strangely mingled.

---

1) To Schumann from Maxen and Dresden July 8th—11th 1838.

"Leipsic, Aug. 15[th 1]) 1837.

You ask for nothing but a simple 'yes'? Such a tiny word — such an important one! Yet should not a heart so full of inexpressible love as mine be able to say this little word with the whole soul? I do so, and my inmost being ever whispers it to you.

Could I paint the agonies of my heart, my many tears — oh no! — Perhaps fate wills that we shall speak to each other before long, and then — Your plan seems to me risky, but a loving heart cares little for danger. And so once more I say to you, 'Yes'. Will God make my eighteenth birthday a day of sorrow? Oh! no, that would be too terrible. I too, have long felt 'it must be', nothing in the world shall make me waver, and I will show my father that a youthful (heart) can also be firm.

In great haste   Your Clara."

On the same day the diary tells us: "Early this morning Schumann wrote my father a note full of feeling in which he returned thanks for the pleasure which he had had."

By this means, so at least it appear, relations were reopened between Schumann and Wieck.

These days of second spring bring a peculiar charm to the diary, between whose lines a barely restrained delight laughs and sings. On the 16th a certain Herr Ritter von Ritterstein comes to hear Clara play, but does not want her to play anything of Schumann's "because he expected to hear him play that much better himself". And on the 20th, "Ritter von Rittersberg (sic) comes back humbly, in order to hear something of Schumann's, because he referred him to me." On the 18th is the suggestive entry: "Departure of Herr Becker after eight days which we have enjoyed very much. He seemed sorry

---

1) Presumably a slip has been made in the date here. In later years Robert and Clara always celebrated the 14th of August — Eusebius' Day — as the day of their betrothal. "We were betrothed on Eusebius' Day, August 14th 1837" writes Schumann in the *Bridegroom's Book*, and in the same book Clara wrote later, "We were betrothed on Aug 14th."

to go." [1])   On the 24th it announces that Schumann has sent her father a critique of her concert by Brendel; on the 25th a "review of Mendelssohn's latest songs, by Schumann — a masterpiece" [2]).   And on Aug. 31st it says in speaking of Schneider's *Weltgericht*, that the "right-honorable Davidsbund authority of this place" has decided that "the music is pretty but dismal".

In the mean time ways and means of private communication were not wanting though as yet only by letter.   How much Clara longed for a genuine meeting and talk, is shown by the following letter.

"Aug. 19th (In great haste).

Dear Robert

I am sending you just a few words by my faithful and silent Nanny [3]).   Yesterday I heard that the cholera was here, and now I must write as every minute I get more anxious.   Do take care of yourself — for my sake — think what my life would be without you! . . . .

And one more bit of advice, do not say anything about us to Father, until you write for my birthday.   He is very kindly disposed towards you, but everything must go slowly.   My longing to see you, to talk to you, is indescribable — if I can find an opportunity, I will let you know.   This morning I had quite deter-

---

1) He took with him as a momento, a copy of the *Phantasiestück Des Abends*, on which was written: —

"August 18th 1837
To his dear Becker
Robert Schumann.
Shyly but with affection there signs herself
Clara Wieck."

Cf. Jansen *Ungedruckte Briefe Robert Schumann's*, Grenzboten 1898 p. 94.

2) In Schumann's paper of Aug. 22nd 1837, No. 15.   The notice of Clara's concert there, which appeared on Sept. 1st — "Concert by Clara Wieck on August 13th" (From a stranger's letter to the editor) — signed B. B. originated from Becker.   Cf. Jansen *Ungedruckte Briefe*.

3) A maid-servant in Wieck's household.

mined to go to you, my spirit had already hurried on in advance, but all at once I stopped — I saw your window, a tear welled from my eyes, ah! how it burned! I went home with a heart full of emotion.

My firm faith in your love makes me happy now — I sent you my heart, my all, with the ring.

If you have anything to say to me tell it to my Nanny; as truly as I love you, so truly is she discrete.

You will see by my writing how anxious I am. — I hope we shall soon see each other. For God's sake be very careful. Ever

Your Clara."

But before the important letter, which contained Schumann's request, reached Wieck, there was a personal meeting and a conversation between Robert and Clara, on September 9th[1]).

They met by appointment as Clara, accompanied by the faithful Nanny, was returning from a call at the Lists. But both of them were oppressed by a certain embarrassment. "The first time we met again," Clara writes afterwards,[2]) "you were so stiff, so cold; I too, should have been glad to be warmer, but I was too much excited; I could hardly control myself . . . The moon shone so beautifully upon your face when you took off your hat and passed your hand over your forehead; I had the most delightful feeling that I ever had, I had found again what I loved best."

At last the longed-for and dreaded 13th of September[3]) arrived, and with it the presentation of the formal proposal

1) According to the contemporary letters of Clara, the meeting took place on Sept. 9th. Schumann writes on Sept. 8th 1838: "A year ago today, on Saturday evening we shook hands again for the first time."

2) To Schumann, from Vienna. Letter from 18th to 30th of January 1838.

3) On Sept. 12th, Schumann wrote that article signed "Florestan and Eusebius" on *Soirées for the piano-forte by Clara Wieck*, beginning with the. words: "Our museum must be adorned with a feminine head too, and besides how could I better celebrate to day as the eve of the morrow which gave life to a beloved artist, than by losing myself with

sent by Schumann to Wieck, with enclosures to Clara's step-mother, and to Clara herself!

The letter to Wieck ran:

"What I have to say to you is so simple — and yet the right words will often fail me. A trembling hand cannot guide the pen calmly. Therefore if here and there I fall short in form and expression, excuse me.

To day is Clara's birthday — the day on which the dearest being that the world contains for you as for me, first saw the light — the day on which I have always taken account of myself, so deep a hold have you taken upon my life. I confess that I have never thought so calmly of my future as I do to day. Secured against want, as far as human knowledge can speak in advance, with fine plans in my head, a youthful heart inspired by all things noble, and hands to work, a magnificent sphere of activity, and still in hopes of accomplishing everything that can be expected of my powers, honoured and loved by many — Is not all this enough! Ah! how painful an answer I must give to that! What is it all compared to the pain of being parted from the very being for whom I strive, and who loves me in return, truly and from her heart! You know stet being only too well, you fortunate father. Ask her eyes, if I have not spoken the truth!

For eighteen long months you have put me to the proof, as hardly as fate could have done. How could I be angry with you! I had wounded you deeply, but you have made me do penance for it. — Try me now for as long again. Perhaps, if you do not demand the impossible, my powers will keep pace with your wishes; perhaps I shall win back your confidence. You know that I persevere in high matters. If you find that I have been proved to be true and manly, bless this union of souls, for nothing but a parent's sanction is wanting to our highest happiness. It is no

---

whole-hearted sympathy in one of her works", which appeared on Sept. 15th in No. 22.

1) Cf. Jansen *Ungedruckte Briefe Robert Schumanns*, Grenzboten 1898 p. 77 etc. (according to Becker's transcript). Since then, published with some variations from the orignals, by Joss, *Der Musikpädagoge Fr. Wieck und seine Familie*. Dresden 1902.

momentary excitement, no passion, nothing external, which binds me to Clara by every fibre of my being, it is the deepest conviction that a union can seldom have come into existence under such a favourable concurrence of circumstances, it is this admirable, exalted girl herself, who spreads happiness everywhere and gives surety for ours. If you too, have come to this conclusion, give me the certain promise that you will decide nothing immediately as to Clara's future, and I promise you on my honour not to speak to Clara against your wish. One thing only, allow us; when you are taking long journies, let us send each other news.

My heart is now relieved of this burning anxiety and at this moment beats quietly, conscious that it desires nothing but peace and goodwill among men. Confidently I lay my future in your hands. My position, my talents, my character deserve a considerate and full answer. It would be best if we spoke to each other. They will be awful moments until I learn your decision — awful as the pause between the lightning and the peal in a thunderstorm, when one does not know whether it will bring annihilation or blessing.

I beseech you, with the utmost earnestness of which an anxious, loving heart is capable: Be gracious to us, be once more a friend to one of your oldest friends, and the best father to the best child!

Robert Schumann."

"ENCLOSURE TO FRAU WIECK.

I commend our happiness, kind lady, to your heart — no stepmotherly heart I think — before all others. Your clear sight, your good wishes, your great respect and love for Clara, will make you find out the best way. Shall the birthday of a being who has already given happiness to such countless numbers, be a day of sorrow? — ward off this great misfortune which threatens us all!

Your most devoted
Robert Schumann."

"TO CLARA.

But you, dear, dear Clara, after this painful separation, must lovingly endorse everything that I have written to your parents, and add all that I cannot say.   Your R. S."

The diary mentions its reception with a brevity which speaks volumes: "Among other letters there came one from Schumann, on my birthday. It would fill pages if I were to write about it." Two years later[1]) Clara wrote to Robert about it:

"You cannot think what I suffered on my 18th birthday. It was not only that my Father did not even show me your letter, but neither did he give me the one which you had enclosed for me; Frau Stegmayer came to see us, and Father and Mother shut themselves up with her in order to read your letter — it was too mortifying, too inconsiderate, and if Father did not feel it so, my step-mother must have realised it; I cannot tell you what I felt. I cried the whole day long; 1 knew a few lines from you had been enclosed and there was I compelled to suffer such tyranny on my birthday! That was the unhappiest of all my birthdays. A few days later I was still unable to calm myself, tears stood always in my eyes, till at last Father began to feel a little pity, and asked me what was the matter; whereupon I told him the truth. Thereupon he took your letters out of his secretaire and placed them before me saying: 'I did not mean to let you have them, but since I see how unreasonable you are, read them.' I was too proud, and would not read them. — The wound which I had received could not be healed in this way. When the thunderstorm burst, that evening, I cried again because I was so anxious about you. My only comfort was your picture."

The fact that they had given up all attempt at secrecy and were acting frankly and openly, made it impossible for an insulting answer to be sent as had been the case a year and a half before, though it did not clear up the situation. Wieck's answer, Schumann wrote to Becker a few days later[2]),

1) June 8th 1839.
2) *Briefe. Neue Folge* p. 84 etc.

"was so confused, wavered so uncertainly between refusal and consent, that now I have not the least idea what to do ... I am very depressed, and cannot think."

More may be inferred from the letters which were exchanged by the two principal persons concerned, during these days.

SCHUMANN TO CLARA.

"Sept. 18th 1837.

My conversation with your father was terrible. Coldness, his ill-will, his confusion his contradictoriness — he has a new method of destruction, he drives blade and haft into one's heart. — — — What now, then my dear Clara? I do not know what to do. Not in the least. Reason is unavailing and emotion has even less effect upon your father. What now, then, what now, then?

Before all things arm yourself, and do not allow yourself to be sold.

. . . .

I trust you with all my heart, and that keeps up my courage — but you will have to be very strong, more than you suspect. Has not your father himself said to me the terrible words that, 'Nothing will shake him'? Fear everything from him; he will compel you by force if he cannot by cunning. Fear everything!

To-day, I am so dead, so *degraded*, that I can hardly conceive a beautiful thought, even your image has fled from me, so that I can hardly picture your eyes. Faint-hearted enough to give you up I am not; but embittered, wounded in my most sacred feelings. He treats me like the dirt beneath his feet. If only I had a word from you. You must tell me what I am to do. Otherwise I shall abandon myself to scorn and mockery, and let fate carry me where if will. Not even to be allowed to see you! He said that we might meet on neutral ground, before everybody, a spectacle to all the world. All this is so chilling, it rankles so! And we may write when you are away! That was all that he would consent to. — —

. . . .

In vain I seek for an excuse for your father, whom I have always considered as a noble, humane man. In vain I look for any nobler, deeper ground for his refusal, such as that he fears that you would suffer as an artist for an early engagement, that you are altogether too young, and such reasons. There is nothing of all this — believe me, he would throw you to the first-comer who had enough money and rank. Beyond this he has no higher idea than concert-giving and travelling. For this, he saps your life and shatters my strength, in the midst of my endeavour to do something beautiful in the world; for this, he laughs at all your tears.

Your ring looks at me so lovingly, as if it would say, 'Do not rail at your Clara's father, like this' — Three times lately have you said, 'Firm, firm', I heard it, it came so truly from the depths of your soul. — Clara that day has done for me — if to day I am weak and have hurt your father, do not be angry with me! And yet I am right.

But let us fix our eyes afresh on the goal. You must do all things by your goodness, and if that does not win its way through, by your strength. I can do hardly anything, except be silent; for each new request to your father I have only a new mortification to expect. Make every effort to find out what has to be done. I will follow like a child ... Ah! how my brain reels! I could laugh for anguish of heart. The situation cannot long remain like this — Nature will not endure it ...

May the good God comfort me, so that I may not be lost in despair. The roots of my life are withered."

The postscript, written on the afternoon of the same day, breathes a spirit of greater self-possession:

"Nothing is lost, I believe; but we have won little enough, too. My letters make me angry. It would have been better to have waited eight or ten weeks. It is important now that we should advance quietly and carefully; I can see that. Eventually he must resign himself to the idea of losing you. His obstinacy will shatter itself against our love; it must be, my Clara ... Only cure your father of his many distorted views.

. . . .
When I asked him if he did not think we should be the happiest people in the world, he conceded it ... and yet we got no further.

Further, he said that we should want far more than we thought, and named an enormous sum. We have just as much as a hundred of the most respected families here. Do not let yourself be persuaded out of that. Then he said, 'You would often shed tears in secret if we did not give large parties etc.' Clara is that true? Is it not laughable? He could not, and can not bring forward anything which has a real foundation. Right and reason are on our side and protect us. . . .

. . . .

If he drives us to extremes, that is if in another year and a half or two years, he still refuses to recognise us, we must seek our right . . . The authorities will marry us. Heaven forbid, that it chould have to come to this . . . Let me have a few words before long . . . soothing and kind. You stand before me now far more distinctly and beautifully than this morning, and your threefold 'Firm' echoes down to me as if from the clear sky.

And before I take leave of you to day, my beloved, swear to me once more *by your salvation*, that you have courage bravely to withstand the trials that are laid upon us, as I do at this moment, lifting up the two fingers of my right hand in token that I take the oath. I will never forsake you. Rely on me.

And so may God help us, and so I remain for ever

Your   Robert.

On your word of honour let me have this letter back at once."

CLARA TO ROBERT.

"Leipsic 1837. (In Robert's writing: 'Read with a thousand joys on Sept. 26.')

Do you still doubt me? I forgive you, for I am after all a weak girl! yes, weak: but I have a strong soul — ahe art that is firm and unalterable. Let this be enough to suppress every doubt of yours.

Till now I have been continuously unhappy, but write me a word of reassurance at the end of this letter and I shall go out into the wide world without a care. I have promised Father to be cheerful and to live for some years more for art and the world. You will hear so many things of me, many a doubt will arise in your mind when you learn of this or of that, but then think to yourself — She does all that for me! Could you ever waver? Well — then you would have broken a heart that loves but once.

Clara.

(Outside) Open it, and then return these lines to me. Do it for the sake of my peace."

ROBERT TO CLARA.

"Leipsic 1837.

Such heavenly words cannot be repaid. I, too, am firm. And now, not another word of what is past, but let us fix our eyes quietly and steadily on life's goal . . ."

CLARA TO ROBERT.

"Leipsic 1837.

(Received on Saturday evening Oct. 11th [1])
the day before their departure.)

. . . Usually I have to listen to a great deal that wounds, that deeply hurts a tender heart. Mother says, you are false — False? Ah God! shall your Clara not know her Robert better than that?

Always write direct to Father, not through my Mother. Do not trust her, if ever you come to see her. It grieves me to be obliged to say this, but believe me, she does not mean what she says; I have often had experience of it.

Could you deceive me? Could you ever forgive yourself for having rewarded my unspeakable love, like that?

I feel brave enough to endure everything; to day I have listened to all that my father had to say, without ever doubting you for a single instant — my faith stands unshaken! — Who knows what brilliant prospects may yet offer themselves to me, but I shall renounce them all with joy, of what use would all riches be to me with a broken heart? Only love can make me happy. I live for you alone, I will give all to you . . .

Now I must part from what I love best. Farewell then — there is no minute in which I do not think of you.

Your faithful Clara."

(On the back of the letter is written in Schumann's hand:)

"I am at once slain and blessed. — Your letter yesterday, my rage with your father, the parting, the whole past time, your goodness, your magnanimity — I am rich in all these. But if once you forsake me, let everything go to ruin. Only, do not forsake me." (The end is undecipherable).

---

1) Schumann's writing.

ROBERT TO CLARA.

"Oct. 9th.

Your 'Good evening' yesterday [1]) when we met at the door, I shall never forget. This Clara, I thought, this very Clara, is yours — is yours, and you cannot go to her, cannot so much as press her hand. Was there in the whole hall a single person who could even imagine the state of my mind? Hardly you, even. I was at once slain and blessed, weary to exhaustion and every drop of blood a wave of fever. How will it all end? Cousin Pfund brought me a greeting from your 'inmost heart' — which made me sleep more softly than on the previous night. But believe me — I am very ill, very very ill; one blow and I should fall.

What has robbed me all at once of the power to work? If I try an improvisation at the piano, it turns to chorales, if I write, I do it without thinking — one thing alone I want to paint everywhere in great letters and chords

Clara."

"Oct. 11th.

I can think and write no more; but when you wept on my heart, then — you showed me Heaven and Hell yesterday, Clara. Do I love you — and you me? Do not forsake me, my own. I cling to you. If you give way, I am lost."

In his letter of Oct. 9th, Schumann refers to the concert in the *Gewandhaus* on the previous day, in which Clara appeared once more, before her departure. Mendelssohn himself led her to the instrument. She played with what was for Leipsic unheard-of applause, and had to repeat the finale of Henselt's *Variations*. The audience would not stop applauding, which is the more significant as the ordinary Leipsic public wa not easily roused to enthusiasm. Certainly the consciousness of the near neighbourhood of her beloved was not the least of the influences which inspired her playing and made her carry those who listened away with her.

---

1) Clara played in the *Gewandhaus* on Oct. 8th.

Their departure followed on October 15th. It was the beginning of a concert tour which separated the lovers once more, for seven months. On October 16th, the day after they left, wrote

ROBERT TO CLARA.

"I kiss you for your last letter — how it has strengthened and exalted me! How happy you shall be with me some day.

Yesterday evening at 9 o'clock I thought of you. — What a charming idea of yours about a special hour. For the first time for many weeks I wept aloud — and it seemed to me as if you must feel it — I had an indescribably exquisite sensation of your presence. Words cannot describe the impression that your last letter [1] made upon me — but deeds shall."

---

1) This letter is lost.

CHAPTER IV.

YOUTHFUL FAME.
1837. 1838.

During the excitements of the last weeks of September and first of October, came, as we see from the letters of both lovers, the preparations for a new concert tour, which took Clara and her father away from Leipsic for many months and in more respects than one was to prove of greater importance in the development of her artistic and personal character than any that had gone before. The goal of the journey was Vienna, the birthplace of German music, which was about to conquer the world. And Clara entered this scene, hallowed as it was by great memories and traditions, and perpetually animated and stirred by an unequalled artistic atmosphere, at the moment when, in spite of her 18 years, the battle which she had so bravely undertaken for her love had given her an inner self-reliance, a ripeness of character, which enabled her to win for herself a new relation to the powers that had hitherto governed her entire life, her father and her art. But in a life such as hers, the two could not be separated from each other. It was necessarily the more painful for her that just at this moment, when love gave her art a new meaning, a new soul, her inmost being came into diametric opposition and warfare with him to whom she owed her art — her father. She felt that in the natural course of events she must become more and more detached from him, and that the harsh antagonism between their views could not but influence the relations between pupil and master. She still appeared in public under his name, as his creation, but already she belonged body and soul to the man whom he never wearied of reviling. And while, as Friedrich Wieck's daughter, she won the greatest triumphs, she felt herself to be nothing but Schumann's betrothed. But at the same time she clearly realised what gratitude she owed to him who had made her what she was — an artist who now triumphantly challenged competition with the greatest, serene in a confidence in her own powers which even passing attacks of faint-heartedness could not shake.

On Oct. 30th father and daughter set out for Prague. There, the first concert took place on November 12th — with no previous subscriptions, and in addition to this with only a soloist and no orchestra, a great venture in the eyes of the inhabitants — and won, as a favourable omen for the further course of the journey, enthusiastic applause from an intelligent, musically educated public, which re-called her twelve times.

The diary speaks of many different sorts of opposition and cabals, as well as of the brilliant artistic and material success, and Wieck is not wanting in strong language especially with regard to the secret opposition of Pixis and his adherents. An epigram of Saphir's, whose acquaintance they made here, is repeated; when a painter [1]) expressed his intention of painting Clara, he said: "Clara is too model a player [2]) ever to be modelled." For the rest, Clara's letters to Schumann both here

---

1) Evidently J. R. Schramm, who drew Clara in November at Prague; a very charming picture which, as Clara once wrote to Schumann, everybody thought "extraordinarily like". For the rest, Saphir showed himself amything but friendly to Clara in Vienna a few weeks later. "We had not given him anything", Wieck remarks in the diary.

2) *Translator's note*: Clara ist so ausgezeichnet, dass sie gar nicht mehr gezeichnet werden kann.

and afterwards, give a truer and more intimate picture of her experiences than the diary which was kept under the eyes, and with the supervision of her father.

CLARA TO ROBERT.

"Prague, Friday Nov. 3ʳᵈ 1837. 9 o'clock in the evening.
(Schumann's writing: Received on Tuesday the 7ᵗʰ.)

Why are you silent? For nearly three weeks I have heard nothing from you — that hurts. Why is there no answer to Father's letter, which he wrote you without my knowledge? Nanny [1]) knows everything that Father does, for he trusts her, but she is too fond of me not to tell me everything.

. . . What do you say to Father's letter, will you answer him? — Write me just a line. B. C. D. E. are the letters. Let Dr. Reuter (to whom I send greetings) write the address, Father might ask to see the letters at the post and recognise your hand. I shall ask for one at the end of next week, on Thursday or Friday — do not let me ask in vain. . . . We left Dresden last Sunday. The morning was so beautiful, the Elbe so clear with the sky, reflected in it, and the sun looked at me in a friendly way, as if it would say, 'Give me your greeting, I will take it to him faithfully.' I could picture to myself so vividly how shyly it would glide through the Park to your window — did it not remind your of a certain —?

I am very distressed to see how unhappy Father is when he thinks of losing me — I am conscious of my duty to him and yet I love you without measure! — He thinks I should forget you, forget? The word makes me shudder! He does not know the strength of a loving heart. — Ah! words fail me so completely. I feel so much and can say so little — an inner voice must say it to you — —

I must tear myself forcibly from you — my spirit is always with you; — the knot is made fast, I will never undo it! — You know what my most longing wish is at present, so send a line to

Your faithful Clara."

_____

1) Nanny accompanied Clara.

CLARA TO ROBERT.

"November 1837.   Prague, Sunday Evening, the 12th.

Dear Robert, your letter made me inexpressibly happy, I trembled all over with joy when Nanny handed it to me. But first let me scold a little, and tell you that you are an insatiable fellow. First you wanted to have a letter every eight weeks, then every 4 weeks, and now I write to you in 3 weeks and you complain — I half believe that you mean to make me feel the mastery of a husband already. — Very good; I think we shall come to an understanding. But what do you write about hopes sinking? Have you drawn that meaning out of my letters? Ah Robert, that hurts! Why I live but in one hope, only one thought inspires me in all I do, and you can say — nay write — such a thing? — Let this go no further! — And now, as to being married, that is certainly to be considered. Supposing a diamond appeared which so blinded me that I could no longer see Eusebius, Florestan and the rest, and you were finally to read in the paper 'Engagement of Fräulein Clara Wieck to Herr von Rope-of-Pearls or Diamond-tiara'. — But seriously, am I a little child, who will suffer itself to be led to the altar as if to school? No, Robert! When you call me a child, that sounds so dear, but, but when you think me a child, then I stand up and say: '*You are mistaken!*' Trust me wholly. Did I not write to you before, 'Necessity breaks iron'; if there is no help for it, I will seek peace in loving arms. Now then — what did I mean to say? I mean the ring. What! you would like to give it back to me? Hm, that must be considered, but I will think it over! — You smile? I do, too — the moon is just peeping in to bring a 'kind greeting' — now, dear Robert, we will leave it all as it was, won't we? and you will call me your true Clara, and *never* anything else, for the future.

You want to know something of my life; listen then! To day I gave a concert in the Conservatoire (on account of the theatre, concerts here are at 12 o'clock, midday, or at 5 in the afternoon) and I was re-called 13 times. Great heavens! I never saw such enthusiasm before. You can imagine that I did not know what to do; again and again I had to come out of my hiding-place, and then there were all the curtsies, which you know I make so abominably! The thought of you inspired me so while I was playing that the whole audience became inspired too. I have already had letters and visits of congratulation to day — the people here have run mad — But look at the clock, how late it is, and I, who need rest so sorely to day, gossip so long! Ah! if only I could always gossip like this! —"

"Friday the 17th afternoon.

At last, after nearly a week, I manage to write a few words to you again. Do not think that that is so easy, for I have to write to you with my door unlocked, as Father is very angry if he finds the room locked. And how suspicious he is now! Think! he told, Nanny, 'I know the dodge, and how to find out if Clara has written to Schumann, it will not remain concealed from me long'. It will be best if you address your next letter to a gentleman, 'Herr Julius Kraus, Poste restante', at Vienna of course. But let the address always be written by Dr Reutter . . . . I have just been reading what I wrote you on Sunday, and it struck me that you might misunderstand my jesting words. But please take it all seriously and also my earnest request to say no more about doubts, it hurts me very much. I am conscious of the most beautiful and steadfast love. Rely on me, as I do on you — then no obstacle can be too great for us, we shall defy them all, if higher powers do not come between us."

"Sunday the 19th.

This was the evening on which I had planned to write a great deal to you, and behold there appears a languishing admirer who spoils my whole nice evening . . . . You will guess, and smile! — There is another enthusiast here too, who threatens to devour me with every glance, and if I sit down to the piano all is over, I make up my mind to an embrace every time; luckly, as you know of old, a stool always stands by my side, over which he falls first . . . . But there is a dreadful chatterbox, Tomaschek, who is wild with you because you have found fault with Drey-schock[1]) (his pupil). Nothing vexes me so much as that I have played some of your compositions to him. Tomaschek cannot, or will not, understand them. — I have quarrelled with him over

---

1) *Ges. Schriften* 4 ed. II p. 46.

Bellini, Spohr (you know my weakness), Mozart etc.: as he was telling me just now that Gluck is the first composer in the world, and that I undertstood nothing of true music, I said: 'If I live to be an old maid then I too will be sentimental over Gluck — but as it is I want to live for all that is beautiful in art, and am happy that I am not confined to one point of view.' He went — and did not come back.

. . . . Mother wrote that you wanted the song of Mendelssohn's, but do not think me disobliging if I refuse it to you. I want to keep that song for myself, I value it. Mendelssohn has at least 50 *Lieder ohne Worte* in his head, some of which he can write down for you . . . .

Yesterday my 2nd concert took place, before an audience of nearly 600, in spite of the fact that the whole aristocracy is not here yet, and there was another storm of applause. Saphir and Uffo Horn were at the concert too, and Saphir has (so he tells me) sent a notice to the *Humorist*, which counts for a good deal in Vienna. . . . .

What makes you think — that I cannot bear your *Davidsbündler* dances? So far I have not been able to get two hours' peace to myself to dedicate to them, and they need that. None but I could decipher such writing. Now, good night, the tea is ice-cold, the room grows colder and colder, but I grow warmer and warmer."

"Friday the 24th. Evening.

To-morrow we set out for Vienna by the flying-coach. You will get this letter on Monday, and now I give you a week in which you can write much and clearly! Nanny has just been saying that my eyes have been heavy ever since the evening when I pored over your letter for 2 hours. See, of what you are guilty! Do not forget, either, to write to me about your plans, for I am much interested in them.

— I have been thinking a great deal about my circumstances during these days, and I must call your attention to something. You rely on the ring! Good heavens! that is but an external bond. Had not Ernestine too, a ring from you, and what is of more importance, your promise? And yet you have torn that bond asunder. The ring is of no consequence. . . . .

.I too, have thought most seriously about the future. One thing I must say to you; I cannot be yours until circumstances have entirely altered. I do not want horses or diamonds, I am happy in possessing you, but I wish to lead a life free from care, and I see that I shall be unhappy if I cannot always work at my art, and that I cannot do if we have to worry over our daily bread. I require much, and I realise that much is needed for a comfortable life. Therefore Robert, ask yourself if you are in a condition to offer me a life free from care. Think that simply as I have been brought up, I have yet never had a care, and am I to bury my art now? . . . .

. . . . Yesterday, I played in the the theatre for the last time, and was (contrary to the regulations) recalled 4 times after each piece. I played my concerto, and Henselt's variations; hardly anyone remembers ever having seen it so full before. I do not, however, want to stay here, Vienna draws me to herself. I am sad when I come into a strange town where I am entirely unknown and many thoughts pass backwards and forwards through my brain. Ah God! I feel as if my heart would burst. If ever I do not write to you within 4 weeks, do not be angry with me, for it will be owing to want of time, and I can only write in the evenings. I shall not have many evenings to myself in Vienna — they will have to be given up to social duties. I can write no more, as it is late. This is a very dull letter — you must put up with it and take it for love, for it is written in pure love

by Your Clara.

On the 3nd or 4th I shall enquire at the post-office for a letter from you. You are not angry with me, are you? Ah God! I do not know what I want, I feel as if I had done something to you."

ROBERT TO CLARA.

"L. Nov. 28th /37.

First as to the most important part of your letter, where you say that you can never be mine unless circumstances have completly altered. Your father's spirit stood behind you and dictated that; but you have written it, and you are right to think of your external happiness. We must be quite clear about this. The only thing that troubles me, is that you make the objection for the first time now, which you should have made to me when I first frankly explained my circumstances to you, as otherwise it would certainly never have entered my head to write to your father, if I had thought that you still had so many scruples.

What I wrote before, first to you and afterwards to your father, about my wealth, was true then and still holds good now. It is not over-powering, but such that many a girl, even many a pretty and good one, might give me her hand on it and say, 'It will be hard to make both ends meet, but you shall find me a good housekeeper etc. etc.' — At that time you thought so too, per-haps — Now you think differently — my mind reels.

To business. Unless a gift falls from heaven, I do not see how I can increase my income in a short time as much as, on your account, I could wish. You know the kind of work I do, you know that it is purely intellectual, that it cannot be carried on at any moment like manual labour . . . . I have shown that I can persevere; mention any young fellow of my age who has made for himself so wide a sphere of activity in so short a time. It goes without saying, that I should like to extend it, to earn more, and in this I shall not fail; but I do not believe that this will achieve as much as you wish, or as you perhaps have now; on the other hand I can with a clear conscience rely upon being able to support one wife or even two wives, in about two years' time, without any great anxiety, though certainly not without con-tinuing to work.

Dear Clara, the last page of your letter brought me down to earth, and I should like to embrace all the clod-hoppers. You might have expressed it more romantically though; I find it difficult to say a word in answer. . . . . As I said, your father held the pen; the coldness of the lines has something killing in it. . . . . And now too, that you think so little of my ring — — since yesterday I have cared no more for yours, and no longer wear it. I dreamt that I was walking by a deep pool, and an impulse seized me and I threw the ring into it — — then I was filled with a passionate longing to throw myself after it. . . .

. . . . I will write more to-morrow; my head is on fire, and my eyes are heavy with grief over you. Farewell, however."

"The 29th (November).

That it is possible so to torment oneself over a few hundred pieces of silver a year which are still lacking to us! But truly,

we must have them. You (know) what I have; I need only half
for myself. If the other half is not enough for you, you will easily
earn something for yourself. It all depends (upon) how we contrive, and you shall hear what I have planned out. I should prefer
to keep my present independent position for a time, have a nice
house not far from the town — you with me — work — and
live happily and quietly with you. You would of course practise
your great art, as ever, but less for the sake of anybody and
everybody and on account of the money, than for the sake of
a few elect and on account of our happiness. All this, if you
like it. A life such as this requires no great expenditure. If you
would be happy in it, and would remain so neither you nor I
can know; people alter, chance and fate often spoil a good game,
other things become involved. But, as I have said, I should
prefer a life like this; I could paint everything to you in still
fairer colours, so that you would fall on my heart and say,
'Yes, Robert, let us live like that'. — Do that for yourself, if
you love me.

It would be another thing if you wanted to live for the great
world; and I would agree to that too. In that case we would
let our house stand empty for three months (I could be away as
long as that, every year, provided I go on editing the newspaper)
and travel (little, or not at all, in German towns), now time to
Paris, now to London — You have a reputation everywhere, and
I have friends, and numerous connections — in short, honour and
profit could not be wanting, and we should come back to our
house, — which alas! is still non existent — richly laden with
treasure. Leipsic would be the centre from which, in the one
case like the sun, and in the other more like the moon, we should
shed abroad the rays of our life — — — Supposing we should
get tired of this sort of life, what would you answer if I spoke
to you like this, some morning: 'Dear wife, unknown to you I
have composed several excellent symphonies and other important
works, and I have also ambitious plans for tours in my head, as
you too seem to have a fancy for crowns and laurels how would
it be if we were to pack up our diamonds and go off and live in
Paris? — You would answer, 'Now, I am glad to hear that', or
'Just listen!' — or 'As you like', — or 'No, let us stay here, I
like it so much' — and then I should go quietly to my writing-
table, and continue editing as before.

Oh! beautiful pictures, may no-one shatter you to pieces! If only I for once lay happy on your loving heart. All these nights of anguish, sleepless with the thought of you, and all this tearless grief — a merciful God must repay them some day. Let me rest for a minute, now. —

In truth, I have reckoned without my host, i. e. without your father. But only you can do anything with him, I can do nothing at present . . . .

This brings me to the place in my letter in which I spoke of 'Making claims'. I need not tell you that I do not look upon the bond between us as a legal contract. Do you think I should place any opposition in your way if you found a more happy man whom you loved and who, as far as could be seen in advance, would make you perfectly happy? No, I love you too well for that, even if it broke my life to pieces; besides, I should be too proud, as you know I can be under certain circumstances.

You say, rather harshly, that I tore asunder the bond with Ernestine; that is not true; it was unloosed in due form, with the consent of both of us. But with respect to this dark page in my life, I must lay bare to you a deep secret, a severe mental suffering which befell me earlier; it occupied a long time, and includes the years from the summer of 1833 onwards. You shall know all about it someday, and you will then have the key to all my actions, to all my peculiarities. For the moment I call to you the words which I read recently in an excellent book: 'He is a fool who trusts to his heart — but do not condemn him[1]).

Once more, therefore, your 'yes' and its external symbol, the ring, certainly bind you . . . . but no-one can force you, and I least of all, to remain true to me. But you are a god-fearing girl and know all this. It is you yourself who have made me talk like this, by your strange words. —

. . . . Clara it hurts so much to think that we must live through our most beautiful, blossoming youth, apart from each other. Where-ever I go, people speak to me of your exquisite nature, people praise you, and I cannot speak to you, hear you, learn of you, rejoice in your spirit — and you too, gain nothing from me, except, perhaps, a few memories which are precious to you of the first never-to-be-forgotten evening when we met again in Sep-

1) Cf. p. 70.

tember — and besides this, a great deal of pain, and the ring, for which you no longer really care, as you say in your last letter on that hateful last page — — though it is true the first contradicts it! One would hardly believe that they could both come from the same girl — you are so passionate and reasonable, so distrustful and kind, you love so warmly and at the same time can make one so angry; in short you are the whole Tuesday evening, with its moonshire, its tears of joy, its surrender. In truth when you wear the cap [1]) you can turn the arrow round and round in my heart, at your ease, I will not quiver — in the cap — put it on sometimes and then think, he loves you best like this. You understood my 'Child': I said it with your my whole heart, which was full of you. As to what you write of your father's remark [2]) .... it is nice of you. I always dislike writing your name in the paper, and should always like to add after it: 'She is my beloved, about whom there is nothing to be said, and with whom none of you have anything to do' — — Would you not like to hear me play again? You know I often use strange middle parts, (they are my sign-manual), you used to stand close by and watch my hand, and I looked into your eyes. We were too happy in those days.

I am far from satisfied with my life for the last few weeks; the separation from you, the pain of so many insults, often weigh down my spirit, and then I can do nothing — then I brood for hours together, look at your picture, which hangs before me, and wonder how it all will end. — Send me often a few words to support me — Then too it frequently irritates me that I have to write about such silly, bad compositions — I feel as if I were a diamond which were used for nothing except to cut common glass. Do not call me vain because of this comparison — I have still several symphonies in my head, of which I am proud. Speak to me therefore lovingly, often .... that I may keep strength and confidence. I might possibly work harder to make money, but it would be more superficial and mediocre; the power of creation has its exact limits; one cannot always draw on one's best powers or they would fail one altogether.

---

1) *Translator's note*: i. e. The mark of a married woman.

2) Wieck had made it a subject of complaint to Clara that Schumann so seldom mentioned her in his paper.

I have still much to say to you. First the question what would you do if your father discovered our correspondence? Give me a decided answer to this. Do not be frightened if he talks about disinheriting and such things. — He cannot deprive you of your heart. Then too, you have a mother. If ever he tries to force you, there is your natural refuge. But I mean, if he finds us out, will you still go on writing to me? If you allowed yourself to be frightened, as you did in Dresden, if you gave me no sign — Clara I would not seek for you a second time; never again. You are not angry with me for that, are you? And be on your guard with the letters! Keep your own counsel. How sad it all is! —

Try to be cheerful on your journey! Your account of the way in which you have been received delights and pains me, for I should like to see it all too.

— Is it always by your own wish that you play your concerto? There are stars of thought in the first movement — yet it did not make an impression of completeness. When you are seated at the piano, I do not know you — my judgment is a thing apart.

Chopin is seriously ill, so Mendelssohn told me yesterday; we were at Voigt's, with Taubert, David, and the rest.

Miss Laidlaw [1]) wrote to me from Posen a week ago; I believe she is fond of me. On leaving, she gave me a lock of her hair, so now you know it. I suppose you could never be jealous? I should like to know you thorougly.

I shall expect letters from you on December 29th and 30th — or else make the holy eve [2]) holy indeed and write then.

. . . . I kiss you in heartfelt love — Adieu my Fidelio . . . . and be as faithful as Leonore to her Florestan, to

Your Robert."

This letter is eminently characteristic, in its abrupt changes of mood as well as in its harsh discords, both of the writer and of the circumstances against which he had to struggle. Before it reached Clara's hands, and, as was only to be

---

1) Cf. P. G. Jansen, *Robert Schumann and Robena Laidlaw.* Grenzboten 1895 p. 320 etc. Also *Zeitschrift d. internat. Musikgesellschaft* Feb. 1902 p. 188 etc.: *Miss Robena Laidlaw.*

2) *Translator's note*: i. e. Christmas Eve.

expected, aroused very mingled feelings in her, she had already received her first impressions of Vienna and its musical powers and ideals. They had thought themselves justified in accepting the remarkably friendly welcome which they received from Bäuerie, the most influential Viennese journalist of the day, who had made himself a power through his *Theaterzeitung*, as a favourable omen, which they needed the more since in artistic circles proper they found here too, a more or less marked reserve. Josef Fischhof [1]), head of the Viennese school, was a striking exception, and maintened their cause vigorously, but he was disappointing in himself, never rising above the level of "a well-educated musician", and missing the highest and most refined culture. Still more disappointing was his, and Czerny's, pupil, Lacombe, who as early as 1831 had been crowned in Paris with *premier prix* for piano-playing. "What expression he has", says the diary, "is nothing but the work of his teacher; where this is the case, there is no true art to be found." In Beethoven's *A* major symphony, which they heard at a concert in the *Redoutensaal* on December 3rd, they found the slow tempi extremely surprising and disturbing. The general impression of the first week in Vienna is summed up by Wieck in the diary, in the words: "Mendelssohn ought to come here — Good God! how a really good musician is wanted here — there is such beautiful material".

Father and daughter were all the more pleasantly affected by the genuinely enthusiastic reception accorded to Clara's playing at a large soirée on Dec. 3rd at Baronness Pereira's, whose house might be called the centre of musical life in Vienna. "The ice is broken", says the diary, "and our faintheartedness has disappeard as if by magic. I achieved a triumph, delighting all Chopinists, Henseltist, and in a word

---

1) Teacher in the *Konservatorium der Gesellschaft der Musikfreunde* in Vienna, a fellow-worker in Schumann's paper. Schumann's letters to him are in the *Jugendbriefe* and *Briefe. Neue Folge.*

all lovers of music (the company consisted of nothing else) and getting a reception which made up to us for the terrible coldness of the local artists, who will not progress with the times, and were afraid of being shaken out of their humdrum way."

Schumann's letter somewhat damped this exalted mood, as is shown by Clara's answer of Dec. 6th. If here she hotly flings back her lover's reproaches as unjustified, yet later [1]) she had to confess that those expressions which so disquieted Schumann, had been the result "of a dark hour", "in which — I can hardly believe it — reason seemed to rule my heart".

CLARA TO ROBERT.

"Vienna Wednesday Dec. 6th 1837.

As great as my joy on receiving your letter, was my sorrow on reading the first page — could you so wound me, draw from me such bitter tears? Is it Robert who so misunderstood me, who read so ugly a meaning into my words — have I deserved this? Yes, I know that many beautiful and perhaps as good girls as I are at your disposal, and better housewives than any artist is supposed to be — yes, I know it, but it is not well that you should mention such a thought to me, to me who live but for you and in you, or that such a thought should come to you, if you love me indeed. . . . . You think that I harbour unattainable wishes? I want but two things, your heart and your happiness.

How could I be calm if you were burdened with cares on my account? Could I be guilty of the base desire that you should turn your genius into a drudge so that I might follow my pleasure? No, my thoughts are not so base; perhaps you will learn to know me better, later. My imagination can picture no fairer happiness than to continue living for art, but quite quietly, so that we may both owe many a pleasant hour to it. So we agree in all things, and I fall upon your heart and say: 'Yes Robert, let us live like this!' Do you think that I too, do not love passionately? Oh yes! I too can be passionate, but passion ceases when our hearts are

1) Letter to Schumann, Jan. 18th to 30th 1838.

full of care, then you would indeed feel yourself brought down to earth. I see that much is required for a simple life — — but do not doubt on this account, that everything will all right. I have steadfast faith, your ring says to me daily: 'Belive, love, and hope'."

"Tuesday the 12th. Evening.

At last I have an evening at home again and can chat with you for a little. I am asked out a great deal here, and am very kindly received. I have roused people to a pitch of enthusiasm which I sometimes find incomprehensible — but really I cannot play badly, if I am treated with such respect after Thalberg! — With rather a beating heart I am looking forward to my first concert! Vienna is quite different from what people say abroad. There are distinguished connoisseurs here and innumerable amateurs with a real taste for art. They know everything of Chopin's, and understand him, but they know little of Henselt, though they are getting to know him through me, and are amazed to hear that he lived here for 3 years. . . . . Mendelssohn is almost wholly un-know, his *Lieder ohne Worte* lie untouched in the music-shops — they do not sing here! They did produce his *Midsummer Night's Dream Overture*, but it was not at all liked. . . . . I wanted to play something of his at my first concert, but I dare not risk it until I have the public on my side — — Your works find a great upholder in Professor Fischhof, especially since he heard me play some of them. He is your only friend — otherwise they are all your enemies; one hardly dare mention your name, they all become so furious; and why? on account of Döhler and Thalberg — — I cannot get a copy of your paper, to read.

Today, the 13th, Fischhof said to me: 'I have a letter from Schumann', and I shook all over as I do every time I hear your name. — The most terrible of all questions is always: 'Who is this Schumann? where does he live? does he play the piano?' — 'He composes'. — 'What are his compositions like?' Then I want to say, like you, 'He is a person with whom you have nothing at all to do, who stands so far above you that you are incapable of understanding him, and who cannot be described in words, etc.' I had to puzzle out several words in your letter to-day, which Fischhof could not read. How glad I was to see the writing, and when I saw your name at the bottom, my heart was at once glad and sad. — I could have wept for pain and joy! — Ah! Robert, believe me, I have many sorrowful hours! No pleasure is complete to me when you are not there! How many polite things I have to say to people, and all the while I am conscious of nothing but the thought of you."

Meanwhile the day of the first concert kept drawing nearer. "Vienna is to decide", said the voice of a critic[1], "whether this modest young artist, who in Germany ranks beside Liszt and Chopin, can be mentioned in the same breath with Thalberg". And although on Dec. 9th, Wieck already announces with triumph in the diary: "Almost all the connoisseurs are on our side", yet he was not blind to the fact that though this was something it was by no means everything, and that a great deal depended on her playing and on the impression made by this first appearance in the city where "Thalberg's name is on every tongue". Under these circumstances the reception accorded to Clara's playing four days before her concert, at a large party at Fischhof's — at which, among others, Grillparzer, Lenau, and Bauernfeld were present — seemed all the more important. The applause roused at the outset by Schubert's piano trio in $E\flat$ major (Op. 100), (in spite of the fact that Clara had "to drag" her fellow-players "along with her") increased after Bach's fugue, which she had to repeat twice, and reached its climax after Henselt's *Vögelein*. Her father states joyfully, "she is being placed before Thalberg by almost everybody, since she plays with enthusiasm, and with far more feeling, she is Thalberg and Henselt in one, and she plays much better compositions than he does". But the real test, which put this to the proof, took place on Dec. 14th in the *Musikvereinssaal*. "My triumph", the diary calls it. "The audience consisted of a select body of the

1) Bäuerle.

most distinguished and artistic people in Vienna . . . . I satisfied connoisseurs and ignoramuses, had to repeat 2 pieces,
and was re-called twelve times altogether." Wieck shed tears
of joy, but Clara writes to Robert the day after: "Yesterday
was the long-expected day at last — the day which was
to decide my fate. I cannot describe the success to you.
Fischhof tells me he has told you something of it. I cannot
write about it properly". But even in this song of triumph,
there were some discords, discords which could not now be
avoided, but must continually trouble and sadden her afresh.
In the same letter she says further on:

". . . . But do not judge Father harshly because of what I
wrote about him; he does not now try to persuade me to give
you up, because he knows that that hurts my feelings, depresses
and disheartens me, and makes it difficult for me to give concerts
and to practise — he thinks his letter has put an end to everything. . . . .

But it hurts me when you wish to cast a stone at Father because he wishes for some small recompense for all the hours which
he has devoted to me. He wishes me to be happy, and thinks
that is to be obtained by riches, can you be angry with him for
it? He loves me above all things, and would not thrust me, his
child, away from him if he saw that my happiness could be founded
on you alone, so, for love of me, forgive him his natural vanity.
Consider that he has treated you like this only for love of me.
You too love me, and you make me happy when you forgive
him; I would not have him misunderstood by you — every man
has his faults; I have and so have you — you will allow me to
say so ! — —

But now for another question, only do not be angry with me, dear
Robert. I know you well enough, but there is one thing — why
do you avoid every opportunity of mentioning me in your paper?
— — — Father is now very unhappy to think that I love you.
He is never really tender, he quickly becomes cold at the thought
that my heart beats for another; he cannot imagine that I can be
happy with you, for he says, 'If Schumann does nothing for Clara
under these present circumstances — will he do anything when

he is married?' I could write more but I know it hurts you, and
I will say no more about it. You are still Robert and I Clara —
nothing else matters. Yet — your secret makes me very anxious
about you — Robert, what am I to understand by this? — —"

"The 21st

My second concert[1]) took place to-day, and was another triumph.
Of the many items in the programme my concerto had the best
reception. You ask if I always play it by my own wish — certainly I do, for it has been well received everywhere, and has given
satisfaction to connoisseurs and to the public in general. Whether
or no it satisfies me is another question. Do you think that I am
so weak as not to know well enough what are the faults of the
concerto? I know them, well enough but the audience does not,
and what is more need not, know. Do you think I would play
it, if it took as little everywhere as it did in Leipsic? Certainly when one has been here one never wants go North again,
where men have hearts of stone (you are, of course, excepted)
You ought to listen to a storm of applause here. I had to repeat
the Bach fugue and the Henselt variations. No pleasanter feeling
than that of having satisfied a whole audience.

So much for me — Now for you . . . . I was much amused at
the place in your letter where you write, 'And so we will come
back to our house, laden with treasure.' Good heavens! what
are you thinking of? Treasures are no longer to be got by in-
strumental art. How much one has to do in order to bring away
a few thaler from a town. When you are sitting with Poppe at
10 o'clock in the evening, or are going home, I, poor thing, am
arriving at a party, where I have to play to people for a few
pretty words and a cup of warm water, and get home, dead tired,
at 11 or 12 o'clock, drink a draught of water, lie down, and
think, 'Is an artist much more than a beggar?' And yet art is
a fine gift! What, indeed, is finer than to clothe one's feelings
in music, what a comfort in time of trouble, what a pleasure,
what an exquisite feeling, to give happy hours to so many people
by its means! And what an exalted feeling so to follow art that

---

1) "Clara," writes Wieck in the diary, "founded a new era of piano-
playing in Vienna, at this (concert). . . . To play a Bach fugue twice in
a concert in Vienna, is unheard of."

one gives one's life to it! — I have done that, and all the rest, to-day, and I lay myself down, happy and contented. Yes, I am happy but shall be perfectly so, only when I can fling myself on your heart and say, 'Now I am yours for ever — I and my art'."

"Christmas Eve.

How can I better celebrate Christmas Eve than by talking to you? I was very sad to-day, because my eye fell on no Christmas-tree. Where may you be now? Are you very happy? But yes — for the tree of love flames for you! — .... One thought has occupied me to-day: how will things be with us in three years' time? Perhaps you too, have been thinking the same? — You received a few lines from me to-day![1) ....

On the 7th (Jan. 1838) in my third concert, and on Tuesday (the day after to-morrow) I am to play to the Empress. I have had a reception here which has made up for the mortifications which I received in the North. ... You may already have heard of one delicate attention towards me. Schubert left behind, among other things, a *Duo* for four hands which has just been printed by Diabelli, and dedicated to me. This has affected me very much, I can hardly say why, myself. It is extraordinary how easily I am upset now, sometimes I think I am quite sentimental. —

I have often played duets with Fischhof but he does not play — he bangs the piano. Ah! that *Hungarian Fantasia* if only I could play it with you again once more — only once more hear you improvise! Believe me, I really do love you dearly. —

I am sorry for poor Miss Laidlaw — she is very fond of you? I am not surprised at that. And you would like to know me better? How shall I answer you? If I say, 'I am jealous', I shall deceive you, and if I say, 'I am not jealous', you will think yourself deceived. So you must wait a little longer.

.... Liszt is not yet here, but is daily expected. But imagine who came yesterday — Eichhorn came with 3 sons and a 10-year-old 'cellist. It seems to me that the eldest has not turned out

---

1) A short greeting: "A few lines for the festival which is being happily celebrated by so many, — we apart and yet together. May you pass the festival very contentedly and happily. I am in strange lands and yet I celebrate it at home — my home is with you.

Vienna Dec. 20th.   Your Clara."

to be much . . . . Infant prodigies are like that, they do not come to much — just as I have not come to very much. At my next concert I am going to play Beethoven's *F* minor sonata and after that, privately, your *Carnaval*. Are not the *Phantasiestücke* nearly ready? . . . . 1 should have liked, dear Robert, to have worked you a little remembrance for Christmas, but do I not employ my time better when I write to you?"

"The 26th. 11 o'clock.

It is late, but I must send a few words. I have just come from the Empress, I am eating a plate of soup, and will finish my letter. Although the Emperor, the Empress, and the rest have been talking to me, do you not think that I would rather talk to you?

. . . . What else is going to happen to me? They want us to go to Pest and Graz also.

. . . . Yesterday, Father again said to Nanny, 'If Clara marries Schumann, I would say upon my death-bed that she is not worthy to be my daughter'. Robert, does not that hurt? My feelings cannot be described; yet I will endure everything if it is for you — I tell you this only because it moves my heart too deeply for me to keep silence about it to you.

. . . . I am quite beside myself when I hear my Father raging in the evening, when his curses rouse me from sleep, and I hear them aimed at my dearest . . . . I am no longer so fond of my Father, ah God! I can no longer be so whole-heartedly affectionate, and yet I should so like to be — it is Father whom I have to thank for everything. It is my highest wish — perhaps it may yet be satisfied and then we shall love each other, untroubled.

. . . . To your question whether I will allow myself to be frightened again by Father, the answer is: 'No, never again!'

Your faithful Clara."

ROBERT TO CLARA.

"Leipsic Dec. 22nd 1837.

Among the thousand voices which give you joyous greeting to-day, you will perhaps, hear one more, which softly calls you by name — you look round — and it is I. 'You here, Robert?' you ask me. Why not — do I ever leave your side, do I not follow you everywhere, although you may not see me? . . . .

And the figure fades again. But love and faithfulness remain. May these lines remind my beloved of   her Robert."

"New Year's Eve 1837, past 11 o'clock.

I have been sitting here for the last hour. At first I wanted to spend the whole evening in writing to you, but I have no words — now sit down by me, put your arm round me, and let us look into each other's eyes — silent — happy —

There are two people in the world, who love one another.

It is just striking a quarter to.

Far off they are singing a choral — do you know who these two are, who love one another? How happy we are — Clara, let us kneel down! Come my Clara, I feel you — let our last word together be addressed to the Highest — —"

"The first; Morning, 1838.

What a heavenly morning — all the bells are ringing — the whole sky is golden blue and clear — Your letter is before me — Here is my first kiss, my heart's darling!"

"The 2nd.

How happy you have made me by your last letters, and in the first place by the one on Christmas Eve. I could call you by every possible term of endearment, but I know no better word than the little German 'dear' — only it must be uttered in a particular tone. Well then, dear, — I wept for you to think that you are mine, and I often ask myself if I am worthy of you. How many things pass through a man's head and heart in the course of a day! One would think, they would burst. Whence come all these thoughts, wishes, pains, joys, and hopes? — and so it goes on, day in, day out, and there is never rest. But yesterday and the day before, how bright things seemed — how much you wrote to me, what a beautiful tone breathed through it all, how firm and true, and how heartfelt seemed your love! If only my Clara, I could do something for love of you. The old knights were better off, they could pass through the fire for their beloved, or slay dragons — but we of the present day must try to serve our ladies by scraping farthings together and smoking fewer cigars, and such things — But truly, the knights notwithstanding, we know how to love, and in this as in all things, the times alone have changed and hearts remain the same.

I have a hundred things to write to you, large and small. If only I could do it properly and in order — but my writing keeps getting more illegible, and I should be anxious if it were a gauge of my affection. In truth, I have my terrible hours too when even your image forsakes me — when I ask myself, with reproaches, if I have guided my life as wisely as I might have done, if I did right in chaining you, angel that you are, to me, if I can make you as happy as I should — your father's treatment of me is the cause of all these questions and doubts. A man easily thinks himself what others think him. After the way your father has treated me, I am forced to ask myself, 'Are you so bad then? Are you so base, that a man can treat you like this?' Accustomed as I am, to conquer easily and to overcome difficulties, accustomed to happiness and to love, and spoiled perhaps, by always finding so many things easy in the world, now I am repulsed, insulted, slandered. I used to read of such things in novels, but I thought myself too good ever to become the hero of such a Kotzebue-ish family-drama. If I had ever injured your father well then he might hate me; but that he should abuse me for absolutely no reason, and, as you yourself say, hate me, I cannot understand. But my turn will come some day — and then he shall see how I love him and you. For, let me whisper it in your ear, I love and honour your father for his many great and noble qualities, as, except for you, no-one else can prize him, it is a peculiar, innate attachment on my part, a submission which I feel towards him, as I do towards all energetic natures. And this doubles my pain, now that he will have no more to do with me. Well — perhaps peace will come now, and he will say to us, 'Well, take each other'. — You cannot think how your letter has cheered and strengthened me . . . . You are a splendid creature, and I have far more reason to be proud of you, than you of me — . . . ."

For Clara, the new year had begun unquietly, but with a promise of happiness and hope in spite of all her secret anxieties. Her third concert, which took place on Jan. 7th, and at which 800 people found themselves in "an indescribable crush", was the occasion of a fresh triumph — "A complete victory over Thalberg", Wieck wrote in the diary, "Clara is the fashion, and drives everything else into the background." He had chinking proof of this in his pocket, as he gleefully notes, in the shape af 1035 florins clear profit. Of more importance, however, was the moral victory which found expression in the open admiration to which Grillparzer as the mouthpiece of Vienna, gave voice in the verses which appeared in the *Wiener Zeitschrift* for Jan. 9th, and which are among the most beautiful that he ever wrote:[1]

CLARA WIECK AND BEETHOVEN.
(*F* minor Sonata.)

A great magician, tired of world and life,
Murmuring, shut his genius in a shrine
Of diamonds, and secured it well from men,
Then cast the key into the ocean depths,
And died.
In vain the busy horde of little men
Strove round about it; for no master-key
Shot back the bolt; and all its magic slept,
As slept the master.
A shepherd child, playing upon the strand,
Watching the hurried, self-imposèd search,
Thoughtless yet thoughtful as girls use to be,
Lets her white fingers fall into the flood
And seizes, raises, holds the wonders key.
She hastens, while her quickened heart beats fast,
And flies to where the shrine is watching her.
The key fits, and the lid flies back. The spirits
Rise from the depths, and bow submissive heads
Before this gracious and pure-hearted mistress
Who leads them with white fingers, while she plays.

Other equally successful concerts followed, and there was a suggestion of Clara's receiving a court-appointment in spite

1) Left among Clara Schumann's papers, in Grillparzer's own writing. The first impression appeared in the *Wiener Zeitschrift für Kunst, Litteratur etc.* No. 4 Jan. 9th. 1838.

of the difficulties created by her being a foreigner and a Lutheran.

CLARA TO ROBERT.

"(March) 3ʳᵈ 9 o'clock.

Fischhof has just been here, and has been playing Mendelssohn's octet with me; a really great work, which, however, has not been in the least understood here. His enemies have made merry over it, and thought it *Schmarn* [1]. . . . These people ought to be burnt together with their works. Before this I played Fischhof some of your *Phantasiestücke*, which he liked extremely. My favourites are *Die Fabel, Aufschwung, Des Abends, Grillen*, and *Das Ende vom Lied*. I like the *Davidstänze* very much, too . . . . but I must honestly confess that often they are too like the *Carnaval*, which I like the best of all these little pieces.

. . . . I like it beyond measure, and revel in it every time I play it. I am not at all pleased that you have sent me such magnificent copies. Why are you so extravagant? If it comes from you, I should love it even if it were on blotting-paper. For the rest, I send my best thanks. I am hugely looking forward to the second sonata, it reminds me of many happy and painful hours. I love it, as I do you; your whole nature is so clearly expressed in it, and it is not too incomprehensible. Rut one thing. Are you going to leave the last movement just as it was formerly? It would be better to alter it a little and make it more easy, for it is really too difficult. I understand it of course, and play it as well as I can, but people in general, the public, even the connoisseurs for whom one really writes, do not understand it. You do not mind my saying this — do you? . . . . You are so industrious that you make one's brain reel. You want to write quartets, do you? One question, but do not laugh at me: do you know the instruments well enough? I am looking forward to it, only please be *very lucid*. It hurts me too much when people do not understand you . . . .

But now for the chief thing. I talked to Father a great deal about you to-day, and he told me that he was quite inclined to be friendly to you when we came back; you are to be the friend

---

1) *Translator's note*: A kind of pan-cake: the phrase is used contemptuously of anything of little value.

of the house again . . . . that he had written to you privately from
Dresden, to say that he would never give his consent in Leipsic,
but that he certainly would if we moved into any other large city[1]),
and I have promised him . . . . that I would never remain in Leipsic,
but that I could never love any other than you. He gave me his
consent, and wrote it in my diary[2]).

. . . . But I have not told you the most important thing. I have
quite decided not to live in Leipsic under there circumstances. Consider, dear Robert: I cannot earn three pfennig by my art in Leipsic,
and you too, would have to work yourself to death in order to
earn what we need. That would depress your mind, and for me?
I could not bear that. No, let us do as suggest: We will come
here, or you can come first, give you paper to Diabelli, Haslinger
(a very respectable firm) or Mechetti (a vigorous, and enterprising
young man). In the fisrt place your work will be paid as well
again here, in the second, you are certainly far more recognised
and respected than in Leipsic, and in the third, it is such a
pleasant, cheap life here, that is, of course, considering the size
of the town. What beautiful surroundings! And then I too, am
thought far more of here than in Leipsic, I am received by the
highest aristocracy, loved at court, and by the public. I can give
a concert every winter which will bring me 1000 thaler (easily)
with the high prices of admission which they have here[3]). . . .
Then I can, and will, give a lesson every day, that will bring in
another 1000 thaler during the year, and you have 1000, what
more do we want? . . . . In a word, we can lead the happiest
life here, while in Leipsic we are not recognized, and Leipsic too
is a town, which a spirit such as yours could not bear for long,

1) Wieck alleged as the reason for his refusal the insuperable difficulties which must arise for them in Leipsic where they had constant
intercourse with Mendelssohn and David, both of whom were able to
live in a grand style.

2) This entry of Wieck's in Clara's diary ran: "March 3rd early (conversation) with Clara about Sch., that I will never give my consent to
Leipsic, and Clara quite agrees with me, and her view will also never
alter. Sch. can opera-tize, philosophize, be as enthusiastic, idealise as
much as he likes; it remains settled that Clara can never live in poverty
and obscurity — but must have over 2000 thaler a year, to spend."

3) The total receipts from Clara's 3 concerts amounted to 1035 florins
C. M.

but where you would live amid nothing but worry, and where too, you could not continue to care for me, for you would become weary of life. Do not think that I have exaggerated at all; Father spent an hour to-day in placing before me everything that I have written to you .... He even said, 'If Schumann does not like to be a long time in Vienna without you, I will do this for him, I will go with you to Vienna'. You see from this that my Father is quite kind, so do not be cold towards him, he wishes us well. .... He quite realises that I will never give my heart to another, and to give my hand without my heart — a father like mine does not do such things."

"The 4th 9 o'clock.

.... I am always dissatisfied with myself now, in spite of the applause. The greater the applause, the more dissatisfied with myself I am, for expectations increase with the applause. Neither this, nor any title[1]), can make me proud. One thing only could make me proud — You! — I do not believe what people say about the title, there is no truth in it, for the religion is an insuperable obstacle.   .   .   .   .

Several connoisseurs, and Fischhof among them, were with us, to-day, to hear the *Phantasiestücke* and the sonata, which made me quite happy again. They liked it all, and I revelled in the music. I liked the former immensely, much better than yesterday. *Fabel, Grillen,* and *Warum?* This question is so charming, and speaks so directly to the heart, that no answer is needed. The *Ende vom Lied* is the most beautiful end a song has ever had; in places it reminds me vividly of Zumsteeg. But the sonata too, is quite too beautiful. Someone thought that there were passages in it which made one half afraid of you — I am not afraid. .... I have not played the *Études symphoniques*, to my great annoyance. Just think! it happened unluckily that all the other solos were in minor keys, and so I had to give in.

.... I am very tired of travelling now, I long for rest; I should very much like to compose, but it is quite impossible here. I have to practise in the morning, and till late in the evening we have visitors; by that time my mind is quite exhausted, as you

1) *Translator's note*: A reference to her possible appointment as pianiste-in-ordinary to the Emperor.

most see by my letters, for they often show signs of an absolutely empty head — but you can always recognise the heart, for that remains unaffected by the events of the day.

It is with me as with you, there are just such alleys in my heart, but they are smaller and there are more of them. My mind has hardly had time to look round in one of them, before it stumbles on another, and so it goes on perpetually. I cannot stick to one idea, another comes at once — but it is your fault, I do not know what will come of it. I always comfort myself with the thought that I am a woman after all, and they are not born to compose."

"The 8th.

I shall arrange to go away from here soon, for these visits from all my adorers are more than I can bear. I can understand that you love me, because I love you so much, but I do not know why these others love me; I am cold, not pretty (I know that), and as for art? that counts for nothing, for the greater number of my suitors know nothing about it.

— But what shall I say? Is this the same Herr Schumann who 3 years ago would not play to his most intimate friends, who now lets himself sink into the depths of the world of tone and improvises before Count Reuss, and to the rusting of silken clothes? Have you become such a good-natured fellow? . . . . But, joking apart, I am really glad that you do not follow your whims so much! Certainly you will once more have won a great many hearts by this means, and I am glad of that.

You want to know what my heart was like in 1837? You think that I had a secret from you? You are not serious, these are only phrases from the past. I will tell you everything, for the present I will only say that that winter in Berlin my heart was more at peace, though it always beat unquietly when I heard your name, or played something of yours. During those 2 years there were days on which my melancholy knew no bounds — one evening when we were at the *Wasserschenke* and you passed by our table. Ah! Robert, — then I could have wished I were in my grave, I became quite ill, and trembled violently, and this lasted the whole evening, and that night in bed I should have liked to weep, but I could not, only I prayed to God I know not what. I never before knew the effect of prayer — now I know it. —

My portrait is finished, it is like, but flattering. To-morrow, I play in the theatre for the 2nd time; on the 18th, at a concert for the benefit of the widows of members of the University; on the 25th for the benefit of the citizens; and on April 6th (if we are still here) at Merk's in a trio with him and Mayseder. I want to leave, something seems to drive me away, I have become so restless all at once. To-morrow, my opponents have determined to hiss me off the platform, but, as you yourself said, I wear a coat of mail. Do not be offended with me became I have written so dreadfully badly, but consider that I am standing, and the sheet of paper on which I am writing lies on the chest of drawers. Each time I dip my pen in the ink I have to run into the other room. — I cannot write you a letter on the way, but only a few lines before we leave.

Now, farewell; write to me, as always, in pure, true love, as I have just been doing to you. —

My spirit is always with you."

Even before this letter was finished the event which Clara had spoken of on the 4th as impossible on account of the "insuperable obstacle of the religion", took place, curiously enough without its having been expressly mentioned in the letter. She was nominated as pianiste to the Emperor, an honour for which Wieck had greatly longed, and which, at the outset of her whole artistic career, placed the 18-year-old girl at a goal which was of the utmost importance in the eyes of the world, and which had the greater weight on account of her being a foreigner and a protestant, and on account of her extreme youth, since by this nomination she was placed beside seven older colleagues, amongst whom were Paganini and Thalberg. Wieck, radiant with joy, relates in the diary, how, on March 7th, the minister, Count Collowrat, personally informed him of the nomination. "The minister assured me", he says, "that it was without precedent, and might never happen again, because she is a foreigner, a protestant, and too young. The Emperor good-naturedly replied to the suggestion, 'Well, if it is agreeable to Clara, and she seriously desires it, I will make an exception'.

On March 15th the letters patent, dated the same day, were given to her. "I never payed 4 florins — which the stamp cost — and a new Austrian ducat, with such pleasure", Wieck wrote in the diary. He knew well enough why, for although it was merely a title, with no salary, yet it was by no means without money value. Not only did it open to her for future journies the prospect of recommendations from the Imperial Chancery, but it assured her, as an Austrian subject, of the special protection and support of the Austrian ambassadors in every country, and finally gave her, as a Viennese citizen, the right to remain in the capital for any length of time.

She had now, more than ever before, to experience the truth of the saying, "Much honour, many enemies", and indeed Grillparzer's poem in the Viennese paper had already given rise to a press feud as to whether or not Clara's interpretation of Beethoven was correct, in which Saphir ranged himself with her opponents. Now, on the other hand her honorary title brought the pianist-in-ordinary many claims, countless requests that she would take part in charity concerts, which could not well be refused, but which strengthened Wieck in his resolve to leave this land, which threatened to become too "dear" to him, as soon as possible. "We must leave," he wrote on March 17th, "Henceforth Clara will only lose." In the midst of these thoughts of leaving and travelling, came Schumann's answer to Clara.

ROBERT TO CLARA.

"Leipsic March 17th 1838.

How shall I begin to tell you what you make of me, my love, my noble love! Your letter raised me from one joy to another. What a life you open before me, what prospects! As I read your letter again and again, I feel as the first man may well have felt when his angel led him through the new, young creation, from height to height, where one beautiful view was continually lost in another still more beautiful, and at last the angel said to him:

'All this shall be yours.' Shall all this be mine? Do you not know that it is one of my oldest and most cherished wishes that it should some day be possible to live for a number of years maybe, in the city in which the noblest in art was called forth — surely in part by the beauty of the world around — in two artist-hearts, the city in which Beethoven and Schubert lived? Everything that you have written to me, in those dear, true words, brings home to me that I must soon leave. — —

.... Shake hands then — our minds are made up, I have seriously considered it, my intense desire, our goal — Vienna. We shall leave some things behind — our native land, our relations, and Leipsic in particular, which is not a bad place after all — parting from Therese and my brothers will be a sad day's work for me — and finally my home, for I love this soil, and am a Saxon, body and soul. You too, are a Saxon and must separate yourself from father and brothers — when we go away together it will be as if morning and evening bells sounded at once, but the morning bells are prettier — and then you will rest on my heart, the happiest heart — *it is decided*; *we go*!

.... If only it were possible to win the love and confidence of your father, whom I would so gladly call father, whom I have to thank for so much of the joy of my life, for advice — and also for sorrow — and to whom I should like to give nothing but joy in his old age, so that he might say, 'They are good children'. If he knew me better, he would have spared me many a pain, he would never have written me a letter which made me two years older — well, the pain is over, it is forgiven — he is your father, he has brought you up in the noblest way, he would like to weigh out the happiness of your future in a balance, to know that you were quite happy and safe, as you always have been under his protection — I cannot blame him — in truth, he wants you to have the best there is on earth.

What you write to me of him, that he talked to you quietly in our favour, has surprised me, and delighted my heart.

.... Write me a couple of words to say what I am to expect, and how I am to behave myself. For I too, do not entirely understand what he has written in your diary. Copy it out for me exactly .... forgive my suspicion; is it possible that your father only wants to get me out of Leipsic? I tell you, I should not like to give up my life in Leipsic until a word from him has made me certain of you . . . . But nevertheless, Vienna remains my goal from henceforth. . . . .

By putting all this into other words you have spread a veritable chart of the heavens before my eyes, which has its own mists indeed, but has abundance of cheerful light, so that I cannot look at it without rapture. A new sphere of activity calls forth new powers. You will rejoice in me when I draw strength from your presence and through it grow ever nobler. Cares will not be wanting; time obliterates one line after the other from the fair poem of youth — but our art will remain to us then, and — above all, the youth of love."

"Saturday afternoon.

. . . . I have . . . . learned that nothing gives wings to the imagination, like expectation and longing, such as I have experienced during the last few days when I was waiting for your letter, and composed whole books full — curious, mad, pleasing stuff. — You will open your eyes when you come to play it — in fact I could often burst for sheer music, nowadays. — And I must not forget to mention another thing that I have been composing. Was it an echo of what you once said, when you wrote to me 'I often seemed like a child to you' — in short, I felt as if I were in pinafores again and then I wrote 30 quaint little things, about twelve of which I have selected and called *Kinderscenen*' ('Scenes from childhood'). You will enjoy them, but you will have to forget that you are a virtuoso — they have superscriptions such as[1]), *Fürchtenmachen* — *Am Kamin* — *Hasche-Mann* — *Bittendes Kind* — *Ritter vom Stecken-pferd* — *Von fremden Ländern* — *Kuriose Geschichte* etc. etc. and how should I know what? In fact it is all there before your eyes, and they just ripple along. But, Clara, what has been happening to you? You say that I am to write quartets — but 'quite clear, please'. — That sounds like a Dresden young lady. — Do you know what I said to myself when I read that? 'Yes, so clear, that she will lose hearing and sight'. . . . . And then, 'Do you know the instruments well enough?' — Yes, that goes without saying, young lady — how else could I venture to attempt it! But I must praise you all the more for being reminded of Zumsteeg by the *Ende vom Lied*,

---

1) *Translator's note*: "Creepiness"; "In the chimney corner"; "Catch-who-catch-can"; "The begging child"; "The knight on the hobby-horse"; „From foreign lands"; "A strange story".

— it is true that when I wrote it I thought, well perhaps after all it will end in a merry wedding — only at the very end the pain about you came back to it, and it sounds like wedding and passing bells mingled.

— I should like to know how things are to be in the summer. I will be reasonable, but 'friend of the house'? — that will not do any longer. There cannot be any pleasure in this situation until I am recognised by your father as the future son of the house, even if he only does it silently and without promising you to me. If he will do this, he shall not repent it. I would do anything to please him. Or was he only trying to give you a pleasant hour in Vienna, by his words, and will he forget it all again afterwards? You have such winning ways — if you speak to him about us again, hold him to his word so that he can make no excuse later. Fall upon his neck and say to him, 'Dear Father, do it, and bring him home sometimes, since he cannot part from me'."

Later.
. . . . "The more I think over Vienna, the more tremendously I like it. In the house such a housewife, in my heart such a beloved and loving wife, and in the world an artist such as it does not get every day and whom it will know how to prize, — I myself, young, respected, in a new cheerful sphere — enough to live on — beautiful country — cheerful people — recollections work which will keep us busy and loving — many pleasant and honourable connections . . . . Who would not live happily there? — Your father must say yes, it would be a sin if he refused.

. . . . In other respects my life has gone on so quietly for the last three months that it can only offer the most glaring contrast to yours, which would bewilder me if I were in your place. I am up early, generally before 6 o'clock; those are my most sacred hours. My room is my chapel, the piano my organ, and your picture, well, that is the altar-piece.

. . . . If only you knew how I value your opinions about every-thing even those which do not directly concern art itself; how your letters refresh my spirit — so write to me of what goes on around you, of men, customs, and cities. — You have a good eye, and I so much enjoy following you and your thoughts. One ought not to be too absorbed in oneself and one's own interests, or one loses one's keenness of perception for the world around. It is so beautiful, so rich, so new — this world. If I had said that to myself more often in earlier days, I should have got further and have done more by this time.

. . . . I am not surprised that you cannot compose at present, when there is so much coming and going around you. To create successfully one needs happiness and perfect solitude. Possibly you may be happy now that you know that I am, but this will not enable you to compose anything that requires thought and hard work. I could have wished you had studied the composition of fugues, since there are good theorists of music in Vienna — do not put off doing so if you ever get another chance; it is a pleasure in itself, and it brings one on. Bach is my daily bread; I go to him to be refreshed and to get new ideas. 'Compared with him we are all children', was said, I think by Beethoven. Why do you never play anything but the fugue in $C\sharp$?

. . . . Apropos, what will you call yourself? Wieck-Schumann, or the other way round, or just Clara Schumann? — how nice that looks, as if it must be that."

"Monday, March 19th.

Sweetheart, if only I could find one word which would comprise everything that you are to me — but there is none. I reverence you — let me say it — as a higher being, I know your heart, and mine. And then how happy you will make me by your art! When I told you that I loved you simply because you were so good, it was but half true — for in you everything harmonizes, so that I cannot think of you without your art — and I love one thing with another.

. . . . And now to end, my dear Clara. — Answer me soon, if it is only a line, to relieve my mind — do you hear? — else you will do me a real injury. . . . What has the Prince done to you, that you can no longer endure him? Write and tell me; it interests me.

. . . . You are always writing to me about connoisseurs, and that one must compose for connoisseurs in particular — why Clara, they are just the stupidest — you can see them all at David's quartet-evenings. You understand what I mean, don't you?

. . . . To the grave, and after, Your Robert."

CLARA TO ROBERT.

"Vienna, 3. 4. 1838.

I am very tired from the journey, but never too tired to gossip
with you, my dear Robert, or rather, since I have become a Viennese
now, my *'herzallerliebstes Schatzerl'*[1]; if only it were always
possible.

. . . . You will ask were I have been; so know, that I have
been in Hungary, in Pressburg, in order to escape from the endless
invitations here, and to get thoroughly rested, though I hardly
succeeded in the latter, as I had to play in the theatre at Pressburg twice during a visit of 4 days, and the day after to-morrow
I have to play at the *Burg*[2] again, by the express wish of the
Emperor. It will be the last time in Vienna. You see how much
I have to exert myself here, though I am always so tired now,
and so weary of playing, and yet, heaven knows, when I play in
public I always play with the same enthusiasm.

There was a great noise in the theatre again yesterday! I only
wished that you could see an audience here for once, the people
have quite an Italian fire. Concerts for the inhabitants Buda-Pest[3]
are endless, and are always crammed. A stall, for the day after
to-morrow, costs 10 florins cash; standing-room 5 florins; and a
box 50 florins cash; and already they have all gone. But now
for our chief business. First of all I must kiss you with all my
heart, for your dear, delightful letters, they are always my best
reward after such great exertions. But I could cry too, to think
that so soon it will all be over, for whatever happens we leave
for Graz within a fortnight; we do not know, however, how long
we shall stay there, and I do not know either if I am to play in
Munich or not, as Lachner gave us a bad impression of Munich;
so you see that I cannot possibly tell you of any place to which
to send a letter, and it makes me quite miserable to think that
perhaps I shall hear nothing from my dear, good Robert, for a
long time to come! But listen! just write another very long
letter, add something to it every day, and at the next opportunity

1) *Translator's note*: "Darling of my heart", this particular form of
the idiom is in the Viennese patois.
2) *Translator's note*: The imperial castle in Vienna.
3) There had just been a flood there.

I will let you know for certain, and then you can send it to me. Please, do not be angry because this letter is so short, but consider that it is 10 o'clock and that I am writing with a heart full of anxiety, standing in my room. For you must have your letter on Sunday, do not think that I could now the heart to let you wait again. You shall have a detailed letter from me, from Graz, in which I will answer many of the things you said in your last letter.

.... In the carriage to-day, we spoke of you, and I told him (father) again that he could say what he liked to me, I would never give you up, and I say to you again that my love knows no bounds, if you wanted my life to-day I would give it for you.

In 4—6 weeks we shall be in Leipsic; what will it be like, when first we meet again? — Oh God! I could cry and laugh over it — shall we ever again speak to each other alone? God knows! .... Excuse this scrawl — I cannot help it. But in haste

Your Clara.

Yes, yes, your Clara is a — I do not know what I want to say. Farewell, my dear Robert."

Already at the beginning of January, Robert had told Clara of a passage in a letter from Liszt to the Music-dealer, Hofmeister, in which, speaking of Clara, he said: "une jeune personne sachant exécuter avec énergie, intelligence et précision des morceaux de ma façon est un phénomène excessivement rare à tout pays, et tout à fait introuvable je crois dans celui que j'habite à présent. Chopin et plusieurs autres artistes m'en ont déjà beaucoup parlé. Je désire vivement de la connaître et malgré ma paresse de locomotion je ferai presque un voyage pour l'entendre". The wish for acquaintance was naturally mutual; consequently it was a great pleasure that Liszt came to Vienna before their departure. From April 11th, the day of his arrival, when, as the diary puts it, he "flung his card in at the window", to April 20th, when Clara and her father left Vienna, the intercourse with Liszt dominated her thoughts "He is," Clara wrote to Robert, from Graz, on

April 23rd, "an artist whom one must hear and see for one-self. I am very sorry that you have not made his acquaintance, for you would get on very well together, as he likes you very much. He rates your compositions extraordinarily highly, far above Henselt, above everything that he has come across recently. I played your *Carnaval* to him, and he was delighted with it. "What a mind!" he said, "that is one of the greatest works I know." You can imagine my joy.

More vivid, however, and clearer, more sharply-cut and more characteristic, is the picture of Liszt's personality and of the effect which he produced on the two travellers, which is given us in the diary, describing the immediate impression made by him.

"We have been hearing Liszt," it says on the 12th, "He cannot be compared to any other player — he stands alone. He arouses terror and amazement, and is a very attractive person. His appearance at the piano, is indescribable — he is an original — he is absorbed by the piano. . . . His passion knows no bounds, not infrequently he jars on one's sense of beauty by tearing melodies to pieces, he uses the pedal too much, thus making his works incomprehensible if not to professionals at least to amateurs. He has a great intellect, one can say of him that "his art is his life".

The 13th. Liszt played Weber's *Konzertstück,* (he broke 3 brass strings in the Conrad Graf, at the outset). Who can describe it? The want of tone in the bass did not hamper him in the least — he must be used to it. His movements are part of his playing, and suit him well. He draws one into him — one is absorbed in him.

The 14th. I played a gallop as a duet with him — he plays Clara's *Soirées* from note, and how he plays them! If he knew how to control his strength and his fire — who could play after him? Thalberg has written the same. And where are pianos to be had which will respond to half what he can do, and wishes to do?

The 18th. A concert of Liszt's — *Konzertstück* by Weber on Thalberg's English piano — *Puritaner-Fantasia* on the Conrad Graf — *Teufelswalzer* and *Étude* (twice) on a 2nd Graf — all three beaten to pieces. But it was all full of genius — the applause tremendous — the artist quite at his ease and very affable — everything was new, astounding — in fact — Liszt. — In the evening, Clara played him Schumann's *Carnaval,* and also his own *Pacini-Fantasia.* He behaved as if he were playing with her, writhing his whole body about."

On April 20th the Wiecks left Vienna and turned next to Graz, where, on the 28th, Clara played in the theatre with great applause but with little satisfaction to herself. "My playing seems to me so dull now," she wrote to Robert on the evening of the day of the concert, "and I do not know why, but I have almost lost the desìre to travel any further. Since I have heared and seen Liszt's bravura I feel like a school-girl."

After this remark of Clara's, Liszt's opinion of his young colleague, given in a letter from Vienna[1]) is of special interest. "I was fortunate enough to make the acquaintance of the young, and most interesting pianist Clara Wieck, who during the past winter has deservedly made an extraordinary sensation here. Her talent delighted me; she has perfect mastery of technique, depth and sincerity of feeling, and is specially remarkable for her thoroughly noble' bearing. Her extraordinary, and remarkably fine rendering of the famous Beethoven sonata in F minor inspired the celebrated dramatic poet Grillparzer to write a poem in which he honours the charming artist."

---

1) From the *Gazette musicale* printed in the *Neue Zeitschrift für Musik* 1838 No. 32 Oct. 19th 1838.

CHAPTER V.

HOPES AND PROJECTS.
1838.

Not without fear of new and severe conflicts had the lovers looked forward to the time when Clara's return to Leipsic should unite them once more in the same place, without, however, removing the external barriers which hitherto had made this nearness to each other a source of bitter-sweet torment. It is true that Clara joyfully believed that she could see a change for the better in her father's attitude of late, and that she would be able to impart this hopeful frame of mind to Robert, yet she by no means deceived herself into believing that even under the most favourable circumstances there were not fresh trials of her love in store. In spite of her concert-weariness therefore, she was by no means pleased when Wieck suddenly gave up the journey to Munich, which he had planned, and decided that after a short stay in Vienna, in order to hear Thalberg, they would hurry home from Graz. She had the more reason to be anxious about this as during their homeward journey it became evident that her idea that Wieck had fundamentally altered his point of view was an illusion; whether it was that he had never thought of it seriously at all, or whether he had changed his mind again in the mean time[1].

---

1) According to the wording of the "Explanation", which Clara regarded as a "Consent", the former, in spite of Clara's conviction, seems the more probable. The "consent" resembles a "prohibition" as much as one egg does another.

The concession of a superficially harmless and friendly inter-cours between her and Schumann, as if nothing had happened, could not disguise the fact that as far as he was concerned it was no more than a truce, by which time might be won to arm more zealously for a fresh outbreak of hostilities[1].

She had sent Schumann news of everything from Graz, and had tried to propitiate him as far as possible: "Listen; be friendly with my Father, and conquer your pride", she had written at the end of her last letter from there. In the same letter she had been able to tell him of a new honour which had been done to her: her nomination as honorary member of the Viennese *Gesellschaft der Musikfreunde* (Society of the Friends of Music).

During her two days stay in Vienna, on her journey through, she was received kindly and simply by Thalberg, who treated her as a colleague, and whose art once more made a pleasant impression on her. As Wieck strikingly expresses it, "Liszt played with inspired affectation and Thalberg with inspired simplicity". But for this very reason his playing did not awaken in her that dissatisfaction, which she had experienced when listening to "the greatest of musical jugglers", as Lenau called Liszt. On May 13th, the travellers, after a short rest in Dres-den, entered Leipsic once more. "Everything is the same", wrote Clara in the diary. She had already received Robert's letter, begun on April 14th, in Dresden: a letter full of mean-

---

[1] In a further communication (referred to below) to the Advocate Einert, on May 30th 1839, Schumann says in speaking of this time, that Clara wrote to him from Vienna in the spring of 1838, "My father has now given his consent, though upon conditions. When, shortly after this, they both returned to Leipsic, Herr Wieck came to see me in my room, but without mentioning the matter. This wounded me, and I avoided him from this time when I could. Irritated by this, he soon began openly to express himself as opposed to our intended union, yes, and to depreciate me in every possible way in the eyes of his daughter, as well as of others."

ing, characteristic of Schumann's inner life at this time, though its enormous length — it is a volume in itself — makes it possible to give only a short extract, having direct bearing on the important points in the situation at the moment.

ROBERT TO CLARA.

"Leipsic April 14th —38th. Saturday before Easter.

First of all I wish my dear, true girl all happiness in her new dignity. — Indeed I spent three of the silliest days, after your nomination, and tried to float, to fly (towards a conductorship, towards a crown) — but at last I withdrew into my own heart once more, looked in it, and found out that all is well as it is, and that even so you will go on loving me. Clara, dear heart, first darling of my soul — my love is worthy of you — you make a child of me — I wander among men like one of the blessed. — .... I have hundreds of things to say to you, and it is with me, as it is with the spring outside, everything is sweet and ready to burst into blossom .... Clara, there are the most important things to be discussed — for in truth, we are not advancing, and it appears that I shall never get a wife if it depends on her.

Well then: That your father has begun to growl and grumble again, has once more made me very angry with him. I begin to think he is a Philistine, who is wholly encrusted by material thoughts and interests, who has become entirely devoid of feeling, who looks upon young love as a kind of childish disease, like measles etc., which everyone must go through, even if he dies of it. Add to this, arrogance because you have received such great honours.

.... It is so human, that .... hatred towards him often rises in me again, so deep a hatred that it does indeed look strange beside my love for his daughter. But if he has so many times taken back what he promised, he will do it again — in a word, I expect nothing from him, we must act for ourselves. Listen, therefore, my Clärchen — as soon as possible, I will go to Vienna, and I wait for your consent to this — Since I made up my mind, and the beauty of your plan flashed before my eyes, the ground has seemed to burn my feet .... There is however one important question as to which you must set my mind at rest. Can you trust yourself, regardless of your father's consent, to give me an

approximate date for our union? I think if we settle on Easter
1840 (two years from now) you will have fulfilled all the duties
of a child, and need not reproach yourself, even if you have to
tear yourself away by force. We shall be of age then, you will
have acceded to your father's request to wait for two years more
— there can be no question of putting our love and constancy
to the proof, for I will never give you up . . . . Give me your
hand then; in two years' time our watchword will be . . . ."

"Saturday afternoon.

. . . . Oh! Clara, there is such music in me now, and such
beautiful melodies always — Just think! since my last letter, I
have finished another whole volume of new things. *Kreisleriana*
I shall call it; you, and thought of you play the chief part, and
I will dedicate it to you — yes, to you and to no-one else — then
you will smile so sweetly when you find yourself in it again. —
My music seems to me, just now so extraordinarily intricate with
all its simplicity, it speaks so entirely from the heart and affects
everybody to whom I play it, as I now often like to do. When
will you stand by me as I sit at the piano — ah! then we shall
both cry like children — I know that — it will overpower me. —
But cheerily, my heart! Your dear, slender form stands ever by
my side, and soon, soon will you be mine. — I will tell you something about last night. I woke up, and could not sleep again —
and then (I) thought myself deeper and deeper into you and the
life of your soul and your dreams, and all at once I cried out
with the whole strength of my spirit, 'Clara, I call you' — and
then I heard quite loud, as if near me, 'Robert, I am with you.'
But a kind of horror fell upon me, to think how spirits can hold
intercourse with each other across great stretches of land. I shall
not try this calling again; it has thoroughly unstrung me."

"Sunday, early.

. . . . I have almost given up all hope of seeing you in the
summer. I have had to put up with it for two whole years, so
let it be the same for another two. What is it, when we have to
steal a few minutes in deadly anxiety in order to get a couple
of distracted words together? — No, I want you altogether, for
whole days, whole years, the whole of eternity. I am no longer

a knight of the moonshine. If you very much want me, I will
come; but otherwise let us leave it, it leads to nothing further
.... I will have you for my wife, it is my sacred, earnest determination.
I have put all else behind me. . . ."

"Sunday afternoon.

.... There are so many things I should like to know about
you, but I understand how difficult it is for you to answer all my
questions. I value your last letter very highly; believe that. As
for me, I write to you only too willingly. I have plenty of time.
And do you know why? Because since the New Year, I go to
bed at 9 o'clock, and get up at 5 — it answers very well. And
then, I feel so well, and am so conscious of the joy of living. It
is a divine thing, this temperate, hard-working life. Yes, I believe
— and you ought to take note of this confession — that my me-
lancholia is nothing much, and that it was only the result of sitting
up into the night. I can be ever so cheerful. But indeed, it is
you, Angel of joy, who now guard me under your wings . . . ."

"Monday, towards evening.

. . . .
My first memory of you goes back to the summer of 1828.
You were painting letters, trying to write, while I was studying
the *A* minor concerto, and you often looked round at me. I remember it as if it were to-day[1]).
.... How little knowledge of the heart your father has shown!
We, who have daily spent many hours together for years past, who
have been brought together so intimately by art, who stand in
such a delightful relation to each other as regards age, who have
such similarity of mind who belong to each other in the deepest
impulses of our hearts, who are bound by a thousand kisses, by
the memory of many blissful hours, and now by ring and word
— and your father thinks to part us — no, my Clara, I no longer
fear anything, and I will win you for myself, under the protection
of a higher Hand, which has united us up to this hour . . . . my
patience is exhausted. I will get the better of such a Philistine.

---

1) Here follows in the letter, the statement — already printed above,
p. 81 — "I must tell you of one mistake" etc.

And if, when he begins about you, he does not treat me with the greatest respect, and speaks of you as of a fortune which I do not deserve, he shall learn to know me. There is no need for him to tell me who you are — I know it without him."

"Wednesday the 25th, early.

Yesterday, I saw everything yellow[1]), all day — in the trees, on the wall, and everywhere I saw postmen — and again nothing came. How sad that has made me! In the evening I went out in the open air, as I do daily for some hours, and went towards Connewitz because that is the road which reminds me most constantly of you. The clouds had created a poem of towering alps — wonderfully deceptive — and I thought, 'Those are the dreams of youth — from the distance, they look safe and firmly grounded — near at hand they vanish in mist. If only one thing is left us,' I thought further, — and then the sun went down, and I thought of you — that you like him, would return."

"Wednesday the 9th (of May) 4 o'clock in the afternoon.

I have just received your letter, my beloved, and I will only tell you that during the last few days I have suffered much on your account, and that your loving letter has banished all my cares. Now, mine shall go immediately, so that you may get it tomorrow. Is it possible that you should be so close to me? . . . .
Now Adieu, my beloved Clara — I am the same as ever, and always   Your Robert."

Among the most interesting events of this summer — apart, of course, from their love troubles and joys — stands the friendship which she formed, with Pauline Garcia, who came to Leipsic on May 24th, in the course of her first tour on the continent, accompanied by her mother and her brother-in-law — the violinist, de Beriot — and who at once made the most favourable impression on Clara. The two young artistes, so nearly of on age, and both alike inspired by the highest artistic ideals, felt themselves mutually attracted, and began an almost

---

1) *Translator's note*: The postmen were dressed in yellow.

daily and most intimate intercourse which was not even interrupted by Clara's visit to Dresden, which lasted from July 2nd
to August 7th, for Pauline also spent this time in Dresden. Thus
they laid the foundation of a friendship, which was to unite
them unalterably until Clara's death. "In her," says the diary,
"I found a lovable, unassuming girl, and the soul of a genuine
artist. She seems to be an exception to all other singers —
she takes a vivid interest in music. She is full of fire, and
seems to resemble her sister, the late Malibran de Beriot.
Pauline Garcia is certainly the most musical singer now living.
She sings very dramatically, always without notes, and ac-
companies herself without looking at the piano, and she can
play anything by ear. They were the pleasantest artists who
had visited us for a long time."

The diary mentions Schumann's name only twice: "On
May 28th I went to Lützschena with Schumann and Wenzel";
and on Sept. 27th, "Alwin and to Sch. to Vienna", and between
these two comes "August 14th — —!" (The day of their
betrothal.)

On August the 7th. Clara who had been in Dresden for
a time went back to Leipsic, accompanied by the de Beriots.
She had been much annoyed during the latter part of her
visit, by the continual persecution of the pianist, Louis Rakemann of Bremen, who unfortunately was not to be persuaded
of the complete hopelessness of his suit, and who besides
depressing Clara by constantly calling on her, endeavoured
to irritate Wieck still more against Robert, and to make her
doubt his constancy. In the latter object he had, needless to
say, no success.

CLARA TO ROBERT.

"Wednesday Aug. 15th 1838.

. . . . Shall I see you to-morrow, or Saturday, or Tuesday?
You were very cold to-day! Were you angry with me? — I kiss
you in all love   Your Clara.

Your *Noveletten* are magnificent! I revel in them — but that is nothing new to you! — Everything about you sings exquisite songs, indeed your whole heart revels itself in beautiful melodies. — *Sei mir gegrüsst!* — Do you know that song? I am very fond of it. —"

ROBERT TO CLARA.

"Leipsic, Aug. 21st /38.

I have kept on meaning to write to you; but my soul is out of tune. Your father embitters my whole life. He treads everything under foot. . . . What lies has he been telling Becker[1]) again? And do you not defend me at all? . . . .

. . . . Enough of this, but all these slanders haunt me even in my dreams.

. . . . In fact, you have a quite insupportable lover at present; there is nothing of Eusebius left in me. Ah! one glance from you . . . . and my heart would have confidence and faith again. So contrive that we may soon be able to see each other. . . .

— Are you really fond of me? —"

CLARA TO ROBERT.

"Thursday, Aug. 22nd /38.

Dearest Robert, you are a good but wicked fellow, and it is true that Eusebius has gone a little way from you. If you are serious when you write that I do not defend you at all, it is very wounding to my feelings, for I should have thought that you must know me well enough to know that I would not sit still and let anything be said of you, but on the contrary I fight to the death if my Father ever begins to me about you, which very seldom does happen directly, now. But you did not mean it, no, no, you are still my gentle Eusebius. Think no more of Father's calumnies, they are not worth feeling hurt about, and you must remember that it will all alter; Father must learn to appreciate you. I think it quite just that you should not make advances to him,

1) Their common friend, Becker, from Freiberg, whom they called "The arm from the clouds", was on a visit to the Wiecks from Aug. 11th to 26th. Cf. Schumann's letter to him of Aug. 6th 1838. *Briefe, Neue Folge* p. 111.

but you must not be disturbed by such petty calumnies and insults, which spring only from a desire for revenge — it would be best if you did not hear them at all, people ought not to tell you of them; I never would.

Fischhof's letter made me extremely happy . . . . *do*, do everything that he tells you. All will be well — only have patience . . . . Do not offend him; and stay with him until you have found a lodging; he would never forgive it you if you refused him this! You will be comfortable with him. You will find a batchelor household and you ought to enjoy that thoroughly, for when once a wife is there, all is over! . . . . You poor man! . . . . . .

. . . . Vesque, indeed, can, as he says, be of use to you, and he is too, an excellent man. Oh yes! I think you will soon find friends. Count Sedlnitzky[1]) was one of my patrons; he seems to me a good man, and has great power. He can rule out anything that he likes, and leave in anything that he likes. It is he who reads through everything before it can be printed.

. . . . It just strikes me that Fischhof has a pretty sister, so now will you stay with him?   .   .   .   .

. . . . Adieu, my dear. Let me know if you will speak to me on Saturday at 11 o'clock. With the greatest impatience

Your Clara."

CLARA TO ROBERT.

"Thursday afternoon Aug. 30th.

Dear Robert . . . . Father suddenly does not want to come with me to Paris, and says I can travel there alone, to which I also have made up my mind, whatever happens I must go there. Possibly he thinks he will get me to give you up when he says, 'Either you will give up Schumann, or we will stay at home for the whole winter!' . . . . Oh! how mistaken all you little people are! — You do not know how fast we are bound to each other. Adieu, my Robert! —

Your C."

"Friday. Mid-day (In Schumann's hand: Sept. 1st /38.)
. . . . Did you pass by our window yesterday? Alwin thought he saw you. Did you happen to hear part of you *Novelette*? —

---

1) Censor in Vienna, under Metternich.

How beautiful the song in the middle is — There is much of Eusebius in it; is not the whole work coming soon? — *Fremde Leute, Fremde Länder* is simply too beautiful! The beginning (that is all I know of it) is simply fascinating. Your music is so entirely your own, it takes hold of one as if it would never let one go and then again it bears one off into the most exquisite dreams; if only I could express the effect it often produces on my mind.

. . . . As you read these lines, listen, and you will hear a soft whispering, and you will easily divine that it is

Your true Eusebiana."

ROBERT TO CLARA.

"Sept. 8th /38 1).

Is it really possible that I am to hear you to-day for the last time, for the last time as Clara Wieck? — A shiver of delight runs through me. Or is it perhaps, for the last time altogether? That is written in the stars, it is our part to be true and to act. A year ago to-day we shook hands again for the first time, with such hopes: do you remember? And to-day? A hundred people crowd between us, you hardly know where I am; often I could cry aloud for very anguish. Now the curtain will soon descend — and then it is future alone that can give us strength. — To-day I feel so dreary again — Yesterday and the day before I passed by your window, thinking that you ought to come — I saw hardly any light, not so much as a shadow. When the thunder-storm was going on I stood for half an hour opposite your house — and you; did you feel nothing? Do you no longer think of me! Do you not know that in a few days' time I am going away? Then your voice will no longer be able to reach me; then for a long, long time I shall hear it no more, that beautiful clear voice. . . . Alas! that common sense must govern every hour and every minute at present. I wish I could write to you in music only. But true love shows itself also in common sense which advances with circumspection and draws ever nearer to the goal. That is better than elopement and languishing — is n't it? . . . . It is settled then,

---

1) Clara's concert in the *Gewandhaus*. "The applause was great," she writes concerning it in the diary, "I had to repeat the *Erlkönig*, which was truly a great exertion."

that I go on the 22nd; I shall go by Zwickau, Schneeberg, then
to Freiberg for a day with Becker, and through Dresden to Prague,
where I shall stay 1 or 2 days perhaps, and will write to you ....
.... Adieu .... When can we speak to each other??"

"Sept. 9th.

All that I heard yesterday, and all that went on around me,
is still like a dream. It was a mixture of rage and blessedness,
which nearly overcame me. I had hidden myself away in the
dark, so as not to catch anyone's eye. I meant to say a great
deal more to you to-day; but I am too excited, and I will go and
dream and think of nothing but you.

Adieu, you most, most beloved, you heart's treasure, you good,
good Clara of my heart you, yours I am, and yours only."

On September 18th the *Neue Zeitschrift für Musik* spoke of
Clara's concert as: "The finest and most fragrant flower of
romance, which has been offered us for a long time; and a
demonstration of technique brought to faultless perfection."
In the following number, on Sept. 21st, a poem appeared at
the head of the page.

DREAM-PICTURE ON THE EVENING OF THE 9th.
To C. W.

An angel-child floats down from on high,
Sits at the keys, and the songs sweep by;
As her fingers wander over the no es,
In magic circles above her floats
    Ring upon ring
    Of figures wild;
    The old elf-king,
    And Mignon mild,
    A hot-mettled knight
    Arrayed for the fight,
    A nun on her knee
    In ecstasy.
And the people who heard it began to rejoice
As if they applauded an earthly voice.
But the angel-child shrank from the tumult, and flew
Back to her home in the heavens blue.

A. L.

And in a later letter Schumann confessed that he himself was the author of these lines.

In October he set out for Vienna, prompted by motives with which we are already acquainted. Wieck made his consent to Clara's mariage dependant upon Schumann's taking up his residence in some city other than Leipsic, and being able to show proof of an assured and sufficient income. This was indeed difficult to justify from one point of view, but from another, his demands were perfectly just, if only he had meant to act fairly. But at the same time he made no attempt to conceal his conviction that Schumann would never have the energy to exchange Leipsic for another place. Hardly had this conviction been upset by the fact of Schumann's migration to Vienna, before he terrified Clara by announcing that under no circumstances would he ever give his consent to their union, and he even went so far as to threaten that he would do everything he could to prejudice Schumann's arrival in Vienna and the plan for the establishment of his newspaper.

It is uncertain if he carried out this openly proclaimed plan, and sent letters of warning to everyone in Vienna on whose assistance and influence Schumann had to reckon for the success of his enterprise. Even without this, things could hardly have come to a happy conclusion. The extraordinary condition of the press in Austria previous to the revolution of March 1848, the slow dragging of the business through endless law-courts, owing to the nervous suspiciousness of the authorities, especially where a foreigner, like Schumann, was concerned, caused the success of his plan to be questionable from the outset. In addition to this, it was difficult for the practical Viennese to understand his nature; straightforward as he was, the very disinterestedness of his intentions made him but little pliable. Hasslinger laughed in his face when he gave vent to the idea that truth, properly expressed, could offend no-one, and would pass the censor untouched.

ROBERT TO CLARA.

"Vienna Oct. 8th 1838.

You will have received my letter from Prague safely[1]). I have much to say to you, my beloved Clara, of things grave and gay, that happened on the journey. . . . .

. . . . I had numerous misfortunes by the way; I found that I was a regular school-boy. Not only did I arrive without a cap — having lost it off my head in the night, twelve miles from Vienna — but I nearly lost my head as well. — A stage from Prague the mail left me behind; I ran after it as fast I could; my powers were already coming to an end; no-one heard, until finally I reached the last carriage and sprang on the step in order to hold on. I had been in this dreadful position for only a few seconds, (the carriage was going at a gallop) when the door to which I was holding, sprang open — how I kept up there I do not know, but if I had fallen, it would have been all over with me. . . . .

. . . . Wherever I go, here and in Prague, you cannot think how fond they are of you; though everyone has a bone to pick with your father. I am using this colloquial expression because he does not deserve such abuse, least of all from people who are barely capable of passing an opinion on his coat, to say nothing of what is inside it.

The young musicians of Prague amused me very much; they were good-natured souls as a set, but they talked perpetually of themselves and their idylls, and such things, and praised themselves a great deal . . . . I found nothing of real interest. . . . .

. . . . I see this much, that the paper will have to be edited in quite a different fashion here — to its own disadvantage and that of all honest people. . . . .

It is a question whether I shall get permission at all. Begin, already, to think over what we shall do then! Shall I confide in Hasslinger? He behaves in a very kind and friendly manner; yesterday, he sent me some remarkably fine Havanna cigars. But I have purposely told him nothing of my plans as yet; one must not ask for everything at once. It will all be decided in the

---

1) *Jugendbriefe* p. 289.

course of the next few days. To-day, I am going to Prince Schön-
berg and to Sedlnitzky, who has promised to receive me. You
shall have news as soon as I can tell you of anything good.

I like Vesque best of all. It is rather unfortunate that his
opera is just going to be given. It contains many nice things, but
is a hodge-podge of what he wants to do and cannot do, and
of what he can do and does not want to do, and seems to me
written in every possible manner and style. He himself calls it
an experiment.

. . . . And, while I can at least distract myself, you, poor thing,
sit still, perhaps crying in your room; or perhaps you are no
longer even in your father's house. — Noble and wonderful being
— how can I ever repay you?

. . . . I could not help smiling a little a I read in your letter
that they promised you, 'You should lead the happiest life, if you
would give me up.' They will dress you in gay clothes, and take
you about the town, and give you oranges to eat. That is what
they call a happy life.

. . . . I had thought it all out so nicely; I thought that your
father would see from this step how serious I am in wishing to make
our future secure, and that he would let everything go on quietly,
and if I won a position, would give you to me with good-will.
But now he has brought forward the deadliest and most hostile
artillery.

. . . . Once more — I can say nothing except, leave him at
once. A poor little simple girl ought not to have been treated
like this — least of all you, whose nobility of character I can find
no words to express.

Farewell, act, act; unchangeably your Robert."

CLARA TO RORERT.

"Evening 8/10. 38.

My dear Robert, I am alone for a minute, and I use it at once
to tell you once more how dear you are to me . . . . and to ask you
if I too, am still as dear to you! Ah! yes, my Robert loves me
still, I know that. I wonder where he is now — in the theatre, or
the coffee-house, or at the piano dreaming of the beautiful times
that are to come? Ah! how I long to play duets with you again,
as we often used to do in earlier days. . . . Father has been at

home for a whole hour, it is 9 o'clock now, Mother is coming, and I can write no more to you! I could cry; cannot I have one little hour to myself!" . . . .

"the 10th.

. . . . Father has decided on a little tour to Dresden for a while, in order to give another concert there; later he means to take me to Munich — and then perhaps I shall persuade him to take me to Paris. Since he came back from Dresden we have not spoken another word on the matter; I have made up my mind to try to obtain by fair means what I shall certainly never get by force, and I mean to carry it through." . . . .

"the 17th.

. . . . I have been much touched, my heart's Robert, by your firm desire that I should go away; I am glad to know, in any case, where to go, and I do not need the money[1]) . . . . I hope that I shall not need it; much pain as my father has given me, yet I should be sorry to leave him before the time comes for which I have given you my promise . . . .

. . . . I am very anxious about you just now! You do not like Vienna, and I feel more and more strongly that you can never like it, and that you must be simply longing for our music . . . . and it is all my fault! — If you do not like anything whatever in Vienna, do not think that I should be unhappy if I could not live there; oh! no, I will go with you where you will, even to death itself!

. . . . Send me some address which I can use when I write to you on the journey, I dare not write to yours as father has said that he would know how to take fresh precautions in every town. . . .

. . . . It will be the third concert to-morrow, but the hall always looks so dreary to me; I keep looking round to see if the door will not open, and then all at once I am torn out of my dream by Frau Voigt, or someone, who asks me if I have heard that you have arrived safely in Vienna! Ah! how I wished that you

---

1) *Translator's note*: In a letter dated Oct. 7th, Robert had told her that Dr Günz of Leipsic had 1000 florins in trust for her, and that she could draw on this at any time.

could come with us to-morrow to hear these magnificent melodies from *Egmont*. How beautiful Clärchen's song is, and how great is the overture — often I cannot contain myself when I hear such music. What a blessing music is to me, what a comfort when the pain is great. . . ."

"The 21ˢᵗ, evening.

I scarcely ever see Reuter now . . . . The other day, when he had just been with us, Father began to talk to me of what Reuter had wanted, and I had to show my Mother every scrap of paper that I had in my pocket; it revolted me, but I controlled myself and did not show it. NB. dear Robert, if you are going to write to Father I advise you not to do it until you have accomplished something in Vienna, and then I believe you will impress him less by anger than by perfect composure . . . . You know all this better than I do, I only wanted to remind you of it, for in your last letter you were too warm.

We have music every Sunday at present sometimes at Mendelssohn's, then at David's, then with us, etc. Whatever anyone brings, is played; next Sunday I am going to play Prince Louis' *F* minor trio, at David's. Verhulst was with us the other day, and brought with him the andante which he had just composed for his new quartet, which I liked extremely, and which showed much talent.

I am playing very badly at present, with so little mastery, and so uncertainly that it is dreadful; I feel it, an yet cannot alter it."

Clara's repeatedly expressed fear that Vienna had proved a disappointment to Schumann, and that it was not after all really the right place for him, seems — if we may judge by his next letter — to have been groundless.

"Vienna delights me," he wrote on October 23ʳᵈ, "in truth I am enjoying myself again, for the first time for many years. I like wandering in the country, and here there is so much to enjoy with everything still in its autumn glory . . . . It often seems to me as if I had been living in prison for these last eight years, without knowing it. . . . But I will in no wise blame my dear Leipsic, in which, on the other hand, the mind can draw freer breath; only it has nothing to offer to the eye, and nothing in the way of enjoyment of life which can be compared with what this place offers."

The present, which separated them, made him more anxious than did their common future. While he did not fail to realise the difficulties of Clara's position, caused by the conflict between her duties towards her father and towards him, and by the necessity, so long as she was exposed defenceless to suspicion and misunderstanding in her parents' house, of avoiding everything that might increase and embitter opposition, yet he was always disturbed by the thought that she would yield too far. In the same letter, he writes on the next day (Oct. 24th):

"I do not know what to say about your having once more come to an understanding with your father. You are — pardon me — like a couple of children together. You cry, he rages — and then it all goes back to what it was before, and we never get any further. I have sent a short, cold, proud answer to his letter. Possibly you know of it; he really must cease to be so petty; I will put up with it no longer, I shall tell him the truth, as is fitting.

. . . . You, with your good heart, stand mid-way between us — and that often troubles me. But that he should care so little for your feelings that he harrows them deliberately . . . . that he should destroy the flower of your youth for all the world to see — we have suffered this too long. It will not be possible for you to belong to him and to me at the same time. You must give up one; him or me."

"Thursday the 25th.

Cross out the previous page if you like, it is very bad-tempered. It is your father's fault. But now let us be friendly again, my Clärchen — — —."

He had in truth misjudged the situation. He could count unconditionally upon Clara's steadfastness, let what would come, but on the other hand his favourable impression of the circumstances at Vienna was soon to prove an illusion, and Clara, with her suspicion, drawn from his letters, that Vienna was not the right place for him, might be right — not only on account of difficulties with the Censor, which dragged on for months, but also for reasons which sprang from the characters of those with whom he came in contact. Wieck, with his keen eye for men's weaknesses, had rightly recognised the difficulties which would arise from this. And Schumann himself, though for the time he was inclined to look only on the bright side, could not be blind to the fact that there was no solid basis which gave promise of satisfactory work in the future: "There is no lack of feeling for what is good, but there is lack of unity and co-operation", he writes in the same letter, and he, like Wieck, comes to the conclusion that some leader, such as Mendelssohn, is required, who would break up the little coteries, and would fuse together and rule over the opposing spirits. It is evident that he did not consider himself suited for the part, and considering his character this is not to be wondered at. It is perhaps, even more suggestive, that in speaking of the characteristics of the chief musicians he repeatedly praises their friendliness, obligingness, and kindliness, even when mentioning his opponents, the "Haslinger Clique", but, with the single exception of Thalberg, whom he calls "The first and only artist, as regards art, society, and manners, whom I met in Vienna", he never placed confidence in any one of them. But his very praise of Thalberg, that he had "something well-bred and simple (in the best sense of the word)" about him, shows at once, in all friendliness, the usual artistic level, and it is easy to read between the lines what he missed in the other artists of Vienna.

The same letter gives other impressions, two days later:

"At the theatre I was extremely delighted with the orchestra, the chorus, and the soloists. Lutzer is a theatre-princess: her curtsies overcome me, and so does her deprecating air when she has sung well, for she can sing, and breathe, for two. But as I have said, I should not like a woman like that for my wife. Gentiluomo is a charming woman, and in Vesque's opera she is really kissable. But I think Wild is the most gifted artist in the *Kärnthnerthor* Theatre.

.... I have also just seen Taglioni. She has, I will not say enchanted me, but at all events, made me strangely happy; she does not excite one so much as calm one; and with this, it is all uncommon and yet natural, everything is new, and yet well-known. See, that is the secret!

Here are a couple of flowers from the graves of Beethoven and Schubert — I found a pen too, on Beethoven's grave, and of steel; was not that splendid?

How sensitive Clara was to the discords which echoed faintly from his life in Vienna, is shown by her comment on the receipt of this letter on Nov. 2nd: "Many of your words made me very unhappy — I do not know why. I believe it is the cares which weigh on you."

It is only natural that such expressions of Schumann's, and still more the news of the probable falling off of subscribers when the paper should be published in Vienna, should have made Clara very anxious, all the more, as she thought that she saw that Schumann, inspired by the most passionate desire to marry her as soon as possible, was inclined to over-estimate his financial position, and had eventually decided to take from his capital the sum which was still wanting to his income. "It need not necessarily be 1840," she writes to him on Nov. 5th, moved by this anxiety, "If it is not possible then, we will wait for another six months." "My heart does not say that," she adds, "You may be sure of that, but my reason does, for not only I, but you too would feel unhappy if we could only just struggle along.... Perhaps I shall be able to earn something this winter, and next, and then everything will go as we wish. Only do not be angry with me for taking such a reasonable tone, but believe me, my heart has already suffered much at the thought that in 1840 I may still be unable to come to you! I will not let you take anything from your capital, if once one does this, one never stops doing it, there are always fresh reasons for it; no, that will not do, I would rather eat my heart out longing for you, for another half year. It will all come right, do not doubt, my dear, dear Robert; we have borne much already, there is no pain which we cannot conquer."

But to Schumann, who in the mean time had worked himself up again into a very optimistic attitude towards the future, an attitude wholly unjustified by the facts, these loving and wise words had a truly crushing effect. "I had not expected," he replied to her on Nov. 13th, "that you would so suddenly lay my last hope in ruins .... I thought that at least we entirely understood each ether .... and now you wrinkle your brow and speak once more of 'Cares for the future' .... and you have so discouraged and enervated me in deed and thought, that I should like to go away from here at once .... If only you could have waited quietly for the time to come, if only you had not snatched away the straw to which I was clinging .... We shall not succeed in living upon our interest alone. But we have between us a goodly possession for which thousands of other couples would fall on their knees and give thanks, we have head and hands with which to earn twice and three times as much as we need, but you want to be a millionaire, and then I should not care to have you. ... Clärchen, what would you call the parents who promised their children a beautiful tree and beautiful presents for Christmas, and then on Christmas Eve led them into a dark room and bolted them in? See, that is what you have done to me; you promised me a reward if I behaved well, and then put me off to an indefinite time, 1850 or -60 when I shall long have lain in my grave."

At the same time he must have written even more miserably and despairingly than he writes in these exaggerated lines to their common confidant, Dr Reuter. For Reuter was induced, Nov. 19th, to send Clara a letter in which, in his desire to help her and Robert, and urged by his knowledge of Schumann's easily excited nature — "You know that he — like you — flings himself with his whole strength into sad thoughts as well as into happy ones" — he begged her to suppress her anxiety as to the future, which he did not entirely share, and as speedily as possible to cheer Schumann again with a hopeful, encouraging word.

Clara, who received all these letters in Dresden, where she was giving concerts, was no less dismayed at her lover's reception of her words. "I am still dead tired from yesterday's concert," she wrote from Maxen on Nov. 25th, "but never too tired to love you and kiss you. Your two first letters[1]) made me so happy, that the last one pained me all the more. You have hurt me bitterly, which I did not deserve. I wrote that to you simply with the intention of quieting your mind, and assuring you that I am prepared for any fate, and if circumstances require it, I too would have patience for another six months. You have misunderstood me. — — Have you so little confidence in my word that you think I would break it? You know that I will come to you in 1840, I have promised you, and here with I promise again."

. . . .

"My good, dear Robert, love me still; for your sake I will give up that which I love next to you — my Father, I will follow you without his consent — that is much for heart to do, it is hard — *but I trust you*, my life will then a feeling lie in your hand alone, and you will make me happy." . . . .

---

1) According to their agreement, the letters had lain at Dr Reuter's during their journey to Dresden, and all three were given her together with Reuter's letter.

In the same letter — which Schumann, on Dec. 1ˢᵗ, greeted
with the words, "Your letter is beautiful, brave, animated, so
heart-felt. Clara, Clara, you surpass me in everything" — she
sent news also of certain events in Dresden.

"Maxen, Sunday the 25ᵗʰ/11. 38. 9 o'clock in the evening.

.... I have driven out here to-day, and have already been
for a walk on the great *Linde*. The winter landscape is so pretty
— it too, has its charm! How beautiful the snow looked on the
pine-twigs — ah! I thought so much of you! You asked me if
I cared for the beauties of nature. I thank you for it, my love
for you; since I have loved you, it is strange, I love nature too.
Formerly my love was too childish, and besides my mind was
not ripe to receive the beautiful, but now it is different, and if
one day I shall be able to enjoy nature on your arm I shall have
a still purer and more untroubled delight; at present your absence
always troubles me. Since you have been away, I suffer continually from oppression of the heart, and head-ache. . . .

I have now successfully got through two concerts here; to-
morrow I go back to the town on Wednesday, to Leipsic. — I
shall not go away again until Christmas, when I shall probably
go direct to Paris, by way of Cassel and Frankfort. . . .

Father's rapid determination to undertake the journey springs
in the first place from an easily pardonable vanity, and in the
second, as you have already guessed, he thinks that I shall forget
you in Paris and London . . . . I will show them all that there is
still such a thing as true love. . . .

I shall have to play in the *Gewandhaus* once more, and I do
it gladly for anyone who has played before a Dresden audience
has learnt what coldness means. I had two good concerts here,
but I care less for money than for the consciousness that I have
satisfied an entire audience — a consciousness which one never
has here, for the public does not know how to stir a finger. They
say that the applause which I have received here has been extraordinary — well God help the mediocre artist then!" [1]

---

[1] In the notice of these two concerts in the *Neue Zeitschrift für
Musik* of Dec. 21ˢᵗ (p. 201 etc.) it says: "Our audiences are decried as
cold and unsympathetic — this is not true; they have shown themselves
just the opposite to Clara Wieck."

ROBERT TO CLARA.

"Vienna Dec. 1st 38.   Sunday morning.

. . . . From you I receive all life, I am wholly dependent on you. I should often like to follow you as a servant and await your slightest sign.   Ah! let me say it once more, come what may — I will whisper to whosoever closes my eyes, 'One alone ruled my life completely, absorbed it into her inmost being, and her have I ever honoured and loved above all.' . . . .

Have you received my little poems?   Everything that I want to say is in them.   You will have to have a poet for your husband, and it is you who have made him one.   Forgive me, therefore.

I grows ever darker outside, but brighter within.   Take care of my little poems for me — they are the first for many years. Did they win a smile from you? . . . . I am now reading Nissen's biography of Mozart; it has struck me how much you were like him as a child . . . . Your last letter has made me happy again; you know the tone which brings me to your feet.   Love can do anything with me.   You are too good, too good for me.   I often pray for you, and wish that everything good may descend upon you.   And so fare thee well, my best beloved

Your Robert."

LITTLE VERSES TO CLARA FROM R. S.
Vienna 1838.

(The following poems were exquisitely written on 4 tiny sheets, which were fastened together and adorned with minute vignettes.)

To a certain Bride
who will have no man in the twenties for her husband.

1. A bride over twenty, a groom over thirty years old —
     So must the bud into the leaf unfold.

2.   Years of wooing more than five,
             No true lover can survive.

3.   · Laurel for the Queen of Art
              Is fit coronal:
              Myrtle for the maiden
              That is best of all.

4.   A sweetheart true belongs to me,
Who looks into her eyes will see
What woman's constancy can be.

5.   Truth hath never ruth.

6.   Egmont's true love Klärchen [1]) hight —
Oh! name of exquisite delight.

7.   Klärchen Schumann's name
Straight from heaven came.

8.   We wander afar —
Star severed from star —
Yet I follow alway
As night follows day.

9.   Decked with her name, my name shall rise
And then our blended harmonies
Will thrill the angels in the skies.

10.   Ransack the earth
For love like ours;
She brings me mirth
In April showers.

11.   We have suffered enough
Of sorrow and care:
Out of leaves sharp and rough
Springs the pineapple rare.

12.   Long, long she bids me languish
Ere she is mine indeed.
Peace, loyal heart, thy anguish
Shall win a double meed.

13.   Yet not too long;
You do me wrong.
The heart grows old,
And men grow cold.

14.   Should Florestan storm,
With Eusebius keep warm.

1) Schumann always writes the name with a K. But as Clara equally invariably wrote it with a C, her way of writing it instead of Schumann's has been uniformly employed in the letters.

15. Florestan wild,
And Eusebius mild,
Sun and foul weather,
Take them together,
Find both in me —
Sorrow and glee.

16. Jealous in truth is Florestan,
Eusebius trusts in his brother-man —
Which of the twain shall be dearest to thee?
Who most true to himself and his love shall be.

17. And shouldst thou seek to domineer
Rebels twain hast thou to fear —
Who will defeated be?
Who will have victory?

18. Then lead we thee with pageant to the throne,
And humbly take our place on either side. —
If one of us thou'rt ready to disown,
Will a like fate the other too, betide?

19. Oft have I let you look into my heart,
And watched how happily you gazed and gazed.
Is it not true, that often you would start
To find yourself there, and draw back amazed?

20. Yet did I show you all my thought,
Dark phantoms would your spirit grieve,
A fear that comes to me unsought —
Question me not! Love and believe.

21. Close, close to thy breast,
On thy heart let me rest:
Then whisper, "The best
Of all things in God's plan
Is an honest, true man."

22. Treat me not too lightly,
And do not prudish be:
Nor coy, nor yet too sprightly —
That's the wife for me!

23. Twilight gray,
Flickering fire:
"Come" they say,
"My heart's desire."

24.   At night, when you were very small
I oft came dressed as a spectre tall
And rattled at your door —
You bade me be-gone, as you shrieked, afraid.
Ah! could I now come in a ghost's disguise
You would open your arms in glad surprise,
And whisper, "A kiss all else before,
From my lover in masquerade."

25.   In a riddle we'd involve
Things that none of us could solve.
Read "Roma", mistress of the world,
Backwards. What meaning is unfurled?
Just now this topsy-turvy town
Between us two has settled down —
A bridge of soft lips we must make,
Kisses our messages will take.

26.   You saw a duck, you thought it a goose.
Certainly things play fast and loose.

27.   "Nay sir, let old times go;
We will forget."
Not so, not so.
Rather with fond regret
Count all the blessed days of long ago.

28.   Heaven smiles on the course of true love, they say.
Now, kiss me, sweetheart, and hearken:
The marriage that heaven has made, one day
No earthly sorrow shall darken.

29.   "Together will we live, together die;"
I spoke, and silence fell.
It was as if we looked across death's stream
And bade farewell —
Your loving eyes, so tender and so true,
Held my eyes in their spell.
"Together will we live, together die:"
In that all blessings dwell.

30.   When thy fair spirit quits this earth
I will follow thee into the dark unknown,
My guilt shall shelter behind thy worth,
And I shall reap where thou hast sown.

CLARA TO ROBERT.

"Leipsic Friday 7./12. 38.

How can I express my pleasure over the beautiful verses? ....
I could never get tired of reading them. I see you before me,
dear and good, and just as you are!

.... I have been back for nearly a fortnight and have not
yet had a minute alone — this is the first, and I am quickly making
use of it. .... I start at the beginning of January with a Frenchwoman — ah! I would rather take Nanny with me. I am so unhappy about her that it costs me many silent tears. . . . .
.... But how can you ask me to take care of your verses?
Are you serious? Long before your request came they were safely
locked up. They are unspeakably dear to me, and are never out
of my thoughts."

ROBERT TO CLARA.

"Vienna Dec. 18th. Wednesday 1838.

God greet you, sweetheart. You have made it Spring with
me, and golden flowers peep out; in other words I have been
composing since I got your letter; I cannot contain myself for
music. Here is my little Christmas present[1]). You will understand
my wish. Do you remember how you fell on my neck on Christmas Eve three years ago? If often seemed as if you were afraid
of yourself when you gave yourself to me like that. But it is
different now, and you rest on my heart, quiet and safe, and know
what it is you possess. You my love, my trusted comrade, my
gracious wife that is to be — when in two years' time I open the
doors and show you everything that I have given you, a cap, many
playthings, new compositions, then you will fall upon my neck in
quite a different way, and cry out again and again, 'How beautiful it is to have a husband, and so excellent a one as you'. And
then I shall be quite unable to restrain your joy, and you will
lead me into your room, where you have laid out your minature,
a writing-block on which to compose, a sugar slipper, which I

---

1) "*Wunsch*. To my beloved bride, Christmas Eve 1838." It is the
"first little piece" of the *Bunte Blätter* Op. 99, which appeared in 1852.
According to this, the inscription on the edition, "composed 1839"
should be corrected.

shall eat at once, and all sorts of things; for you will give me far more than I give you, I know. What happiness! Then we shall grow more and more silent, the Christmas-tree will burn more and more faintly, and kisses will be our prayers that it may ever remain like this, and that the good God will keep us together till the end.

This will be a sad year for me; I shall hum many a melody to myself, I shall often go to the window and look up at the stars as they sparkle, I shall spend the whole evening with you. ...

I mean to end the evening with a young man whom I have recently learned to know, a straight-forward, unspoiled character. I am glad to have found someone who finds it easy to understand me, and whom I believe to be highly gifted. He has run away from his parents for love of music; he thinks and dreams of nothing but music. He will distinguish himself later, so I hope. So far, I always have been most happy and industrious. This young fellow is partly responsible for it, but above all it is due to your two last letters which have so calmed me, and have so rejoiced my heart. Thank you, my Clara, for all that you do for me, a poor artist. ...

. . . . May heaven keep me so contented . . . . Only when I hear nothing of you for a long time, my strength begins to leave me. Then comes melancholy. It is as if it shouded me and wrapped me up in black clothes and garments; an indescribable condition. . . .

A thousand adieus, dear heart!

Do not forget your Robert."

CLARA TO ROBERT.

"Wednesday 26/12. 38.

Best thanks, my dear Robert, for your beautiful tender gift — it was the most beautiful that you could have sent me, for it came from your heart. It is odd that a similar idea had struck me, but I could not get it ready in time, otherwise I should have sent it to you — it was a little romance. Your letter was so dear, and you say how cheerful you are now, but Robert, look me straight in the face, is that really true? Do you not write it simply to cheer me up? — The festival passed very quietly with us, but there was tumult in my heart which felt as if it would break.

To-morrow it will be three months since you went away — ah! that was a dreadful day! I had never felt such pain. —

Thalberg arrived yesterday, and played here for 2 hours, carrying us from one state of amazement to another; he can do much, more than all of us (except Liszt), you are right in that, and if I were not a woman I should long ago have said good-bye to virtuosity; but as it is I calm myself somewhat, I shall always be a match for the ladies. Thalberg is an attractive artist, and I like him much better than I did in Vienna. . . .

. . . . To-morrow Dreyschock, from Prague, is giving a concert. He has a great deal of execution but no mind, and renders things in a horrible way. He had a tremendous success in the *Gewandhaus* — his rapidity imposes on people — Thalberg is a hundred times greater.

. . . . I am dreadfully anxious about my journey to Paris; when I have been listening to anyone like Thalberg or Liszt, I always feel so insignificant, and then I am so dissatisfied with myself, that I could cry! If only I had strength enough and could pull myself together I could do far more, but love affects me too much; I cannot live wholly and entirely for art as Father wants me to. It is through you that I learnt to love art, and hence too often I think of other things — you know what it is I want to say.

. . . . The horrid Frenchwoman is coming soon; I cannot bear to think of the parting from Nanny, the only person who understands me. . . .

The most heart-felt kiss from your true

Clara

Excuse my haste. My love does not pass so rapidly."

The opinion of Thalberg which she expresses in the letter is modified in the diary in a manner that is not without interest. "His playing," it says, "is beautiful, everything is perfect as well as full of expression, but the higher poetry is beyond him; he slurs over much in order to make a greater effect in the last page of a piece—in which indeed, he succeeds. His touch is exquisite, he never fails in anything." At his second concert, however, the applause was considerably less. His fantasia upon *motifs* from Beethoven was not liked as composition: "He ought not to have touched a theme of Beethoven's — he is not the composer for that. As a performer he is great, and yet above all stands — Mendelssohn."

The old year ended, and the new year began with an exchange of new hopes of happiness, pain at their separation, foreboding of new trials, and wishes and greetings, through all of which rings an unshakable faith in the ultimate triumph of loyalty.

CLARA TO ROBERT.

"2/1. 39 Leipzig.

My first greeting and kiss in the New Year, dear Robert. The year that has gone brought us much trouble, may the new one be more friendly towards us. Your letter on New Year's Day came to me like a ray of sunshine — I was sad — I do not know why. . . . . My journey weighs on my mind — what will happen to me? But He who has so often protected me, will not forsake me now. — I travel alone with the Frenchwoman. Father cannot leave on account of his business, and he said too, that he would not come to Paris — and why? Because he thinks it his duty to do nothing that may bring me nearer to my goal, and he would do this if he travelled with me, for I should earn more. Although I quite believe that he will follow me, yet I must say that Father's attitude of mind (he is doing quite right according to his opinion) has hurt me, and deeply."

"7th.

. . . . My heart is so heavy to-day; to-morrow I set out all alone with an unknown person!

I have put in your compositions, *Toccata, Phantasiestücke* etc. — it cost some strife, but I said, 'I will!'.

. . . . It is just striking 11 o'clock, I am dead tired, and I shall have to travel for 3 nights. Good, good night."

Accompanied by the dreaded Frenchwoman Clara set out on her journey to Paris on Jan. 8th at 5 o'clock in the evening. "Father could not come with me now, on account of his business, but he will follow", says the diary; but even at this very time Wieck had already decided not to do so, but to leave Clara to herself. It was a remarkable venture. What caused him to make it was the hope and expectation that Clara, alone in the great city, given over, defenceless, to be the prey of all the annoyances and dishonesties of business dealings, would become so conscious of his indispensability, of the impossibility of carrying on her artistic career without his support, that finally, when the choice was once more placed before her, she would decide for the father and against the lover. It was the last method that he attempted, and once again the weapon turned in his hand and directed its point towards himself. What should have been separated, was bound the more closely together, what was to have been won back, was lost for ever. Only as Schumann's wife was Clara to return to her parents' house.

CHAPTER VI.

IN FOREIGN LANDS.

1839.

The first halting-place on Clara's journey was Nuremberg. Here she was already to receive a fore-taste of the annoyances and difficulties, great and small, which beset the path of one travelling alone, and wholly dependant upon the good will of strangers, who are half indifferent and half hostile. The very elements seemed to have conspired against her. On Jan. 11th she wrote to Robert:

"God be thanked, I can write to you to-day, I did not think I should, for yesterday we were in danger of our lives 10 times; it snowed so hard that we had to drive across fields and ditches. How often did I pray to God that he would let us get happily through it all, just this once more. . . . Now it is all over, and I can write to my dear good . . . . in peace of soul. (I do not write your name down, so that the Frenchwoman may not be able to read it) I was in Zwickau and drank my morning coffee with Therese; ah! how glad I was to see my future sister-in-law, and both she and your brother were so good, so friendly.

. . . . To continue: I came to Hof, and the first thing I did was to go to Grau, the bookseller, and ask for news of Ernestine — what did I hear? . . . . She has . . . . married a Count Zedwitz. I could not believe it, so I wrote to her at once, and begged her to tell me what had become of her. . . . Ah! my dear, if that were true, we could enjoy our happiness as well again.

. . . . It feels so odd to find myself alone in a strange city, without any man to accompany me. I did nothing to show that I was so very unhappy at travelling alone, and that made Father think that I must have written to you to come here, or to Stuttgart.

. . . . Do you not admire my courage in travelling alone with an entirely unknown person? Indeed I did tremble a little the first night that I slept with her."

"Sunday Jan. 13th 38. After dinner.

I had planned to rest for a little — I have not been feeling well for some days — but I cannot, the writing-case lies before me, involuntarily my hand moves towards the pen and writes, 'God greet you, my dearest treasure! How are you? Do you still love me?' Ah! yes, my Eusebius is still true to me.

. . . . Now I must go and practise on a bad piano in preparation for the day after to-morrow . . . . Since I have been here I have been suffering from incessant head-ache, and it is entirely due to bad pianos; they are so harsh, so hard, they tear one's ear to pieces. The *Cantor*[1]) from Nuremberg has just come — good heavens! such a *Cantor*! Now I must end. Meanwhile, a warm hand-grip, my dear, good Florestan. . . ."

"The 14th. Monday.

Every day, every hour, I think that Father will suddenly take us by surprise. The orchestra has refused to play and so I have rapidly to study Thalberg's *Caprice*, in which I am a little out of practice. I have to write every note (which has to do with the concert) myself, send round free tickets, see about tuners and men to carry the piano, and practise in addition. It is rather much; I do not know where to begin first, and then there are all the uninteresting visits!"

"The 15th Tuesday.

To-day is the day for my concert, but there is no concert! Not only have I nearly been snowed up, but we are right in the water and cannot get out. The whole town is under water, for the river has over-flowed; in most of the streets no-one can get out of their house . . . . the water is rising visibly — it is terrible. Many strangers have come for my concert, but it is impossible for it to take place, and it is put off till to-morrow.

1) *Translator's note*: director of music,

.... I played to some of the local musical connoisseurs the whole of this morning. . . . I was very much carried away, *not* by the audience but by the music itself. . . . After the concert I will play the Beethoven sonata, and some of Scarlatti's and Bach's fugues, and your *Carnaval*, to some of them. . . ."

"Tuesday evening.

The *Musikdirektor* from Ansbach has just been here, I played to him, and he was so delighted that he gave me no peace — I must go to Ansbach! . . . .

. . . . To-morrow evening, after the concert, I am giving a little tea-party to which several music-lovers are coming, who have saved me much trouble — Mainberger [1]) in particular.

. . . . In true love, and with my whole soul Your bride."

Even before this news reached its goal, had Robert, on Jan. 15th, had written, in answer to the last letter from Leipsic:

"My beloved. I hardly know how to tell you how uplifted I was by your last letter. What am I in comparison with you? When I left Leipsic I thought I had experienced the worst. And you, a girl, gentle and delicately nurtured, for my sake are going alone into the great, dangerous world. What you have now done is the greatest thing that you have done for me. But since you have done this, it has seemed to me as if there could be no further obstacle in our way. I feel myself strengthened through and through. Someday you will be rewarded for your confidence, your independence. You are a wonderful girl, worthy of the highest reverence. When I wake at night, and the wind and rain drive against my window, and I think of you huddled up in the carriage, with nothing but your art, so absolutely alone except perhaps that in your mind you are surrounded by beautiful pictures of the future, then my whole heart becomes softened and moved, and I do not know how I have deserved so much love. I myself, as I have said, am as if transformed. People must see it in my face. . . . To see such courage in one's betrothed, gives one moral strength. In the last few days I have done work which would usually take

---

1) A music-dealer.

me weeks. It was like the time when we became engaged, in August 37. Everything pours out so easily. It is impossible to fail in anything. See! such power have you given me, my Clara; such an heroic girl must make her lover into something of a hero too . . . . If only I could follow you for a step or two, invisibly (or visibly either); I should like to keep you safe under my wings, like a good genius, so that no harm should come to you. Ah! Clara, how differently people love each other when they have to work and make sacrifices for one another."

"Jan. 16th early.

If only I knew at all how you are getting on! If only I could fly after you across the mountains. I did follow you to-day, on the map which always lies before me now, and saw with terror how great a distance it is from here to Paris. . . . But you would certainly be surprised if I suddenly appeared before you in Paris! You may expect anything of me. I too, believe that your father will come after you. He is probably enduring dreadful boredom, and trouble too. I would not have believed that he would ever have allowed you to travel alone, and indeed he certainly allowed it to come to this only because he did not think that you would have the courage. . . . .

. . . . You have called forth a symphony from me; I thank you for your dear lines; cheer me up sometimes, shake me, pull me up. Now, dear letter of mine, set out on your long journey. Go to her and utter a thousand sweet thoughts to her; tell her that she is loved as sincerely as anyone can be, and that she makes me absolutely happy."

"Saturday, Jan. 19th.

If I could see you just once more, sparks would fly from your eyes. You must look at once like a Madonna and a heroine.

Robert."

Unfortunately this cheery and inspiriting greeting by the way from her lover, went direct to Paris, and, like the other letters which were written after it, did not reach her hands till many weeks later. And yet just at this time Clara needed comfort, support, and advice, more than ever. Stuttgart, the second point on their journey, put her courage, her delight in action, her knowledge of human nature, to still severer tests. In the first place, the inexcusable conduct of Wieck, who simply left her without news, plunged her, — since from what he had said she still expected him to follow her, — into the most painful perplexity and confusion. On Jan. 20th she wrote to Robert from Stuttgart:

"I am very unhappy, since I have been away from home I have had no news from either Father or Nanny, and ah! for so long I have had no word from you, I do not know in the least how you are getting on! My concerts in Nuremberg and Ansbach are over successfully (in Nuremberg I won many hearts, and the parting cost me tears) but it has been a strain, I have not slept for 3 nights. . . .
I do not know yet, how it will be here. Lindpaintner, Molique, Bohrer, Schunke, are none of them here. . . ."

"The 21st.
As usual I could not have the theatre here; they said it could not be managed. To-day it is to be decided if I am to play at court. . . . I do not know what to think of Father! Just think! he has already had three letters from me, and I have not yet had one; all my hopes were fixed on Stuttgart. . . . If he leaves me like this in a foreign land, without news, without everything, I do not know what I shall do, I do not at all know whether I shall go to Paris alone! My situation is really terrible! If no letter comes from him, I shall leave soon, and shall be in Paris by the end of January. My God! what shall I do alone there? But I must have courage, must I not, my Robert? . . . . I believe he does not write because he is so annoyed that I had the courage to travel alone. If it is possible, my dear Robert, I will write to you once again before Paris."

CLARA TO ROBERT.

"Stuttgart Jan. 30th 39 (Wednesday evening).
Ah! dear Robert, what a long time it is since I had a chat with you, and even now I cannot say much. To the most im-

portant thing then, that affects me! By the way, I have at last
received a letter from Father, which only makes me cry; think!
2 pages of nothing but reproaches that I do nothing right, that I
make enemies at every opportunity, and I could see now how I
should get on alone, he was *not* coming to Paris, and in addition
to this, I must have seen for a long time that we no longer suit
each other etc. etc.; I cannot tell you how much all this has hurt
me, that even after not seeing me for a fortnight, Father should not
have a kind word for me. . . . I got the letter just as I was dressed
to go to court and you can imagine with what a lacerated heart
I went.

. . . . Now, listen! I made acquaintance with Dr Schilling [2]);
he became fond of me, and wrote much about me; we were together a great deal, and I did not know how to conceal my relation to you, from him. . . . He told me a great deal about his
paper [1]) . . . . but he also let fall that it would put an end to all
other newspapers (You can fancy how my head went round while
he was talking). He understood, seized both my hands . . . . what
do you think he said? He said, if all went well (which is not to
be doubted, as the greatest authorities are working at it) he would
take you (he cannot manage the editing by himself) as partner,
or some such thing (I could not quite understand him), and from
this time on, our happiness should be his care. The salary is
considerable, a large enough salary for us! . . . . If all goes well,
we must be here in a year's time. He is extremely kind but very
outspoken — I like that! I have confided our correspondence to
him — are you angry? He says, by the way, that if we come
here you must allow him to love me. . . . But now for the chief
point, could you decide to come to Stuttgart? Ah! how beautiful
the mountains are, which surround the whole city; it is delightful,
and the people are genuinely kind and sympathetic. They have
really overwhelmed me with kindnesses at here. . . .

Yesterday I gave a concert, which was fuller than any that
can be remembered here, and was equally enthusiastic. When it
was all over, dead tired as I was I had to play the *Erlkönig*. They
wanted me to give another concert, but I have not the time, and

1) Dr Gustav Schilling, music-teacher in Stuttgart since 1830, founder
and "permanent secretary" of the *German National Society of Music.*
2) *Jahrbücher für Musik und ihre Wissenschaft.*

I do not like playing again so soon, it is too great a strain. . . .
After the concert Dr Schilling and his wife came to me and we
talked about you until 11 o'clock. He spoke a great deal about
you (your individuality and intellectual abilities) but I have not
time to write it all down.

I played to the Queen, two days after my arrival, and was
given a beautiful and valuable jewel, quite to my taste. They
were very nice at court. . . . To-morrow evening I go to Karlsruhe, and the day after to-morrow I shall probably play to the
Grand-Duchess; then I go to Strassburg, stay there Sunday night,
and then on to Paris. How shall I get on? . . . . You will receive this letter through Dr Schilling, answer him in a friendly
manner, he means kindly — he is also the cause of my taking a
young and talented girl[1]) with me to Paris; she is so fond of me
that she left her parents no peace. . . . She is a nice girl, and
is respected by everybody. Her father is poor . . . . but is ready
to spend everything on her, and it was touching when he came
to me with tears in his eyes, and said, 'I am trusting to you the
dearest thing that I possess'. — I could not help crying. I like
the girl, and the thought that I may perhaps make her happy,
makes me happier than it can make her; I will give her as much
attention as I can, for she has talent and she loves the thing. . . .
I believe I have acted as you would wish, have I not, my dear,
good Robert?

. . . . I am curious to know if Father will miss me. Ah! I
cannot tell you what Father's letter made me feel. . . . No greeting from my Mother, ... it is as if I had no parents at all! How
possible it is to have parents, and yet to have none! Now my
life is bound to you, and to you alone, you are my support, my
hope!   Your Clara."

CLARA TO ROBERT.

"Karlsruhe Feb. 2nd 39 Saturday morning.

I cannot leave Karlsruhe without writing a line to you, my dear
Robert, I know you will be glad to have even a word. To-day
I am playing at court, and to-morrow we go to France. Ah! Robert,
now I am no longer in the same country with you, I shall no

---

1) Henriette Reichmann.

longer even hear German! Well, it is in God's hands! To-morrow (Sunday), when you ought to receive my letter and Dr S.'s, and while you are reading them, I shall be on the way to Strassburg. . . .

My heart is somewhat lighter now that I have a real friend with me, who understands me, to whom I have confided everything, and who is the best girl in all Stuttgart. She is very fond of me — she sends you word that she will not be happy till I am — I cannot be so bad, when everybody is so fond of me. . . .

I found it very hard to leave Stuttgart, — I cried all day, and looked at the mountains and thought, 'Who knows if you will not soon be happily climbing these mountains your Robert'. Dr Schilling is really the most self-sacrificing of men, and he desires our happiness. Dear Robert, I beg you to show the greatest confidence in him, he has mine. He says that if he saw the least sign that I should not be happy with you, he would do everything he could against us, just as he is now doing everything for us, because he is so fond of me. . . .

. . . . I have had no further letter from Father. I wrote and told him that I was going to Paris (D. V.) that I really could not make up to him for what he would leave behind him in Leipsic, and therefore I did not urge him, I had courage enough — for everything. . . . . I see now that I can stand alone in the world without my father, and things will not remain as they are much longer, soon, soon I shall be with you, and then I shall know no sorrow, only what is yours shall be mine. Heaven wishes me well. Has it not just given me another dear friend — and some day it will give me the dearest friend of all.

A thousand kisses from your faithful bride

Clara Schumann.

'Oh! name of exquisite delight'!"

The letter which Schumann began on Feb. 4th, told her of his intention of giving music lessons in Vienna — "How am I better than Chopin, Moscheles, Mendelssohn? . . . . In short I mean to become a regular piano-teacher, and to compose in addition" —. Thinking her to be already in Paris, he had written: "But now anxiety and care about my beloved pilgrim and Lady-errant often bring my heart into my mouth". To him Clara's plans for the future, were a by no means entirely pleasant surprise.

"Yesterday, I received your letter from Stuttgart," he wrote on Feb. 6th; "hardly had I recognised Schilling's hand in the address before I suspected what had happened. Clärchen, Clärchen, what have you been doing? I say that with a threatening finger, and yet you meant it so well, and are always thinking that you must do something for me, and do so much, such dear and hard things — ah! you are a dear girl, and once more you have so touched my heart that I do not know what I would not do for you — even join with S., though it would cost some struggles; but must wake you out of some part your beautiful dreams, and not with kisses indeed, but by gently pulling a lock of your hair till you wake. The case is this: S. is a very industrious writer of books, something like what Czerny is as a composer. . . . Thus he has edited one bad book after another, his material is beginning to give out and hence he has been struck by the idea of a musical paper in which he can at once fight himself, and parry all attacks which people may unfortunately take the trouble to make upon his bad books. S., as a sensible, clever man knows the public too well not to realise the value of well-known names, and to understand how to use them to his advantage . . . . in short, — that I may tear you completely from your dreams — he is an excellent speculator and I am afraid, from what he has already done, that he is also a most accomplished humbug and flatterer. He has done the most extraordinary things . . . . and he stands in the worst repute with his book- and money-factory — And you, you Pianist-in-ordinary, you who have been betrothed to me for the last three years, in one word, you, Clara Wieck, can let yourself be so imposed on by a man like this, that, as you yourself told him, you are afraid that his paper will kill all others, and can write to me that, 'All great authorities are taking part in it' etc. to me, who have already had experience in this matter, and have already had my say and truly in a different and deeper sense than S. can ever attain to . . . .

. . . . Frankly, Clärchen, you have hurt me a little; I thought you had a higher opinion of me than ever to think of fellowship with such a braggast. What am I to say when a man like S. writes, 'I will support you if you will promise me to make this girl happy,' in other words: 'If you, who have already edited ten volumes of a newspaper, will promise me, who have not yet begun, such things, then you (that is me), who already make 3—400 thalers a year by the newspaper, shall receive from me (S.), who for the first three years will have a deficit of 3—400 thalers a year, the half of my income —?' Is this not very arrogant, and silly as well and vulgarly expressed; just in a matter which requires such delicate and careful handling? Where is the salary to come from? Besides what is the use of a new musical paper which is not the result of the requirements of the time, and particularly in Stuttgart where there is no music trade, no visits of artists, and no public. And this to me who have every right to believe that I am capable of detecting the slightest signs of advance in the times, who as a composer am making considerable progress and am preparing a sphere of activity for myself in the future, small though it may be. I cannot help smiling at S. speaking of of my 'intellectual abilities', when so far as I know he has hardly even a superficial idea of my aspirations, and I would not give a *Papillon* for all his efforts. Do not say that I am perverse and proud; I know what I can do, and shall be able to do yet, and what others do. But others do not know what I can do, because I am always going on learning, and am always working hard. Or do you really think that one of those 'authorities' could say approximately, where I shall stand as a composer in ten years' time? Not one of them, for they have no creative power themselves, and they see things only when I have long passed on.

Now dear heart, have I not told you the whole truth? And you are satisfied with me, as satisfied as I am with you? What has happened between you and S., seems to me so natural — you came to a strange town, you with your good heart full to overflowing because for weeks you had not been able to give vent to your feelings — S., knowing about us already, sees you, in your most enchanting mood, falls in love with you in all honour, reads in your eyes and lips what you can no longer contain, feels himself fortunate in having drawn a secret from so interesting and famous a young lady, perhaps really means it honestly at the moment, promises to make you happy — and you, my nineteen-year-old fiancée, who know well enough how a little cap becomes you, seize hold of it with both hands, and are delighted that you have found someone to whom you can say what you think — in short, Clärchen . . . . you thought, 'He is my, and our, whole hope, how nice it is to find a man like this, who by dint of the greatest self-sacrifice will make you and your lover happy etc.' This is what my girl thought, and how she speculated in secret. Now, my love, my dear one, indescribably dear, sit on my lap and lay your arms and head on my shoulder so that I may feel the dear burden properly, and may know how happy I am. — Now, do you think I would write a touchy, cold letter to S.? You make a great mistake there. He will receive, by to-morrow itself, the most friendly letters of thanks. . . .

. . . . I cannot, indeed, judge of his enterprise, and besides it is by no means ripe yet. He writes to me quite vaguely, and says little. I shall wait for futher developments, therefore. For the rest, I should like to go to Stuttgart; I know the city; it is charming, and the people are much nicer and better educated than the Viennese. Finally, what would I not do for love of you, so long as it was consistent with the respect which is due to me as your future husband. Above all things, therefore, perfect independence. . . . One thing more, I believe that S. opened your letter to me; there were two wafers on the envelope and two scraps of paper on the top. You never seal like this. Do not forget to write and tell me, if you remember. . . .

Now as to the the dear girl whom you have taken to yourself. You have done a good deed there, and it is quite in accordance with my way of thinking. Such action will always be rewarded in one way or another; it becomes you, and I love you for it. Tell me, is she young? A pianist?

Does she not cost you too much?"

That Schumann dit not immediately refuse the proposal of the questionable "speculator", was due to his diminishing hopes of making his paper succeed in Vienna.

"An official in Sedlnitzky's council," he wrote in the same letter, "told me that Sedlnitzky was not in favour of it, because Haslinger has increased his *Anzeiger* by half, since the New Year. — You see how malicious of Haslinger this is; I believe that he has even drawn up a petition that I may be denied the concession, because it will injure him in his business. If I could see that the paper, if it appeared here, would really be of reasonable advantage to us I would undertake to gain the concession in spite of H. . . . . My conviction that no good paper can succeed here, grows continually, and above all no musical paper, for Vienna is entirely out of touch with central Germany."

This despondency finds even stronger expression in a letter of Feb. 10th:

"If only I had wings and could fly to you, and talk to you for an hour! My situation here grows steadily more and more uncertain, and I am often seized by a fierce anxiety as to the issue of all these complications. You are my only comfort, I look up to you as to a Madonna, from you I gain courage and strength once more.

. . . . Now help me, my brain is really a little confused from much thinking and brooding, and I had better not read *Hamlet* just at present. If only I had my old light-heartedness, when I used to succeed in everything; but now everything takes hold of me, everything irritates and troubles me — it is harder than I thought — is marriage — but there is no longer any choice for us — I cannot tear myself from you — God has forsaken me if you forsake me — I find it so difficult to write to-day — forgive me, I can write no more, I will go into the open air, my heart is so heavy. . . ."

Among these complications, and in view of these difficult and urgent problems, it was especially unfortunate that although Clara had arrived in Paris on Feb. 6th, 3 weeks were still to pass before she received the letters from Schumann, which had so long been waiting for her there. On Feb. 8th she writes in very comprehensible agitation:

"My dear Robert . . . . think, what a misfortune! Your letter is there, and I cannot get it until I present my passport. . . . Write to me at once, if it is only a couple of words; I shall go wild with anxiety if I do not hear something soon. Address to Mlle Clara Wieck chez Mlle Emilie List, rue des Martyrs No. 43, and

then it is sure to find me. I am just going into private rooms [1])
in the same house in which Pauline [2]) lives. — More, in a few days.
I am inconsolable. What a misfortune! . . . . Have you had all my
letters? From Nuremberg, Stuttgart, Karlsruhe? Addio!
Emilie and Henriette send many greetings."

Certain passages in two of the letters which had been
written in the mean time, give the clearest insight into the
over-strained, anxious mood which unfortunately mastered
Clara as a result of the long interruption in their exchange
of thought. In the mean time Schumann — as is to be seen
in a letter written a few days later, which is not printed
here — had become convinced of the entire impossibility of
establishing the newspaper in Vienna in any shape, and he
now wavered between the determination — a difficult one,
because of Wieck's triumph — to return to Leipsic, and the
idea of giving up the paper altogether and founding life for
himself and Clara on a new basis either in Vienna or in
London. . . .

CLARA TO ROBERT.

"Paris, Thursday 14/2. 39.
. . . . Have you answered the Doctor? I had a letter from him
yesterday, which I am enclosing. . . . Do you know, it seems to
me a very eccentric letter, and I think it would be better not to
set our whole hope on him. Henriette agrees with me. . . .
. . . . I have an Erard in my room, which is dreadfully stiff.
I had lost all heart, but yesterday I played on a Pleyel and they
are a little more managable. I must study for another three weeks
before I can play a note in public. I could have three grand pianos
in my room already — everyone wants me to take his. If only
I knew how to begin playing on a Pleyel without offending Erard,
who has shown me every possible kindness. . . .
. . . . So you see that I am really alone in Paris. Are you
nervous about me? Father entirely refuses to come. . . . I have

---
1) Hôtel Michadière, rue Michadière.
2) Pauline Garcia.

written to Frau v. Berg, to ask if she will not come, as I cannot go into society without a suitable chaperon. Probst and Fechner[1]) have been worrying me for the last two days, they wanted to induce me to go home again. Shall I have come to Paris for nothing? Father would give something to have me back again, but I will not go. Possibly I shall stay here for the whole summer, and give lessons, and go to the Lists.

— Write to me soon, soon, so that I may not despair. By this time you have already had 8—9 letters, and I not yet one....

I am staying in the same house with Pauline. She is making a great sensation. My direct address is Hôtel Michadière, rue Michadière No. 7. . . .

I am beside myself to think of your letter being there, and to be obliged to leave it in the rough hands of the officials.

Adieu, my life. —

I would not send you the letter, only I think it will be well for you to read it."

"Here people are not only superficial, but light-minded too", Clara had written in this same letter from Paris. Now that her faith in the complete reliability of Schilling had been shattered to some degree by his "eccentric" letter, and by the revelations made by her new friend, the comments which Schumann, in a state of not unnatural indignation, sent her after receiving her letter, must have fully convinced her that the light-mindedness which she found so painful in Paris was also to be found in Germany.

On Feb. 23rd Robert wrote:

"I am still trembling all over at such unheard of impudence as is displayed in every word of S.'s letter. We have escaped a great danger. Had it been a less foolish rascal who offered to espouse our cause the whole happiness of our life might have been destroyed. But the man is a bungling Don Juan. You must have no further connection with him. . . .

---

1) Probst, a friend of Wieck's, who tried to influence Clara and make her think with her father, thus giving her much annoyance. Fechner, a cousin of Wieck's second wife.

. . . . Do you not see what the man was doing with you? He is the most infamous hypocrite and deceiver, such a man as one has come across only in novels. Do you not see how he goes on from one thing to another in his letter, how he mentions 'his wife's tears', which do not trouble him, how he keeps drawing closer to you, how he says how he hates 'commonplace artists', by which he means me, how, in order to touch you, he brings in his 'late father of blessed memory', giving you to understand that he has money enough to maintain one, or even two women, and adds that 'his house and arms' are open to you, finally how he 'will collect information' about me, how, at the end, he has the impudence, the unheard of impudence, to say, 'I must know that you are happy; we need no *third person* to give you everything else in life', how he goes yet further and writes, 'that we can tear ourselves even from the vocation of heaven', by which he alludes to the cloister, and finally, how he flatly offers you his hand when he says of G.: 'If you had seen the grand scale on which the business was done, we should join with this man, etc.', and how in the end he seems fairly certain of the matter and asks you 'to write and tell him everything, every detail' — He is every inch a rascal — just look at his words carefully. . . .

— I know perfectly that you meant it all well, and to our advantage. But let this be a warning to you for all time. It has made me take a firm resolve, and I beg you to share it — that we will take no one else into our confidence over ourselves and our future, not even if he is clad in the whitest of sheepskins, like this wolf whom we have escaped in time — no-one, no-one else, do you hear? Only do not think that I mean to reproach you in the least. — No girl, no angel in heaven could be more true to me than you are; no other can love like you, more nobly than words can say. — I have no words in which to speak to you, you should listen to me in my sacred hours, or see me in dreams, when I dream of you — for I do not know what to say — I have the exquisite consciousness that I have remained spotlessly true to you. . . . And now for the last words about that vulgar hypocrite, who wishes to leave his wife. — I am not angry because he loves you, or because he is hostile to me — but what is enraging is that he wants to make you faithless, you a lover, a betrothed whom he himself knows to be faithful, — this is so infuriating, so impudent of one whom you have known for barely ten days, that

I boil with rage — and then again he is so stupid with you — and with me. . . .

. . . . I am sorry for your little friend, who has to thank S. for bringing her to you. You write to me so warmly of her that I feel as if I knew her. If you have *proved* her, keep her with you. . . .

Now courage, my own — I know you meant it for the best when you trusted him — do not look upon us as so poor; recognise your strength, believe in mine even though it is not like yours — there is that in our hearts and minds of which no-one can rob us — Never again think of relying on others! Let this be an experience for your whole life! You, kind-hearted and inexperienced as you are, have been brought into contact with vulgarity, — I divined it all, I knew, by a sensation during these last few days such as I never had before, that you were in danger. . . . If you had only read his letter carefully, and had *understood* it all, you would have had to flee to me and say, 'Protect me from this villain' — I cannot forget it — I am shaking all over. . . . You are learning in a hard school, and I will pray heaven that you may come back to me a wise teacher. In none of my letters have I called your attention to the numerous dangers which will come near you here and there, now that you stand so entirely alone; I did not want to make you suspicious, I wanted you to remain the simple artist-maiden whom I know and love. . . .

. . . . Follow the path, then, that you tread for my sake with firm step, and good courage; do not let yourself be misled in anything; some day heaven will reward you; you are too sublime! Shall I tell you something else? I press you to my heart with inexpressible emotion. You shall hear from me again soon — I am in good spirits and feel strong.

And so fare you right well for to-day   Your Robert.

Kind remembrances to Emilie. You can tell her everything. She is certain to agree with me."

While this little spring thunder-shower in the form of a letter was taking its way from Danube to Seine, Clara had at last rescued her longed-for letters from the "rough hands of the officials", and she wrote, radiant, on the 25th:

"My darling Robert

Ah! if only I knew what to do with you! You have made me happier than ever. Think! 4 letters at once, yesterday! As soon as I had your last one I went shivering and shaking to the post with Emilie, presented my pass and got the 3 letters. I must have displayed my joy to the people in the post-office — I could hardly speak. And what letters! . . . .

. . . . And now as to my plan: if it does not prove too difficult, and if I have practised the piano sufficiently, I think possibly of playing at the Conservatoire on March 9th, and should I happen to succeed, of giving a concert in Erard's salon; then I should go to England for 2—3 months, then back again, spending the summer here in order to give lessons . . . . in no case should I return to Leipsic so soon. If I stay here for the summer, I shall live with the Lists, who would then take larger lodgings[1]. Then in the winter I might perhaps make some excursious to other French cities, come back here again, return to Leipsic for Easter 1840, put all my affairs in order, and if my Father will not give his consent, I will come to Zwickau, you come there too, and we will be married and go to Vienna (That is if you stay in Vienna)....

You think that I am not passionate enough? Ah! yes, I am, in the highest degree, but shall I press you to come here, or elsewhere, so that we may speak to each other for once, only to endure the most terrible parting again? . . . . Yes, I will, I must see you again, but when I do, it will be never to part from you more; I cannot survive another parting from you — the pain is too overpowering. . . .

You ask me if I will not live in Leipsic for the first few years? I would gladly do so, if only my parents and relations were not there! To live at enmity with my parents, and in the same town! And then it is so dreadful to me, that they show neither you nor me the respect which is due to us — and yet, if you see a great advantage in Leipsic, we will stay there; I shall be happy anywhere with you. I have read your views about the paper most carefully; and I do think that you ought to go back to Leipsic, the whole thing seems to me unprofitable in Vienna, the coteries there are unendurable and in addition the censor spoils everything . . . .

---

[1] Rue Navarien No. 12. Clara went into the new house as early as March 26th. The Lists followed in the middle of April.

Why do you want to stay in Vienna, to live among people who are not in sympathy with you? Go away, go back to our Leipsic, I believe we should be happiest there after all. And I can give lessons there too, without going round with an umbrella, as Father used to say. . . . .

I am extremely glad that you are composing so much, and a symphony too? Ah! Robert, that is too good! . . . . So you were offended with me for calling you a second Jean Paul and Beethoven? You shall not hear it again. You are quite right, it is not nice to make such comparisons — only always tell me everything that you dislike in me, *I rejoice in every word from you.*

It is nice that you are giving lessons, but when once I am with you, you must not do that any more, that will then be my business . . . . I should like to stand behind you once, when you are giving a lesson . . . . (In the margin) I had not fastened the letter I sent through S. with bits of paper — he broke it open — Inquisitiveness — Vanity — Want of delicacy! —

Now a hasty farewell, dear heart. . . . Write to me immediately, I beg you. Wherever I may be — England, France, America, and even Siberia — I am ever your loyal sweetheart who loves you from her inmost heart. —"

The following letter from Clara, the first which gives any detailed account of her impressions of Paris, notwithstanding the anxieties of which it speaks, is also written in the same exalted frame of mind, a frame of mind which was however upset on the following day by a letter from Wieck, and by Schumann's pessimistic accounts of his Viennese plans.

CLARA TO ROBERT.

"Thursday morning 28./2. 39.

. . . . I have been meaning to write to you, Robert of my heart, for the last three days, but something has perpetually prevented me. . . . .

. . . . Just at present I am weighed down by many anxieties about my stay here. I cannot help feeling how the French judge everything . by externals. People raise their hands above their heads when they hear that I not only have not my Father, but not even a mother or an aunt with me, and the whole world tells me that I shall not be treated with proper respect if I have not an old lady to go into society with me, receive callers etc. . . . This is a real dilemma. Where am I to find one all at once, and where am I to find a lady with whom I can trust myself to go to London, that huge city? I do not know what to do, and I will talk to Erard about it to-day. . . .

. . . . So far everything has gone well, and everybody has liked me; so I am not complaining of this place. . . . It is extraordinary that all the pianists and performers here have suddenly announced concerts! Do they mean to frighten me out of it? Oh! I have courage, and must carry through what I have begun. I shall probably have lessons from Bordogni [1]. . . . I shall also take lessons in French it is unfortunate that almost all my acquaintances speak German, so that there are whole days on which I do not speak a single word of French. I am doing a little English with Emilie, but indeed I am almost always with the Lists; Herr List is most friendly towards me. — To-morrow I am going to see Bertin and Meyerbeer, whom I like.

. . . . I talked a great deal about you yesterday, to Fräulein Parish whom I met here by chance, and who was my best friend in Hamburg; she told me what a sensation your article [2] on the *Huguenots* and *St Paul* had made in Hamburg [3]), and how much people had liked it — and indeed it was a wonderful article. . . . Kalkbrenner asked me to play to him, the other day, for he said he did not yet properly understand your compositions — what is one to say of that? He also said that he had heard that no-one could play your compositions as I do — well, I should hope not! — Loveday is not very good they say; but Laidlaw must have made great progress — don't you like her better than me, now? Why, I must be you not to do that, Herr Robert Schumann. 'Robert Schumann!' indeed, strange thoughts rise in my mind when I see this name, and I always want to add 'Clara' — is it not so? How closely in sympathy we are! I had the same thought, how dreadful it would be to die without bearing your name, and I thought if I lay dying, I would marry you at the very point of

---

1) A singing-master.
2) *Gesammelte Schriften* II, 4. edition p. 59 etc.
3) The reference is probably to the article in *Ges. Schr.* II, p. 62 etc.

death. Let me end for to-day with this thought — it is beautiful!
'Good-night, my Robert', I would say then, — 'We shall meet again!'
and a kiss from you would close my eyes. —"

"Friday morning 1./3.

I have just received a letter from Father — it pains him to
know that I am alone in Paris, and yet he is persuaded that it
will be of great use to me, and in that he is right. There can
be no question of gains, for the journey here long ago cost all
that I earned in Germany, and simply as we manage, living here
is very dear. . . . But do not let this trouble you, one must risk
something if one wishes to go into a large city. . . ."

"Friday evening.

I read your letter over again, and I must answer one or two
things. . . . I cannot think, dear Robert, why you continually say
that I do not like playing your compositions; it is not true, and
it hurts me; it is just because I honour and love your compositions so much, that I play them only to a chosen few. But I
quite admit that one ought not always to be guided by one's
feelings alone, and I will play them as often as possible. You
see, it is so dreadful to me to see someone there who does not
understand — it upsets me terribly. I will try to please you as
much as I can. Do you want me to play Moscheles, Bennet, and
(what is the third called?) Potter?[1] I should be sorry to play
the first (for he is dry; at least in his new compositions), very
sorry to play the second (I simply cannot conceal from you that
I cannot like his compositions), and the third? I know nothing
whatever of him, but he does not sound very hopeful to me. But
in this too, I will please you as much as I can. So what shall
I play of Moscheles, Bennet, and Potter? Write and tell me. —
If only I could hear you again! I so liked to hear you even
when I was still a child. You knew it too, and often improvised
for me alone. Do you still remember how once in Schneeberg you
said to Rosalie's little daughter (you had her on your lap), 'Do
you know who that is?' 'Clara', said she. 'No', was your answer,
that is my betrothed!' I often thought of it, and one day it came

---

1) Ph. C. H. Potter, who since 1832 had been Director of the Royal
Academy of Music in London.

to pass, and that makes me very happy, and you too are contented, are you not, my Robert? —

I was at Bertin's to-day, and he promised to use his interest
for me with the Conservatoire. I met Berlioz there, whom I had
missed three times, ... he at once spoke of you. He is quiet,
has extraordinarily thick hair, and always looks on the ground,
always keeps his eyes down. To-morrow he is coming to see me.
I did not know it was he at first, and wondered who it was who
kept talking about you; at last I asked him his name, and when
he said it, I received a pleasant shock, which must have been
flattering for him. His new opera has not taken at all. . . .”

“How you have wounded my heart,” she writes; “You are
right in saying that I did not read S.'s letter very carefully;
but if I had read it carefully, I should not have taken it all as
you do. But you may be right, you have more knowledge of
human nature than I have — I took it all as being written
in the most zealous friendship. — What he writes about 'being
worthy', did indeed annoy me very much.”

“Did you really write that?” she asks, at once troubled
and roused, but she goes on at once with a hardly won, “Now,
dear Robert, another page. Behave as if I had not written
the last page, look at me kindly and affectionately, and embrace
me tenderly, as I do you.”

The other impressions made by Paris were not calculated
to divert her mind or make her more cheerful. “The concerts
here,” she complains on March 10th, “are really terribly wearisome, they last from 3 to 4 hours. The parties are hardly
endurable; over 50 ladies sit round the piano in one tiny
room, and behave in the silliest fashion. . . . The levity,
idleness, coquetry is unbelievable.

I saw the *Huguenots* the other day, but I did not care for
the music very much; music of this sort is unendurable to
me, it makes one ill. I also saw *Figaro*, at the Italian opera,
but you cannot think how it was done; at every close came
an Italian cadenza, and they sang it without any greatness

of conception; how little do they understand the great master!"

On the other hand, she was relieved at her release from the unsympathetic Frenchwoma, whom she had disliked from the beginning: "I am pleased about one thing, that I am free of my Frenchwomann. I have sent her away, for she was out all day long, and was malicious and deceitful. God be thanked that she is gone; now I am alone with Henriette."

It was her best help during these troublous times, that in Henriette, and in her old friend Emilie List, whom she had found greatly improved, warmer and more pliable than before, she had at her side two friends to whom she could unreservedly confide all her anxieties as to her own and Schumann's future. "A great deal is said about you," she says, "if not to Emilie, then to Henriette, at the piano." And the same letter which contains the complaints over Parisian parties, affords a pleasant glimpse into the common life of the three girls. "Emilie (who has spent the night with us) and Henriette," announces Clara, "have commissioned me to write and tell you that I can cook a really excellent breakfast, and am quite in my element! They are now enjoying it. . . . You must often be anxious lest I should not be able to cook. You can be at ease about it, I shall soon lear nto (when once I am with you). Here Emilie puts in: 'You will only burn your piano-fingers!' What rubbish the two girls chatter to me, about tea, coffee, and heaven knows what; with which I am told to amuse you, you poor fellow!"

But the chief thing was the consciousness of renewed harmony with Robert, who, on his side, did all he could to cheer and encourage her. Thus on March 11th he wrote to her from Vienna in the most cheerful vein:

"My dear Clara, Is it right not to write to you for a week? But I have revelled in the thought of you, and have loved you as I never did before. I sat at the piano all the week, and composed, and wrote, and laughed, and cried, all at once; you will find all this fairly depicted in my Op. 20, the great *Humoreske*, which is already being printed. See, how quickly things go with me! Invented, written down, printed. And this is how I like it. Twelve sheets finished in eight days — you forgive me, don't you, for making you wait a little? Everything shall be made up for now, and in the first place I kiss you for the letter which I received on Tuesday. A beautiful tone runs through it, and it seems as if you wished to please me more and more; in short, I have fallen dreadfully in love with you again, without counting the other, proper love. Your yesterday's letter too, was so dear and good. But I reproached myself for many things that I wrote to you. For instance about playing my compositions. And you will think me vain and thankless; but no, I am not; I only want to be so certain of your sympathy — what else have I in the world, save you?

Thus too, I meant well about the compositions of Moscheles, Bennet, etc. I thought it might be useful to you. Besides, I wanted to play the husband a little, and give you a few significant hints; it was not meant badly. But all these are trifles compared with the chief reproach which I make myself, namely that I give you a great deal of unnecessary anxiety about me. Just consider, what need shall we be in? Out of the 50 first artists in Vienna, there are not 10 who have as much capital as we have; not one of them can live on his income. What more then do we want, or demand? We must earn something in addition, but there is no need to be anxious about that. . . .

. . . . Do not lose courage in Paris; you have been there only a few weeks; they will receive you without a boring old lady, when once you make a beginning. Do not let your father come — listen to me, I beg you — the old song and the old suffering would begin all over again. Now that you have got through the worst of it — the long journey, the first beginnings and preliminaries in Paris — carry it through. . . .

. . . . What you write to me so beautifully and touchingly about the dream of dying, shall spur us on to do our best not to be too old a bridal pair, but to keep to 1840. But we will promise each other that neither of us will die before the other, until after that. . . .

. . . . Apropos of your story of little Rosalie, I remember how once when I wanted to kiss you, when you were a little girl, you said to me, 'No, later, when I am older'; there, dear Clara, 'you showed an uncommonly sharp sight and prophetic spirit'."

He closed this letter with the words, "Write to me at once, and incessantly. Be true and cheerful as I am," and continued in the same tone on March 16th, "You have been crying, have you? Did I not forbid you to? . . . . If I were to give you a kiss for every tear, and always something pretty and amusing, would this content you? First a kiss then — and now, immediately, an amusing idea — Dear Clara, the more I think over our first summer as a married couple in Zwickau, the more does the whole world seem to cover me like a bower of roses, and we sit in it, arm in arm, a young married couple, and feast and work — think it all over, and think of our great happiness — is Zwickau not attainable, then? In the first place (another kiss) young wives must be able to cook and keep house properly, if they wish to have contented husbands, and it would be fun to learn that from Therese, — then next, young wives must not at once under-stake great journies, but they must take care of themselves and spare themselves, and especially one who has for the last year been working hard and sacrificing herself for her husband, — thirdly, we will be exempt from all tedious and inquisitive visitors — fourthly, we will take a great many walks, and I will show you all the places where we boys used to fight — fifthly, your father can do us no harm — sixthly and seventhly, we should need extremely little, and at most we need only cut off the coupons — eighthly, *how* I should compose and you would play! — ninthly, we can prepare ourselves well for Vienna — and now, Clärchen, Clara, you are crying no more, look me once in the face — what is written there? The firmest faith in you, is it not? . . . .

. . . . Now, enough of words, kiss me once, my darling child. People are much fonder of each other when they have been a little angry with each other. It is like a little shower of rain in spring.

From this cheerful and optimistic frame of mind, in which, significantly enough, in spite of all his experiences to the contrary, the continuance of the paper in Vienna once more seemed to him possible, and he comfortably sketched out the details of their wedding in a village Church, "No-one there save the parson and ourselves", sprang the advice and consolation as to the immediate future, which he added on the following day: "Now, one thing more which you should consider, my dear Clara; do not leave Paris until you take a complete triumph with you; put forth all your powers when you make your first appearance; think of me, the while, who listen to you, who stand breathless at your side. . . . I am not in the least nervous for you, but so much depends upon circumstances, upon local conditions, upon sudden chances; therefore if you do not succeed the first time, you must succeed the second; only do not go to London before you are certain that you have been adequately recommended there from Paris. These cities are the largest in the world. You come to them for the first time as a fully developed mistress of your art."

A letter which Clara wrote to her father at this time, may be inserted here. It throws an interesting sidelight upon her personal relations, and upon the general condition of music.

"Paris 19./III. 39.

My dear Father, I can take only a small sheet of paper, I do not know where my head is. The day after to-morrow is Schlesinger's[1] matinée at Erard's (Erard has let him have his

---

1) Moritz August Schlesinger, proprietor of the music publishing house of that name, in Paris, and publisher of the *Gazette musicale*. The matinée

hall for nothing, to please me) and I am playing the $B\flat$ major
trio at it with Batta[1]) and Artot[2]), and then *Lob der Thränen,*
Hexentanz and *Poème d'amour* by Henselt. You can easily imagine
how I feel at playing in Paris for the first time, Afterwards, on
the same evening, there is a soirée at Zimmermann's[3]), at which
I am playing Henselt's *Variations* which have been much blamed
in the *Gazette musicale.* You are sure to have read it . . . . In
spite of this I shall play them here, for I want to see if the Parisian
public will not appreciate what delighted a Viennese public. To-
morrow evening I am going to a countess (whose name I do not
know); and the other day, at Leos', the Saxon consul told me
hat Appony[4]) had said to him that I must play at his house.
To-morrow I will call there again. I went to Koenneritz's[5]) too,
and I was to have gone there for a little this evening, but I wrote
and excused myself, for I cannot bear going out every evening. . . .
        I have been hearing a great many things over again. I went
to a rehearsal at Leos' again, the other day, simply to listen.
Meyerbeer and I may well have been the most unhappy members
of the audience; my ears, at all events, were no longer in tune,
when I got home. Meyerbeer was very nice to me. The next
day I was at a concert of Batta's, who is adored by the ladies
here (he is a 'cellist, and his brother a pianist) because he flirts
with them while he is playing till one can hardly bear it; he
plays delicately, but (as I wrote in my diary) he has an affected,

at which Clara played was the third of a series of matinées which Schlesinger arranged for the subscribers to the *Gazette musicale.*
    1) Alexander Batta, much admired in France as a 'cellist.
    2) Alexander Joseph Artôt, a pupil of Kreutzer's, an excellent violinist
who died at 30.
    3) Pierre Joseph Guilleaume Zimmermann, since 1816 Professor of
piano-playing at the Conservatoire. His "Soirées" had a certain vogue,
but one which Clara, on her first visit, found little justified. "On March 7th",
she writes in the diary, "there was an evening soirée at Zimmermann's.
So these are the soirées which are so famed in Germany? 150 ladies
sit packed together in a tiny room, unable to move; and then there is
music until late into the night; but what music! . . . . Arias, sung very
badly, one after another. Rutini was the only one that gave me any
pleasure, all the rest is worthless."
    4) Austrian ambassador.
    5) Saxon ambassador.

frenchified soul. The concert began with the $B\flat$ major trio; only
by Frenchmen could one hear it played so badly, you would hardly
believe it (his brother played the piano). They dashed it off like
so many Herz *Variations* — I will show them how it ought to be
played.

Yesterday I heard Franchomme[1]) in a charming composition
of his own; he delighted me! He certainly does not pay court
to the ladies, like Batta: Yesterday was Osborne's[2]) concert — a
very mediocre player. Beriot played two duets with him and then,
in answer to a tremendous outcry from the audience, he played
the *Tremolo*. He came to see me recently, and brought me his
new *Études*; I am going to arrange one for the piano, as soon as
I have time. Possibly Beriot will play a duet with me at my
concert — that would be a good thing; he is staying here for the
half the summer . . . . if Pauline is at my concert, perhaps she
may sing, too.

Yesterday I called on a certain Herr Matthias whose son[3])
(12 years old, I believe) is a 2nd Liszt, a genius. You ought to
hear the boy, he has extraordinary talent, and is a pupil of Chopin's.
Shall I describe his talents to you in detail? You know the infant-
prodigy talents, only I must add to these that the boy has been
trained very well, has beautifully supple fingers, and can play
everything that Chopin has written without difficulty. Indeed he
beats all the tinkling players here. Strange to say he has never
practised for more than an hour; he is very delicate (quite like
Chopin) and up to the present time has perpetually been ill. His
father, a very sensible man, does not allow him to play at
parties; he is not one of those fathers who idolise their children.
I was to have given him lessons, but I told him that he needed
no teacher. (Do you know, I should be afraid to give the boy
lessons, for as it is his spirit is too much for his physical strength)
I played duets with him, and I mean to visit this family often,
especially now that I am moving fairly close to them. . . . . .

1) August Franchomme, a famous ˙cellist, a friend of Chopin's.
2) G. M. Osborne from Limerick in Ireland, a pupil of Kalkbrenner's,
noted in his day as a pianist, and no less as a composer of drawing-
room pieces.
3) Georg Amédee Matthias, born 1826, was a highly esteemed pianist
in Paris, and in 1862 became Professor of piano-playing at the Conservatoire, but he was no second Liszt.

Chopin is at Marseilles with Georges Sand, and lies there sick to death, it is doubtful if he will return. Nourrit[1]) (so Meyerbeer has just heard) has flung himself down from a 4th story window in Naples, after singing at a concert and not meeting with approval. He said to his wife, with whom he lived very happily: 'See what the children are doing (it was evening) and bring them to me.' — His wife goes, and comes back with a child in her arms, does not see her husband, the window is open, and when she looks down, her husband is lying below. Not unnaturally she fell to the floor with the child in her arms. When, at last, someone came in they found the husband smashed to pieces. He had gone to the concert in costume and had been hissed, — naturally, since he came in costume. People are quite beside themselves over it.

I have called on Baillot[2]), Paer etc. The former was not at home, nor was Auber, but Paer was very pleasant; he does not in the least understand modern music. A sextet of Kalkbrenner's was played yesterday, which is miserably composed, so poor, so feeble, and so lacking in all imagination? Of course Kalkbrenner sat in the front row smiling sweetly, and highly satisfied with himself and his creation. He always looks as if he were saying, 'Oh God, I and all mankind must thank Thee that Thou hast created a mind like mine' (Probst's words and interpretation — very good, aren't they?)

The article from S[t] Petersburg about Camilla[3]) pleased me very much, after all there are still honest men in the world. I have, as you see, received your letter of March 8th. You ask me to write to you more often, but you do not consider that in Paris an hour is what a day is with us. On no evening do I get home before midnight, and in spite of this I get up every morning at 7, or half-past 7; writing robs me of my best time, and therefore,

1) Ad. Nourrit, for a long time first tenor at the grand opera, and singing master at the Conservatoire, he was also the original Raoul in *The Huguenots.*

2) P. M. Baillot, first violin at the grand opera in the twenties and solo violinist in the royal orchestra.

3) This refers to a notice from S[t] Petersburg in the *N. Z. f. Mus.* No. 13 (X p. 56) concerning the great successes of the beautiful Camilla Pleyel, of whom the writer remarks: "I found that Mad. Pleyel is among the best pianists of the present day, Henselt or A. Gerke alone she cannot make us forget."

dear Father, you must be content to get a letter from me once a fortnight. You can write much oftener, you have much more time. Believe me, with the best of wills I cannot write more, gladly as I would.

Fechner wishes to lithograph me, and I have consented, I should be very glad to extort a portrait that is like me. Could you not send me some of the Viennese portraits, when there is a suitable opportunity, and also I have not got my diamond ring, which I sorely miss[1]) — I cannot very well visit Heine for certain reasons — but possibly I may go there once with Herr List.

Now, farewell, my dear ones; my love to all. I will write to Nanny soon. Tell Verhulst that I am going to play his andante with Beriot very shortly. Greet Wenzel, Pfundt, Reuter, all our relations, and the little blossoming violets, — you still like them better than Parisian violets, don't you? I hope to have another letter from you soon. A kiss to Mother, and an embrace to you, dear Father, with true German love, Your Clara.". . . . . .

"I am quite sick of concerts! Full-stop." — Clara had written in her diary on the previous day. She meant as a listener at other people's concerts. But her own first appearance was to bring her only too much vexation and annoyance. Her hope of showing the Parisians how the $B\flat$ major trio should be played was not fulfilled, for her two partners, Batta and Artôt, to whose ears Clara's verdict on the recent performance may have come, treated their young colleague in such an insulting and rude manner at the rehearsal, that Clara was moved to strike out this item from the programme. This incident made her once more painfully conscious of the lack of a man's protection, and it is easy to understand how she wrote to Robert after it, on the evening of March 13th: "I am devoured by anxiety as to the day after to-morrow; I am incapable of thinking any more. I can think of nothing

---

1) This sorely missed diamond ring, which Wieck had given her as a reward for her brave conduct on the Naumburg concert tour of 1836, she never received again.

but you, and your despair if I should fail — I could not survive it! — I will trust to my good genius. Pray for me, that
will help."

But on the same day on which she received the first cheerful letter from Schumann, March 21st, she could also tell him,
with relieved mind, that she "had come through her first début
gloriously".

"I played at Schlesinger's matinée, and in the evening at
Zimmermann's, and created a great sensation, especially in the
evening when there were many connoisseurs present. They called
me the 2nd Liszt etc. At the matinée I played Henselt's *Variations*
(*Lob der Thränen*), my *Hexentanz*, *Poème d'amour*, Schubert's
Ständchen, and Henselt's *Vöglein*. In the evening I played *Repos
d'amour*, my *Sabbat*, which is much liked, the *Vöglein*, and Thalberg's *Caprice*. I must tell you one joke which will show you
how little musical Schlesinger is. I wanted to play the Henselt
Variations, but Sch. thought that it would not do to put the name
Variations on the programme, and wanted me to play Thalberg's
Caprice, and this was announced. I found it better to begin with
the *Variations*, and play them without saying anything to anyone
beforehand. I thought Sch. would be furious but to my great
surprise he put a good face on it; finally, after I had quite finished, he said to me: 'It would be very nice if you were to let
the audience hear the *Variations* now: will you?' I said to him,
'I have played them already!' 'The deuce!' and a blush, was
his answer. Ah! how I laughed in my heart.

. . . . I am truly delighted with the *Kinderscenen* . . . . how
beautiful they are; to-morrow I must enjoy them again at leisure!
So far I have only been able to play them through once, that
indeed was in Halle's[1]) presence, who was also delighted.

As yet I do not know these compositions well enough to be
able to judge them properly, but *Das bittende Kind*, *Von fremden
Ländern und Menschen*, *Glückes genug*, *Fürchtenmachen*, *Kind im
Einschlummern* und *Des Dichters Worte*, appeal to me particularly.

---

1) Karl Halle from Hagen, a pianist and in Paris since 1836, who
had been called himself Charles Hallé. Later he became a very successful conductor in Manchester and London.

I know the poet, his words have sunk deep into my heart — ....
Ah! Robert, how happy, and yet how unhappy I am! The longing for you takes hold of my life and then when I can bear it no
longer I find relief in weeping on Henriette's bosom. ...

I cannot go to London without a man to protect me. One
important point is that one only goes to London after having been
in Paris, and I am still too little known in Paris, and it is already
too late for it. My intention therefore was to stay here for the
summer and give lessons, perhaps going to Baden-Baden for two
months in the summer, and then coming back here, to give some
concerts at the beginning of the winter, to get some letters of
recommendation, and in January to come to Germany in order to
marry you, my dearest; to pass 2—3 months in Zwickau, Leipsic,
or where you will, and then to go to London together and spend
2—3 months there etc., and then the rest will settle itself. Do
you like this plan? .... I should also get more used to the
pianos, these are so stiff that it is dreadful. And yet I played
fairly well yesterday. Enclosed is little flower from the bunch
which I stuck in my dress yesterday; I received the bouquet from
Emilie, and considered it as coming from you. I believe I should
have pleased you yesterday; I had on a black dress (they like
that here), quite simple, a white camilia surrounded with small
white flowers like the one I enclose, in my hair, and among the
flowers the Empress of Austria's brooch. Do you smile at my
childish description? Ah! but I know you would have liked me,
I looked quite imposing. — My concert is fixed, provisionally, for
April 9th, but there is such a dreadful amount to be done about
it that am not sure if the time is not too short. ...

It is just striking midnight, and I am looking at the moon ....
the thought that we can both see it at the same time always makes
me so happy; it is so comforting.

How happy I always am whenever I read your 2 last letters!
You are so cheerful, so confident, that in truth you banish many
of my cares. You are quite right, what can happen to us after
all, we both have our capital within us, and can that fail us?
So let us step forward boldly, everything will come right, it must
come right. For the rest, I am very glad that you are leaving
Vienna, for the Viennese ladies might end by wishing to keep you
to themselves, and it is better that you should not go back there
until I am with you — it is safer. ...

. . . . Do you know, dear Robert, that I too keep a little account book in which I write down all my expenses, every evening before I go to sleep? Your orderliness delights me; I do not know how to keep on praising you enough, and especially for taking me, and no other, to be your bride — that was, after all, your best deed.

To whom have you dedicated your *Kinderscenen?* They belong just to us two, don't they? And they will not go out of my head, they are so simple, so unpretentious, so exactly like you, I can hardly wait till to-morrow to play them over again. *Fürchten-machen* just comes into my mind, you understand that so well. A few years ago you always had your joke with me, when, for example, you told me about doubles, or pretended that you had a pistol about you. I still laugh when I think of it. . . . . What a silly I was, to believe everything you told me — You story-teller! No *Fürchtenmachen* later thank you, particularly when we sit alone together in the evenings. Good-night, my Robert, my hope, my love, my all." —

"Ah!" she writes three days later, in a similiar mood, "how indescribably beautiful your *Kinderscenen* are . . . . if only I could kiss you! — Yesterday I thought, and I still go on thinking, is it true then that the poet who speaks in this will be mine; is not this happiness too great? Ah! I cannot grasp it! My delight increases every time I play them. How much lies in your tones, and so fully do I understand your every thought, that I could lose myself in you and your music. Your whole heart bares itself to one in these scenes, in this touching simplicity, e. g. *Das bittende Kind*; one can see the child as it begs with its little hands pressed together; and the *Kind im Einschlummern.* One could not close one's eyes to more beautiful music. In this piece there is something so original, so adventurous — I cannot find the words. The first one, *Von fremden Ländern und Menschen,* has always been one of my favourites . . . . I am very fond of the *Curiose Geschichte* too, and *Haschemann* is amusing, it is extraordinarily vivid. *Glückes genug* gave me such a peaceful feeling, the transition to *F* major is so uplifting; did you not feel when you wrote it, as if you were losing yourself in a world of happiness? — I like playing the '*Wichtige Begebenheit*', and play it very impressively; the second part is delightful. *Träumerei* — I always think I see you at the piano in this — it is a beautiful dream. The *Kamin* is German,

this cosiness is not to be found by a French fire-side. It has just
struck me that I am behaving as if I were a reviewer. Do not
be offended at my analyses, I should so like to give you an idea
of the feelings which these pieces arouse, but I cannot. When
you have time, write me something about them, write and tell me
how you wish to have them played, write and tell me your thoughts
about them, and if they are the same as mine. Write and tell
me — tell me also, if you still love me as well as ever?

Have you ever heard the Italian opera? I went to *Lucia*
yesterday, which is the opera of Donizetti's that I like best, and
at the close there is a tenor aria which you could not help liking,
which must carry you away for the moment. . . ."

But already fresh clouds were gathering over their heads.
Towards the end of March, Schumann, who, as he wrote to
Clara, had "summoned up all his strength" in order to finish
two great compositions before leaving for Leipsic, was thrown
into the greatest anxiety and unrest by the news of the serious
illness of his brother Eduard, and determined to leave Vienna
as quickly as possible.

On April 3rd, Clara, without any foreboding of what had
happened, had written concerning her experiences in Paris:

". . . . My concert is to take place on April 16th, think of me
at 8-30, it begins then. Ah! my nervousness! It increases every
time that I have to play, I do not know how it is! I am chiefly
nervous on your account, for I know that if I did not succeed,
you would be beside yourself.

. . . . I dined with Meyerbeer, the other day, and met Heine
and Jules Janin there. The former is very witty, but the latter
is coarse . . . . he continually says sharp things, which are not
without cleverness, but it seems to me dreadful that he himself
laughs at his own wit more than anyone. Heine speaks bitterly
of Germany — he is coming to see me before long, and so are
Auber, Onslow, Halevy etc."

"Thursday morning 4/4.

You did not suspect that I was still sitting at the piano at
2 o'clock this morning, playing your *Carnaval*, did you? — I was

at a certain Countess Perthuis', and all the connoisseurs stayed
behind, and then I played the greater part of the *Carnaval*, and
then things of Chopin's, of my own, Scarlatti, etc. Yesterday I
created a real sensation. It is extraordinary to me that my scherzo
is so much liked here, I always have to repeat it. . . .
      . . . . Listen Robert! will you compose something brilliant, easy
to be understood, something that has no directions written on it,
but is a piece which hangs together as a whole, not too long, and
not too short? I should so much like to have something of
yours to play at concerts, something suited to the general public.
It is indeed humiliating for a genius, but policy sometimes demands it. . . .
      . . . . It is extremely difficult to succeed in playing at the Con-
servatoire, and if one does at last get in, one can only play once,
and it is best to let that be a solo so that one need depend on
no-one . . . . the cabals here are frightful. You are quite right
about England, one must first have won a triumph here in Paris,
and since it is too late for that this year, I shall stay here this
summer, and give concerts here next winter, then I think I shall
be well enough known for England. No-one will listen to Bach
fugues here, not even connoisseurs. . . .
      . . . . Henriette will stay here all the summer, and soon we
shall all live together. I love dear Emilie now even more than
I did before, partly because she loves you. She has far more
heart than one would think if one did not know her intimately."

"My dear Robert," she had ended, "do not be anxious if
I do not write to you for a long time, for all my mind must
be given to my concert, I have a mass of things to see about,
and I dare not make my fingers stiff with writing."

But the news of Robert's heavy sorrows, which she received
in the mean time, made her, herself oppressed by cares, once
more take up her pen.

"You ask," she writes on April 9th, "if I would forsake you
if you became quite a poor man! Such a man as you, with
such an intellect and such a heart, can never be poor. You
can go where you will, the whole world stands open to you,
and my˙ heart is yours — could you put this question to me

in earnest? I will share joy and sorrow with you, my heart belongs to you alone and were you to forsake me, my heart would remain the same, you would be my last sigh."

"I share your grief about Eduard, but I do not abandon all hope", she continues. But one feels in her words that what troubles her in the first place is the anxiety as to how this blow may affect Robert's spirits. She knew too well from earlier experiences how little he could bear such shocks, and she was doubly anxious about him because at the same time a letter had come from her father which declared on them both war to the death.

"A few days ago," says she herself, a letter from Wieck "came (privately) to Emilie, in which he tells her that if I do not give you up he will no longer regard me as his child, he will deprive me of my inheritance, and also of my little capital, and will begin a law-suit against us both, which may last 3—5 years. These are fair hopes, but I do not lose courage. Up to the very moment of our union let us make every effort to prove to him that we shall be able to live (that is the chief ground of his anger) and try to soften him in every way; then if he still will not have it, and repudiates me, well, I shall be able to justify my conduct in God's sight. When I think it all over carefully, it seems to me as if I no longer had parents, for I hear of very little love from home."

"Your brother's illness," she writes three days later, "seems to me of such a kind that you must be prepared for his death. You are a man, and will hold yourself in hand, won't you, my Robert? Ah, how my head reels, and added to all this are the cares of the concert! Unfortunately my second finger has become so sensitive that I can hardly play for an hour without having the most dreadful pain. I shall have to rely entirely on the inspiration of the moment, otherwise I do not know how my pieces would go .... I am very impatient for news of you . . . . I have your health so much at heart, and my anxiety about you is so great."

Schumann's next letters were only partly designed to set her mind at rest on this score. They announced the death of his brother, which had followed on April 6th, and if they soon made clear that Schumann's fears about the state of his affairs were groundless, they also showed, — all the more because he endeavoured to prove to Clara that he was calm-how deeply he had been shaken by this unexpected blow. On April 10th he wrote from Leipsic:

"My Beloved, Our dear Eduard is dead — last Saturday morning at half-past two, as I was travelling I heard a whole choral of trumpets — he died just at that time — I do not know what to say, all these calls upon me have left me as if stupified — I had so looked forward to seeing my brothers and Therese and my friends here again — now everything is turned to sadness, and I dare not think of what Fate may still have in store for me. Perhaps it wants to lead me through all these many trials to happiness, making me wholly self-reliant, and a man. Eduard was the only person on whom I relied as on a protector — he always kept his word so faithfully — we never had an angry word with each other; his last words, when I said good-bye to him, were, 'All will go well with you, you are such a good fellow'. — But I saw something in his eyes which I might call the look of death; he had never spoken to me so warmly at any parting. And I remembered also, how he came to Leipsic again without any reason. Heaven must just have wanted him to see you at my side — do you remember, on the Promenade? And how I said to him: 'Well Eduard, how do you like us?' I know how proud he was that you loved me, and that you would one day bear the name of our family — I remember so much that is painful — but I have the happy consciousness for my whole life, that I have always treated him in true brotherly wise, as he always treated me. — There is nothing like two brothers — and now I have lost him — but wait, I will not let this make me weak. . . .

. . . . I received your remembrance from Reuter, yesterday. . . . Thank you, my dear child — You cannot exist without shedding joy around you — You are ever my joy — without you, I should long ago have been where Eduard is now — Is it possible that I shall never see him again? .... How strange it is that in all our dreams for the future I clung so warmly to Zwickau which is now wholly dead to me, and has nothing but graves for me, and how many of them! Or will mine be added to their number? — Outside, it is a perfect spring day, which carries me out into the very heart of all life, and I have no thought of dying, while you still live — do you not think that something depends on the will, on one's inner force, on the love for another which keeps us longer in life? And so let us faithfully wait out our time...."

This sad news reached Clara just on the day of her concert, and one can easily understand therefore how she wrote to Robert that evening, that she was "quite worn out with crying". Not till the following day did she receive a second letter from Robert which set her mind at rest as to the state of Eduard's affairs, on which their future depended.

"I got through my concert[1]), yesterday," she now informed him, with a lightened heart, "quite successfully, I wished you had been there, I created a genuine sensation, such as no artist has produced for many a day. . . . It was extremely full, but the expenses are so great in Paris that there cannot be anything left over, and indeed I expected nothing else . . . . my name is made, and that is enough for me. . . .

I hope you are composed, my dear. Eduard's death still seems to me impossible, and I am grieved that he could not see us united; yet, my Robert, do not let your courage sink! Remember, that there is one who will be true to you to the grave — even if you were to lose everything — the one who clings to you with a love that knows no bounds!

Yes, I am she!   Your Clara."

But the next few weeks were to bring greater causes for emotion, and more severe storms to them both; causes for

---

1) This "Concert donné par Mlle. Clara Wieck" also took place in M. Erard's salon, rue de Mail 13. Beriot was one of those who took part in it.

emotion in which Clara cannot be said to be entirely free from blame.

Wieck's letter to Emilie List, of which Clara had told Robert, had made a deeper impression upon them, and above all on Emilie, than they themselves would at first confess. This time Wieck had evidently hit upon the favourable moment to make Clara feel the full force of his wishes, worried and depressed as she was by the Parisian cabals; although there was no question of her loyalty to Schumann, which was proof against every doubt. On April 22nd she wrote to Schumann, in answer to his reproach that she was always too weak with her father, "Surely Father must often feel very unhappy; he is to be pitied, and I often grieve over it in my heart: but I cannot possibly alter it at all. Some-day it will be said that I have brought my Father to the grave — but One above will forgive me, have I not fulfilled all my duty towards him? .... Ah! Robert, forgive me if sometimes in later days a sudden melancholy comes over me when I think of my Father — it is so sad."

In this frame of mind she was surprised by a second letter from her father to Emilie, on May 1st, in which, con-trary to the method of threats and reproaches which he had hitherto employed, he suddenly changed his tone and appeal-ed to her heart. Without pausing to reflect, she answered at once:

"Paris 1./5. 39 [1]).

My beloved Father

We have received your letters from Dresden, and I thank you for your dear lines; I have a great longing to see you, my dear Father, again and to talk to you in all love and harmony; so let me at least do so in writing. I read your letter to Emilie and I frankly confess that you stirred much that I have long felt, and

---

1) Curtailed and printed with many mistakes by Kohut, *Fr. Wieck* p. 112 etc. In this, only the unimportant artistic news which comes at the end, is omitted.

have often turned over in my mind. My love for Schumann is certainly passionate, and yet I love him not alone out of passion and sentiment, but because I take him to be the best of men, because I believe that no man would love me so purely and nobly, or understand me as he does, and in like manner I believe that I too can make him perfectly happy, and certainly no other wife could understand him as I do. You will forgive me, dear Father, if I tell you that you none of you know him at all, — if only I could convince you of his goodness! Every man has his peculiarities, and surely ought to be treated accordingly? I know what Schumann lacks, and that is a friend, a man of experience who would stand by him and give him a helping hand; consider, that Schumann has never been about in the world — can it all come at once? Ah! Father, if you were a friend to him — you would certainly not find him ungrateful, and you would certainly respect him; do you think that I should love Schumann so, if I did not respect him? Do you not think that I know his faults well? But I know his virtues, too. Nothing would be wanting to our happiness save a competence, assured, even if small, and your consent; without the latter I should be very unhappy and could never be at rest, and it would be the same with Schumann, who has such a tender heart. What a life would be mine, cast off by you and knowing that you were unhappy! I could not bear that. Dear Father, do you promise me your consent if Schumann can show an income of 1000 thaler? 2000 thaler would be too much to demand, that can only come by degrees. Give us this hope, and we shall be happy, and Schumann will work with quite a different courage in order to win me; I promise you in return not to marry Schumann until we have the prospect of a life untrammelled by care. If Schumann wins a competence, as I firmly believe he will, and we have your consent, you will make us the happiest of mortals — otherwise, the unhappiest. I can never give him up, nor he me — I could never love another man — Please tell me frankly what you demand, what you think in your own heart, hold out no hope if you do not mean it in earnest. Ah! how happy you can make us! My heart is so full of love — will you break it? I have not deserved that! You think that I am not good, you say that my character is spoiled, that I do not know how you love me, that I am ungrateful — ah! Father, in this you do me a serious wrong. Emilie and Henriette are witnesses with what love I always speak

of you, even after your reproachful letters! Often have I wept
by myself at being parted from you, at not being able to accompany
you on your walks, at knowing that you call me ungrateful, and
so much besides. If ever I were devoted to you, 1 am now. You
scolded me in Leipsic for not being cheerful; only think for a
moment of the circumstances in which I was in Leipsic, think
how people usually behave when they are in love, and how much
they need loving and sympathetic surroundings, — had I these?
Durst I ever speak of my love? With whom would one sooner
speak of it than with one's parents? and especially I with you!
How often did I attempt to make you more sympathetic by giving
you my confidence, but on the contrary I always made you
more angry; I could do nothing right! I had to shut up my
love in my own heart, and had — ah! so frequently! — to hear
myself and the object of my love treated with comtempt — a
loving heart such as mine, cannot bear that; you did not know
my feelings; and you did not consider that every word of yours,
yes even a simple look, was able to lacerate my heart! Was
it so unnatural that I should feel unhappy? Ah! my dear Father,
how happy we should be if you would treat me with greater
consideration, and if you would allow but a spark of love for
Schumann to be re-kindled in you you would not find him ungrateful
— we should all be happy! If only 1 could tell you everything
that my heart says, if only I had you here, you would allow your
heart to be touched! — Or do you think me a liar? do you think
me false and hypocritical? I almost believe you do! In truth
you do not really know me! Other people love me because they
think that I am good, and you do not think me so? Oh yes, you
do! so give me a kiss — like that! Please write to me again at
once, I cannot remain long in suspense; you shall see how I will
live in my art. You think I do not love my art? God knows that
if there are moments when I forget all trouble, they are when I
am at the piano. You scolded me for not thanking you for your
letters; think of my situation, of how alone I stand in this great
city! Do I not need to have my courage kept up? And you did
everything you could to deprive me of it — cannot you imagine
how unhappy all this made me?

So you think I ought to go to Baden? I spoke to Meyerbeer
yesterday, and he did not advocate the plan, as expenses would be
heavy there, and concerts do not pay; I also thought it would be

best if I were to remain here for the summer, you would come here,
and I would give another concert in December; thus by gradually
making acquaintances, I would try to obtain recommendations in
Belgium and Holland, and then at the beginning of January we would
go to Belgium and Holland (that is the best time, there is nothing
to be done anywhere, now) and then in May, to England; Emilie
would accompany me on the whole tour, which would make things
much easier for you, if only on account of the language! Write
and tell me if you like this plan? But if you very much wish
me to go to Baden, I will go! But in any case I must come
back to Paris. If we did not go to Baden, perhaps you would
come here quite soon? Let me have an answer to all this, and
also to what I wrote to you earlier in my letter; but I beg you
most earnestly do not give me any hope in order to put me off
— you would only make me the more unhappy. . . ."

Certainly it was comprehensible and natural that in spite
of all that had happened and of what separated her from her
father, she should thus obey her filial instinct. It is less easy
to understand why by this invitation to Paris, which was in
deliberate opposition to what she knew to be Schumann's
views and wishes, she showed herself ready to subject herself
again to her father's influence. And it is quite incomprehensible, and can be excused only on the ground that Clara, like
Emilie, had completely lost her head for the moment, that
after having written to Schumann on April 27th: "You are
my sole support . . . . I have no-one save you upon this earth,
and you are ever dear to me. . . . I will do whatever you
wish, and at Easter I am yours", five days later, on May 2nd,
she could have written the following letter to Robert.

"Paris 2./5. 39.
My most dearly beloved Robert

It is with a heavy heart that I set out write to you to-day.
I must tell you of what has long been struggling within me, and
has to-day come to a head — it concerns the happiness of us both.
The thought of being separated from you still longer makes me

inexpressibly miserable, but keep up your heart, as I do mine! We cannot be married next Easter, we should not be happy. Let me speak to you quite frankly, my beloved Robert. Our happiness would be troubled in two directions, first on account of the un-certainty of our future, and then on account of my Father; I shall make Father most unhappy if I marry you without having an assured future in view; trouble about me would bring him to the grave, and it would be my fault, I should never know a moment's peace, the vision of my Father would be ever before me, and I should have to bear his sorrow, and yours, and my own; from what I know of you, I am sure that you would be most unhappy if you had even on one single occasion to worry about our liveli-hood, as artists we should both perish, overwhelmed with cares. All this came before me so vividly, that at last I could endure it no longer, I had to share it with you, and I spoke to Emilie about it, who thought me right, and you, my Robert, are sure to understand. See, if we have the certainty of even a small income, we shall be secure, we can live quietly and at the same time most happily, Father will then give his consent; he writes yesterday, that he would immediately give his consent if he could see that you could promise me a future free from care — but I am cer-tainly not thinking of myself as much as of you — that you would be very unhappy if your beautiful life as an artist were shadowed by daily cares — I feel it my duty to guard you from such a thing.

Robert, if Father begins his law-suit he can very easily cause us to be put off for a year, by this means we should be made more unhappy, you would have to be able to give proof before the court of — I believe — a certainty of 2000 thaler, and it does not need that to gain Father's willing consent. Father feels only too miserable, I cannot make him so unhappy. He writes that if he could see you acquire a fixed income he would certainly make every sacrifice to help on our marriage, he wants nothing for me but a future free from care, and you also wish for that. Let us wait another half, or whole year, in this way we shall both be able to accomplish a great deal more, and then we shall be doubly happy. Do not you think so, too? I can well imagine how dreadful it must be to you that I should write this, but you do not know how this idea, this decision, has weighed on me. You cannot possibly feel more unhappy than I do, but let us stand firm, and we shall find happiness. I have written to Father to ask if he will promise me to give his consent when you can show him an income of 1000 thaler, I, on my side, will promise him to enter upon no alliance with you unless we look forward to days free from anxiety. I had to do it! But I also wrote and told him that I would never give you up, I could never love again, and I once more assure you of this. Never will I give you up, never will I cease to be your faithful Clara. Ah! what a battle I fought before I decided to write to you this time, to tear you away from your fairest hopes, but I could no longer bear this thought by myself. You are a man, Robert, are you not, and will not abandon yourself to too deep sorrow? You can easily imagine my frame of mind at present, what endless anxiety I feel about you. Ah! if only I were with you! My longing is indescribably great. The thought that you could be angry with me for a moment makes me quite inconsolable, but no, you know how I love you, you know that you can never be so loved again, that no man is loved as you are. Are you convinced of this? Most urgently I beg you to write to me at once and tell me everything you feel, even if it be anger, and write and tell me if you still love me? I love you more every hour — do you believe that? Father means to come here this summer, and then to go with me to Belgium, Holland, England etc.; I realise that I can do much more with him, than alone; not that my courage fails me at all, oh! no, I had made up my mind to undertake all these journies alone, but from the start one is thought more of everywhere, if one is accompanied by a man.

Father wrote me a friendly letter yesterday, but his letter to Emilie was all the more desperate and heart-rending, and it caused the sudden ripening into decision of an idea which I had long been turning over in my mind. I wrote a letter to him, and if that does not soften him, I do not know what more I can say, I will let you know his answer at once, but I beg you too, my good Robert, not to let me live long in this fearful suspense....

. . . .

. . . . I can write you no more to-day, my heart is too full, and so doubtless is yours. If there is a word in this letter which pains you. forgive me for it; perhaps I seem cold to you, but if ever my heart beat warmly for you, it does so now. I can say no more — answer me *at once*, and set my mind at rest.

Take care of your health, I have already told you so often —
your life is mine. I kiss you in most heart-felt, unalterable love

Your faithful Clara.

Remain as true to me as I am to you till death. Let me but
clasp your hand once more! — Ah! if only I could see you, inspire you with courage — share your feelings. Heaven protect
you — may it hear my prayer."

It was the last straw that this unfortunate, and most ill-
considered letter together with an equally ill-advised one from
Emilie List, crossed the following letter from Schumann:

"Leipsic May 4th 1839 Saturday morning.
Most dearly loved wife that is soon to be, I sat with Reuter
yesterday, and made reckonings, and considered, and made out
that we are giving ourselves a great deal of unnecessary anxiety,
and that (if you, you obstinate person, only liked) we could take
each other to-morrow. . . .

I am frightened at our wealth, when I compare it with that
of others; how kind Heaven is to us, in that we have no need to
work for our daily bread; it is just sufficient for two simple artists
like ourselves; this thought makes me happy.

Your fortune	4000	thaler
My fortune		
1) In Government bonds	1000	„
2) In Karl's business.	4000	„
3) In Eduard's business	3540	„
4) From what Eduard left	1500	„
	14040	thaler
That gives an interest of	560	thaler
Other receipts yearly		
From Friese.	624	„
Sale of music	100	„
Earned from compositions	100	„
Receipts during the year	1384	thaler

Am I not a passed-master of arithmetic? . . . . And could you
not come to me at once if I very much wanted it?

LITZMANN, Clara Schumann. I.

And then could we not drink champagne now and then, or send Therese something if she wanted it, or your Mother? In short, do not be anxious, my Clärchen! I am after all as little frivolous-minded as your are! And how I have learned to prize money! Do you know, I often have to guard against attacks of avarice."

After this it is easy to conceive the crushing effect upon Schumann of the letters from Clara and Emilie, and to understand how he, thus hurled down from heaven, lost all composure for the moment. A second letter from Clara, which appears to have treated of the same subject even more harshly (though unintentionally so), was at once destroyed by him; and in later years he also destroyed his answer to both letters. The reply to Emilie's — the only letter preserved — gives an echo of the dissonance which was awakened in Robert's soul by this misunderstanding — for it was nothing more. It was as much a matter of course that Clara should never for a moment seriously have thought of separating her lot from Schumann's, at that Schumann, who was still suffering from the effects of the shock of his brother's death, should consider her behaviour incomprehensible from his point of view, and should take it as a personal insult. His letter itself however, which crossed with the two ill-omened letters from her, and which entirely destroyed all grounds for anxiety, afforded an opportunity for a rapid understanding, which Clara took without hesitation, writing to Robert on May 13th:

". . . . Tell me, my good, beloved Robert, what I am to do in order to awaken once more your tenderer feelings towards me? Please tell me, I cannot be at ease when I know that you are angry with me. You misunderstood me, that was the whole evil, and you doubted me — you ought not to have done that! . . . . Nothing can hurt me more than when you suspect my character and my love for you, I do not deserve that, and I too could be bitterly angry — if I could be! — Kiss me in your old love, as I kiss you with a love that is ever renewed; I love you too much, and I will soon prove it to you, rely upon that. What bitter tears you have cost me again! I am so wretched at having made you unhappy even for a moment, and now I shall have no peace until I have quieting news from you once again, and the assurance that your feeling towards me is restored — please write to me at once. . . .

. . . . Yesterday we were on the point of going out when we were frightened back by cry, 'Revolution'; the drums to summon the National Guard sounded throughout the whole city, and from 3 o'clock in the afternoon till 12 at night there was constant firing; over 50 people were killed. The Tuilleries look like a fort; all night the palace was surrounded by troops, who lay round a blazing fire in the court-yard. . . . To-day it is once more possible to walk through the streets without danger, of which I am very glad as I must go to the post.

It is very gloomy to-day; these dark clouds have such a strange affect on my spirits, and in addition to everything else came your letters to Emilie and Henriette to-day! I should be inconsolable if you had not had some pity on me and had not still called me your Clärchen, at the end. . . .

. . . . The Dukes of Orleans and Nemours are now riding about the streets in order to pacify the people. The King is agitated, the Queen trembles — I am in the worst case for I suppose it is all over with my playing at court, and it had seemed fairly certain.

Now, my dear Robert, I must vex you a little; I am going to have a look at the revolution, it interests me extremely — I hope that nothing will happen to me. I kiss you in warmest love and with all my soul. Your faithful sweetheart before long your happy wife."

With Robert's answer of May 18th, complete harmony was once more restored.

A few days later, on the first day of the Whitsuntide festival, he added the following important continuation:

"Listen, my Clärchen, our plan of waiting till Christmas to write to your father, is no good. It must be done before that. . . . So I am enclosing two letters, one to your father, which I mean to send to him . . . . a few days before your birthday, and another to be at once handed to the Court of Appeal, if he refuses his consent. . . .

We cannot possibly come to a decision in any other way; I cannot impress this upon you with sufficient strength, my dear Clara. . . .

. . . . One thing more, my Clara, so that my character may be entirely clear to you. You often write and ask if I could endure the anxieties of procuring daily bread? We need expect none; but if they came, and if we had only half as much as we have — this could never trouble me; it would only trouble me if I were in debt to people and could not pay — only then — but not otherwise — I am too much of a poet for this — but you will not therefore find me careless, and I have given you proof of how exact I am in everything — for your sake.

Thank God, the revolution is over; but Paris is always in a state of ferment over something or other; so be careful, and do not venture too far inside the barricades — but I rely chiefly upon your timidity, and so I am fairly calm.

Now I will copy the two letters for yon: think them over carefully, they are the most important letters of our whole lives. Courage and confidence, my dearest Clara. In all unending love Your

once more quite happy Robert."

SCHUMANN TO WIECK.

"Once more I come before you, hand in hand with Clara, to beg your consent to our marriage next Easter. Two years have passed since my first proposal. You doubted if we should remain true to each other; we have done so, nothing can make us waver in our belief in our future happiness.

What I wrote to you before, concerning my income was absolutely true, everything has turned out even more favourably and securely; we can look forward to the future with confidence. Listen to the voice of nature; do not drive us to extremes! In a few day it will be Clara's twentieth birthday, give peace on that day; say yes. We need rest after so terrible a strife, you owe it to Clara and to me. I look forward with longing to your definite answer

Your

long since, and still ever attached and confiding

R. Schumann."

"Dear Clara, the letter is cold; it is as if one spoke gave fair words to a lump of ice; I cannot help it; write and tell me your opinion of the letter. The following is largely Hermann's[1]."

"We, the undersigned, have for a long time cherished a common and heartfelt wish to be united to each other in matrimony. But up to the present time there has been an obstacle to the fulfilment of this determination, whose removal is necessary for the attainment of our object, though it gives us the deepest pain to seek to obtain it in this manner. That is to say, the father of the co-signatory, Clara Wieck, regardless of the repeated requests which have been courteously made to him, refuses us his consent. We cannot explain the grounds of his refusal; we are conscious of no faults; our circumstances are such that we can venture to look forward to an assured future. The cause, therefore, which prevents Herr Wieck from giving his consent to this union can only be a feeling of personal animosity towards the other signatory, who yet believed that he on his side had fulfilled every duty which a man owes to the father of her whom he has chosen to be his companion through life. However this may be, we are not willing to give up our carefully weighed determination on this account, and therefore we approach the High Court with the most humble request:

That your worships will cause Herr Wieck to give his consent to our union in marriage, or if you think fit would graciously be pleased to give us your consent instead of his. Nothing but the conviction of the urgent necessity of this step can reconcile us to it, and we are at the same time animated by the confident hope that in this case, as in so many others, time will heal this painful division.

Leipsic, September 1839.   Robert Schumann
                               Clara Wieck
                               at present in Paris."

"For the first time, sweetheart, you must join your name to mine; it is too bitter-sweet. Test every word of the document. . . . . You will want your baptismal certificate for the marriage. Dear Clärchen, it is a beautiful thing that you are in the world. . . . . Remember me to Emilie and Henriette; they must like me

---

1) An actuary and friend of Schumann's.

as much as I like them. Henriette must often whisper to you her fine, strong saying, 'Quickly to the goal'. Well, it will soon be settled. I have complete confidence in you once more. Write soon, my love."

In the mean time, Clara on her side, had told her father that according to the statement which she had received from Robert, his present circumstances entirely fulfilled the conditions which Wieck had himself laid down, and had begged him to lay aside his opposition. Wieck had written a long letter in answer to this, which Clara, always too ready to read what she wanted to read, once more took for a consent which would spare them the appeal to the Court, but which Schumann, when on May 2nd he became acquainted with the text, judged more fairly when he wrote: "You cannot take this letter for a consent, we stand exactly where we were [1])."

In the mean time Robert's birthday had come round; the last, as they then thought, which they would pass as an engaged couple. Clara surprised Robert with her portrait, which she had had painted in Paris, and with a cigar-case which she had worked herself, and she received from him a letter

---

1) The "consent" was bound up with the 6 following conditions:

1. That Robert and Clara should not take up their abode in Saxony, so long as Wieck was alive, but that in spite of this Schumann must earn as much elsewhere as his newspaper brought him in Leipsic.
2. That Wieck should not give up Clara's property for 5 years, but until that time should pay 5% interest.
3. That Schumann should have the statement of his income which he had submitted to Wieck in 1837 formally audited and then given into the hands of a lawyer chosen by Wieck.
4. That Schumann should hold no communication with him either by word of mouth or in writing, until Wieck himself expressed the wish for it.
5. That Clara should give up all claim to her inheritance.
6. That the wedding should take place before Michaelmas 1839.

which strikingly and beautifully reflected the noblest side
of his pure, fine, and tender nature.

"Leipsic June 3rd 1839.

My dearly Beloved

You will receive this letter on my 29th birthday. May it find
you fresh in body and soul, and may it reflect my image more
tenderly than ever. . . . We can look back on the past year
without reproaching ourselves; we have held loyally to each other,
we have advanced, and we are much nearer to our goal. I think
that the worst is over-come; but even now that we are entering
the haven let us be cautious. Fate has ordained that we are to
fight our way inch by inch, but when once we stand at the
altar I believe that a 'Yes' will never before have been uttered
with such conviction, with such firm faith in a happy future.
What must I not do before this point is reached? Become more
and more worthy of you. Do not take this for a mere fashion
of speech. In the face of baseless arrogance I am proud; but
before modesty such as yours I willingly confess my weakness
and try to improve myself. In years to come you will often
worry about me, so much is still needed to make a man of
me; I am often too restless, too childish, too yielding; and I
often abandon myself to whatever gives me pleasure without
considering other people; in short, I have my bad days on which
there is nothing to be done with me — Forbearance and love,
such as you have so often shown me, will gradually mould me,
the mere fact of having you with me always must make me a
better man; but these are mere words. The one thing certain is
that we love each other with all our hearts, and I believe that
in your heart is a rich mine of love with which you will long
make your husband happy. You are a wonderful girl, Clara! In
you are united so many beautiful and various characteristics that
I cannot think how you have contrived to develop them all in the
course of you short life, especially in such surroundings. One
thing I know; that I, with my gentle manner, early made an impression on you, and I think you would have been a different girl
if you had never seen and known me. Let me be happy in the
belief that I have taught you love, your father hate (I mean it in
the best sense, for one must know how to hate), that I have made

you into the ideal bride of my dreams; you were my most gifted pupil, and as recompense you have said to me: 'Take me, too'."

The full radiance of his joy shines through the merry letter which he sent his betrothed the next morning, describing the festival itself:

.... I shall never forget yesterday. If only I could describe all the festivities which took place! Will you listen to your old teller of fairy-tales?

I woke early, with joy bells ringing in my heart. My first thought flew to you. . . . My first birthday greeting came from the sun which poured into my little room on the park; it was one of those mornings when one longs to spread one's wings and soar away at once. I spent the early morning in giving audience to my thoughts and making good resolutions. Not till nearly 10 o'clock was the world admitted. The artists sent me one of their worthiest disciples as representative .... he had on a frock-coat and wanted to make a speech. But I thought to myself, the chief festivities must be held out in the open air, under green trees; and so, proud as a king, I went with gentle little Schmidt[1]) to Connewitz. Butterflies were my satellites, and larks flew on either side to greet the birthday hero; whole fields of wheat-ears nodded their birthday-greetings, and the sky would not allow the tiniest cloud to appear lest there should be any thought that it could be darkened. My heart leaped for joy, and I often thought of my Queen in distant lands. We had our meal at my summer residence, Connewitz, a very moderate and simple one after the fashion of the lords of ancient days, and with many a kind word addressed to my page. After we had eaten, my page suggested an expedition into the surrounding country, and accompanied by the incessant song of the nightingales, we looked to right and to left. All nature was teeming with youth, and I felt proud of my kingdom. We took our mid-day nap under a green tree, and on every side fluttering and humming inhabitants of earth took the opportunity of inspecting the hero of the day more closely while he slept, and

---

1) Gustav Martin Schmidt, music-teacher in Leipsic, and a protégé of Schumann's. See Jansen *Davidsbündler* p. 42.

even touched him with their wings. Hardly was I awake when there came flying over the fields the rapid step of a new ambassador, for foreign lands would not be behind-hand and had chosen Verhulst, who suddenly stood before me and in fitting words most excellently expressed how he wished to see me soon united to my Queen, whom an iron father holds in custody. For his part, the King grew ever more silent and more blessed. Four o'clock had arrived when he felt almost certain of receiving a message of love from his chosen one. But when he came to his palace in the Park there was nothing there. A few light clouds may have passed over his face, but only light ones; for that a message would not be wanting on such a day the 29-year-old lover had good cause to believe. Meanwhile the time was passed away at my faithful piano, and in a few minutes there entered: — first a yellow-clad state ambassador with a letter from my royal betrothed, and shortly after my dear friend and physician[1]) with a myrtle-wreath and cleverly hidden offerings. And as I drew off the covering and your picture shone forth like that of a bride, I forget all consideration of my high rank and of those with me, and kissed it and gazed at it and kissed it again, and then read — and the rest can be imagined."

How justly Schumann had appreciated the situation, Clara was to learn only too soon from her own father, and at the same time she had an opportunity of showing that the experiences of the last few weeks had not passed over her without leaving their mark. At the end of May, or the beginning of June, she received a long letter from her father, with an enclosure — containing his conditions — and the explicit demand that she should at once sign this and return it. "The whole thing," as she wrote to Robert, "was expressed in so extremely insulting a manner, that I was horrified to think it possible that my father could have written it."..... Thus, as she told Robert some days later, her answer, which she sent off on June 9th, in spite of its affection "sounded cold"; she had, she said, written somewhat as follows: "I received your

---

1) Dr. Reuter.

last letter, but I cannot say much to you in answer, since it
would be useless to try to bring you round to other views;
our ideas are too diametrically opposed; you are firmly convinced of Schumann's wickedness, I of the contrary, and that
he alone can make me happy.

Yet let me answer one thing! I have not subscribed to
your conditions, and I tell you that I will never subscribe to
them, I have too much proper pride: besides, how could you
think that I would sign a paper in which evil things are said
of the man I love? You were not serious, and if you were,
I can only say, 'You will never get me to do such a thing'."
On this occasion Schumann could well be contented with his
"brave Clärchen", and Wieck, by over-straining his bow, once
more obtained just the opposite of what he had intended.

On his birthday, Schumann had sent Clara the memorial
to the Court, with the request that she would return the
document as soon as possible, together with her attested
signature, so that if Wieck should send an adverse answer
to Schumann's renewed application, the decisive step might
immediately be taken. He wished to hasten on the actual
application, so as not to leave Wieck time for fresh surprises
and crooked dealings. Wieck's own procedure brought about
the decision. Clara signed the application without hesitation
fully conscious of its meaning. "The moment in which I
signed, was the most important in my life. But I wrote my
name firmly and resolutely, and was boundlessly happy." The
die was cast. She had openly proclaimed herself Schumann's
betrothed wife.

On June 24th Schumann sent the following letter to Clara's
father:

    "Honoured Sir

Clara writes to me that you yourself desire that we should
make an end; I gladly offer my hand in token of peace. Tell
me your wishes; what I can do to meet them, I am ready to do

with pleasure. If you have given no answer to my request by a week from to-day, I shall take it as a decided refusal.

Your most obedient

R. S. "

The answer, which Schumann considered "impertinent", consisted in a letter written by Frau Wieck at her husband's request, saying that "Wieck would have no communication with Schumann".

Now that Clara's certified power of attorney had come from Paris, on the 29th, Schumann, on June 30th, turned to Einert, the Leipsic solicitor, and begged for his legal support in pursuit of the matter. "We wish," he wrote, "the matter to be concluded as soon as possible, in a friendly manner if you advise it, and if you think that an interview with Herr Wieck can lead to anything, but failing this, by means of an application to the Court of Appeal, which cannot deny us its consent, since our income is sufficiently assured."

On July 16th Schumann presented his indictment before the Court of Appeal, and he wrote to Clara at the same time: "You will have to be here in from six to ten weeks. Einert will indeed do everything to prevent it from coming to this, but it does not depend upon him. And if the Court requires you in person, you will have to appear."

On July 27th he had to tell her the decision of the Court: that in the first place they were to attempt to come to a friendly understanding in the presence of the Superintendent[1]), and that on the day fixed the personal attendance of all those

1) On July 19th the Court had already given a decision to this effect, and indeed, as Wustmann has pointed out (p. 512) it proceeded in a remarkable manner from the mistaken premise this was a case of "ordinary matrimonial dispute" in which the law required that any such attempt at reconciliation must take place in presence of the pastor, before the Court accepted the indictment. Robert had already told Clara of this decision on the 23rd, but always in the hope that Einert would succeed in getting them dispensed from personal attendance on the day.

concerned was indispensable. Against this decision no pretext was of avail, and with a heavy heart Clara was obliged to make up her mind to the dreaded journey to Leipsic, without so much as an idea whether, and when, she would return to Paris again.

On August 13th, from the summit of the Pantheon, looking over the sea of houses, she took farewell of Paris for the second time, and the next day she Henriette set out for Frankfort. At the end of April she had written to Robert, "You do not know how unhappy I am among the French, and how home-sick I am for Germany". Thus the parting was not too grievous to her, irrespective of the fact that the prospect of soon meeting Robert again made everything appear in a brighter light.

From an artistic point of view this second residence in Paris can by no means be compared with the first journey undertaken in her father's company; although upon all those with whom she came into contact socially and artistically, she left the impression of a remarkable personality, and although applause and appreciation had not been lacking when she appeared in public. But there was no question of a success such as she had hoped for from her Parisian visit, a success which should strengthen and spread abroad her recent European fame, and above all things should prepare her way in England and Russia. So far Wieck had proved only too right in reckoning that Clara, a 20-year-old girl standing alone and wholly dependent on the doubtful good will of rival fellow-artists, would find how little she could cope with affairs in Paris without a man's protection.

No longer could she rely on that relentless force with which Wieck, the impresario who feared no trouble or annoyance and who well understood how to restrain and intimidate the makers of cabals, had hitherto made way for her. She had painfully realised her own inability to wage war against envy and intrigue. Besides this, with her conception of life, and engaged as she was in internal conflict, she could not adapt herself to the views and customs of Parisian society, and in most of the houses which, like the Erards', were hospitably opened to her at this time — as they had been, years before — she could not feel at home. The protection and friendship of the Lists had indeed been of incalculable service to her during these months; and Henriette Reichmann's self-sacrificing and devoted love had been a stay and comfort to her; but these kind protectors had not been able to provide her with the support and countenance which she — a girl of twenty — needed on entering the world and appearing in public. Other friends, such as Pauline Garcia, whom for some time she saw daily[1]), found more than enough to occupy them in their own concerns; the distances in a large city, her own journies, and the fact that the season was drawing to an end, isolated her more and more.

At the end of May she had already written to Robert: "I am sorry I can send you no artistic news; in the first place there is not much that is new to speak of, and then I know nothing of what there is, for I live quite like a hermit, and for whole days I never see a single soul from outside"; and when Clara and Henriette went into the country, to Bougival, in the summer (from June 22nd) her last connection with society was practically severed. Only with the Countess Dobreskoff, who had taken a great fancy to Clara and who repeatedly invited her to visit her in St Petersburg, does she seem to have held more regular intercourse up to the very time of her departure, though thanks to the various matrimonial plans with which the Russian lady, in entire ignorance of the circumstances, sought to make her favourite happy,

---

1) On Feb. 20th the diary says: "Pauline Garcia has been to see me several times a-day for the last week." On March 12th: "Pauline came to see me again after a long interval."

there was no real intimacy between them. In addition to
this, political circumstances had brought the season to a
close earlier than usual, repeated disturbances in the streets
kept all minds in a state of excitement, and the interest in
Clara's artistic power which had just been awakened at
court, was nipped in the bud. In this manner she had been
living in Paris since April as she might have lived in any
other of the larger cities, but without gaining through this
inactivity the rest for which she was longing. "You ask
me," she wrote to Schumann at the beginning of June, "if
I do not read any Gœthe — what do you think? I have no
time. We go to Montmartre early in the morning, and at
9 I begin to play and play till 12, then we lunch until
1 o'clock, then I have messages to do in the city, which
always take me out for 3 hours, for everything is so far off,
then I come home tired, rest, read French with Emilie till
half-past 5, when we dine, that lasts till 7, then I give Henriette her lesson, that lasts till 9 o'clock, or I write to you,
or write other letters, in fact I cannot manage to read German."
She really enjoyed teaching Henriette. On the other hand,
she absolutely suffered from the lessons which she had to
give twice a week to two entirely superficial, unmusical
English-women, and which, in spite of the time and vexation
which they cost her, she continued after she had moved to
Bougival.

At times she clearly felt that this isolation in a strange
city not only did not help, but actually injured her art.

"Do you know what I long for?" she writes on June 27th
to Robert, "For a lesson from Father; I am afraid of going
back because I have no-one left to tell me of my faults, and
faults are sure to have crept in, as in studying I am too absorbed in the music and often let myself be carried away, and
then I do not hear the bad notes. In this respect I have much
for which to thank Father, and yet I hardly ever did so, but on

the contrary I was usually unwilling — ah! how gladly would
I now listen to his faultfinding!"

Musically — apart from opera — Paris had afforded her
but little stimulus; the particular stars of the moment in no
way impressed her, and she was perfectly aware that they
were incapable of appreciating the best in her[1]). And this
was true not only of people like Berlioz, who met her this
time with coldness and dislike, but also of the mass of the
unbiassed public.

These experiences in Paris had caused her to shrink back
from the still greater venture of trying her fortune in London
without a male protector. And Robert's plan of going to
S[t] Petersburg directly after the wedding, seemed to her premature.

The dispensation which carried her away from Paris before
she had decided on this, proved fortunate in the event, for
Paris at the moment contained comparatively few elements
which were likely to help on her artistic development, and
at best had only grudgingly offered her a means of livelihood.
It seems strange that she received perhaps her friendliest greeting from old Cramer, who had heard her play her *Variations*
at a concert in the St Cécile Musical Club, and who had
sought her out afterwards: "He is a very nice old man," she
wrote to Robert, "but has advanced very little with the times;
he abused Liszt dreadfully, he delights in Beethoven alone,
all others are nothing in his eyes." "Can you believe", she

---

1) We may quote here, as characteristic not only of her circumstances
in Paris, but still more of her particular point of view, the impression
which the 9th symphony, heard for the first time amid these surroundings,
made upon her. On Feb. 10th she heard it at the Conservatoire. "The
symphony," she writes in the diary, "is a great work, but if I am to be
frank, I must say that I did not understand the last movement. My
mind could not grasp it, nor parts of the Adagio. The whole did not
impress me as beautiful. It seems to me that of it here, but the material
is magnificent they have but a very superficial conception."

adds, "that I play Cramer's two first *Études* every morning? I play them first as they are written, and then the first one in octaves which is good practice. I always play one of Scarlatti's sonatas, too; I am so fond of them."

Otherwise we learn comparatively little of her musical studies at this time. She delighted in the themes of Thalberg's *Mosesphantasie* which she studied in May, but she found it full of difficulties. And she thought that some of the Liszt *Études* which she attempted during these months, were too much for her powers. She was naturally interested in the new works which appeared, and never tired of asking for new consignments. But now as always, she naturally found her chief interest in Schumann's own productions. At this time she first became acquainted with his *Fantasie*[1]. "Yesterday," she writes to Robert on May 23rd, "I received your glorious *Fantasie* — and, I am almost ill with sheer delight; as I glanced through it, I found myself driven involuntraily to the window and I felt as if I must throw myself out on to the beautiful spring flowers and embrace them. I dreamt a beautiful dream while I read your *Fantasie*. The march is delightful, and bars 8—16 page 15 carry me completely away; tell me, what you were thinking of then? I never before received such an impression, I heard an entire orchestra, an indescribable feeling came over me."

And four days later:

"I have already learnt the march from *Fantasie*, and revel in it! If only I could hear it played by a great orchestra! It makes me hot and cold all over. Tell me what sort of a mind have you?

---

1) "You can understand the *Fantasie*," Schumann had written, "only if you put yourself back into the unhappy summer of 1836, when I relinquished you; now I have no need to compose in so unhappy and melancholy a fashion. Cf. *Jugendbriefe* I p. 302. Some of the following passages from his letters have been printed in the *Jugendbriefe*.

When once I am with you I shall never to think of composing again. I should be a fool."

And on June 16th:

"— Many pictures pass before my eyes as I play your *Fantasie*, but they are sure to coincide with yonrs. The march seems to me like the victorious march of warriors returning from battle, and the $A\flat$ major makes me think of the young girls from the village, all clothed in white, each with a wreath in her hand, crowning the warriors who kneel before them, and of many other things which you know already; and I often think too, that I am very fond of the composer, and when the $A\flat$ major comes I fancy myself standing among the maidens and crowning you, my dear warrior and conqueror, and doing much besides[1])."

But she was not fated to receive the *Novelletten* in Paris. Schumann told her of them on June 30th, when he wrote: "In the *Novelletten* you, my bride, appear in every possible setting and harmony, and in other ways in which you are irresistible! Yes, only look at me! I assert, that he alone can write *Novelletten* who knows eyes like yours, who has touched such lips as yours — in short, it may well be possible to do better work, but hardly to do anything similar[2])."

During these months she herself composed but little. "I might easily be industrious here," she writes on one occasion, "but I always feel so limp. I do not know what is the matter with me!" But it was very likely the consciousness of Robert's superiority in this respect which involuntarily hampered her, as she had already said when speaking of the *Fantasie*.

All the same this visit did produce some fruits, although she found it difficult to make up her mind to tell Robert about them. "You ask me," she says in a letter of April 23rd,

---

1) *Jugendbriefe* vol. I p. 303

2) They were by no means wholly unknown to her; she had already played them in manuscript in the summer of /38. Cf. Clara's letter to Robert 15./8. /38 p. 158.

"if I am not composing anything; I have written one quite tiny piece, but I do not know what I shall call it. I have a peculiar aversion to showing you anything that I have composed, I am always ashamed."

Some days before, on April 18th, she had already mentioned a little composition: "Yesterday evening I was very happy; I had a beautiful idea for a little romance, day but to-I am already dissatisfied with it." No doubt the entry in the diary refers to this: "April 20th, I composed a little dramatic andante."

But it was not this piece, which by Robert's request she sent to him for the musical supplement to the paper, but another composition, in $A\flat$ major, also dating from this time, which she called *Idylle*. In thanking her for it, on May 19th, Schumann found all sorts of objections to make to this name: *Idylle*, he thought, was not the right word, "it is more elegiac; I recognised you so completely in it, the same girl as ever, with your eyes full of emotion". He advised *Notturno* instead, but Clara liked this as little as she did his later suggestion of *Heimweh* (Home-sickness) or *Mädchens Heimweh*. "It is more of a valse than a nocturne," she declared with decision, but added: "Forgive me, it is only what I think!" But still more decided was her refusal to accept the alterations which Schumann himself made in the composition. And when, on June 9th, he wrote fairly confidently: "Write and tell me if you like your *Idylle* as I have altered it. At any rate it has gained in finish as well as in beauty of proportion", she by no means gave way, but kept to her own opinion.

"I have received the *Idylle*, and thank you for it my dear; but I am sure you will forgive me if I tell you that there are some things in it which I do not like. The end, which I liked best, you have completely altered; and yet it impressed everyone to whom I played it; the theme seems to me too learned from the outset, too little simple and clear, although more skilfully treated. You have added much that is beautiful, but I think it is too learned for the French, and I wanted to ask you if you think it would be a good thing if I were to let it be printed here, together with several other little things, as I had it first, and if you were to take it for the paper as you have altered it and were to call it *Notturno*, though the name seems to me odd — I cannot help thinking it is more like an idyll. You are not angry with me, are you?"

In the mean time Schumann had replied, on May 22nd, in a tone at once yielding and firm: "I seem to have misunderstood your *Idylle* but I wish you could hear me play it; I took the piece very slowly and altered it according to this conception. But whatever happens, do not leave those open fifths at the beginning, they are too common-place and have significance only when justified by what follows, as in Beethoven's ninth symphony." On July 3rd he ended the little discussion in a conciliatory tone: "How can you say that I did not like your *Idylle*? How often do I play it to myself! You often have such tender *motifs*. You too, know rapture, hey? But when it comes to working them out, you girls who are in love stick fast. You have thoughts and hopes of all sorts — send me the romance at once, do you hear, Clara Wieck?"

These by no means isolated experiences of the strength of Clara's power of passive resistance, even towards him, in artistic matters were not without an influence on Schumann, and he let fall some expressions at this time, which betray some slight anxiety: "And yet I believe that we often differ widely in our opinions. May this give us no bitter hours later on." But this very romance, "the little melancholy romance, in which I thought continually of you", as Clara wrote on June 21st, and which she sent him on July 2nd with the request: "Play it very freely, sometimes passionately, and then again with melancholy — I am very fond of it, send it back to me soon please, and do not mind finding fault with it — that can only be of use to me", was to make him once more most happily conscious of the intimate relationship of their musical dispositions. "In your romance," says a letter of July 10th, "I have heard a-new that we must be man and wife. You complete me as a composer, as I do you. Every thought of yours comes from my soul, just as I have to thank you for all my music." And two days later: "It is wonderful! When did you write the piece in *G* minor? I had an exactly similar idea in March, you will find it in the *Humoreske*. Our sympathies are too remarkable." On July 18th he once more lays stress on Clara's fears lest she should not suffice him "in all things": "I like your romance more and more, particularly the idea in the allegro from bar 2 onwards, it is like Beethoven, and is most tender and full of passion."

It was also this romance which, as he himself says, gave him "a beautiful idea": "You shall compose as quickly as possible a nocturne related (perhaps) to the idyll and the romance, possibly in $E\flat$ major, so that this last work may stand half way between $A\flat$ major and $G\flat$ minor and all three may form one whole. You shall call the volume *Phantasiestücke* which seems to me the most suitable — we will write to Mechetti[1]), who has so often asked you for compositions — and then you can dedicate it to the person who loves you best in the whole world, and whom I will not describe to you more exactly."

"It is a sin," she had written to Robert on July 15th, "that I have composed nothing for such a long time. Father is very annoyed, and I too am often unhappy about it, but am altogether more dissatisfied with myself than I can say."

This idea of Robert's, which was at once seized upon and carried out by her with a few little alterations, made it pos-

---

1) Music publisher in Vienna.

sible for her to return home from Paris not entirely empty-handed; which was, indeed, scarcely a cause of pleasure to Friedrich Wieck. The new work, which was published as Op. 11 by Mechetti in November 1839, bore the title:

Trois Romances pour le Piano
dédiées à Monsieur Robert Schumann
par Clara Wieck.

It contained as No. 1 the new *Romance* in $E\flat$ minor, as No. 2 the *Romance* in G minor [1]), and as No. 3 the *Idylle* in $A\flat$ major.

She brought no treasures home this time, and no new wreathes of fame, only the modest handful of an unassuming gleaner. But this was important on account of the union of their names on the title-page. Just so from the lips of the gleaner in the Bible story there rang out to all the world a cry of faithful loyalty: "Whither thou goest, I will go; and where thou lodgest, I will lodge."

---

1) The *Romance* in G minor had already appeared under the title *Andante and Allegro for Pianoforte by Clara Wieck*, in September 1839, in the 7th Volume of the supplement to the *Neue Zeitschrift für Musik*.

CHAPTER VII.

FINAL STRUGGLES.

1839—1840.

"I have not enjoyed my youth at all," Clara once wrote to Robert, "You will make up to me for it; I always stood alone in the world; my Father loved me dearly, and I him, but a mother's love, which a girl needs so much, I never enjoyed, and thus I was never entirely happy."

The lament over the mother's love which was denied her, re-appears frequently in her letters during this period of conflict. She felt strongly that a mother would have found ways and means if not to do away with the dispute between her and her father, at least to smooth it over. That this was not the case, but that on the contrary her step-mother strengthened Wieck still more in his implacable attitude towards his daughter, without herself making the slightest attempt to help the young and inexperienced girl in her dire need, Clara had already had the pain of realising during her stay in Paris. "Please," she begged Robert at the end of June, "and always send me news of Father, I am often very uneasy when I hear nothing at all. It hurts me that my Mother should be so cold, and that she should never even think of writing to me, I never hear anything of the dear little girls; it is as if I had no family left. Six months have now passed, and still I have no letter from home which could give me real pleasure; it is hard! I have always been devoted to them all." Yet she had always felt a stranger in her parents' house. "I have bought everything with my own money," says a letter to Schumann, "I have not received a pin from my parents; they have never given me a thing, my Mother never so much as gave me a cherry or a plum. 'You have money of your own', they always said."

Notwithstanding, it is easy to realise Clara's depression at the thought that she would return home to find her parents' house closed against her; and how, in spite of the joy of seeing her lover again and of all the friendly hands which were stretched out towards her on all sides in order to keep her from feeling abandoned and orphaned, she trembled, and feared the return home.

For this very reason she must have been the more thankful and delighted that a mother's arms were opened to the homeless wanderer just at this moment, and that her own mother did not forsake her child, but remained true to her. It was not only a satisfaction in the eyes of the world, but it gave new life to her, wearied and worn as she was by the struggle with her father. At the beginning of July they had already asked Marianne Bargiel's consent to their marriage. She had replied to Robert on July 18th:

"Berlin July 18th 1839.

Dear Sir

There is indeed no fairer name than that of mother. It has always made me happy, and how should it not do so on such an occasion as this? — I have heard much from Clara of your affection for each other, but not nearly enough! — I am not in the least disinclined to permit it, but further explanations and details are needed for our mutual satisfaction!

I will also write to Clara to-day, in order to comfort her, as I see from her letter that she is in a very excited condition, which makes me very anxious! — I am much looking forward to making the personal acquaintance of the man who has

so completely filled and taken possession of my dear Clara's
heart. —

So there awaits you as soon as possible a very anxious
mother
                                    Marianne Bargiel."

This letter, which in spite of all its cautious and justifi-
able reserve was yet so pronouncedly favourable, had reached
Robert in Zwickau, and had produced a most salutary effect
by rousing him out of the deep melancholy into which he had
fallen there. A few days later — for the first time in his life
— he went to Berlin, armed with Clara's picture, his own,
an entire copy of the *Zeitschrift*, and several new compositions, "so that she may come to know me". "I will so ensnare
her with flattering and imploring words," he wrote to Clara,
"that I will have her 'Yes'."

What success he met with, is best shown by the following letters to Clara from Robert and from her mother.

                    "Berlin July 30ᵗʰ 1839 Tuesday.

My best beloved Clara

I must send you in your lonely village a few words of loving
greeting from this place in which I am so vividly reminded of you.
It is your mother who reminds me of you so much; I quite love
her, with her (your) eyes, and I can never tear myself away from
her. Yesterday I was with her nearly all day, and I kissed her
good-night too. That made me quite happy. We have talked
of nothing but you. . . . She received me so kindly and warmly,
and she seems to like me. If only you were with us; yesterday
evening as we were walking in the *Thiergarten* I thought so sadly
of my lonely, distant girl, who did not know that her mother and
lover were talking of her. . . . .

Your mother is going to write to you herself to-day. . . . You
are afraid that your father will get hold of you; but Clärchen girl,
have you not arms with which to defend yourself. In the first
place I do not believe that he will do it; but in the second —
if he requires that you should return to his house, you can say
quite simply, 'I will not, I will go to my mother', he can do noth-

ing to prevent that. — I have brought your picture with me, as I told you before. When I showed it to your mother the tears gushed from her eyes, and she was quite upset. When the Bargiel children saw it, they all said. . . . 'That is Clara' — that gave me heartfelt pleasure. . . .

. . . . I had not thought this city was so beautiful, and I have been wandering about the Museum with delight. Do you know the Rotunda at the entrance? If one sings a chord there quite softly, it resounds from the roof as if it came from a hundred throats, so that I was quite enchanted. Perhaps I shall soon wander through these beautiful halls with my beloved. . . ."

MARIANNE BARGIEL TO CLARA.

"Berlin 30/7. 39.

My beloved Clara, your Robert has been here since yesterday, and I can tell you, to my real joy, that I approve of your choice, and that I grow fonder of him every hour. . . . . . .

. . . . The first and most necessary thing, my dear child, is that you should come here. — Without your presence in person there can be no possible end to this affair, and as what is most desirable for us all is that you should be married soon, you will not hesitate to carry this through. . . . There is so much to discuss also, even between you two, which cannot be done by letter. You can go back again to Paris; it does indeed cost a great deal of money, but circumstances are such that nothing else is possible. I have written to your father, but he has not answered: however, that cannot be helped; matters must be brought to an end. — If I had you here now, how happy it would make me to see you both with me. — Robert played several of his compositions to us to-day, which gave us the highest enjoyment! What a beautiful talent! — How happy I shall be in your marriage! —"

Much was achieved by this, and if Clara for a time, out of consideration for Wieck, and in order not to embitter her father still more by this means, thought that she ought not to accede to the wishes of them both and take up her residence with her mother, but wished to put off deciding until after the day fixed by the Court, yet the knowledge that at any given moment she could at a word have her mother at her side, made it much easier for her to make up her mind to go back to Leipsic.

"It was time that this terrible situation should be brought to an end," wrote Schumann on Aug. 9th, "It was destroying me; mind and body were giving way, I could not think or work — and as to my art, how I lost ground in that! But now that I am soon to see you, all will be well again."

Clara's diary describes the journey itself, the first meeting, and what happened afterwards.

"On August 14th Henriette and I went to Frankfort by coach. The Hahns, to whom we were recommended by Madame List, came to meet us, and very kindly took charge of us.

On the 18th Henriette went back to Stuttgart, and I went to Altenburg, where at last, after nearly a year's separation, I saw my beloved Robert again. I was inexpressibly happy! From Altenburg, Robert and I went to Schneeberg, where I went to the Uhlmann's [1]. They are a very nice family, and I am very happy with them.

On the 24th, after we had passed three happy days together, Robert went to Leipsic, and I accompanied him as far as Zwickau, where I saw Therese again. I felt so strange as I drove into Zwickau. — I sat by Robert, I felt deeply what must be passing in his mind as he thought of his childhood, and now found no-one left there who loved him. Well, I will try to make up to him for what he has lost, and will be his faithful comrade through life, this is my ambition, and this thought makes me happy. May Heaven only give me strength enough to prevail in the next struggle with my Father. I shall find it hard; my heart is torn to pieces when

---

1) Emilie Uhlmann in her first marriage was the wife of Schumann's brother Julius, who died young.

I think of all that he has done for me, and that now I must openly oppose him. — Heaven will pardon me for it! A good conscience supports my courage and comforts me. Robert's love makes me endlessly happy. — One thought troubles me at times; shall I be able to keep Robert's love? His mind is so great, and in this respect I can satisfy him so little, even though I completely understand him! Understanding must to some extent make up to him.

Now I am endeavouring to combine the artist with the house-wife so far as possible. That is a difficult task! I will not let my art lie idle, I should reproach myself for ever. I think the management of a household must be very difficult; always to keep the right proportion, not to spend too much, and not to be parsimonious. I hope to learn it all in time.

When once I am united to Robert, I shall be really light-hearted — my last 3 years have been miserable; as long as I was at home no day passed without my having to endure the most bitter insults. Often if Father could have looked into my heart he would have pitied me; he is a good man, and has done for me what hardly any other father would have done, but he knows nothing of a noble and beautiful love, and cannot understand it. This does not diminish my filial love for him. I often feel the deepest compassion for him, I would gladly repay him, but how can I go against my heart!

. . . . Now he wishes to deprive me of what I earned by four long years of travelling — it was little, but it would have been a tiny nest-egg, and now I shall not even be able to buy a trousseau with my money — that distresses me! It hurts me too much not to be able to bring Robert anything at all, to be so entirely dependent upon him — it weighs upon me dreadfully, and often makes the whole world look black. But I will not have learned my art for nothing, I will recompense Robert if only heaven gives me health. My greatest wish is to manage so that Robert can live wholly for music, for its own sake, and that no further anxiety may trouble the beauty of his life as an artist.

.... I have had a letter from him in which he writes that I make him as happy as can be, — as happy, that is, as he makes me. — My chief anxiety is his health! If I had to know the pain of losing him — I do not know if I should have courage enough to go on living.

On the 30th I went to Leipsic, and stayed at Friese's.

On the 31st my Mother came — my joy was great!

We have been at Pastor Fischer's[1]), but Father did not come in answer to the summons. He has sent me a letter which has deeply moved me, but he has also wounded me by what he says, as he never did before. May he not repent it some day! If only for once he had a kind word for me! My filial love and gratitude can never cease, but I cannot but draw back shuddering when I think of the means which he uses in order to attain his end.

I have moved to Carl's[2]) in order to be with my Mother.

We have spent some happy days together — they will never vanish from my memory. Robert was always so affectionate towards me that I was quite happy. We played duets, Bach fugues, and 3 beautiful compositions of Bennett's. What a long time it is since I have had the happiness of playing with Robert: — Heaven is kind indeed! When I think of Robert, I forget all sorrows.

On Sept. 3rd we set out for Berlin, and arrived on the 4th."

Thus she was sheltered under a parental roof, and could experience a mother's love. And the fact of living through this hardest of struggles together formed an intimate bond between mother and daughter, an unexpected enriching of

---

1) According to these and the following entries in the diary, and letters, Wustmann's accounts (p. 313) need correcting in certain points.
2) Frau Carl was a sister of Clara's mother.

their lives for which they were thankful at the time, and were still more thankful later.

But the condition of Robert's health, which gave her serious anxiety, cast the deepest shadow upon her path at this time.

During the course of the summer she had already been alarmed by accounts of renewed depression, which seemed regularly to follow moments of happy confidence.

The meeting with Clara had certainly scattered these dark clouds for the time, and as we learned from Clara's diary, they had both passed those August weeks of their re-union in pure and untroubled enjoyment. But the very stress of excitement, which their being together under such circumstances necessarily brought with it, as well as the process of the law-suit, and the various legal appointments which had to be made, were only too soon to overset Schumann's newly won equipoise, and to prove a source of constant anxiety to Clara. Bravely and calmly as she had fought her battle, and continually as she thought how to let her lover feel as little as possible of her own troubles, it is yet no wonder that eventually she felt as if she must succumb to the storms of feeling which swept over her. "I am in a pitiable frame of mind," she confides to her diary on Sept. 19th, "I feel very unhappy, and my anxiety about Robert continually increases. I am especially nervous about his eyes, which, as he himself told me to-day, keep on getting worse."

And indeed, a number of bewildering and disturbing events crowded upon her, at this time.

On her birthday, Sept. 13th, Robert had come to Berlin quite unexpectedly, and had remained there for some days, during which they much enjoyed quiet talks together while they explored the neighbourhood in the beautiful autumn weather. It was the more necessary that they should discuss things because on the eve of Clara's birthday a letter had come from Wieck in which he expressed a wish to break off the suit and to come to a good understanding with Clara, and invited her to meet him in Dresden, "so that he might discuss matters with her". In spite of their experiences hitherto, they were both at first inclined to believe in a change of mind. But when they asked the lawyer in Leipsic, where they had gone together on the 17th — and where Clara again received the friendliest of welcomes from the Carls —, he thought it necessary to warn them most emphatically not to run "into this trap", but, in a letter dated Sept. 19th, advised Clara, on the other hand, to beg her father to meet her in Leipsic (which she did). The entries in the diary tell us in moving terms what was the result of this, and also what Clara felt during these days.

The 20th.

I spent the afternoon with Robert; we played duets, then separately . . . he improvises in the most heavenly fashion — one could lose oneself in his notes, his harmonies carry one into quite another world. Music seems to me like love! If it is too beautiful and tender, it hurts; this is the case with me; often I feel as if my heart must burst.

To-day a deep sadness seized me again at the thought of Father. I am so sorry for him, and yet was he not cruel? But nevertheless I feel an inextinguishable love for him — one friendly word from him, and I should think no more of the pain which he has caused me.

September 21st.

I have just received a letter from Father — ah! he is so cold, my whole heart is full of grief again! I am to go to Dresden; what shall I do? Is it not fearful no longer to be able to trust one's own father! Ah heavens, that is hard! If I had no parents left I would bear it in silent resignation; but I am a child thrust away by its parents, and simply because I have a loving heart; is this just? Indeed, I do not deserve it.

.   .   .   .

Advocate Einert will not let me go — I have had to write to Father, and to write very plainly.

The 26th.

Yesterday and to-day I have spoken with Father again. The sight of him yesterday upset me very much, but if his sad expression awoke gentler feelings, his rough words once more wounded and chilled me. I cannot understand his hardness or his horrible hatred of Robert, whom he used to love so much. He made out that Robert was very bad, and lacerated my heart in so doing; he has no conception of my love, or else he would behave differently. He mentioned four conditions, on whose fulfillment he will give the Court authority to give consent in his place; they were: 1) I should renounce the 2000 thaler which I have saved after playing for 7 years, and should give them to my brothers. . . . 2) I am to have back my belongings and pianos if I pay 1000 thaler later on, and give this too, to my brothers (he withdrew this condition afterwards). 3) Robert shall settle 8000 thaler of his capital on me the interest on which shall fall into my hands, and in case of a separation (what a horrible idea!) I alone shall have power to dispose of the capital. (What man would do such a thing? He has 12000 thaler, and he is to give two thirds to his wife! Is not this unworthy of a man? It is the man's business to control his wife's money, but not the other way round.) 4) Robert shall make me his sole legatee. . . .

Of course we cannot consent to these conditions, and so the matter must be settled by law.

On these pages of her diary material anxieties as to the future become more and more prominent, as she discusses Wieck's conditions. But it is equally evident that anxieties, of quite a different kind, also agitated her heart at this time. She had played many of Schumann's compositions in various houses, and delighted in Becker's delicate appreciation, but at the same time she had once more to realise how difficult it was to make the average audience grasp them. "I would very gladly play them," she complains, "but the public does not understand them. I feel very anxious when I think that Robert must some day see how little his compositions take compared with others which are insipid. He has too deep a spirit for the world, and therefore he cannot be understood!? I believe it would be best if he were to compose for orchestra, his imagination cannot find sufficient scope in the piano. . . . His compositions are all orchestral in conception, and I believe that is why the public understands them so little, because melodies and figures so cross one-another that it requires much training to find out their beauties. I myself find new beauties every time I play them (I am finding this now with the *Novelletten* for example). The *Novelletten* are a very fine work. Mind, feeling, humour, and the greatest tenderness, are all combined in them, there is no end to their delicate qualities. One must know him as I do, then one finds his whole personality in his compositions. . . . The time will come when the world . . . . will recognise (him), but it will come late. . . . My highest wish is that he should compose for orchestra — there is his field! — May I succeed in persuading him to enter it."

On the 30ᵗʰ she returned to Leipsic in order to be present with Robert on Oct. 2ⁿᵈ at the Court of Appeal, for the long dreaded day of the process.

Wieck, however, preferred not to appear but to protest in writing against this day, because the clergyman who had been summoned had not kept to the appointed time. By this delay he attained his object which was to make it impossible for Clara to return to Paris for the winter. At the same time he came forward with a new proposal: Clara was to wait until she was of age, and in the mean time to travel with him for 3 months for a fixed sum of 6000 thaler. Naturally she could not agree to this. "I saw by this proposal," says the diary, "that Father would like to travel with me again, and I was pained at this on his account." But how greatly the refusal embittered him Clara was to learn on the day of her departure. She had sent a message through her maid, asking for her winter cloak. The answer through the servant-girl ran: "Who is Mdlle. Wieck? I know only two Fräulein Wiecks; they are my two little daughters here; I do not know any other." With so harsh a dissonance ended this visit to Leipsic.

On Oct. 3rd she returned to Berlin.

In the early part of September they had still been able to laugh over Wieck's grotesque objections to Schumann — "that no-one could read Schumann's writing", and "that he spoke so softly" — and Clara could answer jestingly: "Father's reasons are really amusing, and besides they are not un-justified. Mother will also go before the court and will plead against you that she cannot read your writing, and I shall complain that I always have to say, 'What?' three times, before I can understand a word." But this laughter died away and there was no more jesting now that Wieck, in the months that followed, let pass no opportunity, direct or indirect, of publicly insulting one or the other of them, and of incensing the whole world against his child. For example, Clara had been warmly received in Berlin in the house of Stadtrat Behrens, and he had promised to let her play upon his ex-cellent piano at a concert. Hardly had Wieck heard of this, when he wrote, so Reuter told Clara, to one of his friends in Berlin and asked him to go at once to Behrens and to warn him not to trust his piano to Clara; she was now accus-tomed to the stiff English mechanism and broke all other in-struments. In the same letter he had expressed the hope that the "noble mind" of the King of Prussia would not allow Clara to appear publicly in Berlin, since she was venturing to do so in opposition to her father's will, and without him. This had no further result, except that on Oct. 21st Clara, assisted by Konzertmeister Müller from Braunschweig, appeared for the first time in the Opera House, played on the Behrens's piano, and both on her first appearance and after the concert was tumultuously applauded. Wieck had even to have the sorrow of hearing that at her second concert, which took place on Oct. 31st in the Theatre Royal, the "noble King" himself was present and with the rest of the audience clapped approval of the disobedient daughter.

What feelings, however, must not have been stirred in her shortly afterwards by a letter of her father's to Behrens (which the latter gave her to read) in which he said: "Out of consideration for me and for my business you ought not to have exposed an instrument of mine to Rellstab's criticism, as the girl whom this wretched man has so thoroughly demoralised shamelessly helped you to do."

She received this blow as she came back from a short concert-tour to Stettin and Stargardt, which she had undertaken at the beginning of November with Konzertmeister Müller and on which her mother had accompanied her. The impressions which she had received, the many and various disagreeables which a concert tour in the provinces brought with it, had depressed her deeply. And if she could still speak with humour in the diary of the kind of supper which followed a concert — "The company looked at me as if I were a strange animal, three young ladies from Pomerania to whom the host paid special attention snapped up my every word with great eagerness. To make my misery complete I had to hear one of the young ladies play something on the piano — it was supposed to be a composition of Chopin's" — yet she found the life of a travelling virtuoso to be "wretched", for both body and mind.

"I live for one person alone," she writes in her diary on the day [of their return, "and if the world will but do him justice — that will be my highest happiness. That I shall never make a great success in the world has become clear to me. I do not possess the qualities necessary for this, and I do not wish to possess them. . . . I wept by myself for a long time to-day, I long so much for Robert and for peace." The weariness and a certain bitterness which breathe in in these words had an especial cause.

During these weeks the picturesque and coquettish pianist, Camilla Pleyel, was celebrating great triumphs in Leipsic. Even Schumann, often as he repeated that she could not be compared with Clara, had not been entirely proof against the charm of her personality, as the naïve accounts in his letters show[1]).

Clara herself had a different opinion as to the importance of Fräulein Pleyel as an artist. "Everything that I read about her," says the diary a fortnight later, "is an ever clearer proof that she is above me; and if this be so I can hardly fail to be completely downcast. I think that I shall submit to it in time, for indeed oblivion is the fate of every artist who is not creative. I once thought that I possessed creative talent, but I have given up this idea; a woman must not desire to compose — not one has been able to do it, and why should I expect to? It would be arrogance, though indeed, my Father led me into it in earlier days."

And just at this time this very father thought good to appear as her rival's patron, protector, and enthusiastic admirer, with the publicly proclaimed intention of wounding

---

1) The two articles, *Camilla Pleyel*, in the N. Z. f. M. 28./10., and 8./11./39, also show this. Cf. *Ges. Schriften* 4th p. 206 etc. He describes her most strikingly in a letter to Clara: "She played Mendelssohn's *B* minor quartet as she plays everything, almost perfectly, and yet, like herself, it was somewhat careless" (Letter of Oct. 27th 39).

and injuring Clara. He appeared beside her at her concerts, paid court to her "with something like tenderness" before the eyes of the audience, turned over for her, and listened to her performance with a estatic smile which had a comical effect. In fact he behaved in a manner, which as Reuter indignantly wrote to Clara, "was as ridiculous in itself as it was wounding to the feelings of those who witnessed it".

Thus heavy blows and pin-pricks came all together. Robert's demeanour also gave her anxiety again during these weeks. He wrote irregularly, often did not answer her letters for days, and when he did write allowed himself to fall into whimsicalities which had a certain frosty humour that half pained, half disquieted her. "I shall not come to your concert," he wrote in answer to a question from Clara, "but I may possibly come the day after, though I will not promise you this, and altogether I intend to keep you in the dark to some extent concerning my plans, so that you shall have no idea where you are with me. These are my bridegroom-whims. I have no other cause to be merry at present, and I am often silent for days — without thinking — merely grumbling to myself. Yesterday evening Frau Voigt died, and that has also been much in my thoughts."

His letters became shorter and shorter, and more laconic in their expressions of affection, finally ceasing altogether. After a long and anxious week of waiting came the explanation that he had not been feeling well, but expressed in a manner which clearly showed that the illness was far from over. Not till the middle of December was there any marked improvement. At the same time came the second of the days appointed by the court. On the 14th Clara went to Leipsic, and on the following day she had the pleasure of seeing Robert again. Two surprises awaited her here: the news that her parents had broken open her desk and read its contents; and an anonymous letter from Dresden, which she at once recognised as being dictated by her father, but which failed in its purpose of frightening her. Then too, she looked forward to the day of appearance before the court with much nervousness. "To-day is the second court-day," she writes on the 18th, "if Father comes, God give me strength." She certainly had need of it. "He was there," she writes on the evening of the day, "I shall never forget it. I could not look at him without feeling the deepest compassion; all the pains he had taken, all his many sleepless nights, the explanation at which he had been working for months — all this is of no use to him. He was most passionate, so that the President of the court had to call him to order, and each time it cut me to the heart — I could hardly bear that he should have to experience this humiliation. He looked at me with terrible anger, but he only once said anything against me. I would so gladly have once more entreated him, there before the court, but I was afraid that he might thrust me from him and I was nailed to my seat. This day has separated us for ever, or at least it has torn to pieces the tender bond between father and child — my heart too, feels as if it were torn in pieces! —

Robert behaved very well, with all his characteristic self-possession, which was the best thing he could do in the face of such passion. I only love Robert the more now that he has had to allow himself to be publicly insulted for my sake. If only some power could control Father's heart how happily and contentedly he might live, as it is he is wearing himself out — all my childish love for him has awakened again and will live in me for ever. So far things have been entirely in our favour. We are almost sure not to have to appear again in person."

On the 20th the President returned her visit, which made her very hopeful: "I could gather from what he said that all stands well for us. On Jan. 4th judgment will be given,

against which, however, Father is certain to appeal. I hope
that it will all be ended by Easter."

On the 21ˢᵗ she went back to Berlin with Robert, and so
was able, for the first time for years, once more to keep
Christmas with him.

She writes in the diary:

"The 24ᵗʰ. This Christmas Eve has been the best in my
life, it makes up to me for many of the sorrows that I have
endured. I was able to keep it with my most dearly loved
Robert and my Mother — the joy of it almost saddens me
for a moment. The whole evening had something sacred
about it to me. I thought much of this time next year.
Robert has given me too much, I could not thank him as I
wished.

The 27ᵗʰ. To-day was a sad day for me. Robert went
away again; now everything is so empty."

This harmonious, hopeful, happy frame of mind shows itself in the letters which passed between them at the turn of
the year.

CLARA TO ROBERT.

"Berlin 1./1. 1840.

How odd the 40 looks to me now it is here at last, this long
looked-for year which is to unite us for ever! I have thought of
nothing but you all day — Shall I be yours in four months time?
And you would like it to be in May? that is the most beautiful
month, and if you love it best, I do. . . .

. . . . I lay claim to the *Romances*; you absolutely must dedicate something more to me as your betrothed, and I know nothing more tender than these 3 *Romances* especially the middle one,
which is the most beautiful love duet. Ah! Robert, you cannot
escape, I will not give up the *Romances*, you have given them to
me — You cannot bear half measures; all, or nothing. But now
give me a kiss so that I may know that you are not angry with
me — perhaps I seem forward to you!?"

ROBERT TO CLARA.

"Leipsic Jan. 2ⁿᵈ 1840.

Your letters make me quite happy, you dear, dear girl. Go
on writing to me always; I am greedy for your letters.

I also owe you thanks, and an answer for your letter yesterday
with the lace cravat and the kind lines from your mother and
from Bargiel. Your last letter was so good and dear, just as I
like it best. If only I knew for what one should love you most.
You could make a number of husbands happy all at once, giving
some special thing to each (do not be offended at the idea) —
but I choose for my own bride warm-heartedness and "home-i-ness"
— You dear housewife Clara.

One thing more! If all goes well, we will be married before
May. The chief reason: The sooner, the better — and your F. is
to be feared as long as you are not married to me.   . . . .

. . . . I will write to you about other things the day after to-
morrow my Clärchen, perhaps with news of victory.

Forgive me for writing so little and so hastily, it has struck
6 already. The *Romances* are indeed not good enough for such
a girl; but I am glad with all my heart if you wish me to dedicate them to you. What shall we write on the title-page? Stop:
I know.

Adieu, my heart's treasure. Your mother must give me another
two days' indulgence. An editor, composer, and lover has much
to do.

Adieu, think lovingly of me.   Your Robert."

But all too soon there came a rough set-back, and a period
of mental torment began for both of them, which threw all
that had gone before into the shade.

On the evening of Jan. 4ᵗʰ Robert announced that all
Wieck's objections had been set aside except one, and that
he had been given six weeks and three days to bring proof
of this one. This meant a new postponement of their hopes.
In spite of this their counsel believed that they might expect
judgment to be given by the end of May.

Schumann wrote very quietly and composedly. "Do not distress yourself about it, my Clara. Who knows what blessings Heaven may be preparing for us in thus delaying our happiness. I for my part promise to wait for you faithfully till the end of my life. Such sorrows and insults as we have borne will surely not remain unrewarded. Give me your hand then, my true girl, rely on God and have confidence."

But this calmness was only temporary and apparent, forced in order to help Clara over the bitter disappointment. As a matter of fact this blow of Wieck's had struck him to the heart. The unkindest act was not the delay itself, which thus put off their marriage for some weeks or months, but the reason for the delay. For Wieck's cunning pretext, of which he was commanded to bring proof, was none other than that Schumann drank. Under the circumstances, since this objection had once been raised, the court could come to no other decision, although its members openly declared that this move of Wieck's might certainly bring about a delay but could not bring a decision in his favour. At the same time so long as this question was at issue the disgrace of such an assertion weighed upon Schumann, and he suffered the most terrible torments under it. "Your letter," he wrote to Clara some days later, "seems to me so sad. But just now, I need comfort and encouragement perhaps more than you do; do not forget that sweetheart, and forgive me if I often write sadly. Turn to your work; set out on your journey soon. Change of air and fresh faces at least distract one's thoughts. If only I too had energy enough to wander out into the world! I do not want to see you until the final judgment has taken from me the disgrace which your father . . . . has brought upon me. . . . .

. . . . If only the strength to work would come back to me, how happy I should be; I think, and think, and think, the whole day long — ah! pray for me often.

I began to compose — a little sonatine in $B\flat$ major, very pretty. But already the strength has left me again. Heavens! are things never to grow better?"

This letter, which he signed "your brother", shows with heart-rending clearness how the brand of shame tortured a nature already sensitive enough; and Wieck took care that Clara should receive her share of the torture. "I am writing to you at length," runs a letter from Robert to Clara on Jan. 12th, "as children try to keep off the ghostly hour by talking. Your father is the ghost. Alwin was with me to-day, and told me to write and tell you that the anonymous letter which you will soon receive, or have already received, was dictated by your father. So you know what attention to pay to it. He wants to bewilder you."

This letter, signed Lehmann, containing accusations and warnings against Schumann, had reached Clara's hands in the mean time, and had at once been recognised by her as coming from her father. The devilish (one can call it nothing else) intention of disabling her by this stab in the back on the day of the first great concert which she had arranged for herself in Berlin and thus preparing a severe artistic defeat for her, was fortunately not attained, as at the last moment the concert was put off on account of an injury to Clara's hand.

One comfort to both the lovers during these terrible days of trial was the loyalty with which Robert's friends stood by him to a man: "The shamelessness of his accusation," Robert writes on Jan. 12th, "is greatly softened as far as I am concerned by the sympathy of so many friends. Count Reuss and David have offered of their own free will to go before the court as witnesses; Mendelssohn will do the same. On the others, such as Verhulst, Friese etc. I can build as on so many rocks." And Clara had similar experiences in Berlin. Thus Geheimrat John, the Berlin censor, assured her that not a word of Wieck's would be accepted.

But of what avail were these alleviations and supports in face of the strong feeling of deep distress and nameless disgust which this method of warfare aroused in Robert and Clara? Even amidst the worst humiliations and degradations which this hard man had made them drink to the dregs in the course of the year, neither of them had ever lost the hope and confidence that when once they had won their victory a reconciliation with the father must and would follow. But now this hope too gave way beneath them. "But one thing more," Robert writes to Clara, "you may think you will be able to reconcile me to your father later on; give up all hope of this. The faintest wish of this kind on your part would be an insult to me. . . .

. . . . Will you be unhappy if for my whole life, for eternity, I remain deaf to this request? Examine yourself. There are laws of honour as binding as those of love. Promise that you will recognise them. Make up your mind on this one point, which otherwise may endanger our happiness. I write strongly, my Clara. . . . I have been betrayed into an angry tone, such as you do not know from me; angry words, angry people, are an abomination to me." And Clara replies: "As to what you urge so strongly, let me say but one thing; I have long since given up all hope of a reconciliation between you. No word shall ever cross my lips, here is my hand on it. I respect your feeling, let this be sufficient to re-assure you. . . ."

Clara suffered no less severely under these perplexities; torn hither and thither by the torturing persecutions of her father and the scarcely less torturing susceptibility of her lover. And at the same time she was thrown upon her own resources and had to bear a burden of her own: she had to make preparations for her two concerts.

But just in this we see once again, in spite of the many secret and excusable tears of which the diary tells us, that she had the more energetic nature of the two, and was the more capable of resistance. Misfortune was heaped upon misfortune: first the injury to her hand, which not only gave her the most violent pain for days, but also made any kind of practising before her actual appearance, impossible, and added to this bodily discomfort, fits of giddiness, nervous attacks of all kinds; then refusal after refusal from the soloists whom she had asked to perform on the evening. And with all this came the strain of Wieck's machinations and the constant fear of new attacks. In her mother's house came anxiety upon anxiety, without the possibility of being able to help; there was the anxiety about Robert, and in addition came the news (not even told her by Robert but coming through Reuter and wholly surprising her) that the end of the law-suit could hardly be expected before Michaelmas. And yet she mastered all these cares and triumphed over cabals as well as over the difficulty of the situation, always finding time and freshness of spirit enough bravely to fight her own tears, to smooth the wrinkles from her lover's forehead and to inspire him with courage.

On Jan. 25th the first soirée at last took place, when she played Beethoven's trio in $B\flat$ major, Henselt's $E\flat$ minor *Étude*, Schubert-Liszt's *Ave Maria*, Mendelssohn's *Prelude* (*E* minor) a piece by Scarlatti, and her own variations on a theme of Bellini's. She was assisted by Zimmermann, Lotze, and the singer Mantius. One misfortune, also due to Wieck, followed her on to the platform itself. On the day of the concert she collapsed entirely, owing to the strain of the last weeks.

"My dearly loved Robert," she writes three days later, "I am still very poorly and can hardly hold my head up, but I must send you a greeting again, and tell you something about the concert. It was a day which I shall never forget as long

as I live. Up to a quarter of an hour before the beginning
of the concert I was lying at home in the most dreadful
state, and finally dragged myself up when I saw that it could
not be helped. I could hardly fling myself into my concert
clothes, I could not stand, my limbs were so weak that I
could not raise my hand. The doctor was caught in the
street at half-past 5, but he could not do much for me, so
I was packed into the carriage and taken to the concert
room. During the concert I strengthened myself with champagne, but in spite of this several times while I was playing
everything went black before my eyes, and the whole evening I was nearer to fainting than to any musical enthusiasm,
and yet no-one noticed it, and everything went splendidly.
The *Prelude* and the piece by Scarlatti went especially well,
not a single note went wrong in either of them, which is
incomprehensible to me, for my hands were shaking all the
time. Rellstab thought I played the latter too fast, and in the
Vossische Zeitung expressed the opinion that it should be taken
much slower — how dull that would be!"

But a reaction was bound to follow. "Since last Monday,"
she writes on Jan. 31ˢᵗ on the eve of her second soirée, "I
have been suffering from face-ache which has almost driven
me mad; up to yesterday I could not do anything, playing
and writing were alike impossible. My last letter to you (on
the 28ᵗʰ) cost me a very great deal of pain, so that I was
almost unconscious after writing it. Yesterday I began for
the first time to study my pieces for the concert. Think of
it! I only began to work seriously at your sonata (for the
first time) yesterday, and I have to play it to-morrow, and
it is the same with the Liszt *Phantasie* etc. etc. Well, dear
husband of my heart, do you forgive me? . . . . Ah! I should
so gladly be merry if only the pain were not so horrible. . . .
As a rule I can conquer a good deal of pain, but now I should
often like to lay myself down and die."

"If only I can play really well, that is what makes me anxious." This is easily comprehensible, for she was going to play Schumann's sonata to a Berlin audience for the first time[1]. She had a secret hope that he would come over for it himself; he had made such minute inquiries as to what she was going to wear: "You want me to dress quite in accordance with your taste? — Does that mean that you will be there? My heart trembles for joy at the thought."

But he did not come, and moreover instead of a specially warm greeting, on which she had counted with certainty, he sent her only a few laconic words; behaviour which can be explained by his over-excited and anxious frame of mind, heightened by the non-appearance of her letter, but which did her a bitter wrong:

"Friday 6- 30.

"Good evening. I have waited till now for your letter. Well, I too will not be intrusive.

Good night and two kisses   Your   Robert."

On the same evening, after the concert, she sat down and wrote:

"You hurt me to-day by not even writing me a kind word for the concert. I should not have thought that you could have done it. That 'intrusive' rang in my ears all the evening, as if I heard you saying it. And see, I am sitting myself down at 11 o'clock and writing to you with a heart full of love, although I am feeling very depressed, as I almost always do after a concert. It all went well, including your sonata — I think I should have played it still better if you had written to me kindly and tenderly beforehand. The audience did not understand the Schubert trio — they did not know if they ought to give any token of applause

---

1) "Now my Clärchen!," wrote Schumann, two days before, "arm yourself for Saturday; play as if it were the day before our wedding, do not take the sonata too wildly; think of him who made it."

before the end or not, but they applauded lustily then. I was very animated on the whole, I might almost say in wild spirits, for the pain was more bearable, and my strength never gave way in the least throughout the entire concert. How pleased one is with the good God when after a shower of rain he lets a little sunshine peep through. At least, that is how it is with me, for I thank God with contented heart that I no longer lie prostrate, and I feel as if I had as much strength again as I had before. The concert . . . . was much fuller even than the first time, and the music sounds magnificent in the hall; even the piano sounded well. The Crown Prince and his wife were there again, which pleased me very much. — He must have liked the previous concert very much.".

"He came yesterday," she continues the next day, "just in time for your sonata — I wonder if he understood it?"

"Marx came to see me to-day . . . . he spoke of your sonata with rapture, and I have also heard other people say that to them it was the best thing in the whole evening — connoisseurs of course. This has delighted my heart, and I am also pleased because people say everywhere that I played it so lovingly that it must be by someone whom I do not hate."

On the very next day, she went with her mother to Hamburg, where she was to play at a Philharmonic concert on Feb. 8th. The invitation to do this, as well as an engagement in Bremen, came somewhat unexpectedly, and had upset other plans.

Not with an entirely light heart had Clara accepted. She knew that in so doing she was exacting a considerable sacrifice from her mother, and in the uncertainty of the whole situation she was also uncomfortable at the thought of being at a greater distance from Leipsic and Robert. And finally she was afraid of all the various surprises which Wieck might prepare for her by the way. Certainly he had done his best in this respect.

The first news that she received in Hamburg was that her father had sent the "Declaration", which had been refused by the law-court, to an acquaintance in Hamburg, asking him to make it known as widely as possible. However, he had as little luck with it here, as in Leipsic and Berlin; the result was rather an increased courtesy and attention towards Schumann's betrothed. Neither old nor new friends were lacking in warmth, so that the awkwardness at the beginning was soon wiped out, and gave place to a feeling of which Schumann caught the infection, and which is vividly reflected in the letters that they exchanged at this time.

CLARA TO ROBERT.

"Hamburg 6./2. 40.

My beloved Robert

You must forgive me for not having written to you yesterday; it was impossible, for the whole day I had to run about looking for a piano, as there are very few here, and no good ones. I found an old one at last, on which I played 3 years ago and which is now quite played out; I am very unhappy about it, and would much rather go straight back to Berlin; I no longer like travelling at all. Yesterday and to-day I have received calls without end, and you will easily believe me when I tell you that I have already been interrupted 3 times in these few lines, and I am so tired to-day — horribly tired, and I cannot play at all, and altogether I think my playing gets worse. . . .

The weather on our journey was very fine, and I thought of you with all my heart on Tuesday evening as I looked at the sky in all its glory of stars. . . . surely you must have felt it. My dear good Robert, if only I could just see you again and embrace you — I love you so that it gives me a pain at my heart.

Everybody here is very attentive to me; the directors of the Philharmonic concerts have already called upon me and show me every possible attention. Ah! if only I play well! I am dreadfully nervous, especially as they understand nothing about music here — fancy, they prefer Dreischock to Thalberg! I shall probably play twice in the theatre next week, and on the 16th we go to Bremen."

"[Hamburg Feb. 1840] Saturday evening.

I thank you Robert, beloved of my heart, for your letter to-day, which seemed to me to have come straight down from heaven to comfort me. Cranz[1]) and Avé[2]) had put me out of humour, they spent 3 hours with me the evening before, and kept on telling me that no-one except Pleyel was of any account. You know, dear Robert, that I recognise all great artists, and that I greatly honour Thalberg and Liszt in particular, as only an artist can, but do you not think that it was most tactless to talk to me for hours in such a strain as Cranz and Avé did? The former said that after he had heard me he thought that he should never care for any other pianist; then Pleyel came, and for the first time he heard the most wonderful playing in the world. This, and much more, he told me. Of course I ought to be above such things, but I cannot help a certain loss of heart and terrible dissatisfaction with myself. They are 3 tremendous enthusiasts for Camilla — the third is Gathy[3]). Nothing distresses me more than not to have heard Pleyel myself. The concert is successfully over, and I roused the audience to at least a North German enthusiasm. On my second appearance I was greeted very warmly, which means something with these cold business men. But one thing vexed me very much, so that the tears came into my eyes — Cranz and Avé did not say one syllable to me about my playing, and at the end of the concert Cranz admired my ear-rings — I should have liked to beat him! You will call me very petty, but I cannot help it. Do not misunderstand me, since yesterday I have had a feeling which cannot be described, but which is certainly not one which could make you angry with me. Grund

---

1) August Heinrich Cranz, proprietor of the great music-publishing business of August Cranz, in Hamburg.

2) Theodor Avé Lallemant, originally from Lübeck, a music-teacher in Hamburg, and, for more than a generation, centre of all musical efforts there. He soon became one of Clara's most enthusiastic admirers and truest friends. In an estatically poetic letter which he sent to Bremen on Feb. 18th, he addresses her as, "Most melancholy friendly music", and adds to this, "Here you have another title besides the imperial one, and one by which I greet you more gladly and from a full heart."

3) August Gathy, from Lüttich, at that time busy as editor of the *Musikalischen Conversationsblatt* in Hamburg.

(the Capellmeister) pleased me, he showed the warmth of a true artist. Just fancy, I played Mendelssohn's *Capriccio* from note, out of sheer, incomprehensible nervousness. . . .

. . . . Tell me, how far do you think Father's memorial can injure us? with the court, in the process of our affair, or with the general public? Father is really terrible. Cranz wrote a letter to him to-day, full of heart-moving words — he hopes to touch his conscience, to awaken the fatherly feelings which do but sleep in him, to make the impossible, possible. I know the answer. The 'Declaration' has not yet come here, it must be in Bremen — if only I knew to whom he had sent it. Ah! Robert, you do not know how painful it is to me to be proclaimed like this to a city, this feeling that people have heard the most humiliating and worst things of me hurts horribly! You are right, I too have long been troubled by the thought that Father can never come to his senses; but perhaps it is well for him, or he would be appalled at his own actions."

"Monday Feb. 10th.

. . . . I am dreadfully nervous about to-morrow, especially as the piano (a different one from that I used at the Philharmonic concert) is so stiff; if only I can get through my pieces! But I cannot practise in peace for half-an-hour without being interrupted, for callers are endless."

ROBERT TO CLARA.

"Leipsic Feb. 9th 1840. Sunday morning.

. . . . Do not be hypochondriacal about your playing, Cläre. You always vex me when you are. You are now nearly 21 and you must know what you can do. Something strikes me — your F. often tried to make you believe that without him — and married — you would soon be forgotten. I do not in the least believe it. Mediocrity is soon forgotten. But not artists like you. Is Paganini forgotten, or Sonntag, or Pasta? So will it be with you, too. Even if you did choose to keep a year or two for home life and then wished to appear again in public — you would not be forgotten, believe me, my Clara. . . ."

CLARA TO ROBERT.

"Hamburg 12./2. 40.

When you wrote your last letter you little thought that it would reach me in the theatre an hour before I had to play. I cannot tell you how this letter cheered me; I lost all nervousness, and played the Chopin concerto . . . . quite well and to my own satisfaction, and that means much. The house was full, the audience at once received me with the livliest and most continuous applause, and went on becoming warmer and warmer up to the end. In Thalberg's *Caprice* I had a fatal misfortune. You know one sits on the prompter's box, and this kept on waggling and creaked every time I got into the treble — I was dreadfully afraid that the thing would collapse, and this made me go wrong in the *Caprice*, but the audience did not notice it. The *Ave Maria*, which I played before the *Caprice*, took extraordinarily well. I did play it well — it was all owing to your letter; I thought of that the whole time. Well, now I have told you enough of my playings — do not take it amiss, when I have been pleased with myself I like to tell you about it. When you receive this letter I shall already have got through my second concert. . . . So that you may know what I am playing, or rather have played: 1) Sonata by Scarlatti, *Nocturno* by Chopin, *Erlkönig*; 2) *Moses-Phantasie*. I am not at all nervous (for the first time for a long while) except about the prompter's box. I will inspect it carefully to-morrow. . . .

. . . . I must thank you for so lovingly comforting me about my hypocondriacism, which had indeed become great. Since yesterday I have been calmer, and have rather more self-confidence again. Write to me again soon, equally kindly.

I embrace you, my dear, beloved Robert, in old and ever new love   Your Clara.

A flower from the bouquet which I carried yesterday."

CLARA TO ROBERT.

"Hamburg 14./2. 40.

Good morning Robert, best beloved of my heart!

If you slept as well as I did to-day, it is a good thing. I played well yesterday, and roused the audience (even if it were not so numerous as on the first occasion) to far greater enthusiasm,

I had to repeat the *Erlkönig*, in which I was very successful. The prompter's box was quite firm, but strings broke, so that it was really funny to hear them. Avé Lallemant insists that when I come back from Bremen I must give one more soirée, at which I am to play a trio of Beethoven's. ...

. . . . The second snub you administered to Banck[1]) was splendid, and how I have laughed over the 'Song-dwarf from Jena'! You wield a dangerous knife; if only your wife never comes under it!

. . . . Tell me then, dear man of my heart, what is it that you are composing? If you do not tell me, I will not bring you any cigars, and that you would certainly find very bitter.

. . . . In his last concert but one (in Vienna) Liszt, with one chord, drove three hammers out of place and besides this broke 4 strings — so he must be well again.

. . . . I am recognised as your betrothed by everybody here, and wherever wine and champagne flow, you are thought of. . . ."

ROBERT TO CLARA.

"Leipsic Feb. 14th 1840.

I received your dear, good, true letter yesterday. I wished that you had heard Pleyel so that you might be at peace for ever. Cranz is a coarse fellow, and the other, Avé, seems to be so too. But, Clara, an artist like you must hold herself erect, and not at once become melancholy. And yet I should like to

---

1) Carl Banck, whom Wieck at this time ostentatiously honoured with his especial favour, was at the same time the subject of repeated ironical remarks in the *N. Z. f. M.*, which most delightfully parodied the remarkable admiration expressed for him by various people, and by himself. At the same time severe attacks on the man of many occupations, were not lacking: and among these is the one to which Clara here refers, No. 10 of Jan. 31st 1840, which arose out of a criticism of Mendelssohn's *Serenade* Op. 48: "Where is the need of many words over such music? What avails it to try and analyse grace or weigh moonlight? He who understands the speech of a poet, will understand this also, and if some paper reported from Jena that Mendelssohn's imagination does not always attain the true height, hang yourself song-dwarf of Jena if the beautiful earth seems to you too lowly. Cf. *Ges. Schriften* II p. 226. 519 etc.

kiss you on the spot for your modest pride, you good Clärchen.
— But do not be too shy and demure. Shakespeare says this is
not the world in which to hide one's talents under a bushel.

Apropos of Shakespeare I am reminded of you, or rather of
it. You want to know what I am composing — in answer to such
a question I will copy a dialogue from *Twelfth Night.*

Fabian: Now, as thou lovest me, let me see his letter.

Clown: Good Master Fabian, grant me another request.

Fabian: Anything.

Clown: Do not desire to see this letter.

When I read that, I thought at once it would do to use against
you some day. Therefore Clärchen, do not desire to know. To
be sure, you made many guesses in your last letter, but it is
nothing of the sort. Next time then — though I could tell you
to-day. Pardon, child; I like playing with children sometimes."

CLARA TO ROBERT.

"Harburg 16./2. 40. Afternoon.

We arrived here an hour ago, by steamer[1]. Mother is getting
a little sleep; I wanted some too, but I thought so much and so
vividly of my Robert that it gave me no peace, I had to seize
my pen. Take a heart-felt kiss, my good Robert! I could do I
don't know what for love of you! You must let me give you one
pleasure, thought it is not an intellectual one. Yesterday, before
we went on to the boat, we eat oysters, the most beautiful oysters
and the freshest imaginable; ah! thought I, if Robert were here
he would relish them too, and in my love-sick mind I determined
to send you a small barrel, and gave the commission to Cranz,
who will send them off to-morrow or the day after, as soon as
they come from the ship. If only I could send you all Hamburg
too, with its beautiful Elbe and its sea-going vessels! Have you
never been there? Ah! Robert, some day we must go there together! I tell you, to live in the Jungfernstieg, and in the early

---

1) The "steamer" (it was the *Primus* which attained such sad notoriety
in 1902) gave Robert the mistaken impression that they had made the
journey to Bremen by sea, which made him very anxious. As a matter
of fact they only crossed the Elbe to Harburg, and from thence went
on to Bremen by land, arriving on the morning of the 17th.

sunshine to see the Alster, with its many swans, is a heavenly view. I never saw it without longing for you to be with me.

.... Just think, to-day, by chance, I have found a wonderful instrument of Andreas Stein's of Vienna, quite new, which is at my service for the whole of my stay in Hamburg. I was inconsolable to think that I had plagued myself with these wretched instruments when I might have had the best. It belongs to a young Viennese, who received it a short time ago as a present from his father, but who never uses it. It is one of the best Steins on which I have yet played.

.... Yesterday a number of Avé's pupils came to see me, and I played to them for 2 hours, chiefly your compositions, and among them I played the *Kinderscenen* twice, they, as well as Avé, were so delighted with them. In the evening, when we played the $B\flat$ and D major trios of Beethoven, all the girls headed by their teacher fell upon me and declared that I must play the *Kinderscenen* again, and also some *Novelletten*. I was intensely pleased, as you can imagine, and played them with real enthusiasm. Now *they* will want to play them and I am afraid they will not find it plain sailing."

She found Bremen far more unfriendly than Hamburg. Here too, the first thing she heard was that lithograph copies of her father's "Declaration" were in various hands. And here she had to find for the first time that the poison had worked. But at the same time she experienced here the proud satisfaction of finding that all lies and calumnies vanished into nothing before the charm of her pure and valiant personality. This change of attitude is shown remarkably clearly in her letters. On the evening of the. first concert she writes to Robert: [1])

"I cannot tell you what I have suffered here in Bremen, I feel as if my very heart were torn in pieces. That dreadful Rake-

---

[1]) She first took part in the "eighth private concert" on Feb. 13th, and gave her own "musical soirée" on the 21st.

mann[1]) has been disseminating the 'Declaration'. Eggers and Möller have read it; I do not know this for certain of the latter, but I conclude he has, from the way in which he received me yesterday — I tell you, it was with an unparalleled coldness and contempt that cost me bitter tears. I am so much accustomed to be received kindly everywhere, that an incident like this hurts me all the more, and especially when I know the cause. Already, before I came, our relations had been depicted in so unfavourable a light that people believe that Father is right, and I cannot bear that. I am dreadfully unhappy here, and feel as if every cheerful thought had left me.

. . . . Möller was quite delighted with my playing to-day, and asked me to dine with him to-morrow, refusing to take any denial — I am annoyed that I let myself be talked into it, I cannot forget how I have been insulted. You must make allowances for me to-day, but I am so irritable and upset that every word affects me, and music makes me cry. Your song[2]) quite delighted me, and resolved the discords in your letter into the sweetest harmonies. It is the tenderest of songs imaginable, and yet with all its naturalness it is so full of meaning — I have already sung it I don't know how often to-day, and revel in it. Best thanks for it, my Robert, and a hearty kiss. If only I could see you soon; I do so long for you! Ah God! what Father has on his conscience in trying to keep us from marrying. I have to see you, my dearest, calumniated and slandered by him, and can do nothing to stop it; people think me blind — and say I see with the eyes of one in love — 'in love' has become so horrible a phrase that the blood rises to my face when it is uttered by such commonplace people, such commercial souls. People are so lacking in delicacy of feel-

---

1) A brother of Clara's old admirer. The latter, who was then living in America, and Banck were chosen by Wieck as chief witnesses to Schumann's dissipation.

2) Probably the *Nussbaum*. She had received with it a letter from Robert, several passages in which had very much depressed her. "Here, my Clara," he had added, "I send you another little song; I have just made it. Read the text well first, and then think of your Robert. It is really the *Scherzino* in another form. I will only tell you that I have composed 4 books of songs and ballads, great and small, for 4 voices. You will like some of them very much.

ing, so coarse-grained, that they do not understand how such talk must hurt me, and that their witicisms (which are not infrequent) are so many stabs. I can only comfort myself with the future. Then you are certain to have justice done to you. . . . The concert is over successfully. I had a good piano of Father's and played well, but felt so unhappy all the while that everything I played seemed sad to me. The public does *not* clap here, and that takes away all one's spirits. (It is a rule in the concerts, because amateurs often take part in them, but North-German coldness is needed for such a law to be conscientiously observed.) An artist needs the outward tokens of approval, or else he does not know where he is. The day after to-morrow I give my concert, on Saturday I leave, and with God's help I run into Hamburg harbour at 9 o'clock on Sunday morning."

"Thursday morning.

Möller has just sent to know if I slept well, and to say that he will send his carriage for us to-day.

. . . . Rackemann is in America. His brother (the youngest) is always with me, he is the image of Rackemann, smiles in just the same languishing manner, and always holds his head on one side — otherwise he is a nice boy! But I shall contrive to get away; the Rackemanns have all taken such a strange fancy to me, that I am afraid even of this boy. . . .

Am I not going to see the other songs and ballads then? I am quite surprised to see you breaking out so delightfully in this direction. — I cannot get the song out of my head. I have played your *Kinderscenen* and sonata and also the *Novelletten*, here — the people were delighted with them, and Töpken was enthusiastic, in a way quite unusual with him.

I have also let a *Novellette* of yours be put into my programme for Hamburg; No. 1 which took so well at a party here, the other day."

CLARA TO ROBERT.

"Saturday 22./2. 40 (Bremen).

. . . . The concert yesterday was good, and I have seldom played so well, a fact certainly due in part to the piano (one of my father's) which sounded wonderfully well. The people of Bremen clapped, and that means something. I played 4 times, the *F* minor sonata, *Moses-Phantasie*, and six other pieces, but I was quite done up, and after the concert I had to go to the Sengstaks' (sister of Grund, in Hamburg) so that I could not write to you yesterday evening, as I like to do. . . .

. . . . I am somewhat reconciled to the people of Bremen; perhaps they have noticed how much their talking must hurt me, and now they are quiet. We cannot get hold of the 'Declaration' in any way; they say Cranz has it. . . ."

ROBERT TO CLARA.

"Leipsic Feb. 24th 1840 (intercalary day).

My dear Clara

— The beginning of your letter to-day once more so affected me that I did not know what to do. But I did do something. I wrote to Rackemann, warned him against circulating the lampoon, and told him that by so doing he was trafficking in vulgarity and ies and that I should sue him. I sent the letter to Töpken[1]), and asked him to find me a legal adviser in case of need. . .

. . . . I am sending you a little song, to comfort you; sing it to yourself softly, simply, like yourself. I will soon send you more. During the last few days I have quite finished a great cycle of Heine songs. Besides these another ballad, *Belsazar*, a volume from Gœthe's *West-Oestlichen Divan*; a volume of R. Burns (an Englishman whose works have as yet been little set), and in addition two volumes from Mosen, Heine, Byron, and Gœthe; with the cycle, that makes seven volumes. There! is that not good of me? And then there is also a volume of songs for four voices, among which is one for four female voices, which must certainly sound uncommon; the words are, for the most part, very emotional. I cannot tell you how easily all this has come to me, and how much I enjoyed doing it. As a rule I compose them standing or walking, not at the piano. It is quite a different sort of music, which does not come first through the fingers — much more direct and melodious. I have already played and sung some of them to Hiller, Verhulst, and others, and I will write, as you

---

1) A barrister and a university friend of Robert's. This letter to Töpken is printed by Jansen, *Davidsbündler* p. 178.

do when you have played well, 'and they were quite delighted with them'. . . ."

This letter came into Clara's hands just at the right time, when, as a result of the mortifications which she had encountered in Bremen, she was overwhelmed by a melancholy and despondency the extent of which can only be guessed from the diary, since, in opposition to her usual custom, she afterwards crossed out almost a whole page in such a way as to make what was written illegible. Immediately after this, stands: "On Oct. 25th I got another dear letter from Robert, which has delighted me unspeakably. With it came a song, tender and heartfelt, betraying the composer in every line."

On the 26th of February she went to Lübeck for a concert, an expedition which left only the most pleasant impressions behind. She was assured beforehand of a friendly reception from the Avés, but total strangers also met her in the kindest and warmest manner. She was much interested in the old town, though the dead silence of the principal streets made her very nervous. The concert too, was a success in every way. But the chief incident in this short journey was her first sight of the sea, which took place at Travemünde:

"There was one day which I shall never forget," she writes to Robert on March 2nd, after her return. "We were at Travemünde . . . . and went out to sea in a little boat with 3 sails, till we could no longer see any shore, and not one of us knew where we were . . . . and although I was rather nervous, still I shouted for joy. The day was misty, but it looked all the prettier when a faint sunbeam broke through the clouds and turned the waves to silver. . . . How many thousand times did I utter your name — ah! if only you could have been with us! . . . .

It is impossible to say anything about your little song, it can only be sung. The other follows, no matter how unwillingly, please send it back to me as soon as possible. . . .

How nice it is that you are composing so industriously! But the songs seem to me suspicious; is there never a young night-

ingale who inspires you? . . . . Are you too, having this lovely
spring weather already? Is the sun shining in your little room?
I should like to know so many things, but I should like best of
all to be with you."

The same day (3./3.) brought her a new and unexpected
pleasure in a letter from Robert which began with the words,
"Dear Clärchen, if you knew who was standing smiling behind
the door and knocking, you would say, 'Come in dear husband and *doctor*!'" It was his doctor's diploma from Jena
that he was sending her; a public honour which just at this
moment, when Wieck's "Declaration" was in everybody's hands,
must have given special satisfaction to her and to all his friends.
Altogether her departure from Hamburg was at the last,
friendly, warm, and — thanks to the consciousness of a hardly
won victory — cheerful to a degree which she herself would
have believed impossible a few weeks before. The final concert, on March 4th, at which she played the *F* minor sonata
of Beethoven, Schumann's *Novelletten*, Chopin's *Nocturnes*,
Schubert-Liszt's *Erlkönig*, the *B♭* major trio, and Thalberg's
Moses-Phantasie, was hard work, but at the same time it was
a great triumph, and the warm applause which was accorded
her was given not only to the artist, but to the woman who had
won respect under such hard circumstances. From this time
forth she was bound to Hamburg by indissoluble ties. Musik-
director Otten, Avé-Lallement, Gathy, and the Parish family,
stood by her with heart and soul, as hardly anyone had
done elsewhere. And while Wieck, in his letters to his Hamburg friends, inveighed against the "degraded, abandoned,
wicked girl who was already reaping the reward of her shame-
ful action", those whom he addressed vied with each other
in perpetually giving the "abandoned girl" fresh proofs of their
esteem and admiration, and the best society in Hamburg
followed their example. It was indeed by no means an unmixed pleasure in one day to take part in a great dinner at

Salomon Heine's and a big supper party at Senator Jenisch's, but at any rate this was not the species of well-deserved punishment which Wieck intended, and expected, her to receive.

On the 11th the two travellers came back to Berlin, well contented with their experiences and with the material success of their journey. For the time being they gave up the thought of a further tour to Kiel and Copenhagen, as well as of one to Mecklenburg; Clara needed rest, and the longing to have Robert within reach again, made her hasten her return. The performance of Gœthe's *Faust*, with Radziwill's and Lindpaintner's music, and with Seydelmann as Mephistopheles, gave her a keen artistic pleasure on the first night of her return. For days after she was full of it, and the memory of those days in Gœthe's house at Weimar became vivid again: "His towering figure", she writes, "is constantly before me, a book in his hand, smiling a little, just as he was the first time I saw him. I was, indeed, quite a child, but his image comes as vividly before my mind as if it were not long since I had seen him." Besides industrious visits to the theatre, no less industrious studies in English and French filled up this interval. But during these days she eagerly kept her ears open for news from Leipsic, where Liszt had arrived and where he and Schumann were daily together. Then began for them both, in spite of all the clouds which stood in the sky, one of those happy periods when the soul has wings. Already, on the 13th, Schumann had written:

"Here is something as a timid reward for your last two letters. The songs[1]) are the first which I have printed, so do not criticise them too severely. When I was composing them, I was rapt in the thought of you. Your eyes haunt me, you romantic girl, and I often think that without such a betrothed one could not

---

1) The cycle of songs from Heine, Op. 24.

write such music, and I say this in your honour. For I love you only too well; every evening I want to run away, and am in perpetual fear of not reaching you in time.

. . . . Have you nothing for my supplement, Clärchen? I am short of MSS., and I cannot go to Berlin until the piano-pieces for the third number are ready. Do you mean to say that you can be idle while I am composing so much? Try your hand at a song! When once you begin, you will not be able to stop. It is too seductive.

I will let you peep a little way into my plan for an opera. Send to a circulating library for the second part of Hoffmann's *Serapions-Brüder*, in which there is a story called *Doge and Dogaressa*. Read it through carefully; imagine it all on the stage; tell me your views, your misgivings. What I like in the novel is its nobility and naturalness. Julius Becker will have to turn the libretto into verse for me. I have already sketched it out."

CLARA TO ROBERT.

"Berlin 14./3. 40 Evening.

My best-beloved Robert

Thank you very much for the songs. They surprised me, and indeed they are quite unusual; they all require good singers who have intelligence enough to understand them. . . . I liked the criticism of the Schubert symphony [1]) very much — if only he were still alive! It makes one so miserable that he did not live to be recognised, as he is now. A curious feeling mastered me as I stood by his grave and Beethoven's. What true friends you would have been! If only I could hear the symphony!

. . . . I cannot compose; it makes me quite unhappy sometimes, but it really is not possible, I have no talent for it. Do not think that it is laziness. And a song indeed! I cannot do that at all; it needs inspiration to compose a song and fully to grasp the meaning of the words. . . .

. . . . You would like to know what I have put by, would you not? I will tell you, although I do not like speaking about it. I took 970 thaler, of which so much went on travelling expenses,

---

1) "The 7th symphony by Franz Schubert" in the *N. Z. f. M.* of March 10th 1840 p. 81 etc.

on purchases for myself and Mother and for the whole household, that I have 490 thaler left. — Are you satisfied or not? I am, very, and think that one can hardly expect more in 5 weeks."

ROBERT TO CLARA.

"Wednesday March 18th 1840.

It will not be much of a letter to-day. I am tired, overdone, and yet excited and restless from the events of the last few days.... As long as Liszt is here I cannot do much work, and I do not know how I shall get done before Maundy Thursday. I am with Liszt almost all day long. He said to me yesterday, 'I feel as if I had known you for 20 years' — and I feel the same. We are already quite rude to each other, and I have often cause enough, for Vienna has really made him too whimsical and spoiled. I cannot put into this letter all that I have to tell you about Dresden, our first meeting there, the concert, yesterday's railway journey here, last night's concert, and this morning's rehearsal for the second. How extraordinarily he plays — boldly and wildly, and then again tenderly and ethereally! I have heard all this. But, Clärchen, this world — his world I mean — is no longer mine. Art, as you practise it, and as I do when I compose at the piano, this tender intimacy I would not give for all his splendour — and indeed there is too much tinsel about it. I will say no more to-day; you know what I mean."

CLARA TO ROBERT.

"Berlin 20./3. 40.

You must just let yourself be pleased at having another visit from me to-day — it seems to me as if I had nothing to do except to keep on writing to you — it would be better if you were with me, and then neither of us would know a pang. When I was so long without having any news from you I thought that it was Liszt's fault, and I must confess that I was jealous of him! But then your dear letter came, and I saw that after all you had been thinking of me.

 .... Liszt is fortunate, for he plays at sight what we toil over and make nothing of in the end. But I quite agree with your opinion of him! Have you heard him play his *Études* yet? I am now studying the ninth, and think it fine, magnificent, but too dreadfully difficult. . . .

. . . . One question: don't you think it would be a good thing if I were to study fugues with Rungenhagen for a little? I should very much like to, only I do not know if my mind, of which I have no great opinion, is equal to such study! I began having French lessons a few days ago; if only I could make something of them! I am often enraged with myself.

. . . . I laughed heartily to hear that you are rude to Liszt; you think he is spoiled, but are not you also a little spoiled? I know that I spoil you. Well, that will all become better when once you are my husband."

ROBERT TO CLARA.

"Leipsic March 20th 1840.

This morning I wished that you could have heard Liszt. He really is too extraordinary. He played some of the *Novelletten*, a bit from the *Phantasie*, and the sonata, in a way that quite took hold of me. Quite different from what I imagined it, but always inspired, and with a tenderness and boldness of feeling such as he very likely does not show every day. Only Becker was present, and I believe tears stood in his eyes. I specially enjoyed the 2nd *Novellette* in *D* major; you would hardly believe what an effect it has; he is going to play it at his third concert here. Whole books could not contain all that I have to tell you concerning the confusion here. He never gave the 2nd concert, but preferred to go to bed, and two hours before gave out that he was ill. That he is not, and was not, well I am quite ready to believe; but it was a diplomatic illness; I cannot explain it all to you. It was pleasant for me, for now I have him in bed all day, and besides myself only Mendelssohn, Hiller, and Reuss, come to see him. If only you had been there this morning, I wager it would have been with you as it was with Becker.

. . . . Can you believe that at his concert he played on a Härtel piano, which he had *never* seen before. A thing like that pleases me more than a little, this confidence in his ten good fingers. But do not take it as a model, my Clara Wieck; keep just as you are; no-one equals you after all, and I often see your good heart in your playing. Do you hear, old girl!

.... This day month, please God, I shall be with you, you good child — then you will rest, quite happy and contented, on my heart, won't you? Cläre, will you not have a little concert ready for me, a quite private one for your lover? I should like to hear the $B\flat$ major sonata (the big one) all through, then a song of mine, which you shall play and sing to me (I care chiefly for distinct pronunciation), then a new scherzo by you, and in conclusion the $C\sharp$ minor fugue of Bach's from the 2nd Volume. I do not want to get the concert for nothing, and when it is over I too will serve up something appropriate, and finally we will each reward the other — you know how. I am much looking forward to this bride and bridegroom concert. — Ah! dearest and best of all humain beings; when first I see you again, I shall crush you to death for bliss.

But now we must part. Liszt will add a few lines to this letter. . . .

Postscript by Franz Liszt.

Permettez-moi aussi, mon grand artiste, de me rappeler affectueusement à votre gracieux souvenir. Combien ne regrettai-je point de ne pas vous trouver à Leipzig! si encore le temps me permettait d'aller vous serrer amicalement la main à Berlin! mais malheureusement cela ne me sera guère possible. Veuillez donc bien recevoir ainsi à distance mes vœux les plus empressés pour votre bonheur et votre gloire — et disposez entièrement de moi si par un heureux hazard je pourrai le moins du monde vous être bon à quelque chose. — Vous savez que je vous suis entièrement dévoué

F. Liszt."

ROBERT TO CLARA.

"Sunday March 22nd 1840.

My dear Child

How I wished you were with me. It is a mad life here and I think you would often be frightened. Liszt came here with his head quite turned by the aristocracy, and did nothing but complain of the absence of fine dresses and of countesses and princesses, till at last I got annoyed and told him that 'we too had our own aristocracy, i. e. 150 bookseller's shops, 50 printing establishments, and 30 newspapers, so he had better behave himself carefully'. But he only laughed, and has not troubled himself in the least about the customs of the place, consequently all the newspapers etc. fell foul of him. Possibly that made him think of what I said about our aristocracy, for he has never been so nice as during the last two days, since he has been criticised."

CLARA TO ROBERT.

"Berlin 22./3. 40.

. . . . The lines from Liszt were a great surprise to me — I will write to him to-day. He must come here . . . . it is dreadful to think that I shall not hear him . . . . I can fancy how he played the 2nd *Novellette* — it must sound splendid. . . .

— When I heard Liszt for the first time in Vienna, I hardly knew how to bear it, I sobbed aloud (it was at Graff's), it overcame me so. Does it not seem to you too, as if he would merge himself in the music while he plays, and then again when he plays tenderly, it is divine. Ah! yes; my heart has still a lively recollection of his playing. What you say about the piano is fine, but that is how it must always be with a true genius. Beside Liszt, all virtuosos seem to me so small, even Thalberg, and as for me — I can no longer see myself. Well, I am happy all the same for I can *understand* music — and I value that more than all my playing, and I am blessed in you and in your music, no-one is as tender as you.

. . . . I am already working hard for the bride's concert, but I am not at all looking forward to it, though I am to the bridegroom's concert which you will give me. What kind of repertoire am I to prescribe then? I really do not know what to say, for I like whatever you play to me, and how happy I shall be when I can once more sit beside you at the piano. . . . I am already scarlet with terror at the thought of singing to you, and as for clear enunciation! That is exactly what is impossible. I can bring out a tone somehow or other if I need not pronounce any words. . . . You cannot think how rusty my voice has got; for two years I have scarcely sung at all, that is the reason."

CLARA TO ROBERT.

"Berlin 24./3. 40.

Ah! poor me! Here I am, and have not the tiniest share in the numerous pleasures which you are giving each other! What

would I not have given to be in Leipsic yesterday, how happy
I should have been, how I sighed for it! I was at the theatre,
but all my thoughts were with you, I saw you in musical ecstasy,
and would so gladly have been at your side! Indeed I long intended to come with Mother, but I thought I should disturb your
life with Liszt, and should not be so welcome to you as I wished
to be. I think we did better to stay here.

. . . . I cannot believe that Father has written against him —
it would be too dreadful! But it was very wrong not to send
Father a ticket[1]). For years he has lent his pianos with the
greatest readiness, he has had more loss than profit, has not
allowed himself to be discouraged by all the trouble which it
has often given him, and now because he is no longer wanted,
he is treated with no consideration! Do you know, that has cost
me bitter tears, and it is not right of you all. . . ."

ROBERT TO CLARA.

"Leipsic March 25th 1840 Wednesday.

My own sweetheart

When you have read this letter you will look at the world
quite differently, and with far friendlier and clearer eyes. That
I will swear to. For Liszt and I herewith invite you to Liszt's
next concert, which is next Monday (for the poor). Liszt is going
to play the *Hexameron*[2]), Mendelssohn's 2nd concerto (which he
has never looked at yet), 2 studies by Hiller, and the *Carnaval*
(or at all events two thirds of it). What you have to do is to
book your seat at once for Saturday, so that you may be here
on Sunday (not later), then to see about your passport, then to get
together all that you want for a fortnight (for I will not let you
leave me sooner and will go back to Berlin with you on Palm
Sunday), and above all to write to me at once, 'Dear husband,
she who comes is your obedient Clara and wife' — will you? do
you wish to? You must.

In no case will Liszt come to Berlin. He says it is too important a city; if he came he would have to give a number of
concerts there, and he has not time for that. . . . Latterly there

---

1) Liszt ignored Wieck out of friendliness towards Schumann.
2) A series of variations by Thalberg, Herz, Pixis, and Liszt.

have been nothing but dinners and suppers, music and champagne, counts and fair ladies; in short he has turned our whole life topsy-turvy. We are all wildly fond of him, and yesterday, at his concert, he played like a god again, and the *furore* was indescribable. All the grumblers and growlers have been silenced.

. . . . Hiller gave a dinner at Aeckerlein's; it was a great affair, and some eminent people were present. Just think how Liszt distinguished me! After he had toasted Mendelssohn, he referred to me in such kindly French words that I turned blood-red, but I was very merry afterwards, for it was a very pleasant recognition. I will tell you all about it, and about Mendelssohn's soirée, which was also an unheard of and magnificent success, on Sunday."

And it was an "obedient Clara and wife" who on the evening of the 28th, immediately after a concert given by the brothers Ganz, in which she had taken part, entered the coach and set out for Leipsic.

The diary says: —

"The journey was successful but for a few little incidents, and I surprised Robert a day earlier than he expected.

On the 30th Liszt came to see me, having just returned from Dresden. He is so genial that no-one can help liking him.

In the evening he gave his concert. He felt most at his ease in the *Hexameron*, one could hear and see that. He did not play the things by Mendelssohn and Hiller so freely, and it was distracting to see him look at the notes all the time. He did not play the *Carnaval* as I like it, and altogether he did not make the same impression on me this time that he did in Vienna. I believe it was my own fault, I had pitched my expectations too high, for he is indeed a prodigious performer, and there is no-one like him — here in Leipsic people did not realise how high Liszt really stands, the audience was far too cold for such an artist. He played his galop, by urgent request, with extraordinary brilliancy and inspiration.

The 31st. Liszt spent some hours with us this morning, and endeared himself to us still more by his refined, truly artistic disposition. His conversation is full of spirit and life; he is inclined to philander, but one forgets that entirely. . . . He played the *Erlkönig, Ave Maria,* an *Étude* of his own etc. I too, had to play something to him, but I suffered tortures while I did it. Otherwise I did not feel at all embarassed in his presence, as I had feared I should be, he behave so naturally himself that everyone must feel at ease in his company. But I could not bear to be with him for long; his restlessness, his lack of repose, his extreme vivacity, are a great strain.

The 4th (April). I went to Connewitz with Robert. I am never so happy, never so much at home, as when I go anywhere with him! There is no need for him to speak — I like it so much when he is just thinking, and I should like to listen to his every thought! And when he gently presses my hand I am happy from the bottom of my heart — I feel so certain that I am his best beloved.

He showed me a number of his songs, to-day — I had not expected anything like them! My admiration for him increases with my love. Amongst those now living there is not one so musically gifted as he.

The 5th. After a long interval, I saw Madame Schröder-Devrient as Fidelio again, and it was an enormous pleasure. The music is too exquisite — I cannot say how it affects me. Madame Devrient's acting to-day was in many respects different from what it used to be — beautifully natural! The highest perfection of art, as she possesses it, seems nature itself, she studies every movement and yet one feels as if it were all the inspiration of the moment. She is a woman of tremendous power — my ideal in art! — No-one can sing the adagio as she does, not Grisi, nor Persiani, with a warmth, a feeling, and yet a masterly calmness and nobility, which must carry away everyone who has a feeling for music.

On the 17th we (Robert and I) set out for Berlin.

On the 21st we went to Charlottenburg and visited the Mausoleum of Queen Louise. . . . The monument is wonderful. . . . a peculiar sadness seized me in the vault. How everything passes away and is forgotten! Why do men live at all? — Thoughts like these came to me, and made me melancholy.

On the 26th I was in Potsdam all day with Robert. We were very happy together.

On the 27th we went to Strahlau and Treptow. They were heavenly days! Ah! I have been more happy with Robert, than I can say.

On the evening of the 28th I was at Mendelssohn's, with Robert. There was a great deal of music; Mendelssohn played Bach's $C\sharp$ minor fugue wonderfully; I played some things of his and Robert's, and then we played the first movement of Hummel's $A\flat$ major sonata together.

On the 29th Mendelssohn spent two hours with us, and let Robert play his songs to him. I was pleased with his appreciation.

The 30th. Robert left me, to-day."

An echo of these happy, fleeting, golden spring days spent with his beloved, is to be found in his setting of Eichendorff's *Mondnacht* (Moonlight Night). Robert sent it to Clara's mother for her birthday, on May 15th.

"Mamma has surely not had so happy a birthday for a very long time," writes Clara, "and I am so heartily pleased about it."

But her days under her mother's roof were numbered. During May she enjoyed above all things the renewal of her intercourse with Mendelssohn, who spent some time on a visit to his family in Berlin. She had not heard him for a long time, and now she found herself delighted afresh, and yet at the same time oppressed by the spell of his unapproachable mastery of the instrument: "You will forgive me for not playing the Bach fugues before," she writes to Robert, "I was always too shy, I know that you have already heard them in their greatest perfection from Mendelssohn, and I would not have played them to you on the last day if I had not been so eager that I quite forgot my resolution. Since I heard Mendelssohn play the $C\sharp$ minor fugue the other day, a new light has broken upon me as to how they ought to be played, and now I play some of them well, I think." And a few days later: "I had a great pleasure yesterday: Mendelssohn played his trio, and the G minor quartet of Mozart. He played in masterly fashion, and with such fire that for a few moments I really could not restrain my tears. He is the pianist whom I love best of all . . . . Apart from the pleasure, I consider that it is very instructive for me to hear him; and I believe that yesterday evening was a help to me."

But the sky was not so wholly free from clouds as would appear from Clara's letters, which overflowed with happiness. In spite of the letter which Clara had sent from Hamburg to the President of the High Court of Appeal urgently begging him to set her and her betrothed free from their torturing uncertainty by hastening the judgment, the suit seemed to drag out more and more, and they both began seriously to accustom themselves to the thought that they might have to celebrate this Christmas too, as an engaged couple. Then too, Clara realised that she would have to think seriously of starting on a fresh tour in order to earn money for the winter.

These pecuniary anxieties pressed on her the more heavily because, owing to an easily comprehensible shyness, she hesitated to take Robert into her confidence in this matter. She had repeatedly made considerable presents to her mother, out of the little capital which Robert had made over to

her, and out of her concert-takings. And if it was a satisfaction to her feelings to be able in this way at least to
give outward token of her gratitude to her mother for the
faith which she had kept with her during these hard months,
yet the thought tormented her that one day her modest means
must be exhausted, and she would find herself thrown entirely upon Robert for support. The longer the law-suit
lingered on, the nearer drew this anxiety: "I am going to
Leipsic with a heavy heart — how shall I tell him; ah! My
God! I cannot do it! But how dreadful it would be if it
came to my having to beg from him for myself. Ah! if only
I knew where to go this summer in order at least to earn
what I need: my situation is sad, and my cares are crushing
and humiliating."

With such gloomy reflections close the comments of the
diary on the events of May 1840.

Her letters of this time betray nothing of this frame of
mind. In June too, though it brought her Robert again — she
went to Leipsic on the 5th for a visit of some weeks' duration
— there was no external change in her state of anxiety and
uncertainty. It was of course a pleasure to them that, for the
first time since their engagement, they kept Robert's birthday
together, and one which the two sorely tried lovers enjoyed
with all their hearts. Besides this there was no lack of interest and diversion — amongst other things they made acquaintance with Lwoff, the composer of the Russian national anthem,
who delighted Clara by his perfect quartet playing, and at
the same time greatly encouraged her to undertake a journey
to S[t] Petersburg, and promised her all support. But the very
prospect of this tour, which was eventually to be undertaken
during the next winter, gave her more pain and anxiety than
she would confess.

To doubts of her own powers, and fear of a possible want
of success, were now added the discords arising from Robert's

bitter feeling towards Wieck — whom he had sued for slander — which made themselves felt in daily intercourse. "I feel that Robert must act in this way, and yet I am sorry for Father," the diary ends in June.

But happiness, so long desired, was already standing on the threshhold and softly knocking at the door; and, as was only fitting, it announced itself in music. In the midst of her most anxious cares for the future, Robert was preparing an unusual surprise for her. "This evening," she writes on July 4th, "as I came home, what did I find? A beautiful Härtel grand piano, wreathed with flowers, and in the next room, there sat he, the dear, most warmly loved Robert. . . . A dainty poem lay among the flowers."

The next day Schumann caused his quartet for men's voices to be sung to her. "I played the piano, which sounds splendid." And on the next day: "I have become filled with a passion for playing, the piano sounds so well."

And then on July 7th: "To-day Robert surprised me with good news! Father has withdrawn his evidence of the reason for his opposition . . . . We expect judgment within 8 days — I cannot say what I felt at this news."

A few days after this they were already house-hunting. On the 16th they at last found a dwelling-place, "small, but cosy rooms in Inselstrasse, in the house of Maurermeister Scheitel". One drop of wormwood mingles with her cup of joy: "That I should not even have what the simplest citizen's daughter has — a trousseau." But she was able to get over even this. And on August 1st the verdict of the court comes at last: "Father has still 10 days in which to appeal: heaven grant that he may leave it alone."

And now came a pleasant distraction in the "terrible anxiety" of the final period of writing — a short concert tour through the Thüringian towns, her last as Clara Wieck[1]).

1) This time she was accompanied by her Aunt Carl.

It was a wonderful journey.

On August 8th she played in the *Rosensaal* of the academy at Jena, and the Thüringian city of the Muses — small, yet not provincial — prepared for her an enthusiastic reception, "such as I have hardly ever known in a small town", she writes to Robert. "I wish you had been there, you would certainly have been heartily pleased to see the enthusiasm which your Clara aroused. . . . The audience cried aloud and clapped frantically, which gave me great pleasure."

Different impressions awaited her in Weimar. First of all, on Aug. 11th, came a performance at the Grand-Ducal court at Belvedere, before a glittering assembly, in the presence of the Empress of Russia and other foreign royalties, "while lively conversation was going on, and some barking of dogs"; the whole thing empty and hollow. But the next evening was all the pleasanter. The foreign guests having gone, only the Grand-Ducal family and the Princess of Prussia were present. "I was no longer at court, but in a family circle. Everybody spoke to me, and they were all so kind that I was enchanted. . . . The Princess of Prussia was very nice; After I had told her that my Father was very strict about my practising, but that I thanked him for it, she said: '*You* thank him, and so do others!'. . . When I was at last going, the Grand Duchess asked me about my plans for the future, and I told her that I was going to be married, whereupon they all congratulated me at once, and the Grand Duchess asked if I meant to drop my art. I answered no, whereupon she said: 'I hope that you may be loved as you deserve.' I am very happy, it was so nice yesterday evening," she writes to Robert.

Pleasant days followed. She met the List family again in Liebenstein, and the Duke and Duchess of Meiningen, who lived close by, at Castle Altenstein, repeatedly invited her to play, and showed a warm personal interest in her, which to some extent compensated for the dreadful instrument out of which she had to try and coax some sound. Here too, the charm of her personality proved irresistible. When she left, the Duchess kissed her with motherly tenderness thereby moving Clara, in her weak and over-strained condition, to tears: "I shall never forget this woman with her tenderness and her angelic gentleness, and yet at the same time with her truly royal dignity."

In the mean time, on Aug. 12th 1), the long desired and feared decision had been pronounced; since Wieck had lodged no appeal, judgment was confirmed in their favour. "I cannot grasp this happiness," says the diary.

On Aug. 16th their banns were published for the first time, and finally, though in strictest secrecy, the mariage was celebrated on Sept. 12th, the eve of Clara's birthday.

Thus August ended in busy happiness. "I wish," she wrote to Robert at this time, "that every bride could remember these days with as heartfelt happiness as I do."

In the diary the heading "September" is underlined:

"September, how strangely this month looks at me. An indescribable sensation of joy and sorrow steals over me — Heaven grant us its blessing! My Robert! if only I see him once again — my heart is well-nigh broken with longing, and with all this I have to see to concert-business — what a contrast!"

Yes this concert-business followed her almost to the bridal altar. On Sept. 2nd, in unbearable heat, she played at a con-

_____

1) "On Clara's day," Schumann wrote, "three years ago to-day, I begged for your hand." This was not exact, for the famous concert did not take place till Aug. 13th 1837, and the Schumanns always kept the 14th as the day of their betrothal. But the three days, Clara (12th), Aurora (13th), and Eusebius (14th) on account of their names, and of the events which occurred on them, always formed a sort of festival for Schumann. Cf. Jansen, *Davidsbündler* p. 220.

cert in Gotha[1]) for the benefit of the poor; and here too, she was received by the reigning Prince with unusual distinction, though she was but little impressed by the *genus loci* as a whole: "A chamberlain, from whom I had the piano, received me in his dressing-gown, with a pipe in his mouth, and stayed like this all the time I was there." Erfurt too, on the following evening, made no better impression. Tropical heat and an indifferent piano did the rest. "I played with only half my strength, and from note."

But then:

"On the 4th. I came to Weimar, stopped at the Montags'[2]), ran up the steps, opened the door of the room, and who came to meet me? Robert! I cannot depict my joy."

On Saturday, Sept. 5th, she gave another musical soirée in the town hall of Weimar. She played the *D* major trio of Beethoven, op. 70, no. 1; Henselt's étude *Wenn ich ein Vöglein wär*, Schubert-Liszt's *Ave Maria*, Chopin's mazurka in *B♭* minor, Schubert-Liszt's *Erlkönig*, and in conclusion Thalberg's *Mosesphantasie*. "That was my last concert as Clara Wieck, and I felt sad at heart."

On the following day she parted from Emilie List, who had been her companion during the latter part of this tour.

On Sept. 7th the lovers went back to Leipsic. Two days later Clara's mother arrived, and on the 10th came the faithful Becker from Freiberg.

And now the diary continues:

"The 11th. *Polterabend!*[3]) My Robert has given me a beautiful bridal gift — *Myrtles*[4]) — I was quite over-come!

---

1) At this concert Elise List appeared with her, as a singer, but not under her own name.

2) Music-director in Weimar.

3) *Translator's note*: The evening before the wedding.

4) A magnificent copy printed in gold, and with the dedication in Robert's writing, "To my beloved Clara on the eve of our wedding, from her Robert."

Cäcilie handed me the myrtle-wreath, a feeling of awe came over me as I touched it.

Some friends spent a merry evening with us."

"The 12th. What am I to say about this day!

— The wedding took place at 10 o'clock, in Schönefeld (near Leipsic), it began with a choral, then the minister Wildenhahn, (a friend of Schumann's youth) gave a short and simple address but one which spoke from the heart to the heart. My whole heart was filled with thankfulness to Him who had at last led us across so many rocks and cliffs to each other; my most fervent prayer was that it might please Him to preserve my Robert to me for many, many years — ah! when the thought that I may someday lose him, comes over me, my head reels — Heaven protect me from such misfortune, I could not bear it.

After the wedding Emilie and Elise List paid me a surprise visit. Reuter, Bargiel, Wenzel[1]), Herrmann[2]), Becker, my Mother, the Lists and the Carls, spent the morning with us in the Carls' house, the afternoon in Zweinaundorf, and the evening at the Carls' again; Madame List came too; in the evening.

We danced a little — there was no romping, but all faces showed heartfelt satisfaction. It was a beautiful day, and even the sun, which had hidden itself for many days past, poured its mild rays upon us as we drove to the wedding, as if it would bless our union. Nothing disturbed us on this day, and it shall be inscribed in this book as the happiest and the most important of my life.

---

1) Ernst Ferdinand Wenzel, a music-teacher in Leipsic, a friend of Schumann's. Cf. *Briefe, Neue Folge* p. 118, 172 etc.

2) Assessor Herrmann, Schumann's friend, who with Reuter, had been of great assistance to him in conducting the suit against Wieck.

One part of my life is now ended; if I have known much trouble in my youth, I have also known much joy, I will never forget that. Now a new life is beginning, a beautiful life, a life in him whom I love above all, above myself, but grave duties rest with me too, Heaven lend me strength to fulfil them faithfully, like a good wife — it has always helped me hitherto, and will continue to do so. I have always had great faith in God, and I will keep it for ever and ever."

CHAPTER VIII.

APRIL SHOWERS AND SUNSHINE.
1840—1844.

"It must be admitted," Schumann writes in the spring of 1840, "that in this Leipsic, which nature has treated in so step-motherly a fashion, German music flourishes, and without boasting it may claim a place among the richest and largest gardens of other cities. . . . May the genius of music long keep beneficent watch over this corner of the world, once hallowed by the name of Bach, as it now is by that of a famous young master, and may he and all who surround him live among us for many more years to the profit of true art!"

Even in this outburst there rings a faint note of anxiety over the transitoriness of all this blossom, an anxiety which in the end was to prove only too well justified. Yet, for a short time, he and those like-minded with himself saw the wish wonderfully fulfilled, more perfectly indeed than the modesty of the prophet had allowed him to suggest.

If up to this time Mendelssohn's name and personality alone had — at all events in the eyes of the outside world — given the stamp to music in Leipsic, during the four years that followed, the life-giving spirit which went forth · was strengthened and deepened by the creative genius of Schumann, whose amazing versatility and exuberant freshness broke through all obstacles like a long pent-up stream. Beside the hearth which he had won so hardly, the goal of so many years, all that had so long been fettered was at last set free.

On Sept. 13th, the first day of their married life, Schumann gave his wife a new diary, in which he himself made the first entry.

"The little book which I begin to-day," he writes, "has a most intimate meaning; it is to be a diary of everything that affects us both in our household- and married-life; our wishes, our hopes shall be recorded in it; and it shall also be a book of the requests which we have to make of each other, when words fail to express our meaning; and also of mediation and reconciliation if we chance to have misunderstood each other; in short, it shall be a good, true friend to whom we will confide everything, to whom our hearts shall lie bare. . . . Every week we will change the secretary; every Sunday . . . . it shall be handed over . . . . What has been writen shall then be read in silence or aloud, as the contents require, what has been forgotten shall be added . . . . and the whole week shall be carefully weighed, to see if it has been a worthy and busy one, if we are building up our life a-right if we are perfecting ourselves more and more in our beloved art.

The entries for a week shall never cover less than a page; whichever of us fails to write as much as this shall receive a punishment which we will devise later.

As I have said, our little booklet shall be graced by criticisms of our artistic work; e. g. it shall contain what you are studying chiefly, what you are composing, what new music you have got to know, and what you think of it; and the same with regard to me. Another great ornament of the book will be character sketches, e. g. of distinguished artists with whom we have come into contact. Anecdotes and jests shall by no means be excluded.

But the best and dearest thing which the book will contain there is no need for me to name to you, my dear wife: our fair hopes — may heaven bless them — the anxieties which married life brings with it; in short, all the joys and sorrows of married life shall have their true history written here, and in years to come we shall enjoy reading it.

If you agree with all this, wife of my heart, sign your name under mine, and as a talisman let us utter the three words upon which all earthly happiness rests:

Industry, Frugality, and Loyalty."

And under Robert's name stands in Clara's writing: "Your wife, who is devoted to you with her whole heart, Clara."

Many of the laws of this "order of matrimony" were neglected or forgotten in course of time, and the lawgiver himself was the chief offender against the first edict concerning the joint management of the diary in regular rotation. — Under the pressure of an impulse towards composition, he began to write irregularly, and later he gave it up altogether, leaving it to his wife to recount the experiences of their life; thus depriving the book of its character as a written dialogue between a married couple about questions which they hesitated to discuss by word of mouth in the bustle of the day. But the key-note which was struck here, the chief object which was placed before them, not so much with regard to the diary as with regard to their journey through life together, was adhered to by both of them to the end, with a loyalty, an earnestness, a simple greatheartedness, remarkable not only in the married life of two artists but in any married life. In the course of their long period of probation both had clearly realised that a life-long union between two artistic natures, both so highly gifted and so strongly marked, must contain difficulties and dangers of a peculiar kind. Not without a struggle, and in no easy school were they to learn the duties which they had undertaken towards each other. It seems inevitable that when artistic gifts such as these were weighed against each other — each claiming recognition — the creative power, in this case the husband's, should out-weigh the interpretive and reproductive, in this case the wife's.

When Clara Wieck gave Robert Schumann her hand there
is no doubt that to the greater number of those interested
in music her name was better known in public than her
husband's. In spite of her youth she stood — so at least it
then appeared — at the summit of her art, and the dis-
appearance of this girl-priestess who — like the star which
shines out of a purer atmosphere, and in quiet silent beauty
sheds its light abroad — had brought happiness to countless
numbers and had awakened and strengthened belief in a
pure and unselfish art, was felt by all to be an irretrievable
loss. For only a very few realised that this temporary loss
was in reality the greatest possible gain for art and for
the artist.

Hebbel once said that he who would attain to self-know-
ledge and to the sure use of his powers must "first steep
himself in some other great soul. . . . One prophet baptises
the next. And he of whom a hair is singed in this baptism
of fire, has not been called".

It is indeed a baptism of fire, and those who come to it
have a threefold need not only of ready devotion, but of unshakable courage and firm self-reliance, if he who wakes life
is not also to destroy it.

And in this respect Clara's power was put to the severest
test. She realised and learnt a-new day by day in her life
with Schumann, that he had reached his highest point of
development as an artist, that he was the master, not only
of his life's companion, but of his fellow-artist, and that it
was at once her highest duty and her highest happiness to
lose herself in him, however much the world, and even their
own friends, might incline to regard the manifestations of his
untrammelled originality as the struggles of immaturity, and
to consider that the harmonious, finished art of his wife, with
her maturity and her reserve, was, within its limits, at least
worthy to be ranked beside his.

But if this clear, personal conviction had caused her, during the last years of their engagement, to abandon all idea of achieving anything as a composer, yet there was a point in her unconditional surrender of herself, at which from the outset her artistic conscience instinctively commanded her to halt, and this was the practice of her art.

There is no doubt in his inmost heart Schumann would have preferred her to renounce all public work as an artist from the moment at which she became his wife. From his point of view this is quite comprehensible. Apart from the desire to have his beloved, whom he had won with such difficulty, to himself, he had more or less clear forebodings of those conflicts which must ensue when he, filled more and more with the creative instinct, felt a corresponding yearning for the quiet peace of home-life, and his wife at the same time felt urged towards a practical exhibition of her art. Her success could be obtained only at the price either of wearisome separations, or through his participation in journies, which, while they seriously hampered his creative work, at the same time put him in a subordinate place, which his own proper pride as an artist must often have found insupportable.

That, in spite of this, the continuance of Clara's public performances was from the outset treated by them both as a matter of course, was due in the first place to financial considerations, since in face of Wieck's dismal prophecies of probable starvation for the young couple, the income which arose from them was of importance.

But for Clara there was from the first far more at stake. Both now and later she emphasized the necessity of turning to account her power of earning money to meet the ever-increasing expenses of the household; and this was indeed no mere pretext, for as a matter of fact, the more her husband delighted in throwing off such anxieties, the more anxious she became. But a very different consideration stood first in her mind. She knew, or at all events suspected, that the moment she renounced the public pursuit of her profession, she would also renounce the right to consider the practice of her art as a factor in her daily life equal in importance to her other duties. And if from the moment in which she gave herself to Schumann, she was determined to dedicate her best powers to him without reservation or condition, yet, from the outset, she realised, more by instinct than knowledge perhaps, that art was first thing necessary to the preservation and development of her individuality, since the woman and the artist could not be separated without destroying the one or the other.

At the moment she naturally did not realise how great a problem she had undertaken to solve in becoming Schumann's wife, and during those early years there were many difficult hours as her own personal artistic powers were day by day forced into narrower limits by household duties to which she was quite unaccustomed, and which increased from year to year, as well as by the creative genius of her husband, which was steadily developing into something richer and grander; so that step by step she was forced back, though at the same time the very life with Robert enriched and deepened her own artistic powers. But this, like every problem which Fate set before this great and good woman in the course of a long life, was solved with admirable certainty, inexpressibly fine tact, and that inner conviction which brings victory, in a way which shows how inspiring an influence must have been exercised upon Schumann's creative power by contact with so pure an artistic and human soul.

"We have been married three months to-day," Clara writes on Dec. 5th, "and they have been the happiest three months of my life. Every day I fall more deeply in love with my Robert, and if I often seem sad, and almost cross, it is but the result of cares which have their origin in my love for him. I hope all the quarters to come will be no less happy than the one that has passed. If anything can momentarily disturb my contentment, it is the thought of my Father, for whom I feel the deepest compassion. He cannot witness our happiness, since heaven has denied him a heart, and he cannot understand a joy like ours. Now he has no happiness left, and his conduct has lost him, not only me, but all his friends — and he had not so very many. It is sad, and the more so to me since I am his daughter. I hope that you, my most dearly loved Robert, are not angry with me for this; a daughter's feelings cannot be entirely suppressed, and you will pardon my sad thoughts about my Father."

It is plain that this matter might, under the circumstances, easily enough become a source of discord and trouble to the young couple. The libel suit which Schumann had instituted against Wieck still lingered on — it was ended by a verdict in Schumann's favour, in the spring of 1841 — but through Major Serre's intervention very painful discussion took place between father and children concerning Clara's property and the rendering up of her belongings and more particularly of her piano. In the end Wieck once more showed the petty and hateful side of his nature to such an extent that Clara's gentle and conciliatory disposition was changed, and in the spring of 1841 the last prospects of even an outward reconciliation seemed to be destroyed indefinitely.

A few months later, Clara, out of the fulness of her happiness, sent her father a birthday greeting, thus attempting to re-unite the severed thread, but, needless to say, this was no sign of weakness or of repentance for what she had done. Neither now, nor at any later time, had she or her husband the slightest doubt or scruple concerning their action. She was simply following the impulse of her heart towards the lonely man for whom, in spite of all the harm that he had done to her, she never ceased to feel a daughter's love. And at the same time the fact that her husband gladly fell in with her wishes was a proof of delicacy of feeling and nobility of thought which cannot be sufficiently recognised. This attempt to approach him was however as little understood by Wieck and as completely ignored, as was the news, which Schumann sent him a few weeks later, that a grandchild had been born to him on Sept. 1ˢᵗ. On this occasion he even sent a letter disclaiming the connection and couched in the roughest terms.

After this it was naturally out of the question that the Schumanns should make any fresh attempt at reconciliation. And neither of them could have been blamed if when Wieck suddenly changed his mind, and in January 1843 (in a letter of which, unfortunately, only a fragment remains) himself sought for a reconciliation, they had replied at least with some hesitation and reserve. But such weighing of the matter was impossible either to Clara or to Robert.

On Jan. 21ˢᵗ 1843 the father addressed them in these words [1]:

"I continue to have a genuine and undisturbed love for art, and it follows that the work of your talented husband cannot remain unconsidered and unrecognized by me. I will prove this to you by asking you to let me know in advance when there is any chance of my hearing in public some of your husband's latest compositions, which are so much praised by all connoisseurs. I would come to Leipsic on purpose.

Your husband and I have hard heads — which must be allowed to go their own way — but we have stuff in us. Therefore he cannot be surprised if I wish to see justice done to his industry

---

1) This fragment is printed by Kohut (with a wrong date), *Fr. Wieck* p. 150, where it is apparently quoted either from the original or from a copy. The letter is not to be found among the letters from Wieck to his daughter preserved among the papers left by the Schumanns.

and to his creative power. Come to Dresden soon, and bring your husband's quintet with you."

And Clara at once replied naturally and warmly, without saying a word in reference to the past[1]).

"Leipsic 23./1. 1843.

Dear Father

I should have been delighted to accept your kind invitation at once, but you know one cannot always get away, and the time of year is too rough for baby now. As soon as it grows warmer again I shall bring her over, and you will be delighted with her.... But I hope to speak to you here before that, for you will easily believe that I long to see you soon.

Perhaps it will be possible to combine this with a musical treat: Sophie Schloss[2]) has invited me to play at her concert on February 9th; I have not yet made up my mind whether I will play the quintet or a *Konzertstück* of Robert's with orchestral accompaniment — but certainly it will be one of them. . . . Can you manage to come here then?

I wished you could have been at our matinée. You would certainly have been satisfied. Robert's quartet and quintet received unmixed applause, which made me very happy; and in this frame of mind I did not play badly, as you can easily imagine. I played one sonata of Beethoven's (Op. 101, you know it well, for if I am not mistaken I once played it to you in earlier days) which I believe had never before been heard in public, and besides this, Bach's Pedal Fugue, concluding with the quintet. Robert's quartets — there are three — are to be published in a few weeks by Härtel. Perhaps you may happen to hear one or other of them this winter; I should be very glad if you did.

It is a great comfort to hear that you are better in health, and I am glad that I knew nothing of your being unwell when you were worse. The summer will make you quite well again.

---

1) Printed here from the original. Kohut gives it, with omissions, *Fr. Wieck* p. 150.

2) Sophie Schloss from Cologne, soprano soloist at the Leipsic *Gewandhaus* from 1839—43, and 1846—48. "The first singer who sang Schumann's songs in public." Cf. Schumann *Ges. Schriften* 4th ed. II p. 556.

Who told you that I was in bad health? I can assure you
that this is not the least true. . . . I should very much like to
hear Marie again; I am told that both she and Cäcilie play extremely well. — Give the children my love, and Mother too, and
as to you, dear Father, write very soon and say something more
exact as to when we are to meet again.   Your Clara."

Schumann's fine character proved worthy of itself on this
occasion. Although this attempt of the father at reconciliation
did not as yet include himself, he did not hesitate for an
instant to make an opportunity as soon as possible for his
wife to accept the invitation to Dresden.

"Clara is in Dresden," he writes on Feb. 17th 1843, "visiting
her relations. Her father has suddenly changed his mind, and
I am rejoiced for my Clara's sake. Parents are parents after
all, and one has them but once."

If we ask for the reason of this "sudden alteration", this
change of mind which is not to be explained by any change
in the behaviour of the children towards the father in the
mean time, we shall do Wieck no injustice if we attribute it
to considerations of common-sense, though affection may also
have had something to do with it.

Notwithstanding his earlier appreciation of Schumann, it
was evident that he had hitherto lacked faith in the power
of his genius to develop; in his own mind he had not believed
in his ability to make a great future for himself, in the sense
of general public recognition so promising an artist. And this
view was certainly one of the grounds· of his obstinate opposition to the marriage of his daughter. But the creative
activity which Schumann developed during the first two years
of his married life, taught him better, and showed him clearly
that if he wished to maintain his position of authority in the
musical world — a position already severely shaken by his
public attack on Schumann's character — he must not allow
the fact that he annoyed him as an individual to weigh against

the victorious artist who was carving a path for himself. And when he had so far conquered himself, it was comparatively easy for one who had always been accustomed quite naïvly to subordinate all personal feeling to the service of material interests to take the step towards reconciliation, for the struggle which it may have cost his pride was amply compensated for by the glory which his son-in-law's star — just rising at that moment — could not fail to shed upon himself and upon his musical plans for the future.

And if the remarks about Schumann's importance — so characteristic in this connection — contained in his first letter to Clara, leave any doubts as to whether these considerations did finally bring about Wieck's sudden change of front, all doubt cannot but disappear in view of the time and the manner in which, some months later, Wieck, after he had reconciled himself with his daughter, sought to re-establish personal relations with Schumann also. On Dec. 4th and 11th the two first performance of *Paradies und Peri* had taken place in Leipsic, and it was announced for Dresden on the 23th. Wieck wrote to Schumann on Dec. 15th 1843:

"Dear Schumann

Tempora mutantur et nos mutamur in eis.

In the face of Clara and of the world we can no longer keep apart from one another. You are moreover the father of a family — what need is there for a lengthy explanation?

We were always united where art was concerned — I was even your teacher — my verdict decided your present course in life for you. There is no need for me to assure you of my sympathy with your talent and with your fine and genuine aspirations.

In Dresden there joyfully awaits you   Your father
                                                                        Fr. Wieck."

And two days later, in a letter to their common friend Becker, he writes: "Schumann obtained extraordinary applause at the first production of the *Peri* in Leipsic and won a laurel wreath, which latter may possibly have made him feel a little awkward. In consequence the *Peri* is going to be given by Reissiger at the subscription concert in the theatre here on the 23rd. However, Schumann is — quite rightly — going to be present at the rehearsal. He and Clara are coming on the 19th, and mean to stay. It is probable that he will visit me, and will stay till the 25th."

Radiant with joy, Clara, immediately after the receipt of his letter to her husband, had written to her father: "A thousand thanks for your letter, and especially for the enclosure, with its friendly words to my husband for which he himself will thank you in Dresden. I am very happy about it, and there is nothing left to weigh on my heart now."

Matters fell out as Wieck had written to Becker. The Schumanns arrived in Dresden on Dec. 19th, and kept Christmas together in the house of Clara's parents, for the first time for seven years.

With this, peace was re-established one more, and at the same time a discord was once for all removed from the lives of the young couple. From this time forward — although there was no lack of momentary rubs and misunderstandings — the relations between parents and children were never again seriously disturbed. That this was so, and that it so remained, was chiefly, if not entirely, due to Clara, who with magnificent self-control, from this moment onwards, would not allow the Wiecks to hear the very faintest echo of the sufferings which she had endured, and in her pure goodness of heart showed herself to parents and brothers and sisters only as a good daughter and a tender sister.

The life which during the early forties unfolded itself in the cosy rooms on the first floor of the house in the Inselstrasse (No. 5) though apparently quiet, was really full of movement. Two artists were at work, both striving to attain the same goal, ·to develop to the highest perfection the mental and moral powers stirring within them, and in this finding the resolution of those discords, great and small, which contact with the cares and problems of daily life, and the little frictions between two highly-strung artistic natures, were bound to bring with them. There were two grand pianos in the house, but they were not both allowed to be heard at the same time, and the diary is not lacking in complaints, both loud and soft, over "the evils of thin walls". "My playing," runs the entry in January 1841, "is getting all behindhand, as is always the case when Robert is composing. I cannot find one little hour in the day for myself! If only I did not get so behind!"

More than this, while abundance of melodies were struggling into shape and reaching the highest artistic forms in song and symphony under this roof, not one note of them sounded in the young wife's lonely room. "Robert has been very cold towards me for the last few days," the diary laments [1]. "There is indeed a very happy reason for this, and no-one can take a more sincere interest than I do in all that he undertakes, yet at times this coldness, which I have by no means deserved, hurts me." Robert himself speaks [2] of the mingled joy and pain which she found in his creations: "For too often she has to buy my songs at the price of silence and invisibility." "So must it be in an artist's life," he adds, "and if two people love each other, it is right enough."

More serious, however, more carefully weighed, even somewhat apologetic, is an entry in Oct. 1842, the second year of their marriage, referring to the first winter concert in the *Gewandhaus*, at which Clara had played: "She played

---

1) At the end of Dec. 1840. He was at that time just giving the finishing touches to the "*Frühlingssymphonie*" (Spring Symphony) (B♭ major) Op. 38).

2) At the end of November 1840, after the completion of the cycle of songs from Kerner (Op. 35).

well and finely, as she always does. I am often sorry that
I so frequently hinder Clara in her study, because she will
not disturb me when I am composing. For I know well that
any artist who appears in public, however great he may be,
can never entirely give up certain mechanical exercises, but
must always keep the elasticity of his fingers, so to speak,
in practice. And for this, my dear artist often has no time.
So far as the deeper part of musical education is concerned,
Clara certainly has not stood still, but, on the contrary, has
advanced; now she lives in good music alone, and her playing
is therefore the sounder and at once more intellectual and
more tender than it was. But she often has not the time to
bring technique to the point of absolute certainty, and that is
my fault; and yet I cannot help it; Clara realises that I
must develop my talent, that I am now at the best of my
powers, and that I must make use of my youth. Well, so
must it be when artists marry; one cannot have everything;
and after all the chief thing is the happiness which remains
over and above, and we are happy indeed in that we possess
one another and understand one another, understand and love
with all our hearts."

In spite of this, or rather, on account of it, Clara's satisfaction when consideration for her husband and her own state
of health, once more allow her to practice regularly, is easily
comprehensible. "I lay myself down to sleep," she writes,
"more peacefully when I have fulfilled this duty to myself."

Nor did she in the least deceive herself as to the justice
of her husband's remarks about the ripening of her musical
powers.

With him and through him she first grew into the deeper
understanding of Beethoven's orchestral works, and above
all, of Bach's.

They had begun the second week of their married life by
studying the *Wohltemperiertes Klavier* together. "Robert," writes

Clara, speaking of this, "points out the passages where the theme continually recurs. Fugues are very interesting to study, and it gives me a great deal of pleasure. Robert scolded me sharply; I had been doubling a passage in octaves, and so had added a fifth voice, incompatible with four-part writing." "We continue our study of fugues;" she writes, a week later, "every time I play them, I am more interested. In almost every fugue one sees such an easy flow and yet such great art. After Bach, Mendelssohn's fugues seem poor, one can see that they are *made*, and that he found it hard work at times. . . . But all the same, I feel convinced that no man now living can write such fugues as Mendelssohn" ("Cherubini, Spohr, Klengel." Schumann corrects in the margin).

In the spring of 1841 these studies were set aside and they began to work through the scores of Beethoven's symphonies, and Mozart's and Beethoven's overtures, together[1]). "Besides this," runs the diary for July 1841, "Clara has been working hard at some of Beethoven's sonatas, and has grasped them in a manner that is all her own without in any way spoiling the original conception. This is a great treat for me."

But revelations which opened new worlds to her, came to her chiefly in studying and playing Schumann's own compositions, which combined with this steeping of herself in classical works, gradually, and yet comparatively quickly, freed her from the fetters of that attitude towards art which, consciously or unconsciously, almost always results from private study with a view to concert-programmes.

The rapidity and completeness with which this change was effected is betrayed by a remark of Clara's in July 1841: "On Sunday afternoon I played some of Beethoven's sonatas,

---

1) In like manner during the summer of 1842 Haydn's and Mozart's quartets were studied.

but neither Becker nor Krägen enjoyed them as we enjoy Beethoven sonatas. They have been taught to think more of virtuosity than of real music. A Bach fugue, for example, bores them, they are not capable of discovering the beauty which lies in the different parts taking up the theme, they cannot follow it. . . . The less I play in public, the more I hate all mere technique. Concert-pieces, such as Henselt's *Études*, Thalberg's and Liszt's *Phantasies* etc. etc. I have grown quite to dislike. . . . Nothing of that sort can give lasting pleasure."

A similar tone is to be heard in her verdict on Henselt, who was staying in Leipsic in Sept. 1842, and delighted her now, as he had done before, by his broad and mellow playing. Yet she felt that something was lacking: "Magnificent as his playing is, clear as is every note, yet I believe that through much mechanical study his attack has lost delicacy. He seems unable to play suggestively and poetically. . . . Otherwise his playing discouraged me as it did 6 years ago, but then it also inspired me. I am unpardonably lazy about playing just now, but I will make up for it as much as possible." If in these words rings a certain confidence that, in spite of all the constantly recurring complaints that want of practice will cause her to unlearn everything, she has something new and individual to set against this, yet the real meaning of what she had learned is shown perhaps even more clearly in a comment on the programme with which in August 1843 Pauline Viardot — whom she rated highly both as a woman and as an artist — appeared before the public of Leipsic. She laments that "a person so musical through and through, who certainly has the mind to appreciate really good music", should believe it necessary to make so many concessions to the public taste.

"Clara," writes Schumann in Aug. 1841, "is studying a great deal of Beethoven (together with much wifely attention to Schumann) with right good will; she has helped me much in arranging my symphony, and in the intervals she is reading

Gœthe's life, and she chops beans when necessary! Music she cares for more than anything, and that gives me great pleasure."

Her intellectual horizon was widened, generally as well as musically, by the stimulus and guidance of books, especially at those times when her health did not allow her to practice her beloved art, and she was all the more thankful for this as daily intercourse with so many-sided and highly educated a person as Robert made her very conscious of her own want of systematic mental training. For example, she now made acquaintance for the first time — by means of a copy which Mendelssohn gave her — with Gœthe's *Hermann und Dorothea.*

With Robert, she now ventured to attack to Jean Paul, and above all, with him she steeped herself in Shakespeare, the study of whose works for a time alternated with that of the *Wohltemperiertes Klavier* [1]). "Our Bach studies," writes Robert at the end of October, "have been in abeyance for a week; and I am now reading Shakespeare instead, in order to pick out all the passages referring to music; Clara is then going to copy them out for me in a beautiful book." He was planning an article on Shakespeare's attitude towards music, "a subject which Mendelssohn ought to treat, if he were also an author". "No-one has said anything finer or more significant about music, than Shakespeare, and that at a time when it was still in its cradle. Here again, we see poetic genius, which ranges over all ages and looks beyond them."

It is easy to understand how, living as she did in the illuminating light of stars like these, in spite of the many physical sufferings which the first year brought to the young

---

1) Clara on Oct. 6th: "We finished the first volume of the *Wohltemporiertes Klavier* with the week, but we have not carried our studies on into the second volume. Robert wanted to rest for a week."

followed the necessary self-abnegation of a married artist,
she found the clouds broken by a feeling of pure and complete happiness such as had hitherto been unknown, and almost incomprehensible, to her. "We enjoy a happiness such
wife, in spite of the moments of despair and depression which
as I never knew before," she writes in Feb. 1841, — "Father
has always laughed at so called domestic bliss. How I pity
those who do not know it! They are only half alive!" [1] — It
was this "domestic bliss" which preserved them from all the
limitations and narrowness of common-place households.
Springing from what was finest in both of them, it developed
all that was best and most individual in their personalities,
and fostered that "high range of thought" which was so
characteristic of them, and which, as Schiller says, gives life
greatness, seeking not to borrow.

In the *Book of Projects* (in which since Dec. 1840 Schumann had been in the habit of making entries of various kinds
concerning his artistic life and work) the list of "Leipsic
Composers", which begins with Mendelssohn, contains the
name of Clara Schumann. Anyone knowing Schumann must
know that this is no mere bridal compliment. He places her
here solely on account of the actual worth of her talent, a
worth which he certainly did not over-estimate, though he
refused to allow it to be under-estimated or suppressed, but
which he considered it his duty to foster, although in this
matter, as in her playing, he was forced to resign himself to
a certain degree of helplessness in the face of external circumstances. "Clara," he writes in Feb. 1843 (during her visit
to Dresden), "has written a number of smaller pieces, which
show a musicianship and a tenderness of invention such as
she has never before attained. But children, and a husband

---

[1] In the diary these words are written in thanks for what Robert
had written about her when he finished the *Frühlingssymphonie* (p. 324).

who is always living in the realms of imagination, do not go well with composition. She cannot work at it regularly, and I am often disturbed to think how many tender ideas are lost because she cannot work them out."

But he never ceased to stimulate and encourage her; stimulating her indeed till he enticed her into following his own path with him. It was therefore quite natural that on Christmas Eve 1840 — the year which he himself had described as "my year of song" — Clara's gift to him consisted of three songs which "with the utmost modesty" she had dedicated to her beloved Robert: Burns's "Musing on the roaring ocean which divides my love and me" Heine's *Ihr Bildnis*[1]) ("Ich stand in dunklen Träumen") and Heine's *Volkslied* ("Es fiel ein Reif in der Frühlingsnacht").

This offering of song re-awakened in him the most ardent desire to publish a volume of songs in collaboration with her. "The thought of publishing a volume of songs with Clara," he writes at the beginning of January 1841, "has inspired me to fresh efforts. Between Monday and Monday 9 songs from Rückert's *Liebesfrühling* (Love's Spring) have been finished." Clara found it harder work, and a week later she confides to the diary, in silent despair: "I have made several attempts to set the poems of Rückert which Robert picked out for me, but it is no use — I have no talent at all for composing."

She then proceeded to prove this lack of talent by writing four songs — all of them composed in the first week of June — which she gave to Robert on his birthday, June 8th: *Warum willst Du andre fragen, Er ist gekommen in Sturm und Regen, Liebst Du um Schönheit, o nicht mich liebe, Die gute Nacht die ich Dir sage*, the three first of which not only found a place

---

1) Published later among the "Six Songs with piano accompaniment, composed and respectfully dedicated to her Majesty Caroline Amalie the reigning Queen of Denmark, by Clara Schumann." Op. 13 Leipsic Breitkopf & Härtel.

in the joint volume of songs, but were to awaken an echo which still sounds to-day. One who did not know, would find it hard to recognise a woman's voice in the storm-trumpets which match the words of *Er ist gekommen*. Thus they shared the thanks for the volume of songs[1]) the first printed copy of which Robert sent Clara on Sept. 13th 1841. Rückert expressed his appreciation in a poem in May 1841[2]). Robert's joy in her work was the chief thing which spurred her on to continue composing songs. With the single exception of a sonatina, consisting of an allegro and a scherzo[3]) — her Christmas present in 1841 — the harvest of the next two years consisted solely of songs.

The summer of 1842 produced *Liebeszauber* by Geibel and Heine's "Sie liebten sich beide"[4]), for Robert's birthday: "The best things that she has yet written," he remarks in the diary. And in the summer of 1843 came Heine's *Loreley*, and Rückert's, "*Ich hab in Deinem Auge den Strahl der ewigen Liebe gesehen*"[5]) and "*O weh, des Scheidens, das er tat*".

Household duties, and preparations for the journey to St. Petersburg, seem, during the latter part of 1843, to have interrupted her delight in composition for the time, although two works, both settings of songs by Geibel — "*Der Mond kommt*

---

1) Twelve Songs from F. Rückert's *Liebesfrühling* for voice and pianoforte, by Robert and Clara Schumann. Op. 37/12. Two volumes. Leipsic, Breitkopf & Härtel.

2) "Friedrich Rückert to Robert and Clara Schumann in Leipsic, thanking them for their musical setting of my *Liebesfrühling*." Dated: Neusess near Coburg June 1842. "On June 15th," writes Robert in the diary for 1842, "we had a great pleasure. We had sent Rückert our songs, and he answered by sending us a master-poem."

3) Unprinted; in Jan. 1842 a last movement was added, but it has not been preserved with the M. S.

4) Both published among the *Six Songs* dedicated to the Queen of Denmark.

5) In the *Six Songs*.

still gegangen", and *"Die stille Lotosblume"* [1] — must date from this period, though the diary makes no mention of them.

In the middle of October 1840 Schumann writes that Clara has been playing a good deal lately, "so that I often forgot the wife in the artist, and often had to praise her to her face, even before other people. Thus, last Sunday, she played Beethoven's sonata in *C* major, as I never heard it before". "I have so much to say about Clara," he continues, "and she so little about me. At present nothing comes of all my efforts to work and create, which often makes me very depressed. I know well enough why it is. Yet I have not been altogether idle, I have ventured into a region in which the first step cannot be successful."

It is curious to find Clara at almost the same moment rejoicing in the diary over the absolutely inexhaustible creative power of her beloved: "Robert," she writes in the first week of November, "is industriously composing songs, and ever more songs; whence do these sparks of divine fire keep coming!" and a fortnight later, "Robert has composed and more magnificent songs. The words are by Justinus Kerner, *Lust der Sturmnacht* (Op. 35 No. 1), *Stirb Lieb und Freud* (Op. 35 No. 2) und *Trost im Gesang* (Op. 142 No. 1). He interprets the words so wonderfully, he enters into their very depths in a way which no other composer whom I know does, no-one has such tenderness as he!" Thus during the last three months of the year, not only did the cycle of songs from Kerner [2] (Op. 35) come into existence, but also a number of others. In October came the three songs for two voices (Op. 43) [3],

---

1) Both in the *Six Songs*.

2) *Sehnsucht nach der Waldgegend* (Longings for the Woodland) (Op. 35 No. 5) was the Christmas present, and in the first week in January came the *Wanderlied* (Wanderer's Song): "Wohlauf noch getrunken" (Op. 35 No. 3) Schumann himself, in the date written on the manuscript copy of his works, gives the date of composition as Nov. 10th—24th, 1840.

3) In the "third week" (Sept. 27th—Oct. 4th) Schumann writes: "I

and the first volume of romances and ballades (Op. 45) — Heine's *Schatzgräber*, Eichendorff's *Frühlingsfahrt*, Heine's *Abend am Strand*, in November *Die Nonne* from the second volume, and apparently the whole of the third volume. Besides these, in January, as we already know, there came the 9 songs from Rückert's *Liebesfrühling*, and before this (on Nov. 2rd) in the midst of other work he had set Becker's *Rheinlied*[1]).

In spite of this, the depression of which Schumann speaks, it quite comprehensible. The ever-bubbling fount of melody of this year of song was to him no more than the chime of swaying bells. That which strove in him for life, and fought its way towards the light, was not to be born without pain.

Three months had yet to pass before the hour of deliverance should strike. It came a few days after the last song of the *Liebesfrühling* had found its music and had flown away to join the others.

Clara begins the 19th week of their common diary (Jan. 17th —23rd) with the words: "It is contrary to our agreement[2]) that I should have the book this week, but when a man is composing a symphony[3]) one cannot expect him to attend to other things — even his wife has to take the second place! The symphony is almost finished; it is true that I have heard nothing of it, but I am enormously pleased that Robert is at

---

have been making two little duets, *Wenn ich ein Vöglein wär* (Were I but a little bird) and *Herbstlied* (Autumn Song) by Mahlmann ("Das Laub fällt von den Bäumen"); during the same time Clara has made a fair copy of the volume of ballades (Op. 31, *Löwenbraut*, dedicated to the Countess Ernestine von Zedtwitz) which has saved me a great deal of unpleasant work."

1) "Patriotic song for solo and chorus, with piano-forte accompaniment" (Leipsic, by Friese) (with no opus number). According to the diary about 1500 copies were printed by December.

2) *Translator's note*: See p. 302.

3) $B\flat$ major symphony.

last turning to the field in which he, with his great imagination, finds rightful place." And on Jan. 25th: "To-day, Monday, Robert has more or less finished his symphony; it has been composed at night for the most part — some nights my poor Robert spent over it, quite sleepless. He calls it *Frühlingssymphonie*[1] .... A Spring poem by **[2] gave the first impulse to this composition."

"I am very happy," writes Clara, and continues, "On Tuesday Robert finished his symphony; begun and completed in four days[3]. If only we had an orchestra here, now, this minute! — I must confess, my dear husband, I did not think you were so clever — you are always inspiring me with fresh admiration!!! —"

But although on the 27th, he set to work on the instrumentation, and went on with it at a great pace, the time that elapsed before she was allowed to hear a note, was a fairly severe test of her patience. She had, indeed, firmly declared at the end of the 20th week: "Next week I shall hand the diary over to you — for the future I demand the regular order without pity." But for the next week, and the week after that, she had "still to practise patience".

Not till Sunday Feb. 14th was her waiting rewarded, when after dinner, in the presence of their friends Wenzel and Pfundt, the *Frühlingssymphonie*, "which really brings one a breath of spring", was played for the first time. "I should like to say something of what I feel .... about the symphony, but I should never stop talking about the buds, the scent of the

---

1) With reference to this the four movements originally bore the inscriptions: *Frühlingsbeginn* (The beginning of Spring)(Andante), *Abend* (Evening) (Larghetto), *Frohe Gespielen* (Merry play) (Scherzo) *Voller Frühling* (Full Spring).

2) In the diary the name is not filled in; Jansen, *Davidsbündler* p. 244 gives it as Adolph Böttger.

3) Sketched between Jan. 23rd—26th 1841 says Schumann's note on his MS. copy.

violets, the fresh green leaves, and the birds in the air, all of
which one sees living and stirring in the strength of youth,"
says the diary. "Do not laugh at me, dear husband! If
I cannot express myself poetically, yet the poetic spirit of this
work has pierced the depths of my heart."

When, at the end, she gave her husband special assurance of
her "fondest thoughts", "not only on account of your symphony,
but for the sake of the heart from which it sprang", she received the best reward for her privation in the thanks with
which Robert, after five weeks' silence, returned to his dear
reader in the diary. Emerging from the depths of a composer's joy and torment he writes: "The symphony has given
me many happy hours; it is almost finished; but one cannot entirely complete work until one has heard it. I am often
thankful to the good spirit who has let me accomplish so
great a work in so short a time. . . . But now, exhaustion
follows many sleepless nigths; I am like a young wife just
delivered of a child — so light, so happy, and yet so ill and
weak. My Clara understands this, and treats me with double
tenderness. I will repay her for it some day. But I should
never make an end if I were to try and relate all the love
which Clara has shown me during this time, and with so
willing a heart. I might have sought through millions without
finding one who would treat me with such forbearance and
consideration."

Everything went now at whirlwind pace. On Feb. 20th
the scoring of the symphony was finished; on March 28th it
was tried through for the first time, "and was received with
delight by all who were present. . . . Mendelssohn was charmed, and conducted with the greatest love and care." Three
days later, on March 31st the first performance took place at
a concert given by Clara Schumann[1]) in the *Gewandhaus* for
the benefit of the Orchestra Pension Fund.

---

1) She herself played with Mendelssohn his duet for 4 hands, as well

"On the 31st," says Schumann himself, "Concert by the Schumanns. Happy evening, which I shall never forget. My Clara played everything in so masterly a fashion and with such profound understanding, that everybody was delighted[1]). In my artistic life also this has been one of the most important of days. My wife realised this, and rejoiced at the success of my symphony almost more than at her own. With God's help then I will follow this road further I feel so cheerful now, that I hope to bring to the light of day many a thing which shall rejoice men's hearts."

A few days earlier he had written: "My next symphony shall be called 'Clara', and in it I will paint her picture with flutes and oboes and harps." But before this came the *Overture Scherzo and Finale for orchestra* (Op. 52)[2]).

"Robert," writes Clara in the middle of April, "to my great delight has finished a dainty, merry, siren-like — to quote his own expression — overture, and is now hard at

---

as the Adagio and Rondo from Chopin's *F* minor concerto, an Allegro of Schumann's, one of Mendelssohn's *Lieder ohne Worte*, a piece of Scarlatti's and Thalberg's *Mosesphantasie*. Besides this Sophie Schloss sang two of Robert's songs — Chamisso's *Löwenbraut*, and Rückert's *Du meine Seele, du mein Herz*, and Clara's setting of Burns's "Musing on the roaring Ocean".

1) Clara herself writes to Emilie List: "I was received with such persistent applause that I turned red and white, it would not stop even when I seated myself at the piano. (I never heard anyone get such a reception, ... not even Thalberg). You can fancy if this gave me courage! I was trembling in every limb with nervousness. I played as I hardly ever remember playing. ... My husband's symphony won a victory over all cabals and intrigues. ... I never heard a symphony received with such applause. ... Mendelssohn conducted it, and all through the concert he was delightful, the greatest pleasure shone from his eyes. The songs too, were a decided success, and Fräulein Schloss had to repeat the last one.

2) According to the description in the M. S.: "Overture, sketched on the 12th and 13th of April, scored between the 14th and 17th. Scherzo and last movement sketched 19th to 22nd, scored between April 25th and May 8th.

work scoring it, which he does with absolute passion. I am
so heartily glad about it, and only wish that I could give
him a tiny bit of the pleasure he gives me." The exalted
frame of mind of the master, and his delight in creation, is
shown further by the idea which took possession of him in
the first week of April, of a symphony for the unveiling of
the memorial to Jean Paul on Nov. 15th, and still more by
the work at a *"Phantasie for piano and orchestra"*, which he
began immediately after finishing the *Symphonette* (Op. 52),
and which Clara speaks of as early as the beginning of
May. It was afterwards the first movement of the *A* minor
concerto (Op. 54) but was completed as a separate piece
by itself — *Phantasie in A minor* — in the course of the
summer [1]).

It had, however, to give way to the second symphony,
which forced its way through during the latter weeks of May
and the first days of June [2]).

On the 29th after a happy day spent in the greatest enjoyment at Connewitz and Knauthayn — Robert's favourite
excursion — when they had wandered home in the evening,
"cheerful, and contented with ourselves and with heaven",
the work began on the Saturday before Whitsunday.

---

1) Clara took advantage of a rehearsal of the $B\flat$ major symphony,
with the new alteration for the press, in the *Gewandhaus* on Aug. 13th
1841, to play this *Phantasie* for the first time. "I also played the
Phantasie in A minor," she writes; "only unfortunately no-one could
enjoy playing in that hall (in any empty hall that is), where one can
hear neither oneself nor the orchestra. But I played it twice, and
thought it magnificent! Carefully studied it must give the greatest
pleasure to those who hear it. The piano is most skilfully inter-
woven with the orchestra — it is impossible to think of one without
the other."

2) Symphony in *D* minor (Op. 120). According to Schumann's note:
"Sketched in Leipsic in June 1841. Freshly scored, Düsseldorf 1851.
First performance in its first form, conducted by David in the *Gewand-
haus* Dec. 6th 1841."

"The holidays," writes Clara on the 31st, "are glorious. Robert's mind is most active just at present; yesterday he began another symphony, which is to consist of one movement, but is yet to contain an adagio and finale. So far I have not heard any of it, but I can watch what Robert is doing, and I often hear D minor sounding wildly from afar, so that I know in advance that this is another work from the inmost depths of Robert's soul. Heaven is good to us — Robert cannot be more blest in composing, than I am when he shows me a work like this. Do you believe that, my Robert? I should think you might."

And a few days later: "Robert is uninterruptedly composing. He has already finished three movements, and I hope it will completed by his birthday. He can look back on the past year and on himself with pleasure I think! It is evident that marriage has not proved prejudicial — people so often say that it kills the intellect, and deprives it of all youthful freshness! My Robert certainly affords the strongest proof of the contrary."

The work did not, indeed, go forward as quickly as she hoped, for "other work", and particularly in connection with the paper, came in between, and a journey to Dresden, which they undertook in July, brought a fresh interruption. And so it came to pass that another sound was the first to give proof of their married happiness, the sound of a tiny human voice which awoke an echo within the walls of Schumann's house, on Sept. 1st.

After many hours of anxiety, "at 10 minutes to 11 in the morning", the first child of this marriage, a girl, came into the world, "amidst thunder and lightning, for a thunderstorm was just going on. But one sound — and life once more stood clear and lovely before us — we were blessedly happy. How proud I am to have a wife who in addition to her love and her art, gives me such a gift!" So writes the happy father as he welcomes in the pages of the diary "the first honorary member of our society" in whose features he sees the mother again.

And when on Sept. 13th, Clara's birthday, little Marie was baptised[1]), he was able to surprise his beloved wife not only with the first printed parts of the first symphony, and with their joint volume of songs, but also with the *D* minor symphony, "which I had secretly finished". "What else could I offer her save my musical aspirations, and how lovingly does she share in them," he writes in the diary, and continues: "One thing makes me happy, the conciousness that I have not nearly reached my goal, and that I must keep on doing better and better, combined with the feeling that I have the power to reach it. Therefore, my Clara, forwards with good courage!"

It was this sense of artistic power, as well as his joy in wife and child — in the latter of whom he of course already discovered a taste for music, ("If ever she is fretful, Clara plays to her, which at once soothes her and sends her to sleep"), — which carried him through the growing cares and anxieties which his literary and artistic circumstances, ever less and less to his taste, brought him during the months which followed. By August he was already occupied with plans for an opera; he thought of Calderon's *Bridge of Mantible* and the *Wonder-working Magician,* and at this period his mind first turned to the *Peri.* "Tom Moore's *Paradise and the Peri* has just been making me very happy," he writes at the beginning of August, "— something good in the way of music might be made out of it."

But the rest of the year was occupied with tentative efforts. It is true that "a little symphony in *C* minor" which

---

1) The godparents were Schumann's brother Carl, Clara's mother Mendelssohn, and Madame Devrient (Schumann's former landlady).

"he had almost finished in his head", by the end of October, was sketched out fully by Nov. 10th, but it was then allowed to stay as it was. A first attempt to compose a song with orchestral accompaniment — "Heine's *Tragödie* for chorus and orchestra" — was indeed finished to all appearance on Nov. 8th, but it was laid aside with the note, "not yet finished" [1]). A *Wiegenlied* [2]) (Cradle Song) composed on Christmas eve the modest, but appropriate ending to all the heights and depths of human and artistic emotion which they had both experienced during the year that was passed!

But there had been no lack either of discords, great and small, during these last months, and these (as well as the events of the first half of the following year) for a time more and more hindered all creative work.

The first performance of the second symphony gave them a little disappointment. It was given with the *Overture, Scherzo, and Finale* at a concert which Clara gave with Liszt in the *Gewandhaus* on Dec. 6th 1841, and at which, owing to the absorbing interest taken by the audience in Liszt, neither of Schumann's compositons had justice done to it. And in other respects this evening was not under a lucky star. Clara played Liszt's duet, *Hexameron*, with him. — "This is a frightfully brilliant piece," writes Clara after the rehearsal — and besides this she played his *Phantasie* on a theme from *Lucia di Lammermoor*. For songs, they had Schumann's *Die beiden Grenadiere* (The Two Grenadiers) and Herwegh's *Rheinweinlied* (Rhenish Drinking Song) for male chorus, by Liszt.

Concerning the rendering of the duet, the *Neue Zeitschrift für Musik* [3]) says: "The duet for two pianos called forth a

---

1) This composition, which was left behind in manuscript, was later worked up for voice and piano, formed the basis of the *Romanzen und Balladen* Vol. IV (Op. 52).

2) Afterwards published in the *Albumblättern* (Op. 124) as *Schlummerlied*.

3) 1841 Dec. 21st No. 50.

really unexampled enthusiasm; all customary limits of applause were broken through, and gave place to frenzy and
wild excitment." But Clara writes: "It called forth storms
of applause and we had to repeat part of it. I was not satisfied, I was even very unhappy on this evening and the
next day, because Robert was not satisfied with my playing,
and I was angry too, that Robert's symphonies were not particularly well played, and altogether a lot of little misfortunes
happened with respect to the carriage, forgotten music, an
unsteady music-stool, nervousness because was Liszt there,
etc. etc. There was so much that was good — Liszt, an
extraordinarily full hall (900 people) — that something was
bound to disturb my pleasure."

It came to this, that neither of them, much as they felt the
charm of Liszt's personality, and fond as they really were of
the "spoiled child", could put up with his followers or with his
behaviour in company. But the chief thing was the consciousness which was awakening in both of them, and especially
in Clara, of the difference in their conception of art at its
highest. As a virtuoso he amazed them, or at all events
Clara, as much as ever, particularly at his first concert, on
Dec. 13th. — "I shall never forget his performance of the
Champagnerlied (the *Don Juan Phantasie*)," writes Clara, "the
abandon and delight with which he played it were unique!
One could see Don Juan in all his recklessness, standing
before the springing champagne corks, just as Mozart
must have imagined him." But their disapproval of his
compositions was all the more vigorous: "I cannot call them
anything but hideous — a chaos of the harshest discords, a
perpetual murmuring in the deepest bass and the highest
treble at the same time, wearisome introductions etc. I could
almost hate him as a composer."

But Schumann's love of composing would have mastered
these, and other, demons of discontent — for by the begin-

ning of 1842 the diary speaks of "working at the text of *Paradise and the Peri*" — if external circumstances had not necessitated an interruption of this creative activity.

Among the plans for the future which they formed before their marriage, concert tours made by Clara in company with her husband, had always played a part, both as a natural exercise of her artistic power and as a means of gaining money to ensure a future free from care. And in fact the Russian tour was already fixed for the beginning of 1841. But to the joy of Schumann, who thought "with terror" of being obliged "to leave our warm little nest", the warlike developments in the East soon compelled them to abandon this project for the first year. Clara was less pleased: "Farewell to the virtuoso!" she writes in Oct. 1840, under the impression made by the frustration of their Russian plans: "If only I could persuade Robert to take me to Holland and Belgium so that I might make some use of next winter! — It is dreadful to me not to be able to make my talent of any use to him, now while my powers are at their best. . . . Consider it well, my dear husband! Let us but make use of a couple of winters. — I also owe it to my reputation not to retire completely. It is a feeling of duty towards you and towards myself, which speaks in me."

Her health, as well as her husband's work, forced this plan into the back-ground, and in the end she renounced it, not unwillingly. But she felt it all the more when, after a visit from Lwoff, who once more offered to use his influence for them while they were in St Petersburg, she was compelled to realise that this plan was not practicable for the following winter, because Liszt was going there: "And one does not want to be in rivalry with him. If he does not delight people by his art, he charms them by his personality — but as a rule he does both. I have long had qualms about this, for if I do really please by my art, yet I am lacking in

everything that is needed to make one's fortune in this world."
"For next winter," she concludes, "I give up all thought of
St Petersburg — it costs me a struggle .... everybody asks
if I am not going — I shall be quite forgotten, and in a few
years' time, when perhaps we shall want to make a tour, who
knows what other things in art people may be interested in."

In face of these complaints and anxieties, which were
never wholly silenced, of her yearning for an active life,
which was never quite stilled, for the kind of life in which
and by means of which she had first developed her personality, and of Robert's easily comprehensible shyness of such
tours, it was really a remarkably fortunate dispensation that
Robert's creative faculty should eventually have afforded
opportunity for her wishes to be satisfied in a way which
was welcome and pleasant to him also.

On March 31st Clara re-appeared in public for the first
time since her marriage, and, as we know, was received with
unparalled enthusiasm by the Leipsic public. On the same
day Robert's first symphony won him his first victory as a
composer of great orchestral works.

The news of these two events spread simultaneously through
musical circles, and it is easy to understand how the desire
to hear Clara play again blended with the daily growing
interest in this new phase of development in Robert Schumann. Only a short time before, Schumann had appeared as
"the herald of a new form of German song" [1]; now he surprised
the world afresh as an orchestral composer, and with the new
interest which this awoke, came the wish to learn to know
this new form of art better. What could be more natural
than to invite the two artists together, and for the wife's
concerts to become "Schumann evenings" in a double sense,
through the performance of the husband's works?

1) *Blätter für Musik und Literatur* 1841 No. 23 (June).

The first invitation of this sort came from Weimar soon after the birth of Clara's child, and in the middle of November they both accepted it. Thus by a strange chance the same city in which Clara Wieck ended her last concert tour a year before, was to be the first halting-place in Clara Schumann's tour. On Nov. 21ˢᵗ she played at a concert in aid of the pension fund for the musicians of the chapel royal, in the second part of which Schumann's first symphony was given; and on the 25ᵗʰ she played at the palace, for the Grand Duchess, when a number of Schumann's songs were sung, and were received with delight and applause — as the symphony had been. Schumann not only expressed himself quite satisfied with the performance conducted by Chelard, but also with their experiences as a whole on this, their first tour together. Their meeting with Liszt, who came to Weimar while they were there and kept them there for another day, and who took advantage of this opportunity to promise that he would take part in Clara's concert on Dec. 6ᵗʰ, contributed not a little to this satisfaction.

But this appearance before the great world seemed at one blow to have made an end of that quiet, contemplative life which had hitherto reigned in the artists' house. Not only did Liszt's presence in Leipsic give the young housewife her first opportunity of displaying her powers in this direction, — for they gave a large dinner-party in his honour, to which, among others, came Liszt's companion, Prince Lichnowsky, whom Schumann described as an "aristocratic adventurer", and other people called a "capricious creature with all the virtues and vices of a fanciful girl" — but her artistic duties suddenly came very much more to the fore.

It was a matter of course that she should repay the friendship which had been shown her, by taking part in Liszt's own concert on Dec. 13ᵗʰ, and since this took the form of repeating the bravura piece of Liszt's, which had been received with such applause, it was no great strain upon her. But the request which David made of her on Dec. 28th, that she would play in the *Gewandhaus* on Jan. 1st, was a great demand, for not only had "the piano rested for three weeks", but it meant studying Mendelssohn's *G* minor concerto. And as if that were not enough, she appeared 10 days later at the *Gewandhaus*, playing, first the piano part of Mozart's *G* minor quartet, and then Beethoven's *F* minor sonata (Op. 57).

She had every reason to be satisfied with the applause of the public — which was friendlier than ever — but she herself felt as if she missed that sense of absolute technical certainty, which regular practice had never failed to give her hitherto. And she became more and more convinced of the absolute necessity, now that she was no longer hindered by physical weakness, of once more devoting all her forces to her art, and above all things of making good her name and place in public, hard as she found the thought of the unavoidable separation from her child which this entailed. Just at this time the name of a new musical wonder came to the fore, a marvellous pianist, whose fame spread abroad from Vienna. "In Vienna," she writes to Emilie List, at the end of January 1841, "there is now said to be an 11-year-old boy, the greatest genius who has been born for a long time, and we have heard this from someone who is usually very hard to satisfy. The boy is called Rubinstein, and is a pianist; he is said to have deep feeling, and in many respects a perfect technique.... I should like to make his acquaintance — he must be a prodigy."

Accounts such as these, added to certain experiences of her own, made her almost physically sensible of the bitter truth of the saying: "If I rest, I rust", and she must have greeted with all the more joy an invitation, from Bremen and Hamburg (in which Schumann was included) to take his symphony there, particularly as this invitation was addressed to her, not as the wife of the composer, but as the artist whom they wished to hear again after a two years' interval.

The journey was undertaken in the middle of February, Schumann having been able to free himself from his editorial work for five weeks. They went through Brunswick to Bremen, where on Feb. 23rd the symphony was given for the first time at the "tenth private concert", and Clara, who also took part in this concert, gave a special "musical soirée" on the 28th, at which, among other things, a singer performed some of the songs from the *Liebesfrühling*. "The symphony (conducted by Riem) went better than I thought it would from the rehearsal", writes Schumann, "the people of Bremen are sparing of applause. . . . Clara played as well as was possible on a tinkly piano." And of the soirée he says, "My poor Clärchen never got away from the piano. After the Mendelssohn fugue in *C* major I was so carried away that I applauded loudly with all the others, Clara played so beauti-. fully."

In spite of the lukewarmness of the public, the travellers, thanks to pleasant acquaintances, were very happy in Bremen, although a painful discord was caused by an incident at Oldenburg, where Clara gave a concert on the 25th. An invitation to court came for Clara alone, which Schumann justly considered extremely rude and unfitting. Although in the end Clara went, and came back well satisfied, yet a sting remained behind; "the thought of my undignified position in such cases, prevented me from feeling any pleasure," writes Schumann. It seems too, as if this occurrence threw a shadow in advance upon their stay in Hamburg, although Grund, as conductor of the Philharmonic concerts, made a very favourable impression upon Schumann both as a man and as an artist. Concerning the performance itself, which took place on March 5th, Schumann remarks somewhat laconically in the diary: "The symphony began, und was very well given. Clara played at first with great care (Weber's *Konzertstück*), but she played the other pieces (a Bach *Prelude and Fugue*, a *Lied ohne Worte* by Mendelssohn, Liszt's *Reminiscenz aus Lucia di Lammermoor*), to which the piano would not do justice, with distaste. The audience was courteous and very attentive."

The friendly, pleasant intercourse with Clara's old friends, and above all with Avé and Harriet Parish who vied with one-another in attentiveness, did but little to clear the atmosphere. The chief cause however, was depression, not on account of the past, but on account of the future, which at this time was being decided amidst bitter struggles; the determination to allow Clara to continue the journey to Copenhagen alone, and to return home himself. A concert tour to Copenhagen had been planned two years ago, and had been given up only at the last moment. This project, owing to repeated invitations from thence, had always kept its place among others. It was therefore natural that in Hamburg, so near the goal, amidst the encouragement of her Hamburg friends, Clara should have grown increasingly anxious to carry out the plan at last, particularly as an instinctive feeling may have told her that if she did not take advantage of these comparatively favourable circumstances to make use of her artistic freedom of action, every later attempt would meet with circumstances still more difficult to overcome. And the difficulties here, were great enough.

She herself writes to Emilie List after her return (May 30th 1842) concerning the reasons which decided her to undertake the journey: ".... Yes, I really went to Copenhagen alone (that is, without Robert, but with a lady from Bremen), and separated myself from him, but this shall never happen again if God wills. I will explain the whole matter to you, so that you may understand our step." After shortly describing how they came to Hamburg, she continues, "In Hamburg they strongly advised us to visit Copenhagen, and we also received various invitations from thence, so that we made up our minds to accept, and at once began to prepare for my concert.

But as the time drew on, Robert saw more and more clearly the impossibility of leaving his paper in strange hands for perhaps two months (the three weeks, for which he had arranged, were ended) and so we decided to give up the journey. I thought the matter over, however. I am a woman, I shall not be neglecting anything, I earn nothing at home, why should I not by means of my talent, gain my mite for Robert? Could anyone think ill of me for so doing, or of my husband for going home to his child and his business? I laid my plan before Robert, and it is true that at first he shrank from it, but in the end he agreed, when I represented the matter to him as reasonably as possible. It was certainly a great step for a wife who loves her husband as I do, but I did it for love of him, and for that no sacrifice is too great or too hard for me. In addition to this I now found a nice girl who with the greatest joy offered to come with me; a girl belonging to one of the most highly respected families in Bremen, and with whom my husband knew that I should be safe. We left Hamburg on the same day, Robert for Leipsic, and I, by way of Kiel, for Copenhagen — I shall never forget the day of our parting!"

Certainly this statement partly explains why, if the journey to Copenhagen was to take place at all, the pair had to separate for a time. But as it was evidently intended to be spread abroad, and to take the edge off the various kinds of gossip which were rife concerning Clara's journey among friends both far and near, the deeper reasons for Schumann's remaining behind, which are to be found partly in the experience at Oldenburg, and partly in the laws of his own artistic personality, are not touched upon. They are expressed, and Clara's statement is completed in the words

LITZMANN, Clara Schumann. I.

which Schumann confided to the diary during Clara's absence, on March 14th:

"The separation has once more made me very conscious of my peculiar and difficult position. Am I to neglect my own talent, in order to serve you as a companion on your journies? Have you allowed your talent to lie useless, or ought you to do so, because I am chained to the paper and to the piano? Now, when you are young and in full possession of your powers? We found the solution. You took a companion with you, and I came back to the child and to my work. But what will the world say? Thus I torture myself with thinking. Yes, it is most necessary that we should find some means by which we can both utilise and develop our talents side by side."

The solution which he now hit on certainly does seem curious enough, especially considering his character, habits, and requirements. He thought of a joint journey to America. This had already occurred to them on their way to Bremen, "which is sister to America", and since then they had both carefully weighed und discussed it, by word of mouth and by letter. It was, naturally, the thought of earning so much in so short a time that enticed them: "It is true that we can work in Germany, also. But what comes of it? What Clara earns, I lose in income and time. So it will be better for us to plan our lives for two years by a grand scheme which, if it succeeds, will make us safe for life. And then I can devote myself entirely to my art, which is my one, most ardent desire."

If these remarks point towards castles in Spain which could never possibly find a place in the world of reality, yet they also serve to show how deeply they had both felt the separation which they had considered necessary. Both. For Clara too had carried with her from her first halting-place a bitter regret which indeed affected her with such physical violence that she was obliged at the eleventh hour to put off her first concert, which she had meant to give in Kiel, and for which every preparation had been made. "The audience, which had assembled, was sent away, and I — had to pay the expenses, 47 marks out of my own pocket, next day — a good beginning!" This was all the more painful since, as has already been said, one of the chief reasons why Clara had so urgent, even passionate, a desire to undertake the journey to Copenhagen, was that she might be able to bring a considerable contribution towards the expenses of the household. The immediate result of this misfortune, and of the unfavourable weather — a violent storm made it impossible for her to leave for Copenhagen — was that the artist, accustomed as she was to misfortunes of all kinds, beside herself with the pain of the separation, lost her head to some extent, and after one fruitless effort to shorten the time of waiting for the next steamer, (which did not leave for a week) and to reduce expenses somewhat by giving a concert in Lübeck — which was frustrated by the presence of the Schwerin Opera Company —, went back to Hamburg. "It was a sad day .... my heavy heart found relief in tears, which flowed without ceasing," says the diary. But fresh disappointments awaited her here: "There was no question of playing. With Easter at the door, no-one would hear of music .... My friends were surprised that in spite of all mischances I still wished to go to Copenhagen. My courage did sink at times, I thought that heaven had sent me all these disagreeables in order to make me give up my plan, but the thought of Robert, the wish that my talent should give me a mite to spend on him .... put fresh heart into me, although this was not very visible, for I never forgot my trouble for a minute, and in addition to all the rest I got no news from Robert, who thought that I was already in Copenhagen, and for a fortnight I heard nothing of my child — oh! it was enough to drive one to despair!"

Nothing could distract her mind. Although her friends in Hamburg, and the Avés in particular, did everything they possibly could to help her through this uncomfortable time of waiting, and although on March 18th she returned to Kiel and had a very friendly and pleasant reception at the Grädners' house, yet on the evening of the 19th she climbed on board "the long-feared, but magnificent ship, *Christian the Eighth*" with anything but cheerful feelings. "It felt horrible as we left the land; how I sighed for Robert, for baby, and came near to thinking that I should never again tread on firm land."

Fortunately, things did not remain like this, and in the end her stay in Copenhagen, notwithstanding the longings for husband and child which would keep forcing themselves upon her and all the little annoyances and disillusionments which a young woman travelling alone in an entirely unknown country could not escape, became a source of many pleasant recollections of various kinds, and both from an artistic and a material point of view repaid the great sacrifice which had been made for its sake. During her visit of nearly four weeks (March 20th to Ap. 18th) she gave three concerts on her own account, two in the Theatre Royal, on the 3rd and the 10th, at the first of which members of the royal band assisted and also a vocalist, and the third on Ap. 14th at the *Hôtel d'Angleterre*. Besides these, she took part in a concert given by the Musical Society on Ap. 6th, and in a charity concert in the Theatre Royal on Ap. 17th, after she had already played with great success at a Court concert on Ap. 5th.

"I felt very moved", she writes after her last performance, at which she had been greeted with great enthusiasm, and at whose conclusion she had been vociferously recalled, "I was sorry to leave a town in which people had been so kind to me, and in which so much consideration was shown me on all sides."

The general level of music, among professional musicians as well as in respect to the public taste, she found noticeably lower than she had expected. "The musicians here are mere mechanics," she says after the concert given by the Musical Society, at which, amongst other things, Mendelssohn's *Hymn of Praise*, after four rehearsals by four different conductors, was finally given under a fifth! — "A really good conductor might perhaps be able to make an end of the disorder." And in addition, there was a rage for Italian opera, which was equally badly performed.

For this reason, if for no other, it was a good thing that Robert did not accompany Clara on this journey. It is true that on March 23rd she wrote to him, "You cannot think how everybody here regrets not being able to make your acquaintance; they all ask after you — everyone knows your paper, and if they do not know your compositions, they know your name"; but this very remark, and still more the comments on the public which follow, and her own programmes — in which Schumann's name appears only once, in the second concert, at which she played Rückert's *Widmung* and the allegro from the *Noveletten* — all show that the ground was not yet in any way prepared for Schumann[1]). The artist had to content herself for this time with the applause and with the pleasantly clinking profits which a public that had learned to love her brought her by their diligent attendance at her concerts[2]).

---

1) "I have to play a great deal of Chopin, here," she writes to Robert on March 25th, "no-one has played him hitherto, not even Thalberg. I should be only too glad to give a performance of your symphony, and could trust myself to study it if only it were possible for me to get the orchestra for more rehearsals. You must know that the orchestra here seems to me very untrained, and has not even given all Beethoven's symphonies.

2) The 3 concerts brought in 940 thaler, 26 groschen (after deducting expenses). The total profit of the whole 7 weeks tour (after deducting expenses) was 100 louisdor.

But of even more value was the mental stimulus which
she received from this glimpse into the peculiar and highly
developed culture of a people whose very isolation gave then
a certain importance. In the Northern Museum it is true that
she found "much of interest" but also "much that was dull".
On the other hand she was fascinated and transported by
Thorwaldsen's art which she came across at every turn, although at home she professed to have little natural feeling for
sculpture. And above all she enjoyed meeting people, the
attractive life on the *Lange-Linie,* daily intercourse with the
Hejbergs and Andersen and with her naïve and youthful admirers, the Princes of Glücksburg and Hesse, who occasionally
walked with her for a short distance "which", as the diary
says, "causes a great deal of talk in gossiping Copenhagen".

Among interesting acquaintances she counted above all
others the Hejbergs, Andersen, and Gade whom she had been
very anxious to meet, but in whom she was at first rather
disappointed.

"Gade came to see me yesterday," she writes to Robert
an March 24th, "a little, round-faced, insignificant-looking
creature, with good-tempered eyes, whom I should never have
credited with such an overture. Another proof that one should
not judge people by appearances. He is at work on symphony
now — I will get him to play some of it to me." But she
soon changed her opinion. On March 31st she writes, "Gade
came to see me to-day, and raved about you. He knows everything you have written, and plays it all — to the best of
his ability. He wants to produce a new overture of his own
at my concert, which is quite different from the first one,
and is very gay. I like him very much; I have told him to
come here again to-morrow, so that I may play him something of yours — he heard the *Nachtstücke* to-day."

On the other hand, she was immediately attracted by the
Hejbergs. "His external appearance," says the diary, "shows

nothing of what must be in him — he is recognised as the greatest Danish author. Madame Hejberg might not only be called the greatest Danish actress, but she would certainly make an enormous success in Germany if only she knew the language. She is one of the most attractive beings I ever saw on the stage, and I shall never forget her in this character; at the same time she has a charming manner and is very pretty and interesting; her personality alone would incline me to like her[1]. I saw both of them seldomer than I wished.

But Andersen interested her most of all, though to her amazement she found the proverb concerning a prophet in his own country once more proved true in his case. She was inclined to attribute this to his personal appearance. "Andersen," says the diary, "has a poetic, child-like disposition. He is still fairly young, but very ugly." "He is the ugliest man that could be," she had written to Robert, after her first sight of him, "but in spite of this he looks interesting . . . . One can only get accustomed to him by degrees . . . . but yet, taking him altogether, he looks intellectual".

On echo of this friendly intercourse is to be found in the dedication of five of Schumann's songs (Op. 40) to Andersen, just as, in another respect, the dedication of Clara's volume of songs (Op. 13) to the Queen of Denmark was an expression of sincere gratitude for her kindly encouragement. Clara had felt it a particular kindness that she not only was invited to play before the queen and a small circle, on Ap. 16th, just before her departure, but that Her Majesty gave her some flowers cut with her own hand from her little winter garden, when she said good-bye, received her for a farewell audience

---

1) Everybody in Copenhagen thought that she resembled Clara. And Clara herself thought that there was some truth in it, "We have the same figure, and similar features," she writes to Robert, "but she is pretty," she adds, "whilst I am ugly."

on the very morning of her departure, and warmly invited her to come back again soon.

Clara in all probability gladly agreed to do this, for on the whole she had very much enjoyed herself in Copenhagen, even if the separation from those dear to her, and still more certain letters from her husband showing a very depressed frame of mind, had given her many black hours and had cost her many tears. She herself says that her faithful and self-sacrificing friend Ohlsen had whispered to her one day when he found her suffering from depression of this kind: "Do not think of coming back to us without your Robert!"

In the mean time Robert had been confiding his loneliness to the diary: "It was one of the stupidest things I ever did, to let you leave me." If he had perhaps hoped at first that he would be able to collect himself and begin new work now that he was quiet, he was soon obliged to realise that solitude is only the friend of those who abandon themselves to it wholly, and that peace and longing do not live together happily under one roof. "This is a wretched life," he says in the notes which he wrote in the margin, beside Clara's entries: "I have been working a great deal at counterpoint and fugues during this time." And a fortnight later: "A dismal time. It was impossible to think of composing."

A letter to Clara on Ap. 1st lets us see still deeper into the dissatisfaction of the lonely husband. Referring to her wish to produce his symphony in Copenhagen, he writes: "As to the production in Copenhagen, I thank you my Clärchen; but do not trouble about it. You can make better use of your time. And what could come of it? In 10 years' time they will give it of themselves — I know that. The world cannot stop at Beethoven. So do not do anything about it unless it comes itself quite easily. I have done no decent work, though I have made many attempts. You occupy all my thoughts. I have not been able to finish so much as a simple song. I do not know what is the matter with me. I can just see you now comforting me and saying, 'Dear Robert, one cannot write symphonies every year' etc. etc. Do you know that our concert was a year ago yesterday? — It was a happy evening. A year ago to-day, we squabbled. But that was a good omen, for it was All Fool's Day, April 1st. I ought to make you an April fool again to-day. Perhaps I shall.

What he says here, does not apply to creative work ripening in secret. The next few weeks brought him distractions of various kinds: the study of the scores of Mozart's and Haydn's quartets, reading of all sorts, now and then a delightful evening at the theatre (thanks to a visit from the Schröder-Devrient company) and from time to time he received visits from friends or from strangers who happened to be passing through Leipsic. On Ap. 18th he notes, after a long interval: "Richard Wagner, who came from Paris."

On the same day Clara, as we know, had left Copenhagen, and with this the period ot their separation drew towards an end. On the 20th she gave a concert in Kiel in place of the one which had fallen through owing to her illness in March. She played with great applause but "to few people". A concert which she had thought of giving in Hamburg, had to be given up on account of the lateness of the season. Thus in the end she came home more speedily than had been expected. On the afternoon of Ap. 25th Schumann went to meet Clara, who was coming by water from Hamburg to Magdeburg. He was "like a bridegroom, at once happy and nervous". Some mischievous spirit contrived that he should miss her, "yet I did not have long to wait", writes Clara, "before Robert's arms opened and I flew into them".

On Ap. 26th they both returned to Leipsic. "A meeting like this, makes up for all the yearning pains that went before — Robert too, seemed very happy, and led me home where I found everything decorated with garlands, and in addition Robert has given me a beautiful carpet. But best of all was the look in his dear eyes, which I could enjoy once more, and the rosy cheeks of my little angel, which I could kiss again."

With this cry of joy from a happy wife and mother, Clara ends her account of her tour. But in the margin in Robert's writing stand the hopeful and significant words: "Now better days will come again."

He was right. It is true that the terrible news of the fire at Hamburg, which reached them a few days after Clara's return, cast a shadow over the festival which was being celebrated by the re-united couple, and a concert which Clara hurriedly got up with the help of David and the *Gewandhaus* orchestra for the benefit of the sufferers from the fire, gave them more outside work than either of them wished, but neither these circumstances nor the swelling flood of artist friends who streamed into their house on their way through Leipsic could destroy their inward satisfaction.

And while Clara devoted herself in the first place to her household duties, and except for the songs already mentioned which she composed for Robert's birthday, confined her musical activity to the study of Mozart's and Haydn's quartets, which she went through, one after another, with Robert, in him the fever of composition raged higher than ever. "The whole of June," he writes, "was a good month, and with the exception af a couple of days and nights of ecstasy . . . . Yet I was also busy in a new direction, and I have almost finished two string quartets in *A* minor and *F* major, and have written them down, too." To these two, a third was added by June — the *A* major [1]) — so that before they took a long-planned holiday to Bohemia, in August, one of their friends could call a toast at their table. — "To the three children who are

---

1) Printed with the two others as Op. 41.

only just born, but are already perfect and beautiful." Clara drank it confidently, although as yet only isolated passages, "overheard", had reached her ears. But when Robert surprised her on her birthday by a performance at home of the three quartets, she once more found her expectations surpassed: "My admiration for his genius, his intellect, in short, for the whole composer, grows with each work .... Everything in them is new, and at the same time clear, skilfully worked out, and exactly suited to the strings."

For herself too, this new phase of her husband's work, meant an important epoch in musical education, since by this means she first became capable of understanding chamber music. "Now, for the first time," she writes in November, fresh from the impression of a repetition (again in private) of the first quartet, "do I begin to take pleasure in chamber music, for hitherto, I must frankly confess, this kind of music has bored me, I could not discover the beauty of it."

Here again, we find that intercourse with the stronger creative genius of her husband and absorption into it, not only in no wise limited or suppressed her own individuality, but that only through the most complete mastery of his work could she learn the true meaning of art.

But when Clara wrote these words the three quartets were no longer the youngest children. Already, during the last weeks of September and the first of October, the quintet in $E\flat$ major[1]) had come to make a fourth with them. It was rehearsed for the first time on the same day on which the first quartet was repeated, and a few days later (Dec. 6th) was played for the first time by Mendelssohn at Voigt's house.

And this was not all: before the close of the year, during November and December, there came into existence the

---

1) Op. 44. According to Schumann's note in the MS. "Sketched in Leipsic Sept. 23rd—28th".

fourth quartet, in $E\flat$ major, for piano-forte, violin, viola, and
violoncello[1]), and a trio for piano-forte, violin, and violoncello[2]).

Unfortunately their pleasure in the work of these latter
months was grievously disturbed by a condition of "weakness
of the nerves" (as Schumann himself calls it) the result of previous over-exertion, which compelled him to let his work rest
for a time. This compulsory idleness brought with it other un-
invited guests to disturb the holiday peace of the household:
daily cares, and worse than these, grave anxieties concerning
the future. For, as their life was now arranged, the burden
of earning a living rested on his shoulders, in spite of Clara's
sufferings at the "dreadful" thought that her husband "was
compelled to work in order to make money", and the moment
that his creative power was crippled — even though it was but
temporarily — it became imperatively necessary to discover
fresh sources of income for the growing household.

Under these circumstances it really seemed fortunate that
the music school which came into existence under Mendelssohn's auspices at Easter 1843, should have afforded Schumann
an opportunity, at once profitable and in accordance with his
inclinations, of turning his activity to the teaching of music.
This assured his future, and prevented him from feeling that
any temporary inability to compose meant that he was de-
barred from work altogether.

For although, thanks to Clara's "most tender nursing", the
illness was overcome far more quickly than had been expected[3]),

---

1) Op. 47. According to Schumann's note: "Sketched, Oct. 25th—30th
1842."

2) Op. 88, later described as "*Phantasiestücke* for Piano-forte, Violin,
and Violoncello".

3) There is a gap in the diary here. Clara's entries end in November. The next entry is in Schumann's writing, and is dated Feb. 17th
(during Clara's first visit to her father in Dresden), and in it the chief
events of the past month are mentioned somewhat summarily.

so that by the beginning of 1843 Schumann could once more give himself up to new duties and new plans, yet with his constitution recurrences were always to be expected.

Concerning these new duties Schumann himself writes in the diary at the end of July: "The music school gives us all plenty of work and plenty of anxiety, but also plenty of joy. I have undertaken the piano teaching just *ad interim*, and later I mean to find myself some other work. The number of pupils has now reached 40."

Fortunately, however, these duties, conscientiously and zealously as his own remarks about his teaching show that he fulfilled them, did not require all the strength of the newly recovered musician. "The *Peri* and the music school took up all my time during the last quarter," he writes at the end of June.

As we know, the subject for this composition had been prominently in his mind since August 1841, and had never been allowed to slip out of his thoughts. In January 1842 the diary speaks of working at the text of the *Peri*. Then, however, the journey to the Hanse towns, and various other plans, had brought the work to a standstill. More than a year passed before it once more got under way; but the ease with which it was all brought into order in less than four months, shows that in the interval the work at the text at all events, cannot have been entirely neglected.

Work at the *Peri* began in earnest on Feb. 23rd 1843 [1]), January and the first half of February having been devoted to the completion of the *Variations for 2 piano-fortes, 2 'cellos, and horn* [2]), which Schumann's illness had compelled him to leave

---

1) So Schumann expressly says in the diary. In his MS. copy of the score, on the other hand, he wrote: "Sketched and scored in Leipsic Feb. 20th—June 16th 1843."

2) Op. 46. *Andante with Variations for 2 pianos*. Owing to the difficulty of getting it performed, he had, as Clara says in the diary, finally

unfinished. Not until the middle of March was Clara, by way
of an unusual treat, allowed to share the composer's joy in
his growing work, when Robert played her the first part,
from the sketch. "It seems to me," she writes in fearful joy,
"the most magnificent thing that he has yet written. He is
flinging himself into it, body and soul, with a fervour which
sometimes makes me anxious lest it should injure him, and
yet it also makes me very happy." The first part was finished
by the end of March; the second, in spite of tiresome interruptions from his editorial business and the music school,
which re-opened on Ap. 5th, — "I have no idea," writes Clara,
"how anyone can teach 8 pupils one after another" — by
the end of April. On May 25th, Ascension Day, Schumann
played Clara the third part, which he had just finished sketch-
ing out, and she was most highly delighted with it: "The
music is as heavenly as the text; what a wealth of feeling
and poetry there is in it!" And on June 16th, as Schumann
himself tells us in the diary, the *Peri* was quite finished "after
many days of hard work. That was a great joy for the
Schumanns".

"Except for certain oratorios of Löwe's," he adds, "which,
however, have for the most part a didactic flavour, I know
nothing in music that is like it. I do not like to write or
speak about my own work; my wish is that it may do

---

decided to arrange the *Variations* for 2 pianos only. The piece sur-
vives in this form. In its original form it was tried over for the first
time in March 1843 at a party at the Härtels; the first public performance was given by Mendelssohn and Clara at a concert of Mme Viardot
Garcia, on Aug. 18th 1843. Unfortunately the impression was spoiled
by the fire-alarm sounding during the performance. (On this same evening a young débutant from Austria, the 12-year-old Joseph Joachim,
suffered from the same misfortune.) A performance, as it originally stood,
was given by Brahms and Clara at a concert of Clara's in Vienna on
Nov. 28th 1868. It was afterwards printed in this form by Clara Schumann in the supplement to the critical edition of the works.

some good in the world and assure me of a loving place in the memory of my children."

This is Schumann all over, with his modesty, and his professional pride, and at the same time his characteristic way of bringing all his artistic work back into the intimate circle of his family — a circle which, to the parents' joy, had been enriched a few months before (Op. 25th) by the birth of a second child, Elise.

But the event of the year was, and remained, the *Peri*. Working at the arrangement of it for pianoforte occupied all the time that Clara could spare for music — less than ever now, thanks to increasing household duties and responsibilities. It cost her trouble, but it also gave her what glimpses of happiness and pleasure there were in a summer and autumn disturbed by various visits from kindred in blood and in art and several journeys made by Clara to Berlin and Dresden. As the time drew near for the first performance in Leipsic it was only natural that they should become more and more feverishly excited. It was a great grief to both of them that the rehearsals began just at the moment when Mendelssohn left Leipsic — as it was then thought, only temporarily — and also that Clara's concert-work repeatedly called her to Dresden just then, as she had an opportunity of taking part in the first performance of Robert's quintet on Nov. 20th, and in the *Variations* for 2 pianos — She found herself terribly torn in two.

A note from Robert, on Nov. 23rd, urgently begging her to come back "to-morrow evening", bears vigorous testimony to the feverish excitement of them both: "I cannot hold a rehearsal without you, it makes me feel as if I had lost my good genius." On the back of this letter there was a note from the post-office: "Addressee left for Leipsic." Her longing to return had driven her back a day earlier. But all the same she was obliged to be absent from the important or-

chestral rehearsal, which was also Schumann's début as conductor of an orchestra and for this reason alone would have
been a great event in their eyes. He himself wrote, well-
contented with the first impression, "It went excellently, and
I think you will gain honour by your old husband. They
were all very cordial, and I was quite inspired when I was
conducting". Others, though they fell under the spell of the
work, straining their ears, heard a few things that had not
gone quite so well. Thus Livia Frege, who took the part
the peri, wrote to tell Clara about this same rehearseal, and
said that everyone thought it had "gone very well" for a first
orchestral rehearsal, and that there was a feeling of universal
enthusiasm, but that she thought the chorus singing, and
particularly the entrances of the sopranos "very far from
good". "If only you could persuade your dear husband to scold
a little and to insist on greater attention, all would go well
at once."

    Clara herself did not hear the orchestra and chorus to-
gether until the morning of the day on which the performance
was to be, when there was a general rehearsal (for the benefit
of the music school), and she was enthusiastically delighted
with the "magnificent instrumentation". "No words can
describe how happy I was that evening (Dec. 4th). There was
great applause, which became enthusiastic at the second performance, on the 11th. Robert was well received when he
first appeared, and on the conductor's desk he found a laurel
wreath, which filled him with some consternation, but which
he could not help liking. He was recalled after each part.
Frege sang the peri exquisitely; after the *Jungfrau's* aria
(Frau Fr. took this part in place of the original performer
who was absent) the audience could not refrain from loudly
applauding her. Herr Schmidt, too, and Kindermann, as well
as the chorus, sang very well, they all sang with their whole
hearts — I had enough heart in it for all of them! If ever I

wished for a beautiful voice it was then! What would I not have given to be able to sing the peri!"

But perhaps the greatest pleasure to Clara lay in the fact that the immediate consequence of the triumph of the *Peri* was a letter from her father in which he offered to be reconciled husband. That he should do so was not only a personal to her satisfaction on her dearly loved husband's account, it was a naïve confession of the position which he had at last won for himself as a musician. Indeed it seemed as if the summit of life's happiness had been reached, and the final reward of faithfulness were won. But during these very weeks they were to become conscious that "the earth belongs to the evil spirit" "not to the good", and that in spite of all, she stood within the ban of those false powers.

"We spend more then we earn", Schumann had confessed in the diary at the beginning of the year, and for this reason he had already promised Clara that next winter they would "certainly do something great" i. e. would undertake another concert tour. In the midst of the unrest and excitement of the *Peri* rehearsals, while Clara was away, and while negociation were going on with Härtel concerning the editorship of the *Allgemeinen Musikalischen Zeitung*, this project suddenly took definite shape and, this time on Robert's initiative, the oft-postponed journey to Russia, was arranged for the early months of the following year. The final work at the score of the *Peri*, and the finishing touches put to the piano score, kept them both breathlessly busy up to the last moment. The children were sent, some days in advance, to the care of their relatives in Schneeberg, and on the 25th Schumann and Clara set out *via* Berlin.

Hard as it was for the young mother to part from her darlings — and both letters and diary bear witness to this — yet as a matter of fact this journey was for her the fulfilment of a long-cherished desire, not only to relieve her husband of material cares and to keep them far from him, but also, naturally enough, to practise her art once more. For Schumann it was another matter; this journey tore him from his quiet, creative work — "I am busy with plans for a couple of operas .... An opera shall come next, and I am burning to set to work at it," says the diary at the end of November — and carried him into a region of distractions and excitements which, as he took part in them merely as a passive spectator, brought nothing to the man, and took from the artist — his most valuable possession, the possibility of collecting his thoughts for his own work. If, notwithstanding this, the original impulse came from him on this occasion — the last, in any case — it was due not only to the necessity which he recognised of adding to their finances, but also to the desire by this means to free himself for some time from the editorial work which he found ever more and more of a burden. The idea that he would be able to find leisure for his own work on the journey, and even during the periods when they stayed for some time at one place in Russia, seems to have been in his mind. He was doomed to entire disappointment with regard to the latter.

The following letters and extracts from the diary, describe the incidents of the journey.

CLARA TO HER FATHER[1].

"Dorpat Feb. 20th 1844 Tuesday.

I have long been wanting to write to you, dear Father, but I could never manage it, for you must know that I have given 5 concerts, one after another. That I may forget nothing I will begin at the very beginning, as I think you will be interested in everything.

---

1) Printed in a mutilated form and wrong order in Kohut's *Fr. Wieck* p. 115 etc. Given here, from the original.

We spent two days in Berlin, and were most kindly received, especially by the Mendelssohns, who were pleased to have a breath of Leipsic air. Mendelssohn gave me 6 *Lieder ohne Worte* (among which were two that you know already) which he is dedicating to me, and Madame Mendelssohn gave me a pair of fur muffetees, which I have already found very useful, and which also look very nice (that is for Mother's benefit). We left Berlin on Saturday evening by the flying coach (the most comfortable in which I ever travelled), and reached Königsberg on Monday evening, where we were most kindly received. It is an ugly town, but that makes the people all the nicer; I gave concerts in the theatre on Friday and Saturday, and had full houses, but the cold was dreadful, for the hall is large and is not warmed. On Sunday we left for Tilsit, where we spent the evening with the post-master, Nernst (a most pleasant family); I played a great deal, in spite of the fact that I had spent half the night packing after the concert in Königsberg, had got up at five, and had been travelling all day. On Monday we got up at three, and at four we set out for the frontier. I must add that in Königsberg there was a pianoforte maker on whose instruments I had played (he was called Marty); he lent us his sleigh as far as the frontier (from here on, we went entirely by sleighs — half-way to Königsberg we found tracks made for them), to which we went with an extra post, which was delightful. At Tauroggen, the frontier, Nernst had already bespoken places for us in the flying coach for Riga, which was also very handsome and comfortable, and had only two inside places. In Königsberg the Russian consul had given us a letter to the custom-house inspector (a very nice man), and we were treated very kindly. As at every other frontier, our boxes were just opened, glanced at, and fastened up again. They never so much as looked at the music. In Tauroggen itself we found a fine posting house and a most appetising breakfast; moreover the consul had recommended us to one of the frontier officials, who looked after everything connected with our passport and luggage etc. etc. Thus we came to Riga very comfortably, but what a hideous city it is! When we reached the posting house we found neither a hackney-coach nor anyone to take charge of our luggage; we had to take possession of a large peasant-sleigh which was standing in the court-yard, put the boxes into it, and sit on them, and so we came to the *City of London*, after threading

our way with difficulty through the hundreds of peasants' sleighs in
the market, and through tiny little alleys. Here we were told that
there was not a single room to be had except on the 3ʳᵈ floor, which
looked dreadful. We once more sat ourselves down on our boxes
and drove off to the *City of Sᵗ Petersburg*, where we got a room,
a back-room, so dirty that it was quite impossible to sit down in
it; Robert at once ran off to Herr von Lutzau, to whom David
had given us an introduction. He had ordered the best room in
the *City of London* for us, which we had never dreamed of, and
now he carried us back to it. You can imagine how unpleasant
an impression Riga made on us. We found friendly and obliging
people here, but we could not feel quite comfortable. The concert
could not be arranged immediately, and in the end this made everything come with a rush. Fancy; on Sunday we had to go to Mitau
(the capital of Courland, where in winter all the aristocracy of
Courland is gathered together, and where they live for nothing but
balls, and concerts, and balls again).

Mitau is 3 hours' journey from Riga, and is a charming little
town in which there is a great deal of artistic culture (all the
artists have given concerts here), and far more culture than in
Riga. There is no artistic feeling in Riga, so it seemed to me
(except in a few people), and no real culture. I gave concerts
on Sunday in Mitau, Monday and Tuesday in Riga, Wednesday
in Mitau again, and Thursday, the last concert, in Riga. Those
were hard days, what with perpetually going backwards and forwards, packing, etc. etc., but I gave all the concerts by myself,
without anyone to support me, as I mean always to do in future;
it is much the best. I found a wonderfully good piano-forte of
Wirth's, in Riga — the Wirth piano in Dresden cannot give you
any idea of it; these instruments are the best English make that
I have yet seen; from top to bottom they have the most splendid
tone, soft and yet so forcible! My husband, whom hardly any
piano satisfies, was delighted with the tone of this one as soon
as he touched it. I am glad to have such good instruments in
Sᵗ Petersburg. It was difficult to get here from Riga as there are
only two coaches a-week, and the places are taken weeks in advance, and even if there is room those coming from the frontier
have the first claim. We did not want to post, as that is very
uncomfortable, so we took an *extra-diligence* as far as Sᵗ Petersburg, which gives us a guard all the way so that we have no

need to trouble ourselves about anything. We can spend 5 days here, and mean to do so. Dorpat is a very pretty town, of far more importance, from the point of view of culture, than Riga, with great feeling for art, and of a very friendly appearance. In Professor von Brocker we found a very pleasant man, who has made arrangements for our concert, and has placed his carriage at our disposal, as everybody does at once in this country; everybody who can possibly manage it has his sleigh and horses. They are extraordinarily hospitable and friendly especially towards artists. I give my first concert to-morrow, and the second on Friday, and on Saturday we continue our journey towards St Petersburg, where we expect to arrive early Monday morning, or possibly Sunday evening; in any case we shall sleep one night on the road, so as to reach St Petersburg by day; you must know that there is a good inn at every posting-station here, where one can spend the night and have anything one likes to eat and drink, and it will be like this all the way to St Petersburg. The journey is not nearly so difficult and dreadful as we expected. German is spoken everywhere — everything is German here, and Russia does not really begin until 10 miles from St Petersburg. Thanks to our furs and fur rugs, we have not suffered from the cold at all so far, though already we have travelled for 2 days with the thermometer showing 12°—15° of frost. All the houses are warm here, there is an even temperature throughout all the rooms, which is very comfortable. Dorpat really does seem northerly, for here, for the first time, we felt real cold — this morning we had 23° of frost.

Now I will leave you alone for a few days — on Saturday I will write again and tell you about the concerts here.

I have just remembered some adventures which Marie will find specially interesting: we have driven, in carriages and sleighs, across the ice of 3 rivers, all larger than the Elbe; on the Duna, near Riga, the peasants hold their wood-market; hundreds of sleighs, laden with wood, stand in the middle of the river, people walk about as if they were in a street, and as if it were quite natural, and we too, drove about for half-an-hour. There are many wolves in the forests here, they often appear beside the high way and watch the travellers as they pass, quite quietly; so far we have not seen any, but everybody who goes from here to St Petersburg meets with some, and I am looking forward so seeing some.

The concert takes place to-day. I have got the university hall, which is very rarely granted as it is by no means intended for concerts. It is not very good for sound, but I like it because of the honour it is to have it. Addio for now."

"Tuesday Feb. 27th.

I have given three brilliant concerts since last I wrote to you, and have aroused wild enthusiasm — I know no more enthusiastic, and at the same time artistic audiences than those here. The third concert took place last night, and after it a fine male chorus[1]) serenaded me delightfully, singing among other things a quartet of my husband's. Robert has caught a bad cold, he has been in bed for the last 6 days, and got up for the first time to-day. He was not able to be at the two last concerts, and of course we have not been able to leave, though we hope to get off on Thursday. The journey from here to St Petersburg is said to be dreadful! 10 miles from St Petersburg the holes in the road begin, and they are enough to make one sea-sick. I wish we had got it over; Dorpat is full of nice people, for the most part the people whom we have got to know have been members of the aristocracy, but they have really been so kind to us that often we have not known what to say. Every day (for the last 6 days) they have sent us various things for lunch — stewed fruit, good soup, wine, as well as eau de Cologne etc.

I must tell you some of things about the ladies here so that you may see how friendly they are. Yesterday, before the concert, an unknown baroness, who had heard of Robert's illness, sent jelly, some pastry, and 2 partridges just roasted, with the request that we would accept these as we should not be able to get anything in our bad hotel. (On the) evening of the concert I told one lady what uncomfortable, dirty beds we had, and added that my husband had caught his cold during the night. At 10 o'clock a servant arrived, bringing 2 beautiful feather pillows and a magnificent great counterpane. . . ." (The end of the letter is lost.)

---

1) It was the trained choir from the *Fraternitas Rigensis*, which sang Mendelssohn's *Wer hat dich du schöner Wald*, and Schumann's *Träumende See* and *Minnesänger*. They were led by the philologist Julius Otto Grimm, who was at that time a youthful student at Dorpat. See J. Smend in the *Monatschrift für Gottesdienst und kirchliche Kunst* vol. IX March 1904 p. 80.

Although Robert's condition gave rise to difficulties and anxieties, they set out to continue their journey towards St Petersburg on March 1st. Schumann became much better on the way, and on March 4th they arrived safely. A letter from Schumann to Wieck tells of their experiences there:

"St Petersburg April 1st 1844.

Dear Father

We are have not answered your kind letter till to-day, as we wanted to be able to tell you of the success of our visit here. We have now been here four weeks. Clara has given four concerts and has played before the Empress; we have made some delightful acquaintances, and have seen many interesting things, every day brought something new — so this is the last day before we go on to Moscow, and when we look back we can feel quite satisfied with what we have done. I have much to tell you; I am greatly looking forward to a talk. We made one great mistake: we came here too late. In a big city there are many preparations to be made; everything here depends on the court and *haute volée*, the papers have little influence. Besides everybody was possessed by the rage for Italian opera. Garcia has created an extraordinary *furore*. Consequently the two first concerts were not full, though the third was packed, and the fourth (in the Michaelis Theatre) was the most brilliant of all. Whilst other artists, including even Liszt, have found a steady decrease in public interest, Clara has found it ever increasing, and she could have given another four concerts if Holy Week did not happen to come in the mean time, and besides, we have to be thinking of our journey to Moscow.

Our best friends, naturally, were the Henselts, who received us most affectionately, and next to them, and before all others, the two Wielhorskys, two distinguished men, and Michael a real artist, the most gifted amateur I ever met — both of them having great influence at Court, and being almost daily about the Emperor and Empress. Clara, I believe, cherishes a secret passion for Michael, who, by the way, has grandchildren already i. e. is a man of over 50, though as fresh as a boy in body and soul. We found also a most friendly patron in Prince von Oldenburg (the Emperor's nephew) as well as in his wife, who is kindness and goodness itself. They took us over the palace in person yesterday.

The Wielhorskys also, have shown us great attention, giving an orchestral soirée for us, at which I conducted my symphony which I had worked up for the occasion. I will tell you about Henselt when we meet; he is just the same, though he wears himself out by giving lessons. He will no longer be induced to play in public; he can be heard only at Prince von Oldenburg's, where one evening at a soirée he and Clara played my *Variations for two pianos.*

The Emperor and Empress have been very kind to Clara; she played there a week ago yesterday, to a family party, for quite two hours. Mendelssohn's *Frühlingslied* has been the favourite piece with every audience; Clara has had to repeat it several times at every concert; and she had to play it 3 times for the Empress. Clara will describe the magnificence of the Winter Palace when she sees you; Herr von Ribeaupierre (who used to be ambassador at Constantinople) took us over it a few days ago; it is like a fairy tale from the *Arabian Nights.*

For the rest, we are quite flourishing; and we have the best news of the children.

Imagine my joy: my old uncle [1] is still alive; in the very first days of our of stay here I was fortunate enough to make acquaintance with the Governor of Tver, who told me that he knew him quite well. I wrote to him at once, and speedily received the warmest of answers from him and from his son, who is in command of a regiment at Tver. Next Saturday he celebrates his 70th birthday, and I think that we shall just be in Tver then. What a pleasure for me, and also for the old man who has never had one of his relations in his house.

People have made us nervous about the road to Moscow; on the whole you may believe that travelling in Russia is neither better nor worse than elsewhere, if anything better, and I cannot but laugh now at the terrifying pictures which my imagination conjured up in Leipsic. Only it is very dear (here in St Petersburg particularly) e. g. lodging is a louisd'or a-day, coffee 1 thaler, dinner 1 ducat etc. etc.

We think of coming back by way of St Petersburg again (in about 4 weeks), then going over-land to Reval, from there by steamer to Helsingfors, and through Abo to Stockholm, and then probably we shall make the canal-trip to Copenhagen, and so get

---

1) His mother's brother the military doctor, Dr Schnabel.

back to our beloved Germany. We are sure to see you once more, dear Papa, at the beginning of June I hope; write to us often before that. For the present continue to write to St Petersburg, to Henselt's address. Henselt will forward the letters to us. The musicians here have all been most friendly to us, especially Heinrich Romberg[1]); they refused to take any payment for their help in the last concert; nothing was expected of us except to have them fetched to the concert, which we did with the greatest of pleasure. Much, very much, I had to write to you; but to-day we have to prepare for the journey to Moscow, so please excuse this little note. Give Clara's and my love to your wife and children, and think kindly of me

R. S."

On April 2nd the travellers left S^t. Petersburg, and after spending Easter with Robert's relations in Tver, they arrived in Moscow on April 10th, much exhausted by the hardships of the journey. Here they intended to spend the next four weeks. The first sight of the city rather disappointed them, „It is not what one imagines it". On the other hand, the Kremlin, to which Robert made his way as soon as he arrived, and the view from it, made the deepest impression on them both. "This sight is indescribable, one feels as if one must be in Constantinople, the city, with its countless minarets, is so extraordinarily eastern." "We found the peasant-women very striking (it was Easter week when all the country-side comes in to enjoy itself) with their silk *Kasaweikas* trimmed with the most beautiful fur, and underneath, as often as not, an ordinary cotton dress." But interesting as the old city of the czars was in its festival attire for Easter-week, the travellers were very soon convinced that it would have been better to have gone there earlier in the year, for the season proper was already over, and if in comparison with the restlessness of life in St Petersburg the narrower limits of social intercourse here proved a pleasant and necessary refreshment,

---

1) Concert director in St Petersburg.

yet the close of the season implied comparatively scanty attendances at the concerts — which was less pleasant. On the other
hand, they found the whole manner in which they were met
by the members of the aristocracy, and in which Clara's artistic performances were received, most sympathetic, and this
made up to them for empty, and half-empty, concert-rooms.
One matinée which she gave in May 2nd before about 30 or
40 people, and at which, contrary to the custom of the place,
ladies of the highest rank put in an appearance, also afforded
her the opportunity which she desired of making the public
acquainted with Schumann's quintet (which could not be performed at the concert, owing to the size of the hall) and the
Variations, and judging from the applause they were apparently
heard intelligently.

For the rest, these weeks in Moscow were chiefly dedicated to recovering from fatigue and to the study of the
country and the people. One day they went to the Russian
opera-house, at which Glinka's opera, *Life for the Czar*, was
given. Schumann wrote, in reference to this, "The first act
contains a good deal of pleasant music, a pretty terzet in
particular — for the most part they sound like national airs —
the instrumentation is weak, and the brass is too prominent.
As a whole it showed strikingly well-balanced talent. The
second part of the opera was lame in every respect, and
lacked any kind of dramatic development." Another day they
visited a Russian monastery: "Bright colours everywhere —
flowers and graves inside the court-yard. We climbed on to
the roof of one Church, from which we had a wonderfully
beautiful view of Moscow with its countless domes and minarets. We called on the abbot, a jovial man who gave us
tea and then presented us with views of Simonoff (the monastery). Vespers was at 6 o'clock. The singing of the monks
is of a peculiar kind, *piano*, with a hollow tone, and very
monotonous — they sing for 5 or 6 hours, and always in the

same way. The music is partly barbaric, partly childish, full
of octaves and fifths. Robert slipped away after two hours
martyrdom from this singing (which, however, is celebrated
just because of its peculiar sound), and I soon followed him."
At another time they paid a long visit to a large orphan
asylum, which, as there was no musical treat connected with
it, gave them far more pleasure.

On May 8ᵗʰ they began their return journey to Sᵗ Petersburg; this time they travelled into the budding spring, and
St. Petersburg greeted them in summer attire. Ten days later
they were at Kronstadt on board the ship which was to take
them to Swinemünde. Schumann's post-script to a letter
from Clara to her father, describes their final impression of
Sᵗ Petersburg.

SCHUMANN TO FR. WIECK[1].

"Sᵗ Petersburg, the middle of May 1844.

The sky promises us a fine journey to-morrow, the weather
is wonderful, and already everything is green. The clear nights
here are of magic beauty; already there is no need to have any
light in the evenings.

Yesterday we had another interesting day; in the morning,
to Tsarkoë-Selo, to which we drove with H. Romberg and Count
Wielhorsky, and in the evening we were at the Grand-Duchess
Helene's, who had invited us to come to her. Clara played
wonderfully. The Grand-Duchess (so Henselt says) treated us as
she has never treated any artists before; she is a really royal
lady, who has already turned the heads of many men, and in
addition she is clever and well-educated; we talked much of the
possibility of founding a conservatoire in Sᵗ Petersburg, and apparently she would have liked to keep us here now.

We have given up the journey to Sweden; we are too anxious
to get back to our home and our children. By the end of the
month, dear Papa, we hope to see you in Leipsic, shall we not?
On our return journey we shall stop only at Swinemünde, in order

1) *Briefe* new series 2 No. 266 p. 239.

to go over to the island of Rügen. Meanwhile here is one more poetic greeting from Moscow, which I do not trust myself to give you in person. Hidden music, for there is no quiet or time to compose.
Best love to your wife and children — may we all meet again happily.   Your R. S."

The 30th of May found parents and children once more re-united in the Inselstrasse. "We could not get used to Leipsic again for ever so long," Clara writes in the diary [1], "everything seemed so dreary, so empty, in spite of the fact that we were in our old homely surroundings, and had our children again. In addition to this came Robert's continued ill-health, which lasted practically through the whole journey though it never came to a crisis."

There seemed, however, no immediate occasion for further anxiety; notwithstanding his physical discomfort, the return to his native land and the quiet of home life seemed to have a favourable effect upon Schumann's creative power. Plans for an opera once more emerged — Byron's *Corsair*, which Dr Marbach was to arrange for him. Above all things, an entirely new work took a prominent place, a setting of the last scene of the second part of *Faust*. On his sick-bed at Dorpat he had occupied himself with the two parts of *Faust*, and the plan very likely took shape then, but the bustle of the journey made it come to nothing. In July an unexpected visit from Andersen brought them some excitement, but also a little disappointment, for their friend from Copenhagen listened somewhat indifferently to Schumann's settings of his songs, which were sung to him by Livia Frege, and to the Beethoven $E\flat$ major sonata. At the beginning of August they both began to teach in the music school (Clara for the first

---

1) These entries relating to the latter half of the year 1844, date from Feb. 1845 as the diary from June to November 1844 was lost in November.

time) and they prepared themselves for a quiet, industrious winter, as their original plan of a tour to Belgium, Holland, and England, had to be given up now that Clara was once more hoping to become a mother.

Then in the middle of August, Schumann became really ill; in spite of this, as soon as he was temporarily better, he continued to work at *Faust*, which he finished down to the final chorus, though, as the diary says, "by the sacrifice of his last strength". An entire collapse followed, "a complete nervous break-down, which made it impossible for him to do work of any kind".

Unfortunately this coincided with an open slight, or at least with what he and his took as such: the election of Gade to be conductor of the *Gewandhaus* concerts for the winter of 1844/45. Although Schumann himself, as matters lay, would hardly have been inclined to undertake the post; yet he felt, not unjustly, that it showed a want of consideration to call a foreigner to occupy the desk which Mendelssohn's absence left vacant, without first offering it to him.

A journey to the Harz mountains, which they undertook in the middle of September by way of distraction, failed completely of its purpose. Immediately after their return, things became worse and worse, so that at last he had to keep to his bed, "and could hardly cross the room without the greatest exertion". After an ineffective "cure" with Karlsbad salts, which still further weakened the nervous, over-strained patient, they finally decided, at the end of September, to go to Dresden for some weeks. "We hoped," writes Clara, "fresh surroundings and fresh people might do Robert good."

Their departure took place on Oct. 3rd. "The journey was dreadful, Robert thought he should never survive it." And in Dresden itself things grew worse, possibly to a considerable extent on account of well-meant attempts on Wieck's part "to rouse" Schumann, "forcibly": "8 dreadful days passed," says the diary. "Robert never had a night's sleep, his imagination brought the most horrible pictures before him, and I usually found him bathed in tears in the early morning; he gave up all hope for himself." The homeopathic doctor ordered plenty of exercise and the cessation of every kind of work. Work would have been impossible to him in any case, and he found walking extremely difficult. Shower-baths, which the patient apparently prescribed for himself, were only temporarily efficacious. For the first week they stayed at an hotel; but as the invalid could not make up his mind to return to Leipsic, they finally settled in private lodgings, at first intending these to be merely a halting-place on their way to Schumann's brother Carl in Schneeberg, where they had planned to spend some weeks. But the illness of Carl's eldest daughter, and at the same time a slight improvement in Schumann's health, made them take a fresh decision in the middle of October: they determined to settle in Dresden — in the first place for that winter only. On Oct. 17th they took a pleasant flat on the ground-floor of No. 35 Waisenhausstrasse, and in the middle of December they moved into it. The intervening time was occupied, apart from the business of moving, by a visit of several days to the Serres, in Maxen, and by various social gatherings in Dresden, all of which give proof that Schumann was better in health. They also made concert tours to Halle and Leipsic. On Nov. 29th all the musical people of Leipsic, headed by Mendelssohn, once more assembled in Härtel's house. The chief artists among them, including the young Joachim, combined to give Mendelssohn's octet once more; Livia Frege sang, and Clara and Mendelssohn played two pieces out of the *Midsummer-Night's Dream*, "the first at such a pace that I did not know where I was!"

On Dec. 5th Clara for the first time played the $E\flat$ major concerto of Beethoven at a concert in the *Gewandhaus*, a thing which she had long wished to do, though she was not without nervousness, "for it is the hardest concerto I know, it requires the greatest staying power, and thoroughly intellectual interpretation". "The audience," continues the diary, "received me with enthusiasm, which doubly delighted me, as it was certainly due in part to a love for the old child of the Fatherland."

On Dec. 8th, Sunday, the Schumanns gave a farewell matinée to their friends, at which Robert's quartet in $E\flat$ major was performed for the first time. It gained great applause. Clara concluded with the Beethoven C major sonata, though she could hardly move her fingers for cold.

On the 13th followed the parting from Leipsic, "not without tears," says the diary, "although there is little to bind me to it beyond the fact that it is my birthplace".

Was this really the case? Had Leipsic really never been more to them than Clara's native city? These questions force themselves upon us and demand an answer, when Robert and Clara Schumann withdraw from the musical life of Leipsic, at whose centre they had been for nearly ten years; and they cannot be answered by insisting on Robert's illness, or on his disgust at Gade's being chosen to take Mendelssohn's place. Both these facts, it is true, explain his sudden breaking away from the city, but they throw no light upon the inner relations of Robert and Clara Schumann to the musical life of Leipsic in the early forties, and hence upon the real reason of their cutting themselves loose from it. In order to understand this it is necessary to glance, however cursorily, at the personages who at this time played a temporary or permanent rôle in the musical life of the city. In the first place we naturally think of Mendelssohn.

At this time Mendelssohn held absolute sway over the musical life, not of Leipsic alone, but of all Germany, and set the fashion in musical taste. For both Schumann and his wife he was at once a source of inspiration and an object of personal veneration, out of all comparison with any other. When therefore Schumann gives as one of the reasons for their leaving Leipsic: "since Mendelssohn left Leipsic we take no more pleasure in its music", this was rather understating than over-stating the real truth. For Schumann's feeling for Mendelssohn, highly as he valued him as an artist, rested chiefly on his boundless admiration for him as a man. "Love and admiration," he writes in 1841[1]), after spending some time with Mendelssohn, "are the two feelings which he rouses every time one has any intercourse with him. He is a diplomatist too; though this is but the hundredth part of his many-sided nature."

It is very suggestive that a man like Robert Schumann, who found it so difficult in face of all the dissonances of life to preserve balance of judgment, should have found the wonderful harmony between the human and artistic temperament in Mendelssohn a sort of moral satisfaction, and should have felt intercourse with him to be an æsthetic pleasure which could not be equalled. It was a satisfaction to find that the highest artistic power and an ideal humanity could be combined in one personality, and a pleasure to watch the effect of this combination upon himself and upon others. "He was like the magic picture," wrote Schumann[2]) after his death, "always some inches higher than one felt oneself to be." All that he was painfully conscious of lacking himself, he found in Mendelssohn, and without a particle of envy he rejoiced that some one, at all events, possessed it. He notes on the pages of the diary for 1846 that Mendelssohn had asserted that "there were no æsthetically educated men", but that exactly what he admired in Mendelssohn was an æsthetically educated man in the highest sense of the words.

---

1) Diary March 14th—21st 1841.
2) Letter to Laurens of April 1848. *Briefe* new series No. 315.

It says much, though after the remarks which have just been made it cannot cause surprise, that two creative geniuses, each possessing so strongly marked an individuality, could live together in close intercourse for years with hardly a single discord, although among the circles of friends and admirers which surrounded each of them there were not lacking those who had both the wish and the power to magnify little unavoidable rubs into matters of great importance. In later years we certainly find Schumann occasionally making sharp remarks about Mendelssohn-cliques, but never about Mendelssohn himself. The two or three exceptions, obviously due to momentary irritation springing from a deep depression which saw all things in a black light, are buried and lost among the innumerable spontaneous expressions of unalterable confidence, which break from him again and again.

A remark of Schumann's in the spring of 1843[1]) is specially characteristic in this connection: "I have spent many intimate hours with Mendelssohn. All the public honours which have been showered upon him have only made him more easy to approach and more modest. He may well feel that he stands at the summit of fame, and that it is hardly possible for him to climb higher. I have several times noticed in him a hint of sadness on this account, such as he never used to have. How glad I am that I belong to the glorious, productive time which is now going on! On all sides interest in good music is awakening; the public sympathy is extraordinary; there is still much to come from here."

These remarks are characteristic too, in so far as the exaltation which rings in the closing words is directly connected with Mendelssohn, whom Schumann honoured as the "greatest critic, with the clearest insight of all living musi-

---

1) Diary 1843 Feb. 17th.

cians"[1]).   Clara's words in the diary[2]), after Mendelssohn's
death, sound like an echo from such hours as these: "His
loss is doubly irreplaceable to Robert, since it was he who of
all artists stood most close to Robert, and with whom Robert
best loved to exchange feelings and views concerning art, finding that intercourse of this kind always strengthened and refreshed his spirit."

That I so strongly emphasise Schumann's admiration for
Mendelssohn as an ideal artist, must not be taken to imply
that he did not equally prize him as an artistically-gifted man.
Anyone who knows Schumann's writings, knows that this was
not the case. Appreciation of the peculiar gifts of the contemporary who was working beside him, and at times showing the
way, no doubt preceded admiration for the man; but it is also
certain that the more strongly Schumann felt himself urged to
express his own artistic conceptions, the more he became conscious of a certain opposition to Mendelssohn, due to the very
characteristics which most strongly attracted him towards the
man, and all the more so because they were denied to him himself.
He likes to compare Mendelssohn to Mozart, and ranks him beside him.   "No-one has a sweeter smile playing round his lips,"
he writes of Mendelssohn and again "I often think that Mozart
must have played like that"[3]).   "He is the Mozart of the 19th century"[4]), he says, speaking of Mendelssohn's D minor trio, "the
most limpid musician, who most clearly sees through the con-
tradictions of the age, and reconciles them. And he will not
be the last musician. After Mozart came a Beethoven." This
comparison shows clearly the boundary line which separated the
characters of Schumann and Mendelssohn; but it is necessary
to realise that this distinction between Mozart and Beethoven,

1) Diary 1842 Oct.
2) Diary 1847.
3) *Schriften* Vol. II p. 146 (1837).
4) *Schriften* Vol. II p. 280 (1840).

and indeed the whole comparison, is intended not so much as an appreciation of their worth, as a summing up of their peculiar temperaments.

It is equally impossible to doubt Mendelssohn's friendship for Schumann, though, as various incidents which have been mentioned have already given proof, it was quite different in character from that which Schumann felt for him. With Schumann it was an matter of affection, with Mendelssohn it was more, if not exclusively a matter of intellect. He respected Schumann, but probably he never found him wholly sympathetic. And his attitude towards Schumann's music was evidently the same. He accepted it intellectually, admired it from outside as a most distinguished artistic manifestation, and spared no pains to further it and to smooth the road of his younger friend and, in one sense, rival; but he never really understood his artistic attitude.

That this was so, was felt — as often happens in such cases — more strongly and more quickly by the woman than by the man, though her personal admiration for Mendelssohn and her confidence in his unselfish friendship did not suffer in consequence. On the contrary, after Clara had become Schumann's wife, there gradually developed between her and Mendelssohn a personal intimacy, in this case based upon genuine understanding, which remained through all the changes and chances of life, through joy and sorrow, and which gave her courage to turn to Mendelssohn for advice and comfort when she was tortured by the most terrible anxiety about Robert and about their future life, and yet hesitated to disturb her dearly loved husband in the midst of his work. Thus during the sad weeks in the autumn of 1843 when Robert was unable to come to any decision about their long-planned journey, her only comfort lay in confiding her anxieties to Mendelssohn. "My husband," she writes to him on Dec. 9th, "now speaks seriously of our journey, and I am very glad of it, but I know well whom I have to thank for this. When I think of the morning when I came to you in despair, I feel ashamed, and think that I must have seemed childish to you, but I shall never forget how kindly and patiently you listened to me, and how you met all my wishes with a sympathy which made me trust you absolutely."

Indeed, Mendelssohn lost no opportunity of making known the friendly feeling for her and the great respect for her artistic power which were doubtless the spontaneous expressions of his deepest convictions, or of displaying them in the warmest and most chivalrous manner in the family circle, at her appearances in public, and in society, without there being the slighest appearance of his ever desiring to treat her as anything but an equal in every respect. The manner in which her self-confidence must have been strengthened by Mendelssohn's esteem, especially during these years which witnessed the most severe struggle between art and housewifery, is obvious. If in spite of this, and in spite of unrestrained intercourse with Mendelssohn, who during those two first years was always in and out of their house — he was godfather to their first child — she never entirely conquered a faint shyness which she did not feel with other artist friends (Bendemann[1] for example), the chief reason for this lay in the fact that for years Mendelssohn had been (and remained) her highest, unattainable ideal in her own art. A significant scene took place in the first year of their married life, March 1841. Mendelssohn came in one evening in order to practise with her his newly composed duet, which was to be played at her first concert as Clara Schumann: "We played it; he did not like it; and he burst forth into comic rage, because he had expected it to

---

[1] She takes occasion to speak of the difference in her intercourse with Bendemann and Mendelssohn in the diary, shortly before Mendelssohn's death.

sound better." Then Mendelssohn sat down at the piano and played some *Lieder ohne Worte*, and among them a particularly pretty *Volkslied*. But the lonely young wife could not enjoy it; she was painfully conscious of the distance between his art and her own. "I saw Robert's look of rapture, and it hurt so dreadfully to feel that I should never be able to offer him this. I was ashamed afterwards of the tears which I shed in Mendelssohn's presence, but I could not help it.

The gentleness and fine feeling with which Mendelssohn helped her to rise above such fits of despondency, and even to prevent them from occurring at all, are shown by a charming incident which occurred in Dresden in March 1846. At a large party, at which the Schumanns and Mendelssohn were present, Mendelssohn was asked to play Beethoven's *F* minor sonata. He expressed his willingness, but added that he could not play the last movement, Frau Schumann must play that. Not having touched a note for 7 weeks she on her side declared that she could not think of it. "He sat down at the piano," says the diary, "but threatened to stop after the adagio, and to make it depend on me whether or no people heard the last movement. He played as far as the last chord, paused on the second diminished seventh, and when I did not come forward, he got up, saying once more that he could not play the last movement — so he forced me to play it, and although the fright made me shake all over, it went fairly well." "I am convinced," she concludes, "that it was only gallantry on his part, for he always pays me attention whenever he can."

Altogether, it is easy to understand that with Mendelssohn's departure Leipsic lost, if not every charm, at least its chief attraction for the Schumanns, and thus made it easier and more natural for them to break away from their surroundings. Yet the fact still remained that Leipsic counted for more in the musical world than any other city. In the first place it contained an unusual number of interesting and distinguished people, who had made, or were making, themselvers a name in art, and whom the favourable situation, and above all Leipsic concerts, attracted thither all the year round. Liszt, as has already been mentioned, was there in December 1841, and Ole Bull had appeared there in the previons year. And here special mention must be made of Berlioz, whom Schumann speaks of in his *Record of Musical Life in Leipsic* for the winter of 1839/40, drawing particular attention to him, and mentioning the omission of his name from the repertoire of the subcription concerts as a decided deficiency. Now, in February 1843, he made his first appearance before a Leipsic audience, at a charity concert at which the *Offertorium* from the *Requiem*, and a *Romance with Orchestral Accompaniment* were given. At once a quarrel sprang up between rival factions as to whether he was "a lesser Beethoven" or merely a *poseur* of genius. Schumann, wishing to show special attention to a man whom he valued so highly, arranged for a performance of Berlioz's quintet and two quartets at his own house, though to Clara's annoyance he received small thanks for his pains: "He (Berlioz) is cold," she writes indignantly, "unsympathetic, peevish. Not the kind of artist that I love — I cannot help it. Robert thinks otherwise, and has quite taken him to his heart, which is incomprehensible to me. As far as his music is concerned I agree with Robert, it is full of interest and genius, but it is not the kind of music which gives me delight, I have no desire to hear more of it."

The music and the personality of Clara's old acquaintance Gade, who won Schumann's heart at first sight (Jan. 1844) seemed to them all the more sympathetic by way of contrast.

After all, this city, the home of so much music, connected so intimately with the names of Schumann and Mendelssohn, with Schumann's *Neue Zeitschrift* (whose promise had been fulfilled in the works which he and Mendelssohn had given to the world during the last ten years) was also Clara's home. Not because she was born here, but because here, after years of stern discipline under her father and later under the influence and in the house of her husband, the *genius loci* had assisted her to develop from a distinguished virtuoso into an independent artistic personality.

The new home must have much to offer, if it is to make up for all that has been left behind.

CHAPTER IX.

SILENT GROWTH.
1844—1850.

"Who once has built his house in native land, on foreign shores will never feel at home." It may seem absurd to take this as the text for a chapter which deals with a change from one German town to another, especially when both towns were centres of culture and possesed an influence which spread far beyond all national boundaries. And yet, in many ways the change was almost as great as that from one country to another. The one was a rich commercial city, which — thanks to its connection with education for centuries past and its interest in book-selling and printing — had always occupied a place by itself among German manufacturing towns; and during the last century its intelligent and active-minded population had raised the level of music to a height which certainly placed it among the leading cities of Germany, if not of Europe, with regard, not only to the performance, but also to the appreciation of music. The other was a royal residence, taking its tone from the luxury-loving family which in the course of centuries had created a city dedicated to the development of art and all other intellectual delights. Its exquisite beauty enchanted every artist at first sight, and the charm of the surrounding country added to its power of artistic inspiration. But above all things it was residential, the court came first, officialdom second, and both showed an unconscious and

naïve tendency to consider that the rank which was theirs
by birth or position enabled them to judge in matters of art.

Nor was the musical taste of Dresden in harmony with
that of Leipsic, and Schumann had neither the heaviness of
hand nor the bitterness of tongue needed to beat down opposition and reconcile conflicting elements. It was not long
before they both realised that the move to Dresden had been
a grave mistake, though neither of them could resolve to
retrace their steps. From first to last, both of them — and
Robert more particularly — in spite of a large circle of
acquaintances, were strangers, whom people respected to a
certain extent but with whom no-one saw any necessity to
enter into closer relations.

"How much," writes Clara[1]) shortly before their departure
for Düsseldorf, "there is of Robert's which we have not yet
heard! it is dreadful! The want of sympathy among the artists
here goes so far that not one of them so much as asks what
Robert may be working at . . . . Such nature here, and such
human beings!" And this was not merely the depression due
to years of disillusionment finding vent in complaints and
accusations, but simply the experience of a critic who made
the greatest demands on herself and on others. She herself
confessed three years later: "Dresden is not an unmusical
hole." A verdict which stands on the same page of the diary,
on a performance of Mendelssohn's *Elijah*, which was given
on the following day (Nov. 1st) at the Singing Academy under
Schneider's direction, affords a striking comment: "We heard
only the first part," it runs, "for the distribution of the
solos, and the thin, miserable accompaniment on the piano,
were so bad that we could bear it no longer. It will be
better therefore to reserve judgment on this work until one
has heard it properly."

---

1) Diary 1850 Ap. 26.

This verdict expresses annoyance, not so much at technical insufficiencies and failures, though she does take occasion to complain of these, as at the inartistic, petty spirit which characterised everything, even when the material itself left nothing to be desired, and which, as she found to her sorrow, was not without its eventual effect upon the weaker-minded of her friends. Thus in 1845 [1]) their friend Hiller, who in other respects seemed to her "too good for the people of Dresden", played Mozart's *D* minor concerto, but in her opinion "did not play it with the care which one has a right to demand from a great artist", while the orchestra came almost entirely to grief after both cadenzas. "I thought of Mendelssohn involuntarily," she writes, "and with what love and masterly power he always performs a work like this." Again, in 1849 [2]), after a rehearsal of Schumann's quintet, in Leipsic, she writes, "I simply revelled in David's powerful playing".

No-where did the contrast of feeling and judgment in all musical questions which existed between Dresden and Leipsic make itself more sharply and painfully felt, than in the household in which it might have been expected that Clara would have been most certain to find further bonds of union: her father's. Already a breach was widening between the Schumanns and the Wiecks in musical questions. It was due in part to the difference in temperament between Schumann and Wieck, but in part also to the difference in the point of view from which the business-like teacher of music, and the master absorbed in new plans, regarded their work. And in this case Clara naturally sided with her husband so completely that the difference of opinion prevented the re-establishment of intimate relations with her former teacher. Since she had parted from him, and especially during the first

---

1) Diary 1845 Dec. 9th.
2) Diary 1849 Jan. 14th.

year of her married life, her views of art and of all that art implies, had widened and deepened, and while this never blinded her to the gratitude that she owed to her father for all that he had done for her, she found it impossible to ignore the fact that her relations to her former teacher were merely those of dutiful respect.

In the first place she felt some anxiety as to the future of her half-sister Marie, whom her father was on the point of producing in public, and whose performance she involuntarily compared with her own at the same age: "She has everything which teaching such as Father's can give," she writes in Feb. 1845, "but she lacks the right spirit, her playing always seems to me mechanical, wanting in enjoyment, and she has neither strength nor endurance. I too, may not have delighted in it as a child, but whenever I played to anyone, or played in public, a certain inspiration came to me. What makes me really anxious is that she is still lacking in technique, and it is impossible not to realise that since I went on tour as a child the public has learned to expect very different performances from children; children now-a-days often give really first-rate performances, which is not the case with Marie — she plays well, but not extraordinarily well. The determination which has enabled Father to bring her on so far is worthy of all admiration, and I was most anxious therefore that he should be fully rewarded but that is now impossible." During the period which followed, this belief instead of changing, became more fixed. Wieck, however, was of the contrary opinion, and consequently all sorts of little irritations and unpleasantnesses arose, especially as later on there were not wanting differences of opinion as to the gifts and readiness for public performance of other pupils of his. It was inevitable that Clara should suffer at the thought that public disappointment and failure might be in store for her father.

"What I endured, this evening," she writes, after the début of his favourite pupil, Minna Schulz, "it is beyond the power of words to express. Father's excitement and anxiety made me so miserable — it was no small thing to him, and I really believe that he had never before been so wrought up." And again, after reading an unfavourable notice in which her father and his pupil "were harshly criticised", she writes; "it distresses me on Father's account, for I know he thinks a great deal of what the newspapers say". "It did not come upon me quite unexpectedly," she adds, "for Father let the newspapers blow their trumpets too soon, great expectations had been raised, which could not be satisfied. If only Father would let her wait for a few years longer and would not fill her head with such great ideas — it is bad for her as well as for him, for now he will always be finding himself disappointed in his hopes, and this grieves me deeply, for his great pains deserve the reward which he has promised himself." Wieck, however, was anything but appreciative of her anxieties on his behalf, and on the contrary allowed himself to be driven by opposition into a really grotesque extravagance, bordering on insanity, which made any real discussion impossible. Thus in 1846, when he was in Vienna at the same time as Schumann, he refused in the rudest manner an invitation from his son-in-law to let a pupil sing at a musical soirée in his house (so that she might have an opportunity of showing what she could do) in the presence of all the musical authorities of Vienna, and roughly declared, "that he recognised only two authorities in the world, Nicolai (Otto, who was then in Vienna) and Meyerbeer. The former had already expressed his opinion of her, the latter would do so before long". "This answer was insulting to Robert," adds Clara, "but I was so sorry for Father, as I could not but see once more how mistaken he is. . . . Amazement at his answer silenced me, common-sense silenced Robert."

Under these circumstances it was fortunate that gradually intercourse between the Schumanns and the Wiecks became confined to stiff visits paid at intervals of several months, painful as Clara found this and warmly as she cherished the wish to lessen the breach by "an explanation". For she had once more to realise from her own experience that explanations of this kind, when they did occur, never improved matters, since the two sides lived in different worlds, and the effect lasted only until some gossip on the part of friends as to unfavourable opinions which they alleged the Schumanns had expressed concerning the performances of Wieck's pupils, once more caused the distrust and rage of the old man to flare up, and he allowed himself to fall into a violence of passion against which they could do nothing. A saying of Clara's, after one of these explanations which she thought cleared the air, is significant. In April 1848 she wrote: "We talked over many things together, some of which (concerning music) we shall never agree over." And it is equally significant that three months later Wieck in so many words forbade his daughter Marie and his pupil Minna Schulz to attend the practices of Schumann's choral society[1].

For similar reasons they found it impossible to have any really intimate and satisfactory intercourse with their friends and acquaintances of earlier days. They found this both with Clara's old friend Sophie Kaskel, now Countess Baudissin, — although they had musical interests in common — and with the Serres of Maxen, who, though always friendly and ready to be of any help, yet were absorbed in their own — often

---

[1] It seemed superfluous to trace out and record here the further phases of this process of estrangement which during the succeeding years of their residence in Dresden unfortunately became considerably more pronounced. It was, however, impossible to refrain from mentioning the fact, as it forms an essential part of the character sketch of Friedrich Wieck and his daughter.

whimiscal — plans, and had no longer any true conception
of what such a pair as this might have brought to their house.
With Becker, the faithful friend and helper in need, they did
indeed always maintain more cordial relations, which received
fresh stimulus later through their interest in his talented children,
but even with him mutual understanding in musical matters,
such as had existed in Leipsic, became more and more difficult.
He could no longer keep pace with his young friends.

But while colleagues and old acquaintances made it practically impossible for them to feel at home or comfortable in
Dresden, in spite of the charm of the surrounding country
which they admired more and more every day, yet in one
respect they were richly compensated by the new ties which
they soon formed with members of the leading artistic circles
in Dresden; ties which years only served to strengthen into
a lasting friendship, and which were to prove a source of
never-failing pleasure to their lives' end.

On Oct. 24th 1847 Clara writes in the diary: "We spent
the evening with the Bendemanns, where a small but pleasant
party was assembled. I played several pieces. Bendemann is
specially interested in Robert's compositions, and takes great
pains to understand them, which always pleases me; Hübner
too, is an attentive listener. The people who have really
artistic minds here are these non-musicians, whom I like better
than all the musicians of Dresden put together."

"One cannot help loving Bendemann," she had written in
Jan. 1845, after her first visit, "he has such a modest, and
at the same time such a really artistic disposition, and there
is something kindly, something which inspires confidence, about
him, so that one cannot but admire him equally as a man
and as an artist."

Eduard Bendemann and his wife[1]), together with Rudolf

---

1) Schadow's daughter.

Hübner and his wife — who was Bendemann's sister — were indeed, as Clara's diary shows, the Schumanns' chief friends and companions at this time. They found a pleasant meeting-place, where people of like taste gathered together, in the house of Dʳ Gustav Carus, the King's physician. Here the little group of friends rejoiced in their music and in the possibility of sharing in the inner life of two such artists as Clara and Robert, both so distinguished and so original in their own way. They came also into personal relations with other artists, Rietschel, Reinick, and Ludwig Richter, though they were never so intimate with them as they were with the Bendemanns and the Hübners.

During their last year at Dresden (1849). The Schumanns first came into personal relations with Eduard Devrient; a bond between them was formed and strengthened partly through their common interests and sympathies in music (they both hated Meyerbeer), partly through literary tastes. At his house they first heard of, "a gifted young poet, Otto Ludwig", and Clara at once "began to speculate as to the possibility of his producing the libretto of an opera!" But for this, however, they saw as little of Dresden authors as they did of the local musicians. Auerbach proved an exception during their last year, but even in his case intercourse was confined to occasional visits and invitations. He had made a pleasant impression on them at first sight (in 1846), with his "merry, quick eyes" which gave one a glimpse into a happy disposition, but this had been partially obliterated a few months later by a public reading of his *Frau Professorin*. Clara thought it "original and full of insight", but the reading lasted 4 hours, and she left before the end. Robert, having a foreboding of the penance, stayed away altogether.

This reading took place at the house Ferdinand Hiller, who could not be classed with those Dresden musicians who so far as the Schumanns were concerned might have been non-existent.

He was not a native of Dresden, and (with the solitary exception
of Johann Schneider, whose organ-playing attracted them) he
was the only person taking part in the public musical life of
the place with whom the Schumanns found it possible to have
any true sympathy. Their points of view were not very different,
but there were discrepencies which could never be entirely
smoothed over, since they sprang from divergencies of character
which implied divergencies of thought and desire, but this did
not prevent the Schumanns from recognising Hiller's fine and
lovable qualities, of which they had experience in good and
evil days during their long personal friendship. Nor were they
blind to the trouble which Hiller took, in defiance of custom,
to bring new life into Dresden music, an attempt for which
he, with his pleasant, man-of-the-world manner, seemed far
better suited than they were.

"They want to start subscription concerts here," Schumann
writes to Mendelssohn on Sept. 24[1] 1845[1]), "but I doubt if it
will come to anything. There is nothing to be done with the
orchestra, and nothing without it. Convention is all-powerful
here. Thus the band will never play a Beethoven symphony
at an extra-concert for fear of injuring the concert on Palm
Sunday and the pension fund."

In reading this criticism of music in Dresden, one name
involuntarily springs to our lips: what of Richard Wagner?

Schumann fully recognised in Wagner a man of intellect
and of ideas, as he had opportunity of realising from his conversation, his poetical writings, his libretti, and he admired
him up to a certain point. But in the musician, the composer,
the conductor, he recognised only a certain originality which
in his eyes was leading in a wrong direction, and therefore
did not count. And he found the whole personality of the man
unsympathetic, and so in the end, preferred to avoid him.

---

1) *Briefe* new series No. 279 p. 250.

"Monday March 17th," runs the entry in Schumann's comments on the year 1846[1]), "I happened to meet R. Wagner in the *Grosse Garten.* He has the most amazing gift of the gab, and is always chock full of his own ideas; one cannot listen to him for long. He had an idea of teaching the public better to appreciate Beethoven's 9th symphony (which is to be given on Palm Sunday), by making a kind of programme full of passages from Gœthe's *Faust.* I could not agree with him over it."

Compare with this, what he says in the letter to Rietz of Jan. 2nd 1849[2]), in which he thanks him for giving his opinion of *Genoveva*: "I know nothing pleasanter than such an interchange of ideas. One can get nothing of the sort here. W(agner) is a poetic fellow, and clever as well, but he is doing his best to break away from what is really musical."

His conducting also calls forth vehement opposition. In speaking of a performance of *Fidelio* in August 1848, the Diary declares that "Wagner took the tempi altogether wrong", and after the performance of the 9th symphony on Ap. 1st. 1849, it says, "parts of it were well-given", but sums up with the remark: "Wagner almost invariably takes the tempi wrong, and very often mistakes the feeling, lessening the character of the whole work, which contains the most magnificent passion and depth of emotion, by trivial ritardandos. How is it possible for an orchestra to produce a perfect whole, when the conductor himself does not understand the work!"

---

1) They are contained in a little book which has notes on the years 1846, 1847, and 1850, in which Schumann, among other things, entered the remarks already quoted concerning Bendemann and Mendelssohn.

2) At other times he takes occasion to praise the conductor. Thus on Ap. 16th 1848, after a performance of the *Elijah* under Reissiger, in which the tempi had been altogether misunderstood, he says, "The 8th symphony of Beethoven was given very well under Wagner's conductorship, and proved most refreshing."

It is true that this does not say that Clara's judgment
entirely agreed with that of her husband. And their opinions
differed with regard to Richard Wagner. Schumann frankly
and warmly admired *Tannhäuser*. "I wished you could have
seen Wagner's *Tannhäuser*", he says in a letter to Dorn (Jan. 7th
1846)[1]. "It contains much that is deep and original, it is altogether 100 times better than his earlier operas, though it also
contains much that is trivial. In fact he may be of great importance to the stage, and if I know him he has courage
enough for it." In November 1845 Clara writes: "I consider
the technique and the instrumentation excellent, incomparably
more masterly than in the earlier ones." "We went to *Tannhäuser* at last, on the 22nd. Robert was intensely interested
in the opera, he considers it a great advance on *Rienzi*,
with respect both to the instrumentation and the musical ideas.
I cannot agree with Robert, this is no music at all to me —
though I do not deny that Wagner has great dramatic power.
I had better hold my tongue about Wagner, for I cannot speak
against my convictions and I do not feel one spark of sympathy with this composer[2]."

That in spite of this there had at first been friendly relations between Schumann and Wagner, is shown, amongst other

---

1) *Briefe* new series 2nd ed. No. 285. This letter — which is most
characteristic — was written after hearing the opera, while the letter to
Mendelssohn of Oct. 22nd 1845 (*Briefe* new series No. 281 p. 251) which
says, "he cannot write four bars well, can hardly make them follow
each other properly and connect them in thought. . . . The music is not
a scrap better than *Rienzi*, if anything it is feebler and more forced",
refers only to the score. After the performance he wrote to Mendelssohn (Dec. 12th 1845): "I must take back much of what I wrote to you
after reading the score; it is all quite different on the stage. I have
been greatly struck by much of it."

2) The letter to C. v. Bruyk, May 8th 1853, shows that Schumann's
opinion of Wagner as a musician more closely approached Clara's, in
later years. *Briefe* new series 8nd ed. No. 433 p. 372.

things, by a letter to Mendelssohn in Nov. 1845[1]), in which Wagner is spoken of as one of the regular weekly visitors, with Bendemann, Hübner, Hiller, Reinick, and Rietschel, and Schumann mentions how he surprised them all with the libretto for his new opera, *Lohengrin.* It was a double surprise for Schumann, for the subject was closely allied to a subject from the Arthurian cycle at which he had been working for more than a year. Possibly this explains why he reserved judgment: "The majority, i. e. the painters, liked the libretto extremely." Clara, 3 years later (Sept. 22nd. 1848, when there was a special performance on the occasion of the 300th anniversary of the founding of the royal band) when Wagner's finale from *Lohengrin* "fell almost flat" while an overture of Reissiger's gained enthusiastic applause, could not help confessing that this was "a pity" though she also says; "It was foolish of him to tear a piece out of his opera, which no-body knows yet, and to give it by itself, like that."

But one, who was afterwards Wagner's chief standard-bearer, found a kind reception from the Schumanns during those years, and on his brief visits was greeted as a coming man. "Young Herr v. Bülow came to see me the other day, says the diary for Oct. 1848, and played Mendelssohn's *D* minor variations to me: he has made marked progress, and plays quite excellently, really musically, only his attack sometimes seems to me hard, and his playing still lacks the true poetic feeling: 'a few days later', Herr v. Bülow came to see us again to-day, and played us a nocturne of Chopin's very nicely, and Beethoven's *C* minor sonata. But he did not play the latter with proper understanding, it was not sufficiently broad and dignified, indeed he lacks life and originality as a whole. I think he will gain something of this as he ripens into manhood."

---

1) *Briefe* new ed. No. 284 p. 255.

In a letter to Mendelssohn[1]) dated Oct. 22nd 1845, Schumann says that the subscription concerts have actually been started, to the boundless surprise of the royal band, and triumphs as he looks back over the condition of music in Dresden hitherto, though at the same time he casts a wistful glance behind him at the neighbouring city: "A Beethoven symphony every year, adorned by flourishes from the band *ad lib.* — we will have no more of that. Will the people of Leipsic support us sometimes? We are building greatly on that, we hope very much that they will."

It so happened that at the very first concert at which Clara was to have played, but was prevented by illness, Leipsic sent a substitute.

"On Nov. 9th," writes Clara, "Father went to Leipsic, in order to fetch little Joachim [2]) to take my place on Tuesday, as I am not able to play;" and on the 11th, "Little Joachim was very much liked. He played a new violin concerto of Mendelssohn's, which is said to be wonderful." This commandeering of "little Joachim" for a concert which was to open a new epoch certainly showed great confidence on the part of all those interested in it, a confidence which rested on the proofs of artistic power which he had given during the past year. It is, however, not uninteresting to learn that even some years later, Clara had moments in which she seriously doubted whether the boy, who had reached the respectable age of 19 in the mean while, really had a great future before him; and it was this very violin concerto of Mendelssohn's which made her doubtful. "We were having music," she writes on June 1st 1850, "one evening at our house, with Joachim; I played a sonata of Bach's to him, and then he played Mendelssohn's

1) *Briefe* new series new ed. No. 281 p. 252.

2) Cf. Schumann's letter to Mendelssohn on Nov. 9th 1845. *Briefe* new ed. No. 282 p. 253.

concerto; delighted as everybody was with him, yet he does not carry us away! His playing is perfectly finished, quite beautiful, with the finest pianissimo, the most wonderful bravura, absolute command of the instrument, but there is nothing to seize hold of one, to turn one hot and cold — he has neither tenderness nor fire, and that is bad, for he will have no great artistic future; his technique is perfect, but who knows if the other will ever come! — For the rest, he is a dear, unassuming fellow, and for this very reason I am doubly sorry that I am not more charmed by him as an artist."

But on July 15th she writes: "Joachim played Robert's 2nd quartet wonderfully, with magnificent tone and extraordinary lightness and to-day I regretted in my heart what I said about him the other day."

In other respects the attempt to make use of the nearness of Leipsic in order to raise the level of music in Dresden by no means met with the success which had been expected. It is true that the inhabitants of Dresden frequently went to Leipsic, but the inhabitants of Leipsic came comparatively seldom to Dresden, and when they did come it was not for music. Hence a visit from Gade, in Aug. 1846, merely by way of a rest, was all the more enjoyed by the Schumanns. "He has a beautiful, strong nature," writes Schumann in his notes, "I have seldom found anyone in such complete harmony with me, I think. He detests Meyerbeer's music[1]." "Gade," he writes, after an evening visit from him in Sept. 1847, "whom apart from his talent, one cannot help loving."

---

[1] As years went on this detestation on Schumann's part increased rather than lessened. To give only one example: Clara writes in the diary, after a performance of *Der Prophet* in Feb. 1850, "Robert hissed audibly several times, and he says, what indeed seems to me very true, that it is godless, immoral music, which cannot but disgust anybody who is naturally clean-minded and unspoiled."

If you burst suddenly into the home of a friend who is
well acquainted with other singing birds but happens never
to have heard a nightingale, crying: "Everything that you have
heard hitherto is worth nothing; only the nightingale can really
sing", it is ten to one that the person addressed with such
vehemence, will conceive a slight prejudice against the singer
who is alleged to be in a class apart, and for whose sake
he is told to consider all his earlier songster-friends of no
value. And this is very much what happened to Clara one
February day in 1846, when her father came back from
Weimar in a state of the wildest excitement, and storming
into his daughter's peaceful sick-room poured the full flood
of his enthusiasm over her defenceless head. "There is no-
one in the world but Jenny Lind; everything must be Lind,
Minna (Wieck's pupil) must sing like Lind, Marie must play
like her; in a word he is beside himself!" she writes, half-
jokingly, in the diary, but she continues more gravely: "My
longing to hear Jenny Lind is very great — I dislike nothing
more than being perpetually told about someone whom I have
never heard or seen, one ends by feeling prejudiced against
them, and in this case that would be unjust." A few weeks
later (on Ap. 12th) the much wished-for opportunity presented
itself. Jenny Lind sang in Leipsic, and Clara at the urgent
request of her relations, went to hear her.

Her step-mother accompanied her. Wieck and his pupil
Minna Schulz, who was to learn to sing in "Jenny Lind's
manner", had already been waiting for days to catch her. A
great surprise was awaiting Clara. "I went first to Mendelssohn," she writes in the diary, "in order to see about tickets,
and he at once got us two good places; he was nearly torn
to pieces in getting them. The minute I arrived he hurled
himself upon me with the request that I would play one
number at the concert instead of him, and urged his request
so insistantly, that in the end I allowed myself to be persuaded,

which was stupid of me, for it made me painfully excited and destroyed all my power of quiet enjoyment." Of the impression made by Jenny Lind, she writes: "Lind" has a genius for song such as can appear hardly once in centuries. Her appearance attracts one at first sight, and her face, though it may not be beautiful, looks so, for her whole countenance is lit up by her extraordinarily beautiful eyes. Her singing comes from the very depths of her being, there is no straining after effect, no passion that takes by storm, it pierces one's heart, there is a sadness, a melancholy in her way of singing which moves one whether one will or no. For the first moment she might seem cold to many people, but she is not so by any means, and it is only because she sings with such sympathy; you never hear her howl, or sob, or let her voice tremble, above all there are no bad habits. There is beauty in all she does. Her coloratura is the most perfect I have ever heard; her voice itself is not large, but it would certainly penetrate throughout any room, for she is all soul. . . . After the concert a great supper was given at Dr Frege's in honour of Jenny Lind. Here I fell doubly in love with her on account of her unassuming, I might almost say retiring, disposition; one hardly noticed that she was there, she was so quiet — in a word, she is not less original as a person than she is great as a singer. "The recollection of this night," the entry concludes, "will never fade from my mind, and it is doubly dear and valuable to me because I have learned to know in Jenny Lind a sweet and natural character."

It was but to be expected that this impression should be mutual. When two such natures meet, this must always be the case. In these two was embodied a type of the highest and purest art, which was not confined to fingers or throat, but inspired and lit up the whole person, a type which is unfortunately so seldom to be found that one hardly dares to speak of it as typical. The utter simplicity with which Clara

had acceeded to Mendelssohn's request to relieve him of a
share of his part in the concert that evening[1]), and bravely
and self-forgetfully to place her art at the disposal of a stranger,
had made a deep impression upon Jenny Lind. She recognised in this a kindred nature, and at once conceived for her a
deep sympathy which, as we shall see, was later, under the
most varied circumstances, to bind the two artists together
in a warm and enduring friendship. A few months later, Schumann also made acquaintance with the artist whom Clara admired so enthusiastically, and here too, that inner sympathy,
human and artistic, for which Clara had hoped and wished,
was established at first sight. How this also strengthened and
deepened in later years will be seen from incidents which
occurred in Vienna and Hamburg (1847—1850). It was in
Vienna that Schumann first really got to know this great, in-
comparable singer. For at their first meeting in Hamburg
(July 1846) he was so far unlucky that his only opportunity
of hearing her was in a part which did not suit her, and
amid unfavourable surroundings, as Donna Anna in *Don Giovanni.* Schumann remarks in his notes: "The final aria was
excellently sung — but it did not impress me as a whole —
the orchestra was mediocre, and the rest of the company were
bad and unworthy of the opera."

The chief point, however, lies in a comparison, which forces
itself on him, between her and another Donna Anna whom both
the Schumanns felt to be unforgetable and unsurpassable: "Comparison with Schröder, is in favour of the latter," is Schumann's first word concerning this evening, and it explains
everything.

Clara's admiration for Schröder-Devrient was passionate
in its intensity. "I would give all the young singers put together

---

1) Mendelssohn had asked her, in the concert-room, to take his place
at the piano.

for her," she writes, "she has more genius and feeling in her little finger."

It is easy to understand why she at first refused, when some months later [1]) Schröder offered her *Schwesterschaft* [2]). "For I thought I could never make up my mind to address as *Du*, the woman who had represented my artistic ideal ever since my earliest childhood. And she consented only when she saw that her refusal hurt Schröder's feelings. With all this passionate devotion and admiration for her genius, Clara had yet a clear eye for human weakness: "She is sometimes painfully insulting in her pride," she writes [3]), "and I realise more and more how impossible it would be for any husband to live with her; she has none of that fine feeling which teaches one how to handle another person's weak side gently; on the contrary, she delights in making such weaknesses the butt of her wit, and no man of spirit would bear that. Added to this is her terrible extravagence, which often really surpasses all belief — what reasonable man could quietly stand by and watch this!" But even here she concludes, "In spite of all this, she remains the artist who most deserves to be honoured."

"May she enjoy the rest of her life in peace and quietness!" she writes [4]), on receiving the news of Wilhelmine's approaching marriage with Herr von Bock, and of her intention of at last withdrawing into private life, "She was a great artist, and has done her best for her art."

While, notwithstanding the great differences in their points of view, and consequently in their manner of life, the absolute purity and greatness of their artistic aims united them more and more intimately with their older friend as they themselves

---

1) Diary 1849 Jan. 17th.
2) i. e. to call her *Du* (Thou).
3) Diary 1849 Jan. 24th.
4) Diary 1850 Jan. 19th.

grew older, the breach widened between the two Schumanns
and Franz Liszt, in whom they thought that greatness in its
highest sense, was lacking.

At their last meeting with the friend whom they had once
taken into their hearts with such warm sympathy, a false note
had been struck, and though, as will be remembered, they
strove to prevent this note from becoming dominant, it sounded
through the following years, during which they neither saw
nor heard from each other, and we catch an echo of it in a
remark which Schumann notes as occurring in conversation
with Mendelssohn in 1846: "Mendelssohn describes Liszt's
vagaries — "So over-violent or over-civil. That every man
with him is god or devil."

In spite of this, when, in June 1848, Liszt payed an unexpected visit to Dresden on his way back from Vienna and
came to see the Schumanns, their first feeling was one of
genuine joy at once more having with them this darling of
the Graces, whom, with all his ridiculous weaknesses, all his
lovableness and freakishness, it was impossible not to be
glad to see. He came with the request that he might hear
Schumann's trio in the evening, and Clara gave herself every
imaginable trouble to collect performers in the few hours in
which they had to prepare for it, and to invite their nearest
friends, Bendemann, Hübner, and the singer Jacobi, to meet
the rare guest. But she was to have no reward for her pains.
When at last everything was happily arranged, the chief person
was missing, "he kept us waiting quite two hours". Eventually
they began with Beethoven's D major trio in a somewhat
exasperated frame of mind, "and as we were at the last page",
the diary relates, "Liszt burst in at the door". It is true that
he expressed great pleasure over the trio of Schumann's which
now followed, but he thought that the quintet was too "Leipsic-ish". That did not exactly improve their tempers, and
when after dinner Liszt let himself go, and, as Clara writes,

"played so disgracefully badly that I was quite ashamed to have to stay there and not to be able to leave the room at once as Bendemann did", Schumann found himself in such a frame of mind that a very little would have been enough to make his wrath with his guest break out. At this moment, Liszt — with incomprehensible thoughtlessness, considering his knowledge of Schumann's attitude towards the two musicians — began to praise Meyerbeer at Mendelssohn's expense. Then Schumann burst out in a violent rage: "Meyerbeer is a pigmy compared to Mendelssohn, the latter is an artist who has done great work not only for Leipsic but for the whole world, and Liszt had better hold his tongue" etc. etc. Having spoken his mind, he left the room[1]). Liszt, who found the occurrence more uncomfortable than insulting, tried to pass the whole matter off as an accomplished man of the world, and to treat it as of no consequence, but at the sight of all their serious, angry faces he finally abandoned the effort and left the company, saying to Clara as he went: "Tell your husband, that there is only one person in the world from whom I would have taken such words as he has just spoken to me[2])."

The Schumanns, judging by their own feelings, took this as a definite breach. "Robert has been too deeply wounded

---

1) This is how it is described by the diary under the immediate impression of the events. J. G. Jansen (*Schumann, Briefe* 2nd series new ed. p. 523) gives a more drastic version, declaring that Schumann "seized Liszt by both shoulders" and cried in an excited voice: "Who are you, that you dare to speak in such a way of a musician like Mendelssohn?" Without in any way impugning the correctness of the description, particularly as Jansen expressly declares that Frau Schumann confirmed "everything" in 1879, I have yet followed the *Diary* here, as being the most immediate, and therefore the most authentic source of information.

2) I have been confidently told that this incident, which is not mentioned in the *Diary*, was often referred to by Clara when she was mentioning this scene.

by this, ever to be able to forget it," writes Clara, and adds:
"I have done with him for ever." At the same time Schumann possibly felt that he had gone too far, and a year later, when Liszt sent through Carl Reinecke to ask him if his *Faust* was suitable for the Gœthe festival at Weimar, and whether they might have it, he seized the opportunity to have an explanation by letter with Liszt, in which he apologised for his brusque manner, but insisted on his point of view if possible still more strongly than before. "But, dear friend[1]," runs the letter, "might you not find my *Faust* too Leipsic-ish? Or do you look upon Leipsic as a miniature Paris in which it is also possible that something may be done? Seriously — from you, who know so many of my compositions — I had expected something more than such a sweeping condemnation of a whole artistic life. If you look at my compositions more carefully, you cannot but find a considerable variety of ideas, for I have always aspired to bring something new to light in all my works, and not only as regards form. And indeed those who were gathered together in Leipsic were not so bad — Mendelssohn, Hiller, Bennett, etc. — at least we could hold our own against the musicans of Paris, Vienna, and Berlin. If our works contain many similar musical traits — you can call it Philistinism, or what you will — the same thing will be found in every artistic epoch, and Bach, Händel, Gluck, and later Mozart, Haydn, and Beethoven, are sufficiently alike to be mistaken for one another in 100 places (though I except Beethoven's last works, which, however, point back to Bach again). No man is wholly original. So much for your expression of opinion, which was unjust and insulting. For the rest, let us forget that evening — a word is not an arrow — and the chief thing is the effort to advance.

Later on, Schumann bethought him of the coming performance of his *Genoveva*, which he expected to take place in

1) *Briefe*, new series, 2nd ed. No. 345. Letter of May 31st 1849 p. 305.

Leipsic in August, and he adds: "Perhaps you will be coming to Leipsic then. . . . If you like I will tell you the exact day, later on." Liszt at once replied most courteously: "Before all things, let me repeat, what you ought to have known long ago, that no-one more honours and admires you than my humble self. We can occasionally differ in a friendly way as to the importance of a work, a man, and even of a town," and in conclusion he speaks of himself in friendly tone as "a *claqueur*" at the performance of *Genoveva*. But this very phrase, which he doubtless meant well in every sense, wounded his old friends, and through it he spoiled the pleasant feeling which was just beginning to re-awaken. The contrast between him and the "French man of the world" became more evident than ever. And when, a year later, Liszt really appeared at the first performance of *Genoveva* and kindly and gracefully complimented both the Schumanns at the festive meal which ensued, the old warmth and freedom from restraint refused to re-appear. They laughed merrily it is true, when the day after, as he and Clara were playing the *Genoveva* Overture and extracts from the "*Pieces for children, big and little*", after breaking a string in the bass he remarked quite gravely, "such a thing had really never happened to him before", and they chatted pleasantly with him, but they did not get beyond polite conversation. And from this time on their intercourse retained this tone. They no longer aroused mutual anger and irritation, but they had also nothing more to say to each other that was personal and intimate.

It was still a youthful household, occupied with youthful, though not necessarily petty cares, that established itself first in the flat on the ground-floor of the house in Waisenhausstrasse, and after Sept. 1846 on the first floor of No. 20 in the Grosse Reitbahnstrasse. Four children were born during these years, three boys and a girl; Julie, born March 11th 1845,

Emil, born Feb. 8th 1846 [1]), Ludwig, born Jan. 20th 1848, and Ferdinand, born July 16th 1849.

There were many joys and many cares for the young mother, and many lonely, sad hours must have been spent in thinking of the future: "What will become of my work?!." "But Robert says: 'Children are blessings,' and he is right for there is no happiness without children, and therefore I have determined to face the difficult time that is coming, with as cheery a spirit as possible. Whether I shall always be able to do so or not, I do not know," she writes in May 1847.

But the chief anxiety during these early years, an anxiety which drove all others into the background, was, and continued to be, Robert's health [2]). It was this that had driven them away from Leipsic, and this care came with them into their new home, and settled there with them. "Robert's nerve trouble will not lessen," she complains in May 1845. A journey down the Rhine to Bonn, which they had planned for the August of that year and on which they had already started, had to be cut short at Weimar in consequence of his severe attacks of giddiness, and continuous ill-health, which the remedies of Hofrat Carus were powerless to alleviate, and in October they made up their minds to take no more allopathic medecine for the future. In the course of the winter, things so far improved that meeting other people often proved a distraction which turned his thoughts and lightened the burden which weighed upon his spirits. But very disquieting symptoms appeared in May 1846. As a result of over-work in

---

1) Died on May 22nd 1847 of disease of the glands.

2) A detailed account of Schumann's illness, given by the homeopathic family doctor, Dr Helbig, is to be found in Wasielewski, *Schumann* p. 200 etc. I cannot, however, but think that many symptoms such as fear of being in high places, which this account places at the beginning, really developed later, when others had disappeared, so that many things which are spoken of here as existing simultaneously, really came one after another.

scoring his symphony, an irritation of the aural nerve was set up, which forced him to break off work in the middle of the first movement: he was specially disquieted by the fact that in addition to singing and rushing in his ears, every sound seemed to him to turn to music [1]. Complete rest, and the use of Biliner water gradually made him better. The move to Maxen, which was undertaken in May for the sake of his health, made him worse again, the attacks of giddiness came back, possibly in consequence of his once more energetically taking up his work of composition, and with this came profound hypochondria: "He cannot," says the *Diary*, "get over the fact that (from his window) he always sees Sonnenstein (a lunatic asylum)." And in addition to all this, he had a feeling of great physical weakness, which made every long walk torture. In June came serious congestion of the blood in the head, and a great restlessness which prevented him from doing any work. But, a journey to Norderney, which they undertook in July and August — and in the course of which the meeting with Jenny Lind, mentioned above, took place — eventually brought about a real improvement, which lasted till the summer of the following year, so that in 1847 Schumann was able to celebrate the 8th of June in good health, for the first time for 3 years. The following months also passed away well on the whole, except for slight variations in his health, and Christmas 1847 was kept cheerily and merrily. But at the end of January 1848, in consequence of over-exertion in connection with the first act of *Genoveva* there came a recurrance of the irritation and exhaustion of the nerves of the head, "worse than he almost ever had before." "Sad days" followed. Towards the middle of February the situation improved, but not until Feb. 21th does the *Diary* announce: "Robert once more begins to do light work," though with the

---

1) Diary March 4th 1846.

post-script: "His old strength comes back to him very slowly."
"Patience and confidence, my dear Robert," says Clara, comforting him, "better times will come again."

The summer passed off fairly well, but in the winter there
came causes for anxiety and this time apparently for the most
part of a mental character — depression and gloom. "Robert,"
says the *Diary* for November, speaking of a party at the
Pfortens', "could not be induced to accompany me, as he was
out of spirits." He was dissatisfied with his own productions
— speaking of the rehearsal of the *C* major symphony on
Jan. 17th 1849, the *Diary* remarks: "Unfortunately Robert's
nerves were so upset that nothing pleased him," and the
following day it says of the performance: "Robert is still very
unwell, he was dissatisfied with himself, and said that he could
not imagine that anyone could like this symphony."

Better days and better months followed, until in 1850, during the preparations for *Genoveva* in Leipsic fresh signs of
over-excitement showed themselves, this time in the form of
a nervous terror of high places. They were consequently
forced to change their bed-room, which was high up in the
Preussers' house, for one on the ground-floor, "since Robert
cannot conquer the nervous excitement into which he is thrown
by any height" [1].

If nothing else had been said of what had gone before,
or of what followed, this statement alone would give us the
impression of a sick man, and of an illness continually showing
itself in constant attacks of over-excitement, which though they
varied in strength, though there were long intervals between
them, and though the symptoms changed, yet recurred with
sinister regularity, and — as may easily be read between the
lines here — were invariably connected with intellectual strain.
Rest from all work of an exacting nature caused them to dis-

---

1) *Diary* May 20th 1850.

appear, but as soon as the patient began to enjoy his newly-recovered strength and to take up his work, they broke out again, as an enemy breaks from an ambush.

And if we glance at the list of Schumann's works for the years 1845—1850, we realise what an over-powering wealth of compositions of the most varied kinds this great spirit, — incessantly haunted and persecuted by such demons, as he was, and with his nerves in this state — wrung from his weak body and delicately wrought mental organism.

No-one, not even his nearest and dearest, fully realised what were the forces against which this man, so often gloomy, unapproachable, irritable, whimiscal, had to fight, and above all, no-one understood that the inexhaustible flood of sheer melody which he poured forth, was purchased — in the truest sense of the word — by the gradual sapping of his vitality[1].

It makes us shudder when, with this end before our eyes, we read the triumphant words of the unsuspecting wife, with reference to this very inexhaustible power of imagination in her beloved husband: "How lucky he is, when all is said and done!" she writes in March 1849[2]: "What a delightful sensation it must be, when an inexhaustible imagination like his, carries one perpetually into higher spheres." And a few weeks later, she writes[3], "I am often quite carried away by amazement at my Robert! Whence does he get all his fire, his imagination, his freshness, his originality? One asks that, again and again, and one cannot but say that he is one of the elect, to be gifted with such creative power."

In November 1843 Schumann had written. "I am .... very .... busy with various opera-schemes .... an opera must be

---

1) Geh. Rat Richarz, head of the institute at Endenich, Schumann's last physician, in on article in the *Kölnische Zeitung* for 1873, on "Robert Schumann".

2) Diary March 18th 1849.

3) Diary April 21st 1849.

the next thing, and I am burning to do it. As we know, the
Russian journey had placed a bar between these plans and
their fulfilment, and when, in the summer of 1849, he once
more awoke to the joy of creating and to strength, the *motif*
which had come to him on this journey, the music for *Faust*,
had been the first thing which had demanded his attention.
He was still working at this in the intervals of his severe
illness in the late summer of 1844. When, at the beginning
of 1845, he once more felt impelled to work — although he
was still far from well — he took up the threads exactly at
the place where he had dropped them a year and a half before.
"Robert," runs the diary for Jan. 16th 1845, "is much occupied
with plans for an opera. Robert Griepenkerl sent him one,
but it was not very interesting, Robert was all the more interested however in the subject of *King Arthur*[1]), which he would
like to have arranged for him. He is now looking out in all
directions, a poet is sure to turn up from somewhere."

It was not this idea, however, which was to pave the way
for fresh musical activity. The new work sprang from the
contrapuntal studies which he began with Clara, a few days
later. "To-day," Clara writes on Jan. 23rd, "we began to study
counterpoint, which, in spite of the labour, gave me great
pleasure, for I saw — what I had never thought to see — a
fugue of my own, and then several others, for we continue
our studies regularly every day. I cannot thank Robert suffi-
cienty for his patience with me, and I am doubly glad when
I do anything right because he cannot help knowing that it
is his doing.

He himself has been seized by a regular passion for fugues[2]),
and beautiful themes pour from him, while I have not yet

---

1) It is the material which he abandoned after he became acquainted
with Wagner's *Lohengrin*. Cf. p. 387.
2) Op. 72. *"Four Fugues for the Piano-forte."*

been able to find one. This "passion for fugues" lasted through the ensuing months, and finally transferred itself from the piano to the organ. "On Feb. 28th, Robert finished a very beautiful fugue in D minor." March 9th: "Robert is working at a second fugue." Aug. 4th: "Robert is working at a fugue on Bach, of which he is making a magnificent success." The sixth, and last fugue, on Bach's name, was not finished until Nov. 1845[1]). These were followed by — or rather, among these were interspersed — the studies for pedal-piano, which, a chance circumstance had inspired him to write. "On Ap. 24th," writes Clara, "we received a pedal for our piano, on hire, which gave us great pleasure. The chief object was to enable us to practice for the organ. Robert, however, soon found a greater interest in this instrument, and composed several sketches and studies for pedal-piano, which will certainly make a great sensation, being something entirely new[2])." He was still occupied with these in May and June, and Clara played some of them and the fugue on Bach's name, to Mendelssohn, who came to see them on his way to the King at Pillnitz. "It was easy to see how pleased he was," she writes. "Among the canons he liked best that very graceful one in B minor, as I thought he would, for this is the one that is most in sympathy with his own temperament."

In March he developed a plan for turning *Hermann und Dorothea* into an operetta, then he asked Julius Hammer to arrange the text of Töpfer's comedy, and in the summer he

---

1) Op. 60. *"Fugues on the name of Bach. For Organ or Pedal-piano."* In the MS. Schumann gives as the date of composition: Dresden, Ap. 1845. The entries in the diary contradict this, however, as according to them the 3 fugues in G minor were finished on Sept. 19th, and a fugue of a "humorous character" on Oct. 2nd.

2) Op. 56. *"Studies for the Pedal-piano. Vol. I: Six Studies in canon."* According to the MS.: "Dresden, May and June 1845 and "Op. 58". *Sketches for Pedal-Piano*, according to the MS. composed in April and May 1845.

wrote to Halm and Annette v. Droste-Hülshoff for libretti. In June and July the *Phantasie* in *A* minor, which had apparently been completed in 1841, was enlarged into a concerto.

On June 27th Clara writes concerning it: "Robert has added a beautiful last movement to his *Phantasie* in *A* minor for piano and orchestra, so that it has now become a concerto, which I mean to play next winter. I am very glad about it, for I always wanted a great bravura piece by him." And a month later, July 31st, she writes: "Robert has finished his concerto, and has handed it over to the copyist. I am as happy as a king at the thought of playing it with the orchestra." But even this only forestalled, and prepared the way for, something greater with which Schumann surprised Clara on Christmas Eve. The 3 first movements of the *C* major symphony[1]) had come into existence, thanks to many days and nights of hard work during the latter weeks of December, without Clara's having any suspicion of what the work was. "My husband," she writes to Mendelssohn on Dec. 27th, "has been very busy lately, and at Christmas he delighted and surprised me with the sketch of a new symphony; at present he is music pure and simple, so that there is nothing to be done with him — but I like him like that!" —

The first few weeks of the following year (1846) were chiefly occupied in finishing off the *A* minor concerto, but a new work forced its way into the midst of this, "some beautiful vocal quartets", which, as the diary for the end of January remarks, were suggested by "the formation of a new society, for mixed chorus (founded in Leipsic by Mendelssohn)[2]). The scoring of the

---

1) Op. 61. On Dec. 26th Clara writes in the diary: "R. finished the first sketch of his symphony". Schumann's note on the MS. says that it was sketched between the 12th and 28th of December.

2) Op. 55. *"Five Songs for mixed choir*; dedicated to the *Leipziger Liederkranz"* must be the work in question. The MS. is dated only "Dresden 1846".

new symphony was begun by the middle of February ("R. began to score his new symphony on Feb. 12th") but it was brought to a standstill by the attacks of nervous irritation, of which mention has already been made. This compulsory pause for rest gave birth to a new plan in the middle of March: "Robert," writes Clara on March 18th, "has devised a delightful plan of writing the biography of a *Davidsbündler*, that is of himself. He will introduce into it all his earlier attempts and old poems, and a thread of romance is to run throughout, although it is to be in no sense untrue." "Robert looked through his old poems," says an entry in this same connection, "and wants to copy the best of them into a special book." This too, seems never to have been done, although Clara welcomed both plans with great sympathy, and determined to remind him later to carry out the idea of a *Davidsbündler* biography. But in the following year his musical powers once more came to the fore, and allowed no other gods near them.

Work at the symphony suffered severely from Schumann's uncertain health. A fresh attack which occurred in the middle of May, had the worst effect, though work at the libretto for an opera — and the discussions with Reinick which ensued — proved a certain distraction. His own composition remained in complete abeyance until the autumn. Then his apparent recovery of health in Norderney was all to the advantage of the symphony. By the end (26th) of September he is already at the last movement, and on Oct. 19th the work is completed. On Nov. 5th the first performance took place in Leipsic, an account of which, as well as of its repetition on Nov. 16th, has already been given. Between the 1st and the 2nd performance Schumann thought of "several very good alterations" so that he had to let Clara go to Leipsic by herself on Nov. 18th, as he was held fast by his work. Clara, who had gained only a very imperfect idea of the whole work from the sketch, who had not been able quietly and thoroughly to enjoy the

two performances in Leipsic on account of the remarkable
series of misfortunes which accompanied them, first fully realised
the greatness and originality of this work which had been
conceived in so sad a time, when it was performed at Zwickau
in July 1847. "This symphony," she writes under influence
of the most vivid impression of that day at Zwickau, "warms
and inspires me to an especial degree, for it has a bold sweep,
a depth of passion such as are to be found in none of Robert's
other writings! It has an entirely peculiar character, a feeling
which is quite-different from all the rest, e. g. from the
Peri ... These two works, each in its own way, are among
my keenest musical pleasures."

Clara, too, had not been idle during this time, in spite of
her anxiety about Robert, although her ever-increasing duties
as wife and mother — two children were born, one in March
1845, and one in Feb. 1846! — continually narrowed the circle
of her artistic activity, and the task of settling down amidst
new surroundings brought all sorts of interruptions and distractions. But it is possible that she was less conscious of
these hindrances than she would have been in earlier years,
for during this time her artistic efforts were moulded and
directed by Robert's works more than ever, and she realised
that besides the continual deepening of her own musical understanding her chief task was to interpret Robert's genius to
the world, and that in interpreting him her own powers found
their highest expression.

With this, all the sense of being torn between her duty
to herself and her duty to her husband which had given her
so many unhappy hours during those first years, gradually
disappeared. And this service, which might have broken a
smaller nature, was her salvation, "it forced her upwards".
As she penetrated with Robert more and more deeply into
contrapuntal studies, and led by him worked through the
"grayness" of Cherubini's *Counterpoint and Fugue*, at the

same time absorbing herself in the practical exercises which new production necessitated, works of superficial interest gradually lost charm for her, and her eyes were opened to the sublimity of Bach and the divine depth of Beethoven.

This practice in counterpoint, which began in April and was continued without interruption till November, was of immediate service to her own compositions. It bore fruit in the *Preludes and Fugues* (Op. 16) with a printed copy of which she surprised Robert on her birthday in 1845, and in the *Trio for Piano-forte, Violin, and Violon-cello* (Op. 17) which was begun in May and finished on Sept. 12th, the 7th anniversary of their wedding-day.

Her husband's studies for the pedal-piano seem to have been the immediate cause of her once more taking to regular practising, which had long been interrupted, for in almost direct connection with them the diary says (May 1845): "I am beginning to play every day, again." About the same time she began to arrange the overture and scherzo from Schumann's *Overture, Scherzo, and Finale,* for four hands, as a surprise for Robert's birthday.

Into the midst of this quiet time of creative work, a certain excitement was brought by the news of a great event in the world of music, "which is setting all France on the alert", and which even overflowed into Germany. At the beginning of June, Hiller brought the piano score of Felicien David's symphony *Le Desert.* Clara and Robert, however, "find nothing particular in it, neither beautiful melodies, nor anything of harmonic interest, nor anything remarkable in the conception, and the whole thing is really no symphony at all, merely a series of little pieces strung together".

And when, a month later (July 12th) the new prophet himself appears in Dresden and has *Le Desert* performed, the impression is still the same: "there is talent, and the scoring is clever, but there is no originality anywhere, and there is cer-

tainly not, as the Parisian papers say, a new era in art."
"His music," Clara concludes, "left me with absolutely no
desire to hear it again; once was enough." This holds true
of the composer himself, whose acquaintance — he and Hiller
spent the evening with them after the concert — was to have
a curious little sequel for Clara, very characteristic on both
sides. Clara had asked him for his autograph for her album.
It is evident that he had no idea of what she wanted, or of
her own position as an artist, for a short time after the great
man sent the following testimonial:

"Avant mon départ de Dresde, je dois remercier Madame
Schumann de tout le plaisir que j'ai éprouvé à l'entendre. Je
puis lui dire sans flatterie, qu'elle est du petit nombre des
artistes qui sentent véritablement le beau et qui l'expriment
sans emphase, avec force, noblesse et simplicité. C'est le
cachet de l'artiste élu. Je suis heureux de rendre cet hommage
sincère au beau talent de Madame Schumann.

Felicien David."

Clara was annoyed, and wrote the following answer:

"Madame Schumann n'ayant pas demandé une attestation
pour son album remercie Monsieur David pour sa bonne
volonté et prie du reste d'accepter l'assurance de sa parfaite
estime."

Meanwhile Clara was preparing for the concert-season, and
began by studying Henselt's new piano-concerto, which proved
another bitter disappointment to her, great as was its success
in the concert-hall afterwards. She thinks it lacking in "invention", and considers his chief aim is brilliance. "These
passages are laborious, far-fetched, and patched together. The
first movement is not a whole, at all .... it is not well carried
out, and (except for the first) has not a single beautiful, fresh
motif in it.... It is not so easy to write a concerto, poetic
feeling and warmth and creative power are needed if the

composer is to awaken lasting interest. Henselt is not entirely lacking in the first of these, it is true, but even this is lost in his desire to produce something technically remarkable; thought must come first, and then the other will follow!"

Involuntarily one's eye falls on the opposite page of the diary, and it is as if all at once the artificial light was extinguished and the clear sunshine entered: "On Wednesday, Sept. 3rd, I began to study Robert's concerto. What a contrast between this and Henselt's! How rich in invention, how interesting from beginning to end it is; how fresh, and what a beautiful, connected whole! I find real pleasure in studying it."

During this winter (1845—6) her performances — apart from a concert of her own, which she gave on Dec. 4th — were given in three public places: at concerts in the *Gewandhaus* (Oct. 5th and Jan. 1st), at the new subscription concerts in Dresden, under Hiller's direction (Nov. 25th), and at matinées[1] to which Robert and Clara Schumann invited the public (1846: Ap. 7th, Ap. 19th, May 3rd). Her impromptu share in Jenny Lind's concert in Leipsic (Ap. 16th) has already been mentioned. It is noteworthy that, at all events as far as the concertos were concerned, — she now appeared before the public more than hitherto as the interpreter of Robert Schumann. At her own concert, and at the 2nd *Gewandhaus* concert she played the *A* minor concerto (in Dresden she also played Mendelssohn's duet for four hands, by way of novelty) and at the matinée she played the piano quartet in $E\flat$ major (Op. 47) and the quintet, as well as a number of little solo pieces, It is further noteworthy that bravura pieces of the old school are replaced by works of Beethoven, Bach, and Mendelssohn, and finally, that as these great names took the first, instead of the second place in her repertoire, in other

---

1) The two first took place at their own home, the third, in the hall of the Cosel.

respects too she began, quite involuntarily, to develop new standards of criticism as she practised her art, standards which became a second nature to her.

Two instances are typical:

On Oct. 2nd 1846 she rehearsed her trio for the first time, and at first she took a naïve delight in it, as its creator: "There is nothing greater than the joy of composing something oneself, and then listening to it. There are some pretty passages in the trio, and I think it is fairly successful as far as form goes." But the joy soon lessens: "of course it is only a woman's work, which is always lacking in force, and here and there in invention." A few weeks later, on Nov. 18th, she writes: "This evening I played Robert's piano quartet and my trio which seems to me more harmless each time I play it." And a year later, in September 1847: "I received the printed copies of my trio to-day; but I did not care for it particularly, after Robert's (D minor), it sounded effeminate and sentimental."

And the second instance: In November 1846 the two first performances of Schumann's C major symphony in Leipsic were clouded, as has already been said, by all sorts of misfortunes and misunderstandings. Clara herself won the greatest success at both concerts, a fact which in earlier years, when she herself was satisfied with her performance, would have helped to atone for the audience's lack of sympathy with Robert. On this occasion, however, this was swallowed up in distress and vexation because the symphony was not played as it should have been in order to bring out its full meaning.

These two concerts, and an appearance of Clara's at a *Gewandhaus* concert — on Oct. 22nd — at which she played Beethoven's G major concerto for the first time, with two cadenzas of her own composition, were to be the last for a long time on this ground, for immediately after, on Nov. 24th, they set out an their long planned concert-tour to Vienna, which brought 5 months' interruption to his work, and an interruption not caused by ill-health. The two elder children accompanied them.

There is no doubt that Clara's residence in Vienna during the winter of 1837—38, formed the most brilliant climax of her career. It was here that her star had first risen, and from hence Clara Wieck's name had gone forth to the musical world as that of one called and chosen. Her fame dates from Vienna, where Grillparzer had dedicated to her his poem, where the imperial household and the general public had vied with each other in overwhelming this quiet, grave, magic-fingered girl, with attentions and with every possible mark of admiration. And for Schumann, too, his visit to Vienna had the pleasantest associations.

It is therefore natural, and indeed a matter of course, that they should both have set out upon the journey with the highest expectations. If, almost a decade ago, the coming artists had found so kindly and sympathetic a reception, what might not be expected now when they had so far surpassed the hopes that had been conceived of them? Seven years before Schumann had been known only to the close corporation of connoisseurs, and even to these chiefly by hear-say: now he had won himself a place beside Mendelssohn!

As soon as she heard of the projected journey, Clara's old friend Emilie List, who was then living in Augsburg, asked them to come to her, and at the same time suggested that the visit might prove worth their while in other respects, as they might call upon a man who had great influence in mu-sical circles in Vienna, and who might be of great use to them in inserting notices in the Viennese press. Clara, who was rather annoyed by this, replied: "What are you thinking of, dearest Emilie? I am to come to Augsburg so that Kolb may write articles on me! Not one step, for that. You show little knowledge of me, and Vienna too, where I am better known and loved than anywhere else in Germany!"

As far as the past was concerned this was no doubt true; but she was to learn, to her bitter disillusionment, during the following months, that there is no place in the world where people live at a faster rate and forget more quickly, than in the imperial city on the Danube.

From first to last an extraordinarily unlucky star governed their stay in Vienna. Everything seemed to combine to place obstacles in their way, and even the few rays of light, such as their meeting with Jenny Lind, only served to throw into sharper relief their many calamities. Incidents which at first seemed favourable, turned to their disadvantage — even their re-union with Clara's old friends Emilie and Elise List. The death of Friedrich List followed quite suddenly, under specially tragic circumstances, and this news, which reached his daughters in the midst of the rehearsal for Clara's first concert, threw a deep shadow upon Clara also, since she witnessed the uncontrollable anguish of his children.

She found no change in the kindliness and warm sympathy of her old friend Fischhof[1]), but his was the only face in Vienna which she saw as she had pictured it. And though the tone of the instruments which they heard at the philharmonic concert, under Nicolai's direction — "which are far better here than with us" — made a great impression on them, yet they missed "all real understanding" in the performance as a whole, as well as in detail.

The Vienna of 1846 sang and played beautifully up to a certain point. It had wonderful instruments, wonderfully skilled

---

1) But she did not, as Hanslick says in his *Recollections*, stay in his house. After arriving at the *Stadt Frankfurt* the Schumann's, at the end of 3 days, transferred themselves to private rooms in the *Bauernmarkt*, *Grundelhof* on the 1st floor of No. 549 Kammerhofgasse, for which they paid a ducat a day, and where they stayed till the end of their visit.

hands and wonderfully flexible voices, but it had absolutely no understanding of what the two musicians from North Germany, with their pure and great art, had brought with them. The reason why it now entirely failed to understand what 9 years ago it had seemed to understand so well, was, not that it had changed in the mean time, but that it had not changed. If Clara Schumann had appeared with the same virtuoso-programmes that she had played in the old days, she would probably have been fêted with the same enthusiasm by the Viennese. They would also have accepted her interpretation of Beethoven with close attention and interest, as they had done then. But the Clara Schumann who brought them Robert Schumann's music, meant nothing to them.

In the course of a little over two months she gave four concerts. The first, which took place on Dec. 10th and at which she played, in addition to the G major concerto of Beethoven, Chopin's new *Barcarole* (Op. 60), a piece of Scarlatti's, Mendelssohn's *Frühlingslied*, and a canon and a *Romance* of Schumann's, "was fairly full". "We had a few ducats over expenses. The audience received me (especially after the G major concerto) very kindly," says the diary, but adds, "I found, however, none of the enthusiasm of 9 years ago."

The second, 5 days later, at which Schumann's quintet, and the *Andante and Variations for two Pianos* (with Anton Rubinstein) were performed, as well as Chopin's polonaise in $A\flat$ (Op. 53) a scherzo of Clara's, Henselt's *Wiegenlied*, and one of the *Lieder ohne Worte*, just paid expenses! "They liked Robert's quintet very much," Clara tells us, "it was very well received and he himself was called for." But it was little more than success in name. My other pieces (except for the A minor fugue of Bach)[1] did not take so well, I was reproached with playing things that were too good, which the

---

1) It does not appear in the programme.

public could not understand. I preferred this reproach to the
opposite. But I soon saw that Vienna was not the place for
me, and I quite lost all desire to stay here. Robert will enjoy
himself still less in the long-run. The means to produce the
best work are here, but the right disposition is lacking — the
Italians ruin the public taste.

In addition to these circumstances Clara was obliged to
postpone her third concert on account of severe indisposition,
and it is only too easy to understand that there was not a
very merry Christmas in the *Gundelhof*.

"We lighted up a tree and gave the children some little
things, but Robert and I could not give each other anything,
for we had earned nothing! In the depths of my heart I was
very unhappy, it was the first Christmas at which I had not
only been unable to give my dear Robert pleasure by some
gift, but was forced to make him anxious.

This sad Christmas was followed by a scarcely less gloomy
close of the year. On Dec. 31st the second rehearsal for the
third concert — which was to take place on Jan. 1st — was
held. Robert's $B\flat$ major symphony and A minor concerto were
to be played at it. "I was in a dreadful frame of mind today,"
writes Clara, "I thought that everyone, even Mechetti[1]), was my
enemy, and all this as the result of misfortunes in connection
with the concert! First, I had seen no bills in various places,
then few tickets had gone, then the singer wrote to withdraw
because he was hoarse — in short, I was in such a state that
I should have liked to swear never to give another concert in
my whole life. Thus New Year's Eve found me in the most
depressed frame of mind, and I did not begin the New Year
very happily. I was sorry for poor Robert, who was now
drawn into this wretched concert business."

---

1) Who had undertaken the business arrangements in connection
with the concert.

And the third concert itself proved the climax of disappointment. "I had the sorrow of having a deficit of nearly
100 florins, which has never happened to me in my whole life,
before! In spite of this, I pulled myself together and played
well. Robert's concerto (he conducted) it and the symphony
took extremely well; which was one thing that pleased me.
Robert was recalled several times after both of them.

It almost seems as if, so far as the success of Schumann's
works with the public is concerned, this statement is painted
in too rosy colours. Hanslick, who was an eye- and ear-witness,
says: "The attendance was very moderate, the applause cool
and apparently expended on Clara alone. The piano-concerto
and the symphony found but slight approbation."

The same witness mentions a remark of Schumann's on
that very evening, which involuntarily reminds one of the lines
from Goethe's *Wanderers Sturmlied*:

> He who is led by the immortal spirit,
> Shall fear nor rain nor storm;
> His heart shall ne'er grow cold.

"After the concert," he says, "I and a couple of Schumann's
admirers were with him. The minutes passed in uncomfortable
silence, for all of us were oppressed by the poor reception
afforded to this magnificent evening of music. Clara was
the first to break silence, complaining bitterly of the coldness
and ingratitude of the public. Everything that the rest of
us said, endeavouring to soothe her, only increased her
vexation. Then Schumann said these never-to-be-forgotten
words: 'Calm yourself, dear Clara; in ten years' time all this
will have changed'."

No-one could have been blind to the fact that after these
events, and in face of the steadily diminishing receipts, the
prospects for the fourth concert were as bad as they could be.
But it almost seemed as if they had under-estimated the feeling
for art in Vienna, for at this last concert — which took place

on Jan. 10th, and at which Bach's *Prelude and Fugue* in *A* minor, and Beethoven's *F* minor sonata were included, amongst other things, in the programme — the hall of the *Gesellschaft der Musikfreunde* (Society of Music-lovers) was "full to suffocation, so that many people were unable to obtain places". But encouraging as this appeared at first sight, it was a sort of Pyrrhic victory, for these crowds came, not to hear Clara Schumann play, but to hear Jenny Lind sing.

Jenny Lind, who had arrived in Vienna on the day before the last concert but one, had been among the audience, and no sooner did Clara visit her on the following day, than she offered to sing at her fourth concert, putting aside all thanks with the simple words that it was only her duty, and an honour into the bargain, to sing for Clara Schumann. The attention which had been shown to her, or rather to Mendelssohn, earlier [1]), could not have been repaid in a kinder or more delicate fashion. And the consequence, as has been said, was what she had intended — the hall sold out. "The concert was the best and the most brilliant that I have given," Clara writes in the diary, "it paid for our whole journey, and we brought 300 Thaler back to Dresden with us." "And yet," she adds, "it belongs to my saddest recollections. ... I could not get over the bitter feeling that one song of Lind's had done what I, with all my playing, could not do. ... None the less was I enchanted by Jenny Lind's rendering of her songs, and especially of Mendelssohn's *Auf Flügeln des Gesanges.* I had never heard this song sung so well, but there was a double influence at work for as I see from everything she says about Mendelssohn, she loves him no less as a man than as a composer. ... She did not succeed so well with Robert's *Nussbaum,* she had slightly mistaken the tempo. "This comparison of their success was, however, the only shadow thrown

---

1) See above, p. 390.

on Clara's mind by meeting Jenny Lind again. In other respects, intercourse with her brought the purest joy to both the Schumanns. She bewitched all with whom she came in contact, the Schumann children, as well as the Schumann servants: the former were found by their parents when they returned, sitting quite happily and confidingly on the strange lady's lap; and man and maid "stood with eyes and mouth open when she was there, vying with each other in exclamation of the highest delight."

Schumann writes of this time together: "We often used to meet Jenny Lind, dear and admirable artist that she is. She offered, of herself, to sing at our concert on the 10th, and did sing. The rehearsal of a number of my songs, which preceded it, I shall never forget. I have never before met so clear an understanding of music and text at first sight, and simple, natural, and deep comprehension of a work at first reading in such perfection. ... She has told Clara much of herself, much of her inmost feelings, for she has taken a great fancy to her, and Clara is enthusiastic about her! We also talked a great deal about Mendelssohn, whom she calls 'the purest and most refined of all artists', and she says that she thanks God for having sent this artist into her life. She said that this might be the last time that she would sing in Germany, as she was going to retire to Sweden altogether, — but no sea would be too wide for her to cross in order to hear Mendelssohn once more[1]. — When we went, she loaded us with apples and sweets for the children; we parted with her as with an angel from heaven, she was so lovable and gentle."

Their intense desire to see her on the stage, was fulfilled at a performance of the *Regimentstochter* (Daughter of the Regiment) and it was a great pleasure to be enabled in this

1) There is an asterisk here in the text, and in the margin stands in Schumann's hand: "She was never to hear him again. Nov. 19th 1847."

manner to complete the picture of her as an artist, which the
only opera part in which they had seen her before — Donna
Anna — had hitherto left incomplete. "Jenny Lind," writes
Clara, "is a charming, refined daughter of the regiment, her
acting is very characteristic, and she sang magnificently in
places, though I shall always be sorry that it was this opera,
and not another! — She did not seem to have much strength
and I am afraid that she will not be able to stand it much
longer. I have never seen anyone act as she does, her every
movement is full of charm, grace, naïvité, and her face —
which is not beautiful if one criticises it — has a sweetness,
and a poetic charm, which carries one away involuntarily."

If their meeting with Jenny Lind left behind the most
purely harmonious impressions of the highest mastery of art
combined with the most distinguished and lovable personality,
the other inhabitants of Vienna — native and foreign — saw
that they did not forget that such meetings on the highest
plane of human nature, 'are exceptional. The Viennese journalists, with Saphir at their head, took care of this, apparently wishing to revenge themselves for the refusal to give
them free tickets; Wieck took care of it, finding himself —
neither to their pleasure nor to his own — in Vienna at the
same time that they were, having come there in order to
bring his pupil, Minna Schulz, and displaying all the unpleasant
side of his character towards them in word and deed; and
finally, others, who awoke quite different feelings, took care
of it. The meeting with Meyerbeer, who was staying in Vienna
at the same time, and who was enthusiastically extolled and
flattered by Viennese society, was a scurvy trick on the part
of the Fates. With an amazing want of tact, considering
Schumann's well-known attitude towards Meyerbeer's music,
they were both, so Hanslick tells us, invited to a "friendly
gathering" at the "Authors' and Artists' Club". "Fortunately,"
he says, "they sat at a fair distance from each other, but

neither of them appeared to feel quite comfortable." The diary, which only makes a brief reference to this incident (on Dec. 12th) represents this affair in a more favourable light for the club, as a chance meeting. "In the evening, Robert went to the club, an assemblage of artists, men of letters, poets, painters etc. . . . There is a meeting every Saturday, and Robert often goes to it. They welcomed him very kindly the first time, and invited him to be their guest while he is here. To-day, he met Meyerbeer and Flotow. . . . The former is an unpleasant, flattering, fawning courtier who knows how to get hold of people, the latter is an imitation Frenchman, not very intelligent, but apparently good-natured, he calls the most exquisite things in music, 'very nice'; — when I hear that of a musician, I always feel that I know all there is to know of him and his music."

If these, and similar, proofs of the standard of intelligence which prevailed among the official champions of Viennese art and literature, did not exactly encourage Schumann to win himself a place in the neighbourhood of Meyerbeer and in opposition to him, yet friendliness and sympathy were not wanting, even in these circles. Grillparzer renewed the old relations, and left the most pleasant impression behind him — "an intelligent man, who spoke in a very striking manner, particularly of Vienna. Adalbert Stifter, too, put in an appearance, but he somewhat disappointed the admirer of his Muse: "We had thought of him as quite a different person, his looks and his dialect were anything but poetic; but in the course of a long conversation it was impossible not to realise what a gifted man he is." Eichendorff, who was as anxious as they were to come into personal contact, unfortunately met them only at the end of their visit. This meeting occurred at the second matinée[1]) given by the Schumann's in their compara-

1) Hanslick in his *Recollections* speaks of these matinées, and mentions one at which Eichendorff was present, and at which he heard the

tively small dwelling, for their social and musical friends, at
which "many interesting people" were gathered together. At
the first, on Dec. 26th, they were given, amongst other things,
Schumann's E♭ major quartet, and Beethoven's D minor sonata,
played by Clara. At the second, "farewell matinée", which
took place on Jan. 15th, and at which "all the artistic nota-
bilities" were gathered together, first the brothers Hellmesberger,
with Zäch and Borzaga played the A major quartet, then Clara
played her trio, and in conclusion some trifles of her own.
In addition, von Marchion, sang Schumann's settings of Eichendorff's lyrics. Eichendorff himself was, as has been said, among
the audience — his children with him — and he was much
delighted. "He told me," Clara writes, "that Robert had given
life to his poems," but I answered "that on the contrary his
poems gave life to the music:" "The matinée," she concludes,
"was one of the most interesting that we have given, and we
were glad to take so pleasant a farewell of Vienna."

Less pleasant was the last musical treat which they gave
themselves on the evening before their departure, when they
went to the *Kärntnerthortheater* in order to hear a German opera,
and heard Meyerbeer's *Robert der Teufel*. "Hesselt-Barth sang
Alice," writes Clara, "but so badly, and with such a tremolo
that it was hardly bearable. The Viennese, however, were
beside themselves over it, the greater the tremolo the greater
the applause. But the men are very good, the Viennese have
no idea of what they have in them — they do not yell like
the Italians." The music itself seemed to her to contain much

---

E♯ major piano quintet and the *Variations for 2 Pianos* for the first
time, played from manuscript by Clara Schumann and Anton Rubinstein.
It is evident that he is confusing a rehearsal of the quartet and the
Variations which was held at the Schumanns' house on Dec. 14th (in
readiness for the concert next day) with the concluding matinée, mentioned above, at which Eichendorff was present. At this matinée neither
the quintet nor the *Variations* were played.

that was "really clever and skilful", and by its means "Robert's heart was somewhat softened towards Meyerbeer. But if we were to suggest that there was anything of this softening in the more cheerful spirits in which they left Vienna, we should give a false impression of the feelings with which the travellers actually set out early on the morning of Jan. 21st. For although they were by no means blind to the kindness and constancy of old friends such as Fischhof and Vesque von Püttlingen, and the social recognition which had been shown to Clara in the highest circles — she had played once at court, before the young Empress — yet their final impression was one of painful, bitter disappointment.

"How different," Clara writes at their departure, "our feelings were at leaving Vienna from what they were when we came! Then we thought we had found our future haven of refuge, and now all our desire for it had vanished."

Their journey took them through Brünn to Prague. A concert was rapidly got up in the theatre at Brünn, on the 22nd, and was given in frightfully cold weather. "I shall never forget this evening," Clara writes, "my fingers kept growing stiff while I played, my teeth chattered, in fact it was indescribable. After each piece I thought, 'I cannot go on any more'." To their own surprise, they met with a reception which was in every way a marked contrast to that in Vienna. At the first concert Schumann's quintet was vehemently applauded by a house crowded with the best society, it was the same with the Eichendorff songs, both gave occasion for a personal ovation to the composer, and Clara was so much pleased that she hardly minded a little misfortune which befel the piano piece by Scarlatti, in which, after the strain of the Bach *A* minor fugue, she was not entirely successful. "In the evening we sat in the *Schwarzer Ross* with Dr. Ambros and young Hofmann (music-dealer) and drank a glass of champagne. We were very merry — I, except for the Scarlatti!"

And after their Vienna experiences the events of the following day must have raised their spirits still more. "On the
30th," says the diary, "there was a great stir. Count Nostiz
had finally succeeded in arranging with the theatre-director
for a concert in the theatre (which at first he had roundly
refused to allow), but on condition that Robert's $B\flat$ major
symphony should be performed. As it would have to be given
with only one rehearsal, Robert declared that this would
never do, and eventually Hofmann (the theatre-director) had
to give way. Hofmann, rather to our surprise, declared that
no-one would go to the concert if Robert did not produce
the symphony — another proof of the sound taste of the inhabitants of Prague."

The days passed in the most delightful social intercourse
until the second concert, on Feb. 2nd, at which Schumann
himself conducted the A minor concerto. "Robert's concerto
took extraordinarily well," Clara writes, "I did well, and the
orchestra accompanied and Robert directed *con amore*. He
was recalled, much to my amusement for he was too funny
on the stage; I had almost to push him on when the audience
would not stop calling for him."

Delighted as they were with the attitude of the Prague
public, and above all with the attentiveness of the Austrian
nobles who resided there, yet they found it impossible to think
highly of Bohemian music itself. Majourek's opera, *Ziskas
Eiche*, given at the Bohemian opera-house, seemed to Clara,
"unprecedentedly bad music", and young Smetana, who brought
Robert a composition betraying Berlioz' influence — which
was not to their taste — found little favour in their eyes.
"Berlioz himself," says the entry concerning this, ". . . . had
a great success here as well as in Vienna. I cannot understand how this could have been the case here!"

On Feb. 3rd they started on the return journey to Dresden,
where they arrived on the afternoon of the following day, after

an absence of over two months. Their delight at once more
seeing their two younger children was darkened by the sad
state in which they found little Emil. But they had little time
to give to anxiety, for after a few days' rest they set out on
Feb. 10th for Berlin, which they reached on the 11th, breaking
the journey for a short time in Leipsic.

The immediate cause of the journey to Berlin was a performance of the *Peri* at the *Singakademie*, which was then
under the direction of Rungenhagen and Grell. The inclusion
of the *Peri* in their répertoire was a concession to modern
tendencies and an entirely new departure from the conservative
tradition which they had followed hitherto. The result was that
the rehearsals — especially so far as the soloists were concerned — left much to be desired, as neither of the two conductors really had his heart in the work. Endless troubles
and difficulties resulted for the unfortunate composer and his
wife, who had to take the matter in hand themselves, and
who met with opposition at every turn. To begin with there
was no peri! Fräulein Tuczek, who had been chosen for the part,
"apparently did not wish to sing it". Rungenhagen accordingly
called upon Madame Burkhardt, who expressed her willingness
to undertake it. All at once, however, Fräulein Tuczek declared
that she had never thought of not wanting to sing, she could
sing and she would sing. Upon this, they had to write to
Madame Burkhardt again, and break with her. Then Herr
Kraus, who had been chosen for the tenor part, suddenly refused to take it, and an amateur whom Rungenhagen suggested
as substitute, proved so absolutely impossible that Schumann
plainly declared that he would not conduct if he sang and
that the gentlemen of the *Singakademie* might manage the
affair by themselves. It was only with difficulty that Rungenhagen could induce him to hold a rehearsal for the band, but
as this orchestra, which was partly composed of amateurs
from the Philharmonic Society, played unexpectedly well,

Schumann eventually gave way. All this, however, was but
a little introduction to the symphony of hindrances which
now began. The diary may be allowed to speak here. "On
Sunday, the 14th, there was a full rehearsal in the *Singakademie*
at 11 o'clock. Rungenhagen presented Robert to the assembled company — Robert bowed silently — without speaking
to the company, which Mother says has never happened before. Frl. Tuczek came to the rehearsal and sang (after the
usual fashion of singers, she had never looked at the part
before) pleasantly and easily, — but Herr N. was dreadful, and
Herr Z. so rough that one would have liked to beat him. The
Contralto parts were well taken by Frl. Caspari, and Madame
Busse (née Fesca). The 'Jungfrau' (Frl. Z.) is not behind her
father in absence of feeling, and does him credit! — Robert
was very tired; the rehearsal lasted 3 hours — I sat at the
piano, to the great amazement of Rungenhagen and Grell, both
thoroughly good fellows but quite of the old school, who cling
to the past with iron resolution, and consequently found it
difficult to get used . . . . to Robert's work. Rungenhagen liked
the chorus of houris best, as was only natural.

On the afternoon of the 15th there was to have been another rehearsal. At 2 o'clock I was practising with Frl. Tuczek,
and she promised to be at the *Singakademie* at 5; instead of
coming, however, she sent word that she could not sing as
she had to go away. As if this were not enough, Herr
Kraus[1]) was waiting for us in the hall to say that he could
not sing as Küstner (the manager) would not permit it. This
was too much, and we should have been glad to have run
away from the whole thing! Robert was in the deepest depression. Madame Burkhardt would now have to sing the
peri without any rehearsal with the orchestra, this was dread-

---

1) Apparently he had expressed himself willing to sing, in the
mean time.

ful! Robert wanted to put off the performance, or not to conduct it, but the directors would not hear of postponing it. . . . Naturally the rehearsal (except for the choruses, which were good) went badly. Robert was quite exhausted, and hurt Grell's feelings dreadfully by scolding him for interfering — he kept on wanting to (prescribe) to Robert how, and from where, he ought to conduct; in like manner, one of the directors, Councillor H., pushed himself into everything, and wanted to give Robert good advice as to how he ought to stand when he was conducting; in short, everything combined to-day to make us absolutely miserable (for I have part in everything that affects Robert) — but Rungenhagen and Grell thought it all excellent."

The next day, the greater part of which Schumann spent in bed, half-ill with excitement, Clara dedicated to individual rehearsals with the peri and the bass. In the evening there was a another rehearsal for the chorus, at which Grell accompanied on the piano, but, according to Clara, so badly that she could not understand Robert's patience "in not chasing him from the instrument".

On the 17th the performance at last took place, after one more rehearsal of the quartet in the morning — there had not been one proper rehearsal of the whole. "It began at 6- 30," says Clara, "Robert lost all nervousness at sight of the beautiful orchestra with all its smartly dressed ladies, and stepped boldly to the desk. The King was there from beginning to end, and listened very attentively; the hall was quite full, and great attention was paid. Robert conducted very well (though afterwards some people blamed him — most unjustly[1]) — for conducting with too little energy — this had

---

1) Not so entirely unjustly! For, as far as I can see, it is a "reproach" which is made —loudly or softly — about Schumann's method of conducting by everyone without exception. Cf. Livia Frege's remarks upon the first rehearsal of the *Peri* in Leipsic, p. 352.

been spread abroad after the first rehearsal at which he was too out of heart to take any pleasure in being energetic, and when everybody were quite unknown to him). — The two first parts went well, except for Neumann who was dreadful, but the third part went badly, the three first soloists broke down entirely, so that Grell had to play the melody on the piano till they recovered themselves. I was in agonies and thought I should sink into the ground. What must it have been for the poor composer! In spite of the bad allotment of the parts the work was very much liked, and was mentioned very favourably in the papers, although some of them could not understand the recitatives being treated *arioso*.

For some time Schumann cherished the thought of repeating the performance with better forces, the only difficulty was to find them. Clara's old friend Pauline Viardot, who was then singing in the Berlin opera, and whom Clara next asked to sing the peri flatly refused. Willing as she was at any time to take part in a concert of Clara's, she had not time to study the part. Clara was bitterly disappointed; for although she had been forced to realise at their last meeting, that, without detriment so their old friendship, their musical interests and tastes were becoming more and more divided, (for Pauline considered Meyerbeer and Halévy the greatest dramatic composers — greater than Weber, Beethoven, and Mozart) —, yet she had believed that when once she had heard the *Peri* she could not help being charmed with the music; and instead of this she only mentioned the chorus in *B* minor, which is the least remarkable number in the work. "I saw once more," "Clara writes, "that she is not capable of understanding this tender German music."

With Viardot's refusal the whole plan collapsed, and all that happened was that she took part in two concerts which Clara gave at the *Singakademie* on March 1st and 17th. At both concerts Clara set herself to interpret Robert Schumann, as she had done in Vienna and in Prague. At the first she played the Bach *Prelude and Fugue*, Chopin's *Barcarole*, some little pieces of Mendelssohn's, and Schumann's quintet. At the second, in addition to playing Beethoven's *F* minor sonata, she repeated the quintet. The reason why she confined herself to the quintet, and played none of Schumann's other larger works, was very likely the difficulty of collecting performers to play with her, and above all of getting together an orchestra. She did play the $E\flat$ major quartet at a matinée in her own house on March 8th, at which Countess Rossi (Sontag), Fanny Hensel, Count Redern, and Geibel were amongst the audience. The critics received the pianist very warmly — though at times they thought her very serious, and almost too severe, as if she had steeped herself almost too much in Bach — but they maintained an attitude of chilly reserve towards Schumann's compositions.

In spite of this, rather to their suprise, they began to feel at home in a few days. Comparisons with Vienna continually forced themselves upon them, and without exception these were in favour of Berlin. "It seems quite odd," Clara writes, a few days after the performance of the *Peri*, "when one comes from Vienna to Berlin! How different people are here! grave, cold, but at the same time highly-cultured, as they are in scarcely any other part of Germany, they yet take a vivid interest in music, there is none of the slackness that there is in Vienna, but rather, an interest in good music; and journalism too, stands on a better footing here than in Vienna."

Robert received a similar impression of high intellectual culture in the scholarly and literary circles, an despecially at the *Montagsklub* (Monday-Club) into which he had been introduced by Prof. Lichtenstein, and where he was always certain to find a large circle "of distiguished people", "but here, in almost all educated circles, one is almost certain to meet one or two interesting people, and so hardly ever returns home empty, one has always listened to interesting talk, or has taken part in it oneself". "But here," Clara adds discreetly, "I am speaking, not of myself, but in Robert's name."

Most of all they enjoyed social intercourse in the musical houses of the Court book-seller, Decker, Prof. Wichmann and Prof. Lichtenstein, and Dr Frank. At Dr Frank's they met von Keudell, afterwards ambassador, "who means to take his law examinations here, but who is a musician, body and soul. He knows every work of importance, and almost everything of Robert's"[1].

At the old Bendemanns, the parents of their Dresden friends, they made acquaintance with old Schadow, of whom Clara says suggestively, "I believe that the more one knew him the better one would like him".

A musical matinée at the house of Countess Rossi brought them in contact with quite a different class of society. But although it was graced by the presence of hignesses of all sorts, the mistress of the house proved by far the most attractive and distinguished-person present. "Her singing delighted me more than any I have heard for a long time," writes Clara, "I have never heard so beautiful a pianissimo, and at the same time she sings naturally, with no hint of exaggeration; her voice still sounds very beautiful, and she herself looks charming; when she is singing her eyes, which have great attractiveness and sweetness gain a peculiar brightness. . . . I never listened to a singer more peacefully, whatever she sings gives one a sense of the most perfect satisfaction." Clara was still further exalted on the plane of civic, or rather noble

---

1) In the middle of February 1849 Clara writes: "A few days ago we spent an evening with Baron von Keudell, and Robert and I played the arrangement of the C major symphony which we had just received, and which greatly interested young Herr Keudell. It is a pity that he does not always live here, as he is a person with whom it is easy to hold musical intercourse, and he appeals to Robert in every respect and especially as an companion."

rank, by an invitation to a soirée given by her old friend and patron Count Redern: "All the best society was there, in cluding the King, the Princess of Prussia, the Duke of Meck-lenburg etc.," writes Clara. "I met the Frl. von Arnims, and clung to them, for I did not feel quite comfortable among all this exalted company, and I did not want associate with the artists who were kept waiting in the next room until their turn came. I felt indignant with them as well as with Count Redern, whose arrangement it must have been. I played, and then went back to the rest of company, where Robert was. Dreyschock played a piece of his own, called *Inquiétude*, for which he deserved to have his ears boxed! It was unspeak-ably bad. A great deal of bad stuff was sung . . . . And so we went away early, before the music was over."

It was in the houses of Mendelssohn's two brothers-in-law, Dirichlet and Hensel that she felt most at home. "They are all so kind to me here, that I have but one thing to say of them all," Clara writes after a little luncheon-party at the Dirichlets, at which the Hensels and Jacobi, the mathematician, had been present, and at which, to their great surprise, their host had proposed their health — "in beautiful language, though a little difficult to understand" — with special reference to the *Peri*. But the chief attraction to both the Schumanns, was to be found at the Hensel's house in the person of Fanny Hensel. "I have taken a great fancy to Madame Hensel," runs the entry for March 15th, "and feel especially attracted to her in regard to music, we almost always harmonize with each other, and her conversation is always interesting, only one has to accustom oneself to her rather brusque manner." She admired her as a pianist too, though not as a composer, "Wo-men always betray themselves in their compositions, and this is true of myself as well as of others."

The Schumanns had one peculiarity which manifested itself on almost all their journies. Whenever a place pleased them for any reason, they seriously debated the possibility of settling there. Even in Moscow this question had arisen. It is comprehensible, because they felt themselves so out of place in Dresden, but as a rule these projects lasted only for a day. When, however, under the influence of all these pleasant impressions, they began to discuss the possibility of migrating to Berlin, there were serious reasons behind, and the thought that by so doing they would establish permanent relations with Fanny Hensel was frankly of great weight. It is by no mere chance that in the diary this project is mentioned immediately after the passage about Fanny Hensel, which has just been quoted. "All our acquaintances advise us to settle down here, Robert would be certain to find a sphere of work in time, and I should get many pupils at a high price. We have a great wish to, and now that we have got to know Berlin we have lost all desire for Vienna. In Vienna one would always be afraid of ending by floating about on the surface with the others, without even knowing it."

And if eventually this plan, which seemed so promising, came to nothing, not the least of the causes which brought this about was the death of Fanny Hensel in May 1847. "I was very much upset by this news," Clara writes on May 18th, "for I had a great respect for this remarkable woman, and should much have enjoyed getting to know her better (in Berlin)."

They had at first thought of going through the cities of Silesia immediately after their visit to Berlin, but their longing for rest and their longing for their children — who were all left at home this time — became so overpowering that on the day of the last concert they suddenly decided to give up all other plans and to return to Dresden as speedily as possible. On March 24th the travellers — rich, not in material treasures, but in pleasant memories — left Berlin. They passed through Leipsic, where they had a glimpse of their friends, and among them of Mendelssohn — without any foreboding that it was the last time they would see him[1] —, and on the evening of the 25th they arrived safely back in Dresden, where they found all the children well except the youngest, the end of whose sufferings was slowly approaching.

"Happy as I was to be with the children again," Clara writes, "yet the sudden quiet, after so active a life, was unpleasant for the first few days, but I soon became used to it, and began to arrange Robert's last (C major) symphony for four hands[2]. This occupation soon made me feel at home, although I was twice as conscious as before that I have no intimate friend here, with whom it is possible to speak frankly. People keep at a certain distance from each other, they hardly see each other once a month — I should not like to pass another winter here!

It was so pleasant in Berlin to have my Mother, who sympathised with everything, who rejoiced with me, and at the same time was so fond of Robert that she could well understand my love for him. It is not that I do not love my Robert and the children above all things, but with a woman-friend one can talk about many things which one cannot discuss with one's husband or one's children, and besides my children are still so young."

It is easy to see from these words how deeply the idea of migrating to Berlin had taken root in her mind, and also how severely she — who among her other gifts possessed to a marked degree that of cherishing and preserving friendship — suffered from her loneliness in Dresden. It is not surprising that from this point of view, and with the vivid memory of those weeks in Berlin and of the good friends there fresh

1) In the margin of the diary, beside Mendelssohn's name, is written in pencil, in Robert's hand: "The morning of Thursday March 25th for the last time."

2) Between March 31st and April 12th.

in her mind Dresden friends — who did after all exist — should
have been a little underrated. Friendship with the Bendemanns for example, and especially with Frau B., developed
slowly. It is all the more easy to understand, what Schröder-
Devrient's return to Dresden in the following year must have
meant to her.

During the next few months her life took its colour and
meaning more than ever from the personality and work of
her husband. It was for him she had finished her work at
the *C* major symphony, that she arranged the *Faust-Szenen*
(*Scenes from Faust*), between Ap. 27th and May 3rd, for him
that at the end of May she began to work at the first movement of a concertino in *F* minor, by way of a birthday present
for him — a work which she found very difficult, but for which
she was afterwards rewarded by Robert's approval, "who liked
some things in it very much." But the greatest pleasure at
this time was that for the first time for 3 years he celebrated
his birthday in good health. And the radiance which the sight
of his delight in his work threw upon their path, shone with
healing power even into the shadow of death through which
they had to pass, when at the end of June little Emil's sufferings ended. She found her own art almost a burden this
summer. "I am lazy" she writes at the end of July, "but I
cannot help it, for I am never well, and am dreadfully weak.
Ah! if only I could work! That is my one trouble."

Schumann however, although he |had repeatedly suffered
from the effects of his illness both, at Vienna and at Prague,
seemed all at once to have received new life, and was fired
and possessed by a passionate delight in creating. In Berlin
he had already begun to busy himself with plans for an opera,
in the second half of March. And directly after their return
the diary notes on March 27th: "Robert is busy looking for
the libretto for an opera; he has just been reading *Mazeppa*
(from the Polish), and he likes it in parts." He had chosen

Reinick to write the libretto, and he talked it over with him on March 31st. "They came to an agreement, and Robert gave him *Maxeppa* to look through."

But a few days later another subject bore the palm from *Maxeppa*. "On April 4th," writes Clara, "Robert went to Reinick and took him another book, *Genoveva*, by Hebbel. It is a good subject for an opera, and we both decided on it at once."

We shall have to speak of *Genoveva* in detail later on, and of the time which Schumann and Reinick devoted to it during the summer months. Here, it is enough to say that it was the means of making Schumann study Hebbel's other poems, and thus of bringing about their acquaintance. It is characteristic of Robert's æsthetic development in poetry as in music that he should have become so possessed by Hebbel, a poet whose work stood in the sharpest contrast to that of Jean Paul, the idol of Schumann's youth. He was learning to appreciate austere strength and tragic greatness, and even to be capable of preferring these qualities to all others. He insisted on Clara's reading *Judith* immediately, and by the middle of May he had already endeavoured to establish personal relations with Hebbel. With touching modesty[1]) he thinks it necessary to explain to the poet his interest in *Genoveva*, adding in parenthesis — "I am a musician." — An entry in his note-book — intended for no eye but his own — made shortly after meeting Hebbel in the summer of 1847 shows what he imagined he had found in him and how he looked up to him: "A great honour has befallen our house — Fr. Hebbel came to see us on his way through. He is certainly the most gifted man of our day. His whole personality is striking. If he does not over-strain his powers he will attain the highest and his name will be enrolled among the immortal artists of all ages."

---

1) *Briefe* new series 2nd ed. No. 300 (May 14th 1847) p. 267 etc.

The work of those spring months resulted first of all in the finale of *Faust*, which was finished between the 18th and the 25th of April[1]), and in the course of the summer in the new *D* minor trio. On June 13rd Clara writes, "Robert is very busy just now, writing a piano trio[2]) which is to be published in the same opus with the first; I am glad that he is once more turning his thoughts to the piano. He himself seems to be very satisfied with his work." On June 16th the sketch was finished, and on Sept. 13rd Robert surprised Clara with the completed trio, which was played on the same evening by Clara, Konzertmeister Schubert, and Kummer; and in the following months was twice repeated in private house (the first time at a party at the Bendemanns'). The first public performance, however, did not take place before January 1849. "It sounds," Clara thinks, "as if it were by one from whom much is to be expected, it has such youthful strength and force, and yet at the same time the execution is so masterly. . . . The first movement is to my mind one of the most beautiful that I know." But for this, this summer appears to have produced only the *Lied beim Abschied zu singen*[3]) (*Song to be sung at parting*) by Feuchtersleben, for chorus accompanied by 2 flutes, 2 oboes, 2 clarinets, 2 bassoons, 2 horns, which, the diary tells us, Schumann composed for his native city, Zwickau, (whither they went on July 2nd for a performance of the *C* major symphony).

This visit to Zwickau, which lasted nearly a fortnight, proved to be almost an ovation offered by Schumann's native town to her great son, and it left the pleasantest and most inspi-

---

1) But at the end of July the final chorus was completely re-written, as he was dissatisfied with the first conception.

2) The *Fantasiestücke f. Pianoforte, Violin, und Violoncello* is meant, Op. 88, which dates from 1848 (cf. p. 348) and which Schumann had originally described as a trio. The *D* minor trio has the opus number 63.

3) Dated June 21st Op. 88 in the MS.

riting impressions on both of them. It was a sort of family festival on a large scale, with all the intimate and affectionate character of a festival of this kind, only in this case the family consisted of all the lovers of music in the town. Grave and gay, high and low, all met together in the most friendly manner, for everything came from happy and grateful hearts, and each one gave of his best.

They found comfortable quarters in the house of Stadtrat Oberländer, an old acquaintance of Schumann's (afterwards Minister). One evening they were serenaded by an orchestra and chorus; Dr Klütsch had set to music a delightful poem, appropriate to the occasion, and round the garden, in the evening light, stood hundreds of Zwickau-ers, old and young, enjoying themselves. And not one of them enjoyed himself more than old Kuntzsch, Schumann's former master, who handed him the text of the work, beaming with joy, and, as the diary says, went about for the next few weeks "swelling with pride" over his former pupil. When they went to the Church-yard on the following morning, they found a beautiful orange-tree standing on the grave of Schumann's father. And while Robert was holding his rehearsals — in which good-will prevented slender powers from ever jarring — Clara wandered about among the houses where Robert had gone in and out as a boy and a youth, and occasionally paid a visit to "one of Robert's old flames". On July 10th the concert took place in the midst of the most dreadful heat, but all went radiantly well. "When Robert went to his conductor's desk and I went to my stool, we found them beautifully decorated, and so was the platform on which the piano stood, and a lovely bouquet was on the piano itself. Robert conducted with greater energy than I ever witnessed in him before, and so the symphony went very well." Clara played the A minor concerto that evening, and at the end some little things. I have already mentioned what an effect the symphony had upon

Clara in this room, in these surroundings, and how through it she first became fully conscious of the height Robert's creative power had reached.

On the following Sunday there was a sort of pendant to Faust's Easter walk. In the afternoon all the world went to the *Burgkeller* where there was a concert, and thousands assembled for "a regular people's festival". As the Schumanns crossed the bridge they were greeted by a thrice repeated flourish of trumpets and loud cheers, while on every side hands were thrust out towards them by old and new acquaintances, and old flames of Robert's, and the daughters of old flames, came forward, so that, as Clara says, there was no end to his surprise. In one word, it was a day of unmixed festivity, on which the sun shone brightly from beginning to end.

All the harsher sounded the discord with which the winter began.

During the first weeks of November, Gade brought news from Leipsic of Mendelssohn's serious illness, "his mind wanders, without there being any fever, so that the doctors do not know what to make of it. . . . They are very anxious about him in Leipsic, but we hope that it may pass over", says the diary for Nov. 1st. But the following entry shows that their worst fears were confirmed: "Friday, the 5th, I was at the Bendemanns', and to my great alarm heard that Mendelssohn had had a stroke, and that there was little hope of his recovery; we thought that things had probably been exaggerated, but shortly after came a letter from Reuter in Leipsic, telling us that Mendelssohn had passed quietly away on Thursday the 4th, at 5 minutes past 9 in the evening. He died from the effects of three strokes which came one after another in the course of a fortnight, just as happened with his sister Fanny — it is as if his sister had drawn him after her, for he himself said to his family, 'I shall die like Fanny', and this seems to have become a fixed idea with him . . . . Our grief is great, for he was dear to us, not only as an artist, but as a man and a friend! His death is an irreparable loss for all those who knew and loved him. . . . A thousand cherished memories rise, and one feels tempted to exclaim, 'Why has heaven done this?' But it has taken him from earth in the full splendour of his powers, in the flower of his age . . . . as an artist he stands at the highest summit of his fame — is it not happiness to die thus? If only we could have seen him once more! We saw him last on March 25th, and the last time he conducted in the hall of the *Gewandhaus* was at my concert on Nov. 16th last year, when I played his *G* minor concerto. If I tried to part into words everything that one loved in him, and of his, I should never make an end. I feel that our grief for him will last all our lives."

The days that follow are still wholly under the influence of this grievous loss. The entries in the diary reflect this feeling most vividly.

Saturday 6th, Robert went to the funeral at Leipsic. Bendemann and Rietschel had both gone early in order to sketch and model Mendelssohn's face. How painful for Robert! I cannot get over it at all, a feeling of the deepest sadness oppresses my heart. In the evening my Mother came with Marie and Cäcilie — but nothing could rouse me out of my depression. Marie stayed with me for the night.

Sunday 7th. It is a beautiful morning! I think incessantly of my dear Robert; how prostrated he will be by all this sadness! How I want him, now when my heart is so full! — I am only partly alive when I have not got him — God preserve my highest happiness for me!

In the afternoon I went with the children to Frau Bendemann's, where of course we spoke of nothing but Mendelssohn. In the evening I went — induced by Hiller's request — to the rehearsal of the oratorio, *The Destruction of Jerusalem*, but

I enjoyed it but little — the music only made me more low-spirited! — After the rehearsal I went to Hiller's for a little while, really in order to shake off something of my depression. But Hiller's whole tone jarred upon me horribly. . . . It all seemed to me so dreadfully material in comparison with what was moving my heart so profoundly. Rietschel was there too and he saw me home afterwards.

Monday 8th. Robert came . . . . back.

Not only had this sudden "home-going" of his friend come upon Robert as an irreparable loss, but the appearance of death in this form had shocked him to the very soul. The thought that a similar end awaited him never left him from this time on, and at times of excitement became a fixed idea.

Another loss, which was indeed less painful and was not for ever, but which nevertheless made life somewhat the poorer, followed immediately: Hiller left Dresden. He received a call to become director of music at Düsseldorf. Two days after the funeral ceremony of Mendelssohn, came the farewell dinner to Hiller on the *Brühlsche Terrasse*. "What a mixture of feelings!" writes Clara. "In spite of all their sorrow Mendelssohn's friends could not possibly stay away. . . . The company is said to have been cheerful, Robert says that Devrient, in proposing Hiller's health, made the best speech that he ever remembers. . . . Robert was toasted also, and was greeted as Liedermeister (conducter) of the *Liedertafel* (men's choral society), a position which Hiller had held before him."

This inheritance from Hiller was not without influence upon his work. He composed a chorus for male voices, to words of Rückert's, for the very first evening on which he entered upon his official duties, and a number of other compositions for male voices followed before the end of the year — "Rückert's *Ritornelle* in canon form for men's voices in several parts" [1]), and "Three Songs for Male Chorus" [2]) (Eichen-dorff's *Der Eidgenossen Nachtwache*, Rückert's *Freiheitslied*, and Klopstock's *Schlachtgesang*) with which Robert himself was well satisfied. But these occasional pieces, flung off at odd moments, were not the sole results of the year's work.

On Oct. 26th the diary had announced, "Robert finished the sketch for his 3rd piano trio [3]), and he is now copying out the two last movements. He has already written down the two first, which I like extremely but which are quite different in character from the first movement of the second (first) trio." It afterwards became one of her favourite pieces. "It belongs," she writes in April 1849, "to the pieces of Robert's which warm and delight my whole heart, from beginning to end. I love it passionately, and should like to play it again and again!"

But the greatest surprise and pleasure of this year came on Christmas Eve when Robert presented her with the overture to *Genoveva*, ready scored, which he had sketched, without Clara's suspecting it, in the spring, between the 1st and the 5th of April, immediately after finally deciding on this subject. And between Christmas und the New Year he began to work at the first act with keen delight.

Clara too, although her health continued to leave much to be desired, towards the end of the summer of 1847, had started on a course of renewed activity which was obviously not uninfluenced by the composition of Robert's trios, and the desire to be able to play them as soon as possible. From September onwards she played regularly to herself, and from October she studied trios with the Schuberts regularly, on a fixed day

---

1) Op. 65. Composed at the end of November.

2) Op. 62. According to the MS. 2 and 3 were composed on Dec. 6th and 1st on Dec. 9th.

3) It was the 2nd. Op. 80. Cf. note 2 p. 434. According to the MS.: Dresden, August—October 1847.

every week. It was a particular satisfaction and pleasure to her that more and more pupils of all classes wanted to take lessons from her. "This week," she writes on Dec. 11th, "I have been fairly industrious! I gave two lessons nearly every day . . . . it is a very pleasant feeling to earn something daily."

One can understand therefore, how, among these impressions and in face of the alteration of circumstances in Berlin, which had taken place since her return, the thought of migrating retired more and more into the background.

When in December she received news of the death of another friend, whose acquaintance she had made only last spring, she wrote: "For me Berlin is now entirely without attraction (except for my Mother). Fanny Hensel dead, Marie Lichtenstein gone, and now this dear, kind woman dead too. — I think that we shall end by not going there at all, but shall stay here. Robert is now flinging himself heart and soul into the formation of a society for a mixed chorus, the chief object of which is to study new works of importance, and songs. He has christened it the *Cäcilienverein* (Society of St Cecilia). To-morrow the invitations go out; I hope many people will join, for there is so little opportunity for practising music of this sort, since the *Singakademie* performs only sacred music. I shall be very glad if Robert creates a pleasant sphere of activity for himself by this means, and one of this sort would suit him."

By the end of the year, the new society — which in the mean time, as a *Cäcilienverein* was already in existence, had called itself the "Society for Chorus-singing" — numbered 110 members. And to make the end altogether good, on Dec. 31st came news from New York that the American *Musical Institute* was preparing for a performance of the *Peri*. "It is being studied with the greatest care," says the diary, "and has awakened the livliest interest in all those who are taking

part in it. The great beauty of the work cannot fail to make
it a brilliant success." The old year ended with these happy
prospects, and on New Year's Eve Clara played Robert the
whole of the *Faust* music from her own arrangement for
the piano.

Its successor began no less promisingly.

On Jan. 5th was held the first practice of the new Choral
Society: about 40 or 50 singers were assembled. Robert opened
with a little speech, which must really have been very little,
for Clara herself writes: "Robert's address might well have
been somewhat longer." "But," she adds, "he has always
understood how to say much in a few words, and he did so
now." They began with a Bach choral; and some solfeggi for
the whole chorus, "which interested them all very much," and
some songs of Mendelssohn's and Hauptmann's, provided rich
material for the first practice. "Robert had been feeling very
unwell to-day," Clara writes, "but all this suddenly disappeared, and he became quite cheerful and contented; I
too, for all day I had been suffering from stage-fright."

During the next few months the society, which soon grew
to have 70 members, claimed more attention than Schumann
always found desirable, but at the same time it often brought
a distraction from gloomy thoughts and a change of work which
were all the more welcome on account of the fluctuations in
Schumann's health. For during these months and those which
followed (till August) he was working hard at *Genoveva*.

"On Jan. 3rd," writes Clara, "Robert finished the sketch of
the first act of *Genoveva*[1] .... but it never leaves his thoughts,
day or night, which cannot but affect his nerves."

---

1) Robert's notes on the MS. give the following dates for the sketches:
Overture sketched Dresden 1st—5th April 1847

Act I	„	„	26th Dec.—3rd Jan. 1848
Act II	„	„	31st Jan.—4th Feb.
Act III	„	„	24th Ap.—3rd May
Act IV	„	„	15th—27th June.

On Jan. 10th the diary announces that he has been scoring the first act for the last two days. "He says that no work has ever given him such pleasure." On Jan. 23rd this was accomplished. But then, as has been said, this over-stain revenged itself, and grave symptoms of over-excitement compelled him to pause for some weeks. Even after the work had been taken up again, on Feb. 27th, it was necessary to break off more than once, till at last on Aug. 4th the finishing touch could be given.

For Clara, life during the early months of 1848 was chiefly passed in household duties and cares. On Jan. 20th Ludwig was born, and almost at the same time, Robert collapsed under his work at *Genoveva*. She worked her way bravely through these hindrances and shadows, and when she had overcome the uncertainty resulting from her long, compulsory rest, she took pleasure in the exercise of her art. At the first performance given by the Choral Society on March 26th, she reappeared in public for the first time, playing Bach's *A* minor organ fugue, and accompanying the performance of Gade's *Comala*, on the piano. And if, in spite of ample applause, she was not wholly satisfied with herself on this occasion, the last of the *Gewandhaus* concerts, on Ap. 6th, at which she played Robert's *A* minor concerto amidst enthusiastic applause, gave proof that she was once more able to interpret works of the highest genius, and above all those which Robert's muse set before her, a proof which was further supported by her performance of the *D* minor trio (with David and Grabau) at a large party at Härtel's on the following evening.

"At this concert," she writes after the *Gewandhaus* concert where she had the melancholy satisfaction, of playing as encore the *Frühlingslied* which Mendelssohn had dedicated to her, "one might have thought that Germany was more peaceful than ever, the audience was so enthusiastic. After Härtel's soirée, however, she writes: "It was a very pleasant party, but at present there can be no entirely comfortable meetings, those fatal politics always pursue one."

And during the summer months that followed, these wretched politics brought gloom and discord into the quiet, cheerful, artistic life of the Schumanns' house, in which Clara, with ever increasing delight in its beauties, was devoting her chief strength to the piano score of the growing *Genoveva*. They even force their way into the crevices of the diary. Clara begins to make political comments as to the necessity of establishing the freedom of the press, and of dismissing the detested ministry from office: "Everybody is reading the papers just now, and God knows what is still to come. In Lombardy the outlook is dreadful, and it is the same in Switzerland, in Vienna Metternich has resigned — it would take volumes if one were to write down all the things which have been stirring the world for the last 3 months." And now came alarming news from Berlin. "On the evening of March 13th the most dreadful news came from Berlin, the King will not give way, and the citizens are fighting horribly with the soldiers." "Over 1000 people are said to have been killed," she writes on the 22nd: "What things a King has on his conscience!" Excited explanations concerning Prussia and its politics followed, and vehement differences of opinion among friends. In April 1848 the slowness of Prussia in the Schleswig-Holstein affair led to a discussion between Bendemann and Robert, "which was not unlike a quarrel". And the women also disagreed among themselves. Clara carried on a vehement quarrel with a lady from Berlin — whom she also disliked in other respects — and concludes: "It is sad to see how few really liberal minded people there are in the educated classes." And a day later: "I went to see Madame Hübner, but I had a regular quarrel with her — and (is it credible?) over politics!" A couple of days later, at a party at Hübner's, "she is very depressed,

and all on account of politics. None of these people are in
the least liberal minded."

Even the sanctuary of art itself was invaded by the flood
of political feeling. A performance of *Egmont*, for example,
which usually awoke nothing but enthusiasm for Gœthe's poem
and Beethoven's music, was now looked upon as having a
political tendency, with reference to the struggles of the present
moment: "The subject of this work applies so directly to our
own time." In March 1848 she writes: "Poland and Russia
are said to be at war! How glad I should be if Poland were
to free herself again!" And when on May 23rd 1848 a musical
and dramatic matinée was given in the hall of the *Hôtel de
Saxe*, announced, somewhat mysteriously, on the bill, as being.
"For charity", we find among those who took part in it, beside
the names of Johanna Wagner, Eduard Devrient, and Fräulein Böger, Frau Clara Schumann appearing with a *Nocturne*
of Chopin's and "two *Lieder ohne Worte*". The concert opened
and closed with solos on the 'cello and — the guitar — by
Herr Szezepanowski, which was most fitting since the "charity"
was the unfortunate Poles. "It was very well attended," declares the diary, "almost entirely by Poles. There was great
applause, good or bad — it was all one!" The next day some
Polish ladies sent a charming flower-table, as a mark of gratitude. Wholly unpolitical, however, — though it was brought
about by the distress at the time — was a charity-matinée
which was got up by Konzertmeister Schubert a week later,
"in aid of the poor Saxon inhabitants of the Erzgebirge", and
at which Clara and the two Schuberts played Beethoven's
B♭ major trio. She also played Mozart's *Variations* for four
hands with her sister, Marie Wieck.

Greatly, however, as politics influenced her trend of thought
and her relations to the outer world, her own quiet, artistic
work remained entirely unaffected by them. The piano-score
of *Genoveva*, the ever-increasing number of pupils, preparation

for Robert's Choral Society, and occasionally acting as his deputy, occupy the foreground. And though at the end of May she complains: "Unfortunately I play but little now, for I have no time. As to composing — I never do any at all," the fact that she caused Robert to be awakened on June the 8th by the sound of four part-songs "which I had composed for the purpose", shows that she knew how to find time for her own personal work. And with the beginning of the winter (1848/9) everything that she had been obliged to leave unfinished during the past year, was once more taken up with renewed energy in spite of the fact that once more — and this time to her great distress — her physical condition began to make it necessary for her to be careful.

The year closed under cheerful auspices. For the first time they could feel that even on this barren and inhospitable soil a rich and fair harvest might ripen in time. The work of these 4 years seemed, after all, not to have been wholly in vain. "We can neither of us be thankful enough," writes Clara on New Year's Eve, "for all the good things and the happiness which heaven has granted us this year."

Once more, at this time and during the months which follow, she breaks forth into expressions of wonder and delight at Robert's inexhaustibility and many-sidedness, and in view of what was taking place before her very eyes every expression seems inadequate. Immediately after the completetion of *Genoveva*, he set to work at a new composition. "On Aug. 4th," says the diary, "Robert ended his opera. But he at once began a new work, a sort of melodrama, Byron's *Manfred*, which has inspired him in the most amazing way. He read it to me, and it took hold of me extraordinarily . . . . Robert has arranged the poem according to his own ideas, in order to make it possible for the stage, and he is going to begin setting it as soon as ever he has finished the numerous other things which are waiting to be done by him.

The chief of these (hindrances) were the arrangement for four hands of the *C* major symphony, "a work which he found very dull", and which he began on Aug. 26th, and the *Kinderstücke*, the first of which he gave to Marie on her 7th birthday. "The pieces which children usually learn at their music-lessons are so bad, that Robert hit on the idea of composing and publishing a volume (a sort of album) of children's pieces. He has already written a number of charming little pieces," writes Clara on Sept. 1st. The reference is to the collection which appeared under the title: *40 Piano Pieces for the young* (Op. 68), with a frontispiece by Ludwig Richter, and which according to Schumann's notes came into existence between Aug. 30th and Sept. 14th 1848.

In the second week in November, we first hear once more of hard work at *Manfred*. "His overture, which is finished already, seems to me one of Robert's most poetic and perhaps his most moving works," Clara writes on Nov. 4th; and on Nov. 14th, "Robert brought a small bottle of champagne home with him, in honour of the birthday of the first part of his *Manfred*, which he finished to-day. She had to share in the birthday festivities without as yet knowing the birthday child, but she did not long remain in uncertainty, for on the 22nd Robert played her the first part," which must have a magnificent effect upon the stage and with the orchestra — apparently the scoring is of quite an original kind!" Immediately after this came the *Adventlied* [1] (Advent Hymn), the *Kirchenstück auf einen Rückertschen Text* (Sacred piece with words by Rückert) as Clara calls it, "6 charming pieces for 4 hands" [2], with which Robert surprised Clara at Christmas.

---

1) Op. 71. According to the MS.: "Sketched Nov. 25th—30th 1848. Scored Dec. 3rd—19th."

2) *Bilder aus Osten* ("Pictures from the East") *6 Impromptus* Op. 66. According to the MS., "Composed in December 1848".

1849 brought a further advance. Indeed, with regard both to wealth of invention and inexhaustible variety of form, it marks the summit of Schumann's creative power.

The passage from the old year to the new was marked by the *Waldszenen* ("Forest Scenes") [1], and these were followed in February by three connected pieces for piano and clarinet [2], which by Feb. 18th Clara had already tried through with Kroth, the clarinet-player, to her great pleasure. The fascination of trying the effect of the piano with other instruments drew from him, immediately afterwards, an *adagio* and *allegro* for piano [2] and horn, which Clara tried over with the horn-player Schitterlau, on March 2nd, "with real satisfaction". "It is a magnificent piece, fresh, and passionate; just what I like!"

"All the instruments are having a turn," Clara had written just after this was finished. But it was the effect of the horn which enticed him to make further experiments, and the result was a concerted piece for 4 horns [3], which was completed on March 11st. On the 13rd, the diary speaks with surprise of a new phase of development. "Robert is now composing *Romances* and *Ballades* for a mixed chorus [4], a *genre* in which as yet nothing has been written .... what a lucky fellow he is! what a glorious feeling it must be to have such an inexhaustible imagination, and to be perpetually being carried on to higher and higher planes!" Three days later, this too

---

1) *Waldszenen* 9 piano-pieces dedicated to Frau Annette Preusser. Op. 82. According to the MS.: "Dresden Dec. 29th 1848—Jan. 6th 1849. Not mentioned in the diary."

2) *Phantasiestücke* for piano and clarinet. Op. 73. "Sketched, Dresden Feb. 11th—12th 1849."

3) *Konzertstück für 4 Hörner und grosses Orchestra* Op. 86. "Sketched, Dresden Feb. 18th—20th 1849."

4) *Romanzen und Balladen für Chor* Vol. I. Op. 67 (*König in Thule. Schön-Rothraut, Heidenröslein. Ungewitter. John Anderson*) "Dresden, March 1849". Vol. II. Op. 75 (*Schnitter Tod. Im Walde. Der traurige Jäger. Der Rekrut. Vom verwundeten Knaben.* "Dresden, March 1849").

was finished. "On March 16th Robert finished his *Ballades* and *Romances* for chorus, 12 in number[1]). Most of them are of the nature of folk-songs, some Scottish in character, which must have a charming effect as a chorus." Immediately after these came the *Romances* for female chorus.

A few days later, fresh works forced their way to light. "On March 29th," says the diary, "Robert finished the sketch of a Spanish cycle of songs for 4 voices[2]) — a sort of little love-story! — 'The first meeting'; 'Longing'; 'Despair'; 'Meeting again'; and 'Union'. It is a piece of quite an original kind, with piano accompaniment, and the 4 voices having in turns songs, duets, and quartets . . . . Robert has not yet played any of it to me, he has only told me what is the idea of it. I am most impatient for it." At the beginning of April we find him busy polishing the two trios, but already on Ap. 19th he played Clara "his new pieces for piano and violoncello"[3]). "These pieces are of the nature of folk-tunes, and have a freshness and originality which delighted me," she remarks.

That he now rested from work for a month was due, not as had been the case earlier, to physical exhaustion which made a pause absolutely necessary, but to external circumstances — chief among which was the sudden death of his brother Karl, — which affected him profoundly. "With the deepest sorrow," writes Clara, "I realise that I and the children are now all that he has, may heaven grant that I may long be able to give him the support of my love, and make up to him for what he has lost."

---

1) In addition to the 10 songs included in Op. 67 and 75, the **MS.** contains, *Das Schifflein*, by Uhland, *Willie*, by Burns.

2) *Spanisches Liederspiel.* "A cycle of songs from the Spanish, for one and more voices, with piano accompaniment. Op. 74." "Sketched March 24th—28th 1849".

3) "Five pieces after the manner of folk-songs, for violoncello and diano. Op. 102." "Dresden, Ap. 13th—15th 1849."

But political events disturbed his repose both of body and mind, even more profoundly than the grief awakened by this loss; a grief which Clara successfully endeavoured to soften and distract by plunging at once into the study of the Spanish cycle. This cycle was performed, together with the *F* major trio, at a matinée on the 29th. The political situation in Dresden in May, came like a sudden flash of lightning from a clear sky, and startled them out of the deepest peace. The diary says, in speaking of this:

"Thursday the 3rd, we went to dine at the villa in the *Plauenschen Grunde* and revelled in the exquisite scenery — we little guessed what was happening in the city at that moment. We had hardly been at home for half-an-hour, when the drums sounded a general alarm, bells rang from every tower, and soon we heard firing. The King had refused to recognise the imperial constitution before Prussia had done so, and they had taken out the poles of his carriage — in which he meant to flee — and so compelled him to remain; they had also attempted to gain possession of the arsenal, from which, however, the crowd had been fired upon. It can easily be imagined that this aroused the greatest bitterness. The night passed fairly quietly, but on Friday, the 4th, we found all the streets barricaded when we went into the city, and on the barricades stood men armed with scythes, and republicans who made them keep on building the barricades higher. The utmost lawlessness prevailed everywhere, hatches and paving-stones were torn up as well as the stones from the streets and were turned into barricades. In the town-hall the democrats were gathered together, and they chose a provisional government (the King had fled to Königstein during the night) which issued various proclamations concerning the soldiers, who were encamped with cannon in front of the castle and in *Neustadt*.

As we walked through the city we saw the terrible sight of 14 dead bodies, men who had fallen the day before and now lay in dreadful array in the court of the hospital, a spectacle for the people. I could not forget this sight for a long time, and only the great tumult which was yet to follow obliterated the terrible impression. That day and the following night passed without fighting, the barricades grew into regular fortresses, the tension was dreadful; how would it all end? in what spilling of blood!

Saturday 5th: a terrible morning! A guard of safety formed itself in our street, and they wanted Robert to join. After I had twice denied that he was in, they threatened to search for him; we escaped with Marie, by the garden door, to the Bohemian Station. Here we met Oberländer, amongst other people, who wanted to go to the King at Königstein in order to make one more effort for concession. Here stood men with scythes, who gave warning that no-one would be allowed to depart armed. At 1 o'clock we went as far as Mügeln. — I was very distressed that we had not at least taken Elise with us, but we went off as best we could, and had no time to take the children with us; besides Robert thought we should be back by the evening, though I did not believe it, especially as shortly before we left they began to storm the city and to fight.

From Mügeln we went on foot to Dohna, there we ate, and waited for news by the next train, which brought nothing comforting, and at 7 o'clock we went to Maxen[1]), where we found a fair number of people. . . .

My anxiety all day was frightful, for continually one could hear the thunder of the cannon, and my children were in the city. In the evening I wanted to go into the city and fetch them, but it was too late, and I found no-one who would accompany me so late. Robert could not come with me, for it was reported that the insurgents were searching the neigh-

---

1) Major Serre's estate.

bourhood for all men capable of bearing arms, and were com-
pelling them to take part in the battle. On Monday, 7th, I
went to the city at 3 in the morning, accompanied by the
daughter of the estate-agent. Frau von Berg also went with
us. It was a terrible drive. I was anxious lest I should never
come out of the city again! I did not think that I should
return that self-same way, to-day. We drove to Strehla,
and there Frau von Berg went her way, and we went ours
across the field to the Reitbahngasse. We entered amidst
the continuous thunder of the cannon, and suddenly we saw
40 men with scythes coming towards us. At first we did
not know what to do, but we plucked up heart and went
quietly through (and with us a man whom we had met in
the field).

We arrived safely in Reitbahngasse, where the doors of all
the houses were shut. — It was horrible! Dead silence here;
in the city incessant firing. — I found the children still asleep,
tore them at once from their beds, had them dressed, put together a few necessaries, and in an hour we were once
more together in the field outside. Henriette, who was ill
when I left, I found still suffering, she lay quietly in one place
and took no notice of anything. This made me very anxious,
especially just now when I needed her so much. — In Strehla
we got into the carriage again, and before dinner we were
back in Maxen, where at last we were all re-united once more;
my poor Robert had been spending anxious hours, and was
therefore doubly happy now. — In all the villages we had met
fugitives who told us dreadful things about what was going on
in the city. The people are behaving splendidly, I should never
have expected such courage of the Saxons. Reinforcements
pour into the town incessantly, and in particular a large number of people have come from the Erzgebirge. But the soldiers
also continually receive fresh contingents from Prussia, which
exasperates the people to the highest pitch.

Tuesday 8th, passed without anything decisive. The battle
in the city continues without interruption. I have taken the
nurse and 3 children to the doctor with whom we stayed
3 years ago, so that we may not all be a burden on the
Major. Amongst others Herr von Albedyll and his wife and
daughter, and Frau von Hann, who live close to us in the
city, were there, and so was the von Stephanitz family.

All these were aristocrats who spoke of the people merely
as *canaille* and rabble, till it made one quite uncomfortable —
the Major is the only liberal minded person in the whole house,
and he sometimes tells the aristocrats roundly just what he
thinks!

At 11 p.m. Mathilde (our cook) came from the city — a
good and most useful girl, who has been of real service to
me during all this time.

Wednesday 9th. All this morning we saw clouds of smoke
rising from the *Räcknitzer Höhe*, and we imagined that they
were bombarding the city from that side. We were anxious
about poor Henriette, who, so the cook told us, had developed
small-pox. At mid-day, however, we learned that everyone
had left the city, after the soldiers had threatened to bombard
it since they could not capture the chief barricade. The provisional government, and a great many other people, had fled
to Freiberg during the night.

Thursday 10th, we heard of terrible cruelties practised by
the soldiers; they shot down every insurgent that they found.
Our landlady in the city told us later that her brother, who
owned the *Goldner Hirsch* in Scheffelgasse, had to look on while
the soldiers shot 26 students, one after another, whom they
found in a room there. They are said to have thrown dozens
of people from the third and fourth storeys into the street. It
is too terrible that we should live to see such things! How
men have to fight for a little freedom! When will the time
come when all men will have equal justice? How is it possible

that the belief can so long have been so deeply rooted among the nobles that they are a different species from the the bourgeois!

In the afternoon we drove into the city, but Robert waited in Strehla as we heard that the soldiers let no-one leave the city without a pass, and it was too late to get one to-day as we wanted to return to Maxen. We left Ludwig very unwell, which made us anxious. — On reaching our flat, I busied myself in re-arranging all my things, Mathilde fetching them out of the cellar where she placed them a few days ago on account of the danger of fire. Before long the doctor came, and advised me not to send Henriette away (which I had thought of doing) as harm might come to her, but he also advised us not to bring the children back to the flat, and so I had to make up my mind to pack up a few more things, and to remain with the Major in Maxen for another fortnight or 3 weeks.

Very soon Father came, but he would not believe the horrors of which I had heard. After he had gone, Robert came, as he found it impossible to stop away. We now went together through the principal streets of the city, in order to look at the main battle-field. It is hardly possible to give a picture of the desolation. One sees thousands of holes made by bullets in the houses, whole pieces of wall are broken away, the old opera-house has been destroyed by fire, and a like fate has befallen 3 fine houses in Zwingerstrasse, and in Kleine Brüdergasse, in short it is terrible to see, and what must not the houses look like inside! The walls were broken through to enable the insurgents to correspond with each other through several houses. How many innocent victims there have been, killed in their own rooms by bullets, etc. etc. The *Frauenkirche* (Church of our Lady) is full of prisoners, already there are close on 500. Kapellmeister Wagner is said to have played a part among the republicans, to have made speeches from the town hall, to have caused barricades to be built after a system of his own, and many other things! — The streets are still torn up for the most part, and paving-stones are lying about, only the barricades have been taken away. Martial law has been proclaimed. The city swarms with Prussians — they are lying about on straw in the *Altmarkt*. The streets as they are now make a terrible, but interesting picture. In the evening we drove back to Maxen, and on the way Robert was struck by the very happy thought not to stay in Maxen but to remove to Kreischa which is quite close; it is much more pleasantly situated and has a milder climate. There we drove on the morning of Friday the 11th, with bag and baggage."

Good cause as they must have had to be satisfied in this asylum which they had been happy enough to reach, yet neither of them — and especially Clara — liked "this sudden complete political peace after such violent excitement". "The contrast is too great, all at once." The *Augsburger Allgemeine Zeitung* which they began to take in and hastily devoured every day, "especially Robert, who never stops reading it", gradually restored their mental equilibrium, and reconciled them to their idyllic surroundings. But the vibrations of the storm were long felt, the news of bills issued for Wagner's apprehension, the indictment of Semper and others, agitated them afresh.

"The confusion in the world is frightful at present," writes Clara on May 18th. "God knows what will come of it all." However, the day before, she had tried over Robert's newly finished *Liederalbum* [1]) "on the Kantor's piano".

"It seems to me extraordinary how the terrible events without, have awakened his poetic feeling in so entirely contrary a manner. All the songs breathe and spirit of perfect peace, they seem to me like spring, and laugh like blossoming flowers."

---

1) *Lieder für die Jugend* Op. 79 (Title-page by Ludwig Richter) "Dresden and Kreischa from Ap. 21st to May 13th 1849".

On May 23rd the diary announces: "Robert has written 5 hunting songs for men's voices, with an accompaniment of 4 horns[1] (ad lib.) during the last few days, and we hope to try them at the Choral Society before long." On May 23rd: "Robert is still hard at work composing. He is now writing a sacred cantata; how and in what manner he has not yet told me." And on May 29th: "To-day, Robert finished his sacred cantata for double chorus of men's voices[2], and was very pleased with it."

A glance at the text: — "Despair not in the vale of pain" etc. suggests that the echoes of the storm without were still reverberating and found answer in these words of peace and comfort. That these stormy times did directly affect his music is shown by, "4 Marches from the year 1849"[3], whose completion Clara mentions on May 15th, declaring them to be "extremely brilliant and original. They are popular marches, stately in character. He is going to have them printed immediately."

These, however, came into existence after their return to Dresden, which, to Clara's great distress, took place a few days after Robert's birthday. Schumann — probably as a result of over-work — suddenly declared that he could no longer endure to be out there.

---

1) "For a grand hunt. *Habet acht! Jagdwagen. Frühe. Bei der Flasche.* Five songs from H. Laube's *Jagdbrevier* (Hunter's Breviary) for male chorus in four parts (With an accompaniment *ad lib.* of 4 horns) Op. 137. May 18th—21st."

2) *Verzweifle nicht im Schmerzenstal* (In the Valley of Death thou shalt not despair) by Fr. Rückert. Motet for double, men's chorus with organ accompaniment (ad lib.) Op. 93. According to the MS. "Sketched: Kreischa, near Dresden, May (?) 25th—31st 1849. Scored for orchestra, Düsseldorf May 1852. First performed in Leipsic at the *Paulinerkirche* (Church of St Pauline) July 4th 1850, under my direction."

3) *Vier Märsche für Pianoforte 1849* Op. 79. "Dresden June 12th—16th 1849."

Previous to this, in Kreischa, the *Minnespiel*[1]) from Rückert's *Liebesfrühling* had already been produced. Unfriendly as was the reception afforded to the fugitives by Dresden, now turned into a martial camp, and oppressive as Clara, in particular, found the quartering of the detested Prussians — "First they come in order to shoot down our citizens, who have done nothing, and then we have to supply them with food and drink for nothing — it is an outrage! — Dresden swarms with Prussians, one runs against them wherever one goes till is it quite unbearable," she complains — these distractions seem to have had no ill effect upon Schumann's productive powers but even to have increased them, as if he sought to free himself from the discords of the outer world, which thrilled his soul too, by burying himself deeper and deeper in his art.

He had already begun to set Mignon's songs from *Wilhelm Meister*, in Kreischa, and early in July this led to the *Requiem*[2]), whose music, when he played it to Clara on July 3rd, "profoundly affected" her. Even more powerfully was she affected by the deep melancholy of the *Harfnerlieder* two of which, just composed, he played her on July 6th.

It seemed as if he had to wander thus through the depths and shadows of Goethe tragedy before he could sound those abysses of human suffering from which the anguish of Gretchen's soul cries out to us in *Faust*. On July 14th he played Clara the newly finished scene "In the Cathedral", the "Garden Scene", and *Ach neige, du Schmerzenreiche.* "It is long since anything has so taken hold of me as this combination of words and music, it make one feel as if both had sprung from the same

1) *Minnespiel* from Fr. Rückert's *Liebesfrühling* for one and more voices with piano-forte accompaniment. Op. 101. "Kreischa, near Dresden May 1st—5th 1849."

2) Songs, Lyrics, and Requiem from Goethe's *Wilhelm Meister*, for voice and piano. Op. 98. "Songs in Kreischa in May 1849. Requiem sketched July 2nd and 3rd 1849 in Dresden."

soul. I can find no words in which to express the sense of rapture which once more completely over-mastered me at the sound of this magnificent music. When Robert has written anything which fills me with such delight, my joy in it can find vent only in tears."

Two days later, the third boy — Ferdinand — was born.

The choice of the Mignon songs had doubtless been chiefly suggested, by the coming centenary — on Aug. 28th — which naturally filled Schumann's mind. This event may have led him to renewed study of *Faust*, and in July the Choral Society had begun to prepare for the performance of the concluding scenes of part II, which was to take place on August 29th. While official Dresden contented itself with the performance of Gutzkow's arrangement of the Helen scenes in the 2nd part and Reissiger's music, there came almost simultaneously from Weimar and Leipsic requests from Liszt and Härtel that he would send them the concluding scenes from *Faust*, so that eventually at the Gœthe festival Schumann's music formed the accompaniment to Gœthe's great poem in three places at once. The performance in Dresden which evidently made a deep impression on the audience took place on‘ the afternoon of Aug. 29th in the *Grosse Garten*, when in addition to the concluding scenes from *Faust*, Mendelssohn's *Walpurgisnacht* was sung. The soloists, headed by Mitterwurzer, were excellent throughout, and the chorus "sang with all their hearts, for they were all inspired by it". From Weimar too, "young Bülow", who had heard *Faust* there, and "was quite delighted with it", brought good news. But, judging from the newspaper reports, the celebrations seem to have been less successful in Leipsic; and they were particularly surprised to hear that the final chorus — which is incontestably the climax of the whole work — produced least effect there, "possibly", as Clara thought, "because its opening phrase is not in perfect accord with the words, and in spite of all its beauties it is some-

what more material than all the rest of the music". "Robert,"
she concludes, "when the work is published will certainly retain
the final chorus which he composed afterwards, for it stands
above the other in musical worth. All the same I am sorry
to give up the first, and if it lay with me, both choruses would
be printed." For the rest, she set her hopes upon a speedy
repetition of the performance, conducted by Robert, for Rietz
had evidently entirely mistaken the tempo. "Robert takes it
with an indifference which I cannot understand."

Robert's thoughts were already wandering down new paths,
which led him far away from those exalted regions, and in
which he was nearer than ever to his loved ones. He was
once more in the land of childhood, and beside him ran his
little daughter Marie trying to keep pace with him, however
big were the steps her father took. On Sept. 13th he surprised Clara by a *Geburtstagsmarsch* (Birthday March) which
he and little Marie played to her together. And besides this,
two other pieces for four hands lay on her birthday table,
Bärentanz (The Bears' Dance) and *Gartenlied*[1]) (Garden Song).
Her hope that a series of others would follow, so that there
might be "another album", was speedily fulfilled[2]). On Sept. 20th
she writes: "Three more pieces for four hands have followed:
Am Springbrunnen (At the Fountain), *Reigen* and *Turnier-*
marsch (March to the Tournament). The first is most charm-
ingly original — dream-like; one feels oneself carried inside
the fountain, and sees all sorts of curious things in it, such
as the ball which turns about so funnily and at last comes
back to its first position, in short one dreams with the music
without knowing it until the end of the piece, when in high
delight one turns smiling to one's neighbour. This is what
happens to us when we (Robert and I) play it together."

---

1) Printed as *Gartenmelodie*.
2) 12 Piano-pieces for four hands, for children, big and little. Op. 85.
"Sept. 10th—15th 1849, and Sept. 27th—Oct. 1st."

On Sept. 28th came in addition *Beim Kränzewinden* (Making wreathes) and *Gespenstermärchen* (Ghost Legends).

But amidst these laughing children's faces a more serious note had also been sounded. On Sept. 20th, Clara writes: "To-day, Robert finished the sketch of a concert allegro and introduction 1), and he is now beginning to score it. I very much enjoy playing it — it is very passionate, and I shall certainly so play it. The introduction, which has become quite clear to me (now Robert has played it only once) is very beautiful, the melody deep and thoughtful — I must get to know the allegro more intimately in order to have a complete impression of it."

The "four cantatas for double chorus" 2) which came into existence in October, are not mentioned by the diary, but it refers to a setting of Hebbel's words, for chorus and orchestra 3) in November (Nov. 5th); and at Christmas Robert surprised her with "his hundredth work, three *Romances* for oboe, with piano accompaniment" 4), which at once renewed and concluded his experiments of the year.

A new experiment, in a different direction, was made in the "Three Songs from Lord Byron's *Hebrew Melodies*" with harp accompaniment 5) which were written at the beginning of December, and another equally new experiment — recitation

---

1) *Introduktion und Allegro appassionato.* Concert piece for the pianoforte, with orchestral accompaniment. Op. 92. "Sketched, Dresden Sept. 18th—20th, 1849."

2) Op. 141. According to the list of Schumann's works the three first were written Oct. 11th—16th, and the last, at the end of October.

3) *Nachtlied von Fr.!Hebbel für Chor und Orchester.* Op. 108. Sketched in Dresden Nov. 4th 1849, scored between the 8th and the 11th.

4) *Drei Romanzen für Oboe ad libitum Violine oder Klarinette mit Begleitung des Pianoforte.* Op. 94. "Dresden, in December 1849."

5) *Jephthah's Daughter. Drei Gesänge aus Lord Byron's Hebräischen Gesängen für eine Singstimme mit Begleitung der Harfe oder des Pianoforte.* Op. 95. "Dec. 4th and 5th, 1849."

to piano accompaniment — was the setting of Hebbel's *Schön Hedwig*[1]) at the end of December.

At the turn of the year 1849/50 came the sketch of a new work for chorus and orchestra, Rückert's *Neujahrslied*[2]) whose words, written under stress of recent political agitation, inspired him.

Serious questions about the future were pressing for some decision. The longer Schumann stayed in Dresden the more he felt his position there to be untenable. Without doubt the musician of greatest intellectual capacity in the place, after five years of the greatest creative activity he still found himself as much a stranger to official Dresden and to the leading musical circles as on the first day. Not only did they make no attempt to get into touch with him, but they kept out of his way, and took every opportunity of letting him understand that his presence was not welcome. For example, not only did Intendant von Lüttichau consider it superfluous to do himself and his theatre the honour of voluntarily putting seats at the disposal of Robert and Clara Schumann, but he refused to make good the blunder, when Schumann eventually re-

---

1) *Schön Hedwig*. Ballad by Hebbel for declamation with piano accompaniment. Op. 106. "Dresden Dec. 22nd 1849."

2) *Neujahrslied von Friedrich Rückert für Chor mit Begleitung des Orchesters*. Op. 144. According to the list of Schumann's work Dec. 27th 1849—Jan. 3rd 1850.

The following quotation shows the spirit of the poem.

> Mit eherner Zunge da ruft es: gebt acht!
> Ein Jahr ist im Schwunge zu Ende gebracht.
> Ihr freudigen Zecher, hebt tönende Becher,
> Begrüsset das junge, das Jahr das erwacht.

> Im Dunkel geboren, im nächtigen Schoss,
> Da tritt's aus den Toren des Lebens wie gross!
> Was führst du im Schilde? Was zeigst du im Bilde?
> Was rüsten die Horen für wechselndes Los?

quested him to do so, on the ground that free seats were given only to musicians "who write for the Dresden stage".

And when in response to this, this Robert Schumann who "had as yet written nothing for the stage", allowed himself to say by way of excuse and explanation, that he was even now at work on an opera, and on this very account was extremely anxious to go to the opera often, a still ruder refusal followed. In like manner the authorities had recently refused him the use of the *Frauenkirche* for a memorial service which he wished to hold for Chopin[1]).

In the midst of this came suddenly in November a confidential question from Hiller, as to whether Schumann were inclined to become his successor in Düsseldorf.

It was a difficult matter to decide. Schumann expected *Genoveva* to be performed in Leipsic in February, and a success might at one stroke alter his whole position in Dresden[2]).

"We were beseiged on all sides," writes Clara on Jan. 13th, "with petitions not to leave Dresden, and on the other side the people in Düsseldorf strongly urged Robert to make up his mind to accept the post of director of music there — in short, we live in a state of fatal indecision. The move would be troublesome, but the position has many attractions — 10 secular and 4 sacred concerts a year, and a choral practice every week with a Society which numbers 130 members. The choice of pieces rests solely with the conductor. The salary is 700 thaler, which if not much is yet not despicable as an assured income. Robert will receive the full salary from the first of April onwards, and he is not to enter upon his duties till August, a very acceptable stipulation which almost covers

---

1) *Briefe* new series, 2nd ed. No. 365. Letter to Hiller Dec. 3rd 1849 p. 323.

2) Cf. Schumann's letter to Hiller, Jan. 15th 1850. *Briefe* new series, 2nd ed. No. 370, p. 326.

the expenses of the move. And yet, here, he is so strongly advised to try for the post of second Kapellmeister! But he cannot do this, his rank as an artist would not permit it."

She was perfectly right, and right, too, in thinking only of him in this case. In a letter to Hiller, Robert had expressly formulated the question: "Would there be any sphere of action for my wife? You know her, she cannot be idle." But for her, at this time, the only consideration was what Robert Schumann owed to his name.

And if, a voice was suddenly raised in the *Dresdener Anzeiger*, saying that Schumann was the greatest living genius, and that it would be a disgrace to Dresden if such a man were allowed to leave, this was counter-balanced, the next day, by a second, "very malicious", article which left them no illusions as to any change in the general level of taste in Dresden. But they could not yet come to any unbiassed decision, to say nothing of any official one. At the same time friends and acquaintances took the matter as settled.

Thus, when they were in Leipsic, at the beginning of February, Friedrich Brockhaus, whose guests they were on this occasion, surprised them at the farewell festivities, by giving tableau from the *Peri*, with the assistance of their most intimate friends in Leipsic.

In other respects they found nothing but disappointments of all kinds in Leipsic this time. The worst thing — which they experienced on the very first day — was the news that the performance of *Genoveva*, practices for which ought already to be beginning, was put off in favour of Meyerbeer's *Prophete*, until after the fair.

Their second disappointment was the reception of Schumann's *Introduktion und Allegro appassionato* (Op. 92) which Clara herself played for the first time on Feb. 14th at a *Gewandhaus* concert, not to her own satisfaction "for terrible nervousness possessed me". It is true that the player was very

warmly and kindly welcomed, and that the composition was
not received with entire coldness. "But taking it altogether,"
writes Clara, "I was very unhappy to-day, and the cause lay
first in vexation, or rather grief, that I could let myself be
overpowered by nervousness in this way, and secondly in the
feeling that the audience did not appreciate the beautiful work
as it deserved, and I kept on thinking that at bottom I was
responsible for this; in short, I was deeply distressed." And
this feeling was renewed a few days later when at a soirée
given by Moscheles, she played Schumann's *Bilder aus Osten*
with him, and "greatly exasperated" the composer because
she "perpetually hurried the tempo". "But," she adds by
way of explanation, "it is unbearable playing with Moscheles,
as he makes such frightful *ritardantos*." And on the self-
same evening she succeeded "in making her peace completely" with her offended husband, by a successful performance of Beethoven's *C* minor sonata, which she played with
David.

The comments and expressions of this time, the rapid alter-
nations of light and shade, and the unusually sharp and bitter
opinions which she lets fall even in speaking of friends, make
it only too evident that they were both suffering from a
nervous irritability which is partly to be explained by the
emotions which January had brought with it, but chiefly
by their deep depression at the repeated postponement of
Genoveva.

Even the enthusiastic reception of the *F* major trio (Op. 80),
which she played with Rietz and David at her first concert,
on Feb. 22nd, and the applause won by the *Variations for two
Pianos* (Op. 46) were not able entirely to dispel the depression
caused by the fact that neither of her fellow-players said a word
to her about the "magnificent" piece, at the rehearsal on the
preceding day. On the other hand, they both felt it a pure joy
and great satisfaction that the *Genoveva* overture, which was

played by the *Gewandhaus* orchestra under Schumann's direction, at a concert on the 25th in aid of the orchestra pension fund, aroused the greatest enthusiasm on all sides. They were the more inspired to hope that the whole work would achieve a brilliant success, by the fact that a few days before, the text had apparently made a deep impression upon a little circle of hearers (including among others, Moscheles, Schleinitz, and Dr Härtel) to whom it was read, and besides this, "the very day before the concert", Peters had offered to print the whole opera, "An offer," writes Clara, "which is not so often made to a composer for his first opera." Feb. 26th brought them a serenade, which included the *Ritornelle*, among other things; and this and a merry evening at the Brockhauses' at which Robert and Clara played some of the *Kinderstücke* for 4 hands to the great delight of those present, brought their stay in Leipsic — chequered as their feelings were at leaving — to an harmonious close. But they did not yet say good-bye, for they meant to come back in May, this time really for the performance of *Genoveva*.

The unexpected postponement of the opera, which had at first been so bitter a disappointment, was eventually to have its good side.

"At the beginning of the winter," writes Clara, "we had received an invitation to go to Hamburg, Robert to produce his compositions, and I to play. We had refused it as we could make no definite plans on account of the opera in Leipsic, and also Robert had no wish to undertake anything else. But now that there was nothing to do for the opera, and that we had already arranged to be away for 6 weeks, I wrote to Hamburg again, and at once received a delighted answer and a renewed invitation for the philharmonic concert. We had written in the same manner to Bremen, meaning to take it on our way, as we had plenty of time left and had no more to do in Leipsic."

It would, perhaps, have been wiser if they had not taken Bremen "on their way", for at their last visit, 8 years before, they had made an enemy in Egger, the influential director of the so-called "Private Concerts", who had the first word in musical matters in Bremen. The quarrel apparently arose in consequence of a piece of rude tactlessness on Egger's part, which had led to a somewhat irritable and sharp altercation between him and the Schumanns. They might have thought that it would all have been buried in the interval, and that their other friends, in conjunction with Carl Reinecke — who had recently come there — would see that everything was going right. They felt it, therefore, all the more deeply when immediately on their arrival, friend Töpken, Marie Garlichs — Clara's travelling-companion of 1842 — a niece of Egger's, and others, declared that a visit of apology to Egger was the first, unavoidable necessity. "Such a thing never occurred to us," writes Clara, "and when even Töpken remarked how sad it was for the people of Bremen that under these circumstances they could not hear any orchestral work of Robert's, as Egger would prevent it, Robert's patience gave way completely — I believe nothing in the world would now have induced him . . . . to take one step towards such a braggart. If this fellow were not so conceited . . . . he would have written a couple of lines to Robert, and we should have let the past be *tempi passati*, and have gone to see him. But enough of these trifles, which I should not have mentioned at all if they had not made our stay in Bremen unpleasant in so far as Egger counts as an authority on music and the rank and file could not get over the fact that for once this authority was not recognised."

Clara consequently contented herself with giving one concert in the *Union* on March 7th, with Reinecke's help, "to a small but most enthusiastic audience", which was capable of fully appreciating the second trio (Op. 80 played with Königslow and Cabisius), and the *Variations for two Pianos*, which she played with Reinecke.

In spite of this, they were glad to turn their backs on Bremen and one more they felt the contrast between the two Hansa cities to be altogether to Hamburg's advantage. "Hamburg again pleased us enormously, how much more of a metropolis it is than Bremen! How magnificent the *Jungfernstieg*[1]), the life, the wealth! and how kind and attentive are all our acquaintances!"

The reception afforded to the new works which they brought Hamburg, also gave them steadily increasing satisfaction. To begin with, at a philharmonic concert at which Robert himself conducted the *Genoveva* overture, and Clara played (among other things) the *A* minor-concerto, they were again surprised by the coldness of a Hamburg audience. "The people of Hamburg do not consider it becoming to clap much, and if they do clap, it is like a shower, soon over." But only two days later, at her own concert, the quintet and the *Variations for two Pianos* (which she played with her old Dresden pupil, Otto Goldschmidt) and Beethoven's *C* major sonata, were received very much more warmly. "In fact it was a very animated soirée," says the diary. It was to have a tragi-comic sequel, which somewhat upset people for the moment, but which later appeared in a humorous light. "After the soirée, we went with Schuberth, Grädener and some others, to an oyster-cellar (again), and we were very merry at first, though it ended very unmerrily! Robert had recollected that to-day the first day of spring, Bach and Jean Paul were born, and in his joy he proposed their healths." "Grädener," the diary continues, "under the influence of the wine declared that he would drink Bach's health, but he could not drink Jean Paul's, and began

---

1) *Translator's note*: The Park Lane of Hamburg, on the bank of the Alster.

to elaborate this theme until, Robert jumped up, and after telling him he was a impudent fellow, left the room. Schuberth was with us. The fright quite paralysed me." As Grädener apologised to Schumann next day, the incident had no further unpleasant consequences. Clara herself, may describe the events of the days that followed.

"The day before yesterday Robert wrote to Jenny Lind in Berlin, and told her that we should soon be going back to Dresden by way of Berlin, and that it would give us great pleasure if we could spend a day with her. Robert had told her that we should be staying here until the 23rd — possibly she may come here before we leave. We await her answer with impatience.

Wednesday, 20th, In the morning we went with Schuberth to the daguerreotypist's who made at beast half-a-dozen pictures of us, the best of which he will use to print from. One of Robert was quite excellent. We also had an early practice with Böie and Kupfer.

After dinner I had just lain down for a little while, and was reading a letter from Emilie about Jenny Lind's appearance in Dresden, when she herself came in, having just arrived from Berlin.

I was highly delighted, and Robert was no less so; all day he had had a sort of presentiment that she would come. She was very nice, and said that she had come so quickly from Berlin because she wanted to sing at my concert in Hamburg. She was not a little surprised to hear that it was over, for she had thought that it was on the 22nd, as Robert had written that we were leaving on the 23rd. She at once offered to sing at my concert to-morrow in Altona, and I naturally accepted with joy. I could have hugged her for joy and gratitude! After she had gone, I at once drove out to Altona in order to make it known there, but the hall is very small and it is almost filled by subscribers, so that only a few more can be let in. The surprise of Altona was great! —.

Thursday, 21ˢᵗ. In the morning Jenny Lind came to us in
order to have a little rehearsal of the songs, which grew into
something more, however, for she sang quite a number of
Robert's songs; and how she sang them! with what truth!
what heart-felt understanding and simplicity! how she sang
at sight *Marienwürmchen* and *Frühlingsglaube* — I shall never
forget it. What a magnificent, divinely gifted creature she is!
What a pure, genuinely artistic soul! How refreshing is everything she says! She always hits on the right thing and expresses it in few words! In short, I never loved and admired
any woman more than I do her. These songs will sound for
ever in my heart, and if it were not unjust I should like to
say that I will never again hear them sung by anyone except
her. I need scarcely say that Robert is no less enthusiastic
about her than I am; it is a joy for any composer to hear
his songs sung with such heart-felt feeling. She went, and
whenever she went, I was left in great agitation, her tones
and words making incessant tumult in my heart. — What will
you say, dear Robert, of this passionate outburst? Yet not I
alone, but you too, felt the same, only I give more vent to
my feelings! —

The soirée in Altona that evening, was splendid! Seldom
had so much been combined, as was to-day! — a full room,
an extraordinarily enthusiastic audience, magnificent singing,
my playing — which was not bad — Robert's wonderful trio
(with Böie and Kupfer), in short there was nothing wanting
for a perfect whole! I was very happy, and not least because
I did not come behind Jenny Lind as an artist in the estimation
of the public, but awakened like interest and experienced
equally enthusiastic applause. This inspired me to put forth
my intellectual and physical powers to the utmost; I had been
very much afraid of the humiliating sensation of being slighted,
and I was over-joyed that this was not the case! But now,
for her! How she sang! How she sang Mendelssohn's *Rhein-*

isches Volkslied, how Robert's *Sonnenschein* — no, it cannot be described! Robert said to her, One really feels the sun on one's back. One wants to listen to freshness and child-like innocence and simplicity such as this, again and again — and indeed the audience took care to make her repeat it. And how she sang *Der Himmel hat eine Träne geweint,* with what distinction, and heart-felt emotion! Words cannot ex-press the heavenly impression made by such singing of such songs! One thing only could we suggest to Jenny Lind; that she should sing only good music, and discard all that stuff (which she has sung in other places) of Meyerbeer's, Bellini's, Donizetti's, etc., for she is too good for that.

Friday, 22nd. In the morning there was a rehearsal of Robert's first trio for a soirée in the evening at Lallemant's (Avé) Jenny Lind came to the rehearsal, too. Otten had come in earlier, and had strongly urged us to induce her to sing at another matinée to be arranged for to-morrow, but much as I wished it I did not like to ask her to do it for me! I asked her if she would not give a concert at which I might play, or if we could not give a matinée together, for the poor; but she did not want either of these, only if I wished to give another matinée for myself, she would sing, and instead of leaving for Lübeck in the morning, she would not go until the afternoon — she had to be there by Saturday. She pressed me very much, and (who could have withstood so tempting an offer) I accepted. She was evidently prompted by the wish to be of pecuniary assistance to us, and frankly expressed her great satisfaction when she heard that the matinée was going to be very full. She also wanted to have quite high prices, but I did not like that, and she agreed with me in the end. But now we had to be busy, for in the first place there had never before been a matinée in Hamburg, and then, we had hardly 24 hours before it. Here Schubert's stupendous activity displayed itself. In an hour he had bills and placards ready, by evening he had given notice to the newspapers, etc. etc. Otten and Avé also bestirred themsleves.

Towards evening, dear, kind Jenny came to us, and we had another song-practice, which, however, again turned into something much more. She sang *Nussbaum, Widmung, Früh-lingsnacht, Stille Liebe,* and a number of others, also the aria from the last act of Robert's opera. I would a thousand times rather have passed the evening with her, like this, than have gone out to a party, but it was of no use, we had to go. Jenny Lind ought also to have gone to Avé's; but she wanted to devote her last evening to the people with whom she was staying (Madame Brunton and Frl. Semenoff, both kind, pleasant ladies, with whom I should think it was agreeable to stay), and she has no love for parties in any case, and is difficult of access — inquisitive people she will not allow to come near her at all. She takes extraordinary care of her voice, she does not dance (she used to love it passionately), she drinks neither wine, nor tea, nor coffee — in every respect she is an etherial being! — Besides her great kindness in singing at two of my concerts, and staying on purpose, etc. etc., she was also most attentive in other ways! For example, she never let me come to her to rehearse, she herself fetched us for each concert, and many other things of the same kind! — What a contrast to the pretentiousness of other singers! I had to climb up three flights of stairs to Frl. Wagner on the morning of the first concert, and then she had not learned a single song, not even the words. · It always the way; the greater the artist, tho more modest the person!

Saturday, 23rd. Matinée. Immensely full, great entsusiasm. Jenny Lind had seated herself behind the lid of the piano, which caused a general restlessness as but few people could see her, and everyone wanted to do. so. She sang wonderfully again, — Mozart's aria from *Figaro* with enchanting simplicity (Frl. Wagner would have had an opportunity of learning respect for the composer), and in like manner some songs of Mendelssohn's and four of Robert's, and of course she sang *Sonnenschein* at the end — twice. She gave another 'proof to-day of how she makes everything that she sings part of herself, when in turning over in *Frühlingsnacht* the pages got wrong, and she sang it by heart to the end. She sang all Robert's songs, as I have always imagined they should be sung, but as I never expected to hear them. She never misses the slightest inflection, such as others would pass by without noticing, when she listens to the music of others it is a real pleasure to watch her and see how nothing, not the subtlest and most delicate modulation, escapes her. — I too, played very well to-day, played as I seldom have done before, which was no wonder when I was inspired as one always is by Jenny Lind! — At this concert too, the audience received me with equal enthusiasm, and I had to repeat one of Mendelssohn's *Lieder*.

After the matinée, Jenny Lind would not hear of our seeing her home, but said good-bye to us, which made me very sad. Who knows when we shall see her again, now she is going to America? And how quickly had these few hours with her flown by! That is always the way in this world: one can never live with those who understand one, and whom one loves and admires! Few were the hours we spent with her, but to us they are unforgetable."

Robert, in his notes on this incident, writes under the heading: "In the spring of 1850":

"We met Jenny Lind again in Hamburg. She has steeped herself in my music. I shall never forget the kind and noble words she spoke to me. Other things too we discussed. Clara was happy during these days. We were deeply grieved to bid her farewell."

The substantial gain, also, was not to be despised. "We have never yet made so profitable a journey in Germany," writes Clara, "I should like to say now: 'What a good thing that the performance of the opera did not come off'!" After deducting expenses, there was a clear profit of 800 thaler.

They had but a short rest in Berlin. "Our first visit was to Mendelssohn's grave; Robert plucked a leaf from a laurel-wreath which was lying there, and took it with him as a keepsake." They spent one evening with Cäcilie Mendelssohn. "I had to play a great deal of Mendelssohn — the *C* minor trio, *Variations serieuses* etc. Madame Mendelssohn was kind and dear, but it fills one's heart with grief to look at those beautiful children who have so early lost such a father. Neither of us could quite shake off this feeling." A daguerrotype of Mendelssohn, done from the picture by Magnus and brought to her by Magnus himself, gave her great pleasure. "It seems to me the best likeness of all."

On March 29th they were once more in Dresden, and on the 31st the diary says that "Robert wrote to Düsseldorf and agreed to go there; but he says he is very uncertain whether he will go or not — he still hopes that a post may be found nearer at hand. However, in no case shall we stay here. We are dreadfully bored, everything here seems to us so conventional. One never sees a live person, everybody looks so common-place! — And as to musicians — one never gets a glimpse of one!

But since their eyes were fixed hopefully on the future, all this was borne with good humour: it would not last much longer. "Yesterday," writes Clara on May 8th, "Robert received his first quarter's salary from Düsseldorf. Will he not sometimes long for golden freedom? Well, a man must have experience of all kinds . . . . I am most pleased at the prospect of being able to hear Robert's new things there, which we yet heard with the orchestra. He really must get an orchestra have not under his own direction. . . . Here we may sit still for years with all his treasures buried."

Full of pleasant anticipations they set out for Leipsic on May 18th where, after long delay and numerous disappointments, the rehearsals of *Genoveva* were at last to begin. Only an indisposition of Robert's, which at the last moment obliged them to put off for a few days the journey which had been planned for the 17th, cast a slight shadow over them, a shadow which was to be deepened by various unavoidable agitations during the weeks that followed. Signs of violent nervous excitement manifested themselves on several occasions, apparently, however, without causing further anxiety. On this occasion they stayed at the Preussers' house, which, was situated in a charming garden, and thanks to the kindness, attentiveness, and delicate tactfulness of their hosts, they found it as comfortable and cosy as they had found the Brockhauses' in February. "But nowhere here is it as nice," writes Clara, "as it is at the Preussers', where we are staying! We are as if in Paradise, all around us nothing but exquisite greenness, and the most restful stillness broken only by the twittering of the birds. We have early breakfast in the garden, and our kind hosts forestall our every wish; in short, we could not wish for a pleasanter stopping-place."

On May 22nd was the first private rehearsal. "The singers already read their parts so well that it goes almost without a hitch," says Clara. "It was a great pleasure to us at last to hear some of it. I accompanied at the piano. The chorus is already learning it by heart." And the first rehearsal from proof sheets with the orchestra, on the 29th, at which Clara played the voice parts on the piano, also left nothing but favourable impressions. "I cannot describe the treat that this rehearsal was for me! The magnificent instrumentation throughout completely enchanted me, and then how the orchestra makes everything stand out. . . . I am looking forward enormously to the next rehearsals. The musicians were very much surprised that the music was so easy to play — it all went quite easily on." And the first rehearsal for soloists and chorus, on June 7th, was, as Clara writes, also "a great pleasure to me." Robert's birthday, for which the two eldest children were fetched from Dresden as a surprise, fell in the midst of this happy time. The *Paulinerchor*, together with some of the orchestra, serenaded him early in the morning, with a choral, two of his songs, and the 4th march from the *Klaviermärschen* (scored 1849).

But the nearer the performance drew, the more did sorrows ally themselves with joys. It is true that the rehearsals, notwithstanding several battles over the coming and going of two choirs, and the occasional absences of some of the soloists, continued to go tolerably well, and they got the impression that "everyone at the theatre" was doing all they could to help him. But this was more than they could say ot many of the other musical connoisseurs of Leipsic. Thus they felt the coldness with which the *Minnespiel*, and the *Stücke im Volkston* were received at the party given by the Preussers in honour of Robert's birthday, to be almost insulting. "Whatever do the people want! It seems to me that among connoisseurs a stupid tone prevails here, they refuse to like anything unless it is by Mendelssohn, and only when they find that the public appreciates it, do they turn round and like it. — David stands at the head of them. — I do not want to play any more to these people here, they are too cold and ungrateful, with some exceptions of course, including the general public. I am only speaking now of the Mendelssohn-clique."

This irritability was probably due to the nervous strain of theatre-rehearsals, which no-one can experience without suffering for it. On June 21st she writes significantly of an performance of "*Kabale und Liebe*" on the preceding evening: "I was very unwell to-day, partly from the effect of last night's play which always makes a tremendous impression on one; and then this whole time of strain affects me, especially just now when the performance of the opera is drawing near." On the same page, the diary says: "A visit from Spohr, who arrived yesterday." My Mother also came from Berlin to-day, for the opera, and Reinecke from Bremen, and several people from Hamburg, with Schubert and their head.

Sunday, 23rd. Orchestra-rehearsal in the theatre. Many guests as listeners — Spohr, Gade, Hiller, Moscheles, Hauptmann — one could not easily find such another gathering of artists, nor such a quartet as yesterday's (at a party at the Preussers) when Spohr, David, Joachim, and Gade played in Spohr's sextet. The rehearsal lasted until 2 o'clock. . . .

Monday, 24th. Final rehearsal of the opera. In the evening there was music at the *Gewandhaus* in honour of Spohr. I began by playing Robert's *A* minor concerto, which went excellently, unusually well, and that without rehearsal! I played to my own satisfaction, and felt extraordinary animated. . . . Everybody was electrified and it really is a fine piece. After this, Spohr played three little drawing-room pieces for piano and violin, which (except in a few little places) sounded charming . . . . he played them so tenderly and beautifully that one could not help liking them. Finally he conducted his new symphony, *Die Jahreszeiten* (The Seasons), which, like all Spohr's work, bore the stamp of a masterhand and was not without imagination, only Spohr is always so monotonous in character, harmonization, and instrumentation, that one cannot bear it for long . . . . It was extraordinary to me, to realise how time changes people! Formerly, as a young girl, I raved about Spohr, and his very softness seemed heavenly, and now I should very soon have too much of it. . . .

Tuesday, 25th. We had a very lively time here. Early in the morning friends from Dresden arrived for the opera, and of course they came to see us. In the afternoon I paid a farewell visit to Spohr, who unfortunately has to go to-day. . . .

He said many nice things to me about Robert's *Genoveva* —
in his opinion this opera contains a wealth of imagination,
and magnificent dramatic vitality!"

In the evening Pauline Schumann came from Schnee-
berg, also Kuntsch (Robert's old master) and Klitsch (from
Zwickau), besides several people from Hamburg (Grädener,
Bierwirth, etc.), Herr Ehlers from Königsberg, Liszt from
Weimar, and Hiller from Dresden, in short it was a remark-
able gathering.

In the evening the first performance at last took place.
"All the singers took great pains, the first two acts went
very well, but in the third Wiedemann (Golo) had the misfortune to forget the letter for Siegfried. They both ran
about in despair, and the scene was entirely ruined; the
singers themselves were thrown into consternation by it,
so that the two last acts went less well, and added to this
the magic room was very poorly staged. However, the
audience was very attentive, and at the end the singers and
Robert were twice recalled, amidst great applause, and a
laurel-wreath fluttered down, which Frau Günther set on
Robert's head.

Looked at clearly, this means little more than a *succès
d'estime*, which the following performances, though disturbed
by no accidents and consequently more uniform and dramatic
in effect, could not change into a real triumph, although Clara
and Robert carried away the impression that a great victory
had been won, and that a wide path had been opened for
the future.

Clara, who had lost all equanimity and all her good spirits at
the first performance, owing to the misfortune about the letter,
writes concerning the second: "The house was crammed, a
pin could not have fallen; the audience was far more lively
than on the first occasion, the singers sang and acted very
much better, and they, and Robert with them, were rewarded

with great applause and many calls.... The music filled me
with delight. What dramatic feeling, what instrumentation,
what characterization are in it!.... Here we have once
again real, beautiful, German music, that does one's heart
good, it is not noisy, and yet its instrumentation shows a
power of invention which ranges from the most forcible to
the most tender! — This is real genius, such as heaven gives
only to its chosen ones. May you, my beloved Robert, be
more and more conscious of this, and ever be as happy at
heart as you deserve to be.... I cannot describe the feelings
of delight which stirred within me during these days, but certainly they were enough to fill a life-time!

At the third performance (May 30th), conducted by Rietz
this time, before a crowded house, the singers were recalled
after every act, and at the end they called so loudly for
Robert that he had to thread his way through the labyrinth
of passages which lead to the stage; naturally this took
some time, and the longer they waited, the louder became
the cries; at last he appeared in a frock-coat (he had not
even a dress-suit), and was received with a regular storm
of applause. I could have wept for joy to see how he came
forward, so simply and unassumingly; if ever he seemed to
me lovable, it was at this moment, as he stood there, true
artist and man!"

On July 10th they went back to Dresden, whose midsummer
stillness, however, could not content them after the weeks of
stormy excitement in Leipsic. "It is really as if the people
here had no blood in their veins," writes Clara, "no enthusiasm
for anything."

"I must say," she writes on July 31st, "that I shall leave
this place with pleasure, and I am glad that Robert is in no
way fettered to it. What a position it must be for him here!
with all these gossiping, insincere men in the band, who want
nothing except to go on in the old humdrum ways. They are

altogether a fine and worthy company now . . . . who throw
'dear colleague' and 'my good friend' about on all sides, and
would then like to scratch out each others' eyes."

"A concert in the '*Grosse Garten*'," runs the entry for
Aug. 14th, "in aid of the people of Schleswig-Holstein; to
Dresden's shame it was not nearly so well attended as one
had a right to expect. There were four military men, and
none of the nobility, in short Dresden once more displayed
all the prejudice and conventionality of a residential city!
Everybody looks to, and bows to the Court. It is pitiful!
Words fail to describe it! — And look at the way an
audience like this receives a symphony of Mendelssohn's!
They sit there like logs, not a spark of vitality shows itself
in their withered faces — I should like to fall. upon them
hand and foot, and cry, 'Have you no drop of blood in
your veins'?"

The extreme sharpness and drastic energy with which the
vials of wrath are here emptied over the whole of musical
Dresden, are partly explained by the fact that the very society,
small and select as it was, which Schumann had formed into
a Choral Union, and whose practices and excursions had often
given him renewed strength and stimulus in exchange for the
stimulus which it received from him, during the last few
months had given much cause for complaint on account of
the bad attendance at the practices, and had shown signs of
the unconquerable force of musical dilatoriness in Dresden.
Robert had already declared in April, that if gentlemen did
not attend regularly, he should leave. And the last practices
had been able to be held only partially or entirely without men."

It is comprehensible that the farewell dinner which the
Society gave their departing conductor on Aug. 30th, on the
Terrace, should have suffered somewhat from these ups and
downs of feeling. "As is so often the case in Dresden," writes

Clara, "it was very dull, and then in addition to this we kept on hearing the scraping of the basses in the concert underneath, which was very disturbing, particularly when Reinecke proposed our healths in a delightful speech which we should have liked to listen to in peace. Robert was at first very much out of spirits, but towards the end he revived a little. His song for a chorus, '*Wenn zweie auseinandergehen*' was very effective; besides this, they sang old, well-known songs. . . . The orchestra from Kuntze played several pieces in Robert's honour, only, though the intention was good, the choice of pieces was curious — it seemed to me once more a piece of regular Dresden pedantry."

Official Dresden, and the local musicians who held official posts, took no notice of Schumann's departure from Dresden. On the other hand, on Aug. 25th, a few days before they left, a farewell party was given by the Bendemanns, at which Clara played once more, and Fräulein Jacobi sang some of Robert's recent settings of Lenau's songs, "which are all very melancholy". "It is strange," writes Clara, "that the songs end with a requiem for Héloise, which Robert had chosen in order to soften the feeling at the end to some extent . . . . at the same time believing that Lenau was dead. This was not the case, but, wonderful to relate, this very day Robert read that he had passed away, and so the first requiem sung for him was Robert's. This, and the music of the songs, made everybody strangely melancholy, until Robert's magnificent, fresh hunting-song which I played, banished low spirits. We stayed a fairly long time together — it made me very sad to think that I was here for the last time. But the Bendemanns are the only people (the Hübners of course included) to whom I find it hard to say good-bye!"

There were many who were grieved at their departure, as they realised during the last few weeks or months, but these were those who were indebted to them on various accounts.

And when the wanderers turned their backs on Dresden early on the morning of Sept. 1st, perhaps the thought stole over them that the weight of their luggage would not be materially increased by all that they had gained from the city and its inhabitants in return for the inexhaustible artistic treasures which for 6 years they had royally lavished on all sides. The family had a roof, the growing children elementary schooling, but the artists received practically nothing.

INDEX.

Printing by Breitkopf & Härtel of Leipsic.